HOME & GARDEN SERVICES
for Garstang & surrounding areas

DEAD STRAIGHT GUIDE TO

GUNS N' ROSES

Tel 07912 888 178   **Email** enquiries@hgs-garstang.com
Web www.hgs-garstang.com

MICK O' SHEA

GUNS N' ROSES

This edition © Red Planet Publishing Ltd 2019
Text © Mick O' Shea 2019

This first edition published July 2019 by
Red Planet Publishing Ltd
www.redplanetmusicbooks.com

Email: info@redplanetzone.com

Printed in the UK by TJInternational

Design / Cover / Layout: Harry Gregory
Publisher: Mark Neeter

A catalogue record for this book is available from the British Library

ISBN: 978 1 9127 3309 5

WWW.REDPLANETMUSICBOOKS.COM

CONTENTS

GUNS N' ROSES

AUTHORS NOTE

When I first heard the rumours about how Slash had supposedly made his peace with Axl, and that they – along with Duff McKagan – were set to "regroup" under the Guns N' Roses standard for the 2016 Coachella Festival, I pretty much dismissed them out of hand. If only because I couldn't imagine a scenario where Axl would admit to being at fault over Slash's walkout from Guns N' Roses some two decades earlier. And yet the seemingly impossible – or "the most significant and anxiously awaited musical event of this century" according to the GN'R website – was confirmed in early January with the regrouped Guns N' Roses set to make two headline appearances at Coachella. This was followed soon after by news of two consecutive headline appearances in Las Vegas in the run-up to Coachella, as well as a brace of shows in Mexico City. And then March brought news of a 21-date US summer tour – the Not In This Lifetime . . . Tour (the title tongue-in-cheekily lifted from one of Axl's many barbed responses to the possibility of an *Appetite*-era GN'R reunion).

There were always going to be naysayers bemoaning the reunion, of course; the gripes generally about Axl's failure to hit the high notes on the *Appetite* classics during recent tours. There's an easy solution, of course. If you want the songs to sound like they do on the record, then stay at home and listen to the record. The same grouches probably castigated Axl, Slash, and Duff for not looking like they do in the old posters. The overwhelming reaction among GN'R fans to the "regrouping" – both young and old – has proved positive, however, as the Not In This Lifetime . . . Tour is the second-highest grossing tour of all time (behind U2's U2 360° Tour of 2009-2011), earning a cool $563,300,000. Taking the cash out of the equation, Axl, Slash and Duff's regrouping has allowed those of a certain age to relive their yesterdays, if only for one evening. It also gave those who were too young first time around the opportunity to see what all the fuss was about.

To give the reconciliatory regrouping a homely touch, Guns announced a warm-up show at the Troubadour in West Hollywood on April 1. The "Troob" was where it had all started for Guns some three decades earlier, of course. The show quickly became the hottest ticket in town, with clued-in fans queuing through the night for the chance to catch Axl, Slash and Duff sharing the same stage for the first time in 23 years. It had been hoped the regrouping would include Izzy Stradlin and Steven Adler. Steven was supposed to make an appearance during the Troubadour show but had to withdraw at the eleventh-hour because of a back-related injury that required surgery. He would, however, make occasional guest appearances on the Not In This Lifetime . . . Tour. Petty squabbles over money were to derail Izzy from joining the party, alas.

I was 25 at the time of the release of *Appetite For Destruction*. Many of my friends were bemused at how an ex-punk could suddenly get a yearning for heavy metal. To my mind, however, "heavy metal" was the dominion of Iron Maiden, Judas Priest, Saxon and their studded leather armband clad brethren, whereas Guns N' Roses were a gritty blues/rock band in the Stones/Led Zep/Aerosmith mould. It was most likely Izzy's famous quote about rock 'n'roll having "sucked a big fuckin' dick since the Sex Pistols" that first grabbed my attention. There'd been plenty of great music in the intervening years since the Pistols, of course, but I readily got Izzy's drift.

Izzy was my fave Gunner (most likely because I played rhythm guitar in a band at the time). As luck would have it, my first GN'R show – at the old Wembley Stadium on Saturday, August 31, 1991 – was to prove Izzy's last – at least as a full-time member. The surge as the band came tearing out onto the stage that night was unbelievable (even surpassing the frenzied rush to grab the comb Madonna had teasingly stroked betwixt her bare thighs before tossing it back into the crowd four years earlier).

The Use Your Illusion albums were still a couple of weeks away from release at the time of the Wembley show so the only track I was familiar with – aside from the 'Live and Let Die' and 'Knockin' on Heaven's Door' covers – was 'You Could Be Mine', the theme song to *Terminator 2: Judgement Day*. But you just knew from songs such as 'Civil War', 'Double Talkin' Jive', 'Estranged' and 'November Rain' that Guns were hitting another level.

I'm not going to try to pretend I was, or ever have been, privy to the band's innermost thoughts. But Slash, Duff and Steven have all penned their respective memoirs, while Matt Sorum is also in the process of committing his recollections to print. I don't even delve into the band's personal lives unless it pertains to the GN'R story because this book is exactly what it says on the cover – a Dead Straight Guide to the band once proclaimed the "most dangerous in the world".

Mick O'Shea
Still Living the Dream
June 2019

"Los Angeles is the loneliest and most brutal of American cities; New York gets godawful cold in the winter but there's a feeling of wacky comradeship somewhere in some streets. LA is a jungle."

JACK KEROUAC

PART ONE

OUT IN THE STREET

Los Angeles, the fabled "City of Angels", is where dreams were said to come true. Not all dreams, of course, just enough to keep the illusion alive; to keep wishful wannabes from Soda Springs, Idaho, Coupon, Pennsylvania, Three Way, Tennessee, American Fork, Utah, and a plethora of other far-flung cornpone outposts, boarding Greyhound buses with a one-way ticket clutched in their hand. Those with possessions that couldn't be stuffed into a holdall – say a guitar and drum kit, for instance – hit the road in their own wheels. Happy-go-lucky Jeffrey Dean Isbell was 19 when he waved goodbye to "Bumfuck Indiana", or Lafayette, as the civil parish of Tippecanoe County is more commonly known. "It's a small town so there wasn't much to do," he reflected. "We rode bikes, smoked pot, got into trouble.
It was pretty *Beavis and Butt-Head*, actually." His caustic opinion of Lafayette was to mellow over time . . . even to the point where he considered it "cool" to have grown up there.

Jeff, or "Izzy", as he would soon be known by one and all, was born in Florida in April 1962, but the family had upped sticks and relocated to Lafayette, or some ten miles out in the neighbouring countryside, by the time he was ready to start school. His father was an engraver by trade, while his mum got a job with the local phone company. The marriage had already strayed onto rocky ground, however, and while the move to Lafayette delayed the rot somewhat, Izzy's parents were divorced by

the time he reached third grade. Following the split Izzy, together with his kid sibling Joe, stayed with their mother and moved into Lafayette itself. There still wasn't much to do, but at least he could now hook up with his friends from school and do nothing together.

By the time Izzy lit out for LA, he'd been playing drums for the past six years or so; his paternal grandma having relented to his ceaseless pleading and bought him a set for his thirteenth birthday. The old girl still played drums herself and even had a band going, according to Izzy. Another early influence on Izzy came with watching *The Partridge Family*, ABC's popular musical sitcom that ran for four seasons from 1970 through to 1974 and served as a launchpad for David Cassidy's solo career. The two child actors portraying Chris, the family's drummer – Jerry Gelbwaks (Season 1) and Brian Forster (Seasons 2-4) – were roughly the same age as himself. "I'd watch it on TV and think, 'that looks good, I'll do that.'"

Izzy's best friend's older brother had a band of sorts that would get together most Friday nights at an old farmhouse that was close enough to home yet far enough out in the sticks to ensure some privacy. On occasion they'd ask Izzy to come up and jam with them. These ad hoc keg parties were to provide an adrenaline rush release against the stagnating boredom of his everyday life that Izzy still looks back on with fondness.

GUNS N' ROSES

Izzy's drive and determination might well have seen him make it as a drummer in one band or other – maybe even with Guns N' Roses. Yet his loose-hipped, Johnny Thunders-esque frame was undoubtedly best suited to playing gutsy rock'n'roll guitar. His only thought upon arriving in West Hollywood in his beat-up Chevy Impala was to make a living from playing and making music. Never in his wildest, pot-fuelled fantasies could he have imagined that he'd end up as the rhythm guitarist in the hottest rock band of the mid-to-late Eighties and early Nineties. "At some point in the mid-Eighties I heard a song of mine on the radio and for the first time I felt that something really important had happened," he revealed during a May 2011 interview with www.gunsnfnroses.com. "Still, from time to time I listen to songs that I composed and recorded in the Eighties on the radio, and I to say myself, 'Wow, incredible, there I am.' But I was still just a teenager who just wanted to play the guitar."

Speaking with the unofficial Izzy Stradlin fan page, On Down The Road, Izzy explained the futility of getting something going in his home town. "When I wasn't in school, I was practising. I was trying real hard to put together a solid band in Lafayette, but it wasn't working out. After graduation, I just said, 'Fuck it – I'm going to LA, because the weather's better and that's where everything is.'"

Izzy found himself a tiny one-bedroom apartment in Huntingdon Beach, taking occasional work and selling drugs to meet the rent. He also perused the Musicians Wanted ads in The Recycler (LA's free musicians' paper) and music store notice boards. At night he would trawl the Strip, calling in at the Starwood, the Cathouse, Gazzarri's, the Roxy, and the Whisky a Go-Go, checking out bands or hanging about the Rainbow Bar and Grill parking lot seeing and being seen. His first foray into the West Hollywood music scene came with drumming with a low-rent drag punk outfit called Naughty Women. "They were kinda like the Stooges," Izzy reflected. "The guitarist looked like Gene Simmons. He had this apartment covered in rock posters, with a ton of records. And to me, straight from Indiana, I thought, 'He's really got it goin' on!' I had a car, a kit and a PA, so they figured, 'This guy came from heaven!'

Izzy's debut with the New York Dolls copyists came at the LA Studio, a seedy punk hangout frequented by an unruly hardcore punk element. Naughty Women were the opening act of a three-band bill featuring Hollywood gothic punksters 45 Grave, along with the headlining Adolescents. The mood inside the club was antagonistic from the get-go. Don Bolles, the ex-Germs drummer who was now playing with 45 Grave, was set upon by the hardcore skinhead punks for his glam-orientated style.

Naughty Women were used to their shows being interrupted by the macho elements in the crowd who obviously felt their masculinity was being threatened by a bunch of Spandex-wearing fags. Their arrival onstage had been greeted by a barrage of beer bottles, but midway through the third song several skinheads charged the stage; the ensuing melee resulting in their frontman Larson getting a beating, while guitarist Mike Dratch suffered a broken finger. Izzy, fortunately, came away unscathed. "The audience was like the angry guys in The Decline of Western Civilization," says Izzy. "I'm sitting there waiting for the rest of the band to come onstage, and they finally get out there – and they're all in drag. The singer's wearing pink Spandex and this big Afro. I'd never thought twice about the name Naughty Women. The crowd hated us. They were throwing beer bottles and jumping onstage. Finally they started beating the shit out of the singer. They knocked over the guitar player's amps, and he got his hand busted. I just grabbed a cymbal stand and stood on the side trying to fend them off, yelling, 'Get the fuck away from me, man!' That was my introduction to the rock scene in LA. I was like, 'Wow, this is exciting!'"

Exciting it may have been, but Izzy's tenure with Naughty Women would prove short-lived, as would his time with the long-forgotten Atoms; this time owing to an opportunist thief making off with his Chevy Impala with the drums stashed in the back. Deciding the theft of his car was fate's way of telling him his future didn't lie behind a drum kit, Izzy bought himself a cheap bass guitar.

News of Izzy's hauling ass to LA would have been big news among his friends from Jefferson High, the school from which he'd graduated the previous year (the only one of Guns N' Roses' classic line-up to do so). The doubters and nay-sayers no doubt expected Izzy to come slinking back into town with his tail between his legs, yet others had been impressed at their friend's derring-do and had cast an envious eye towards the I 65 turnpike.

One of these was Izzy's best buddy, William "Bill" Bailey; the soon-to-be-rechristened Axl W. Rose. "[He] used to come down and crash on the floor," Izzy recalled. "He was always coming out to visit [and] getting lost. Then, at the end of '82, he came back out with this girl (Axl's first serious girlfriend, Gina Siler) and rented an apartment. That's when he stayed."

Izzy's abiding memory of Axl from their time at Jefferson High was of seeing him tear-assing down a corridor with several teachers giving chase. It made a favourable impression on Izzy, and a chance pairing in Driver Education class soon thereafter was to provide the first tentative step to a solid friendship. Izzy was already known for his easy-going, laidback attitude, so befriending a hot-headed firebrand such as Bill Bailey would have raised the odd eyebrow or two. And yet it was Bill's unpredictable craziness that had drawn Izzy moth-like to the flame.

Izzy was already involved in what passed for Lafayette's music scene, but each outfit in turn would soon flounder because none of them could find someone willing to stand in front of a microphone. The majority of Bill Bailey's peers at Jefferson High tended to keep him at arm's length, but to Izzy's mind there was something

indefinable about him that screamed "rock'n'roll frontman". Bill was to prove amenable to the idea, even if the unpredictability Izzy loved about his friend drove him to distraction on occasion.

The opening scene from the 'Welcome to the Jungle' promo video shows Axl as a naïve, freckle-faced hick alighting from a bus at the Greyhound terminal in North Hollywood. This was exaggerated for effect because, in reality, he had tested Lafayette police department's patience to the point that, by his own estimation, he ran up some 20 arrests resulting in ten days spent cooling his heels in the county jail on charges ranging from public intoxication and contributing to the delinquency of a minor, to criminal trespass. When Axl lit out of Lafayette for the last time he was technically skipping judge's bail. And while this hardly saw him placed on the FBI's Most Wanted list, an ocean would flow through the Wabash River before he set foot in his native Indiana again.

Axl's upbringing had largely proved a joyless experience at the hands of his religious zealot stepfather, L. Stephen Bailey. An uncompromising Pentecostal preacher of the "hellfire and brimstone" variety, he was of the unwavering belief that sparing the rod did indeed spoil the child; a conviction young Axl and his younger siblings, Stuart and Amy, came to understand all too well. Rock'n'roll was wholly condemned as being devil's music, and the only singing Bailey Snr countenanced was that which venerated the good Lord. Indeed, the only positive that could be said to have benefited Axl during this puritanical period was learning to sing and play piano at the thrice weekly church recitals the family were forced to attend.

Axl, of course, had no reason to suspect that Bailey wasn't his natural father, so when he accidentally happened upon some documentation that proved otherwise when he was 16 or so, it hit him hard . . . Very hard. On confronting his mother, Sharon, he discovered that his biological father, William Rose, was a drunken, misogynistic wife-beater, of whom nothing had been seen or heard since The

GUNS N' ROSES

Beatles claimed the top slot on the *Billboard* chart with 'I Wanna Hold your Hand'. Axl had been two at the time Sharon had finally bucked up the courage to flee the marital home, and so obviously had no memories of his father, either good or bad. In later years, however, once flush with the trappings of success, Axl would undergo extensive regression therapy, the results of which left him convinced that Rose had sexually abused him.

Axl was already displaying the usual traits of teenage rebellion: bunking school, growing his hair, drinking booze, smoking joints, and popping pills, but the discomfiting disclosure of his real father's identity was to push him over the edge. He stopped paying attention in class before giving up going to school altogether. In a fit of pique, he also began calling himself W. Rose. When Bailey threw him out following yet another argument – this time over the length of his hair – Axl moved in temporarily with his grandmother and remained there until stoking enough courage to make the move to LA.

By the time of Axl and Gina's arrival in LA, Izzy was playing bass with Shire, a Scorpions-esque heavy metal outfit featuring Alan Santalesa on lead guitar. Speaking about Izzy's brief time in Shire on the *Appetite for Distortion* podcast, Santalesa described him as a "very enthusiastic and energetic, Nikki Sixx lookalike" owing to his teased black hair. "He'd only recently switched to bass, but he was so keen to learn that he had stickers with the notes of the songs taped in front of him to help him play along."

Santalesa goes on to explain how he first met Izzy – who was calling himself "Izzy Bell" at the time – circa 1982. "He (Izzy) was learning bass by playing along to Ramones records, and to appease him we'd play the song 'Commando'. I didn't know punk at all so I played a lead in the song. When Axl came to see us play he couldn't believe it – 'Ramones with guitar solos?'"

Izzy played only five or six shows with Shire and Santalesa says he was sad to see him go

because his enthusiasm was so infectious. "There was no falling out; David (Anthony, Shire's frontman) just came in one day and said that Izzy was leaving but was going to play one more show. He'd started teaching himself rhythm guitar to help with his songwriting so I guess that's the way he wanted to go."

Being on the West Hollywood scene meant Santalesa was able to follow Izzy's career path first with London, then Rose and Hollywood Rose, and finally Guns N' Roses. "Hollywood Rose were very entertaining," he recounted. "Their bass player, Steve Darrow, used to do these crazy runs across the stage and Axl would leap on his shoulders. I saw Guns N' Roses at the Troubadour. I don't remember if it was their first or second show, but they introduced themselves as being from two bands, LA Guns and Hollywood Rose, so I thought it was a side project or something. I don't think it was their first show because Duff was the bass player and Ole Beich was the first bass player."

♫

Two other teenage tearaway wannabe musos that were set to feature large in Axl and Izzy's lives had both migrated to Southern California years earlier. Steven, a 19-year-old surfer-dude with an easy smile and laidback style, had relocated from his native Cleveland following his parents' separation. His buddy Saul Hudson, or "Slash", as he was known owing to his seemingly zipping hither and thither at lightning speed, was a transplanted English kid some three years older than himself. For some inexplicable reason, Slash chose to kick off his 2007 eponymously titled autobiography by stating he was born in Stoke-on-Trent (a polycentric West Midlands city famed for its pottery), when he was in fact born in Hampstead, north London (which he does at least confirm in Martyn Atkins' 2014 documentary, *Slash: Raised on the Sunset Strip*).

Slash lived in England until the age of four, the majority of which was spent with his artist dad, Tony, and his paternal grandparents in Stoke-on-Trent. In the aforementioned *Slash: Raised on the Sunset Strip* documentary, Slash jokingly cites this period as the "last years of stability I ever had".

Slash's American-born fashion designer mum, Ola, had returned to her native LA while her first-born was barely out of nappies in order to expand her business. In hindsight, it seems strange that Tony would choose to return to the Potteries to live with his parents as his relationship with his father was somewhat fractious owing to his steadfast determination to make a living through his art; returning from Paris with an equally carefree and strong-willed black American girl was to cause further consternation.

Reflecting on this period of his life, Slash said that once Tony was reunited with Ola in LA, his dad never spoke to his parents again. Indeed, Slash wouldn't see any of his English relatives again until Guns N' Roses rocked into London midway through the Use Your Illusion Tour in June 1992; his abiding memory from that night being his uncles, cousin, and grandfather laying waste to the backstage rider – a GN'R backstage rider to boot!

At the time of the Hudson family reunion, Ola was renting a bungalow in "Hippy Hollywood" off Laurel Canyon Boulevard. During the mid-to-late Sixties and early Seventies, Laurel Canyon was a countercultural enclave with the cream of LA's rock fraternity setting up home there including Mama Cass, Frank Zappa, James Taylor, Joni Mitchell, Jim Morrison, Carole King, John Mayall, Neil Young, and Micky Dolenz and Peter Tork of The Monkees. Indeed, Tork's drug-fuelled all-night parties have since gone down in West Hollywood folklore.

Joni Mitchell was something of a semi-permanent fixture at the bungalow as Ola designed her stage clothes, while Tony, having since channelled his creative talents to graphic art, designed the cover for her 1974 album

Court And Spark. Jim Morrison was living close by at the time, which may account for Slash's earliest LA memory being hearing The Doors' classic 'Light My Fire' blasting out from his parents' record player all day, every day. Another close family friend was David Geffen who at the time was looking after the interests of Laura Nyro and Crosby Stills & Nash, but would go on to found both Asylum Records and Geffen Records, the label that would beat all others to the punch in signing Guns N' Roses.

Geffen, of course, didn't oversee signings personally so for a time remained blithely unaware that he'd once babysat the corkscrew-haired guitarist within the label's latest acquisition. "We were bound and determined to make sure David Geffen didn't know who Saul Hudson was until it got to a point where [*Appetite for Destruction*] was sufficiently successful and David wanted to know who was involved," Guns' one-time manager Alan Niven revealed. "David's sitting there going, 'This is Saul Hudson? I know Saul Hudson. What do you mean he's in one of my bands on one of my labels? How did that happen?'

"We wanted to avoid a sense of nepotism; we wanted to avoid any baggage that might come with that. He (Slash) wanted to stand up on his own, so we kept that completely quiet."

By the time Slash's brother, Albion ("Ash"), arrived in December 1972 the family were living on Doheny Drive, a major north-south thoroughfare meandering through Beverly Hills and West Hollywood. Though only seven, he was old enough to acknowledge the change his sibling brought to the family dynamic, while savvy enough to also recognise the sea change taking place in his parents' relationship. The ensuing separation would at least prove an amicable one, with Tony continuing to live in the area and remaining in close contact – even after a new guy had entered Ola's life . . . A certain David Bowie.

Ola's career had really taken off and young Saul had thought nothing of accompanying his mum to various film and TV sets, being introduced to the likes of Stevie Wonder, Helen Reddy, Linda Ronstadt, Diana Ross and Ringo Starr. (He was also introduced to Ringo's fellow ex-Beatle, John, but much to his chagrin has no recollection of the occasion.)

Ola had started designing clothes for Bowie while he was recording *Young Americans* around November 1974. This in turn had led to her being invited to design the costumes for his first cinematic starring role as the humanoid alien, Thomas Jerome Newton, in Nicolas Roeg's *The Man Who Fell to Earth*. During the filming in New Mexico, Ola and Bowie embarked on what Slash describes as a "semi-intense affair"; the intensity levels proving sufficient for the Thin White Duke to record *Station to Station* at LA's Cherokee Studios.

Following her separation from Tony, Ola moved to a house on Rangely Drive in West Hollywood, and such was her relationship with Bowie that the latter would often bring his wife Angie and son Zowie along. "It seemed entirely natural for Bowie to bring his wife and son to the home of his lover so that we might all hang out," Slash recounted. "At the time my mother practiced the same form of transcendental meditation that David did. They chanted before the shrine she maintained in the bedroom."

While recording *Station to Station* Bowie played a show at the LA Forum, and Ola and Saul were his invited guests. Saul was captivated from the moment Bowie walked out onstage, recognising the familiar elements of the guy he'd come to know, only exaggerated to the extreme. "He (Bowie) had reduced rock stardom to its roots: being a rock star is the intersection of who you are and who you want to be."

Ola's laissez-faire attitude to life meant the teenage Saul had free rein – within reason, of course – to experiment with booze, cigarettes, and occasionally with soft drugs. As with many other kids his age he'd been captivated by the latest extreme sport, BMX racing. Indeed, he was to prove such a natural that winning races quickly became as easy as, well, riding a bike. He lived and breathed biking, spending most of his free time hanging around bike shops. He was soon invited onto the racing team for a local bike store, and everyone who knew him anticipated he would land a sponsor and turn professional.

> ## "It seemed entirely natural for Bowie to bring his wife and son to the home of his lover so that we might all hang out,"

Slash also proved something of an adept shoplifter. If he wasn't lifting cassette tapes of his favourite bands from music stores, he'd be walking out of pet stores with a snake or two strategically wrapped about his forearm. He'd then raid a local bookstore for books on how to rear snakes. As with most kleptomaniacs he was stealing for the thrill rather than the booty and, as such, it was only a matter of time before the inevitable happened; the inevitable occurring during a raid on Tower Records on Sunset Boulevard, where both his parents were regular patrons, serving to heighten his discomfiture. Though he'd thought to purchase a couple of albums to distract the cashiers, the store's in-house security had been watching – and filming – his nefarious activities. Fortunately, the store elected not to press charges but seeing his mum's pained expression when she came to collect him proved more of a deterrent than anything the juvenile courts might have thrown his way.

It wasn't long after his near brush with the law that Slash had first encountered Steven while he and his friends were hanging out in the Laurel Elementary School playground, a regular haunt for the neighbourhood kids. Steven, new to the area, was trying to impress with his skateboarding skills and failing miserably. After a particularly spectacular tumble, Slash had ridden over to help dust him down.

 12

♫

Steven had in fact been born Michael Coletti after his father, in keeping with Italian tradition. His elder brother, Tony, had been named after his paternal grandfather so the next son would take the name of the maternal grandfather or in Steven's case, his father's. When reflecting on his early life in his brutally honest 2010 autobiography, *My Appetite for Destruction*, Steven describes his dad as an "Italian gangster-wannabe with a bad gambling problem and a worse temper." He then goes on to say how his parents' marriage hit the skids while his mum, Deanna, was carrying him; that she was suffering both mental and physical abuse with frightening regularity and was most likely "plotting her escape" by the time he entered the world. His arrival did little to salve Mike Coletti's volatile temper, however, and when Deanna did finally rustle up the courage to leave her sorry excuse of a marriage, he left her battered and bleeding on her mother's front lawn.

Deanna was Jewish and naming one's offspring after the living is against Jewish tradition, yet she would have been too terrified to point this out to her husband for fear of another beating. Steven says he never saw their father from that day on, and his mom never saw so much as a red cent of the $30-a-week child support the judge had ordered Coletti to pay towards the upkeep of his sons. (Years later, Tony sought to trace their father via an online search and discovered Coletti had died in 2004.) Marrying a "capicola Catholic" had also flown in the face of the Jewish faith, and as such Deanna's relationship with her parents had been non-existent from the moment she'd announced her intentions. Though loath to go crawling cap in hand to her parents, she was 24, separated, with two young mouths to feed and had nowhere else to turn.

Steven's grandmother, Big Lilly, agreed to assist her daughter, but only after laying down two conditions: the first of which Deanna was only too happy to comply with in giving her sons new names

(brother Tony was renamed Kenny). The second condition came completely out of leftfield, however. Deanna was to give up Steven to live with them while she and Kenny moved into an apartment in the same complex. "I literally became their son and spent most of my childhood under their care," Steven goes on. "Mom was completely crushed [and] couldn't believe her son was being stolen away from her by *her parents.*"

By Steven's own admission, Lilly spoiled him rotten, usually turning a blind eye to his bratty behaviour. On the rare occasions when he did overstep the mark, however, he would be packed downstairs to live with Deanna. He would then purposely drive his mum to distraction until his grandma came to collect him and the process would begin all over again.

Steven describes himself as "one wild, crazy, fucked-up kid", and was imbued with a fervent contrarian streak as wide as the Cuyahoga River. Indeed, his earliest memories away from the ongoing familial war of wills betwixt his mum and grandmother primarily consist of creating mischief. He was thrown out of preschool after, among other things, locking one of the other kids in the toy cupboard and attacking the teacher when she tried admonishing him.

One of Deanna's older sisters was now living in Southern California and, with each of their bi-weekly phone conversations, Deanna became more and more enamoured with the idea of starting anew in sunnier climes; a life away from her mother's grace-and-favour clutches. Steven had come to note the lighter mood and conversational tone whenever his mum was on the phone to his auntie, and so wasn't all that surprised when Deanna mooted the idea of paying her sister an extended visit; a visit, that all being well, would lead to a permanent move.

Steven had lived and breathed his mum's marital miseries but overhearing her phone conversations to a boyfriend back in Cleveland had caught him completely unawares; his surprise was compounded when a beaming Melvyn Adler arrived at the door of their tiny North Hollywood home with a suitcase and promises of a better

GUNS N' ROSES

life for them all. So it was to prove, as Deanna and Melvyn were married in 1973, with a bouncing baby boy, Jamie, arriving not long after; the domesticity being completed with Adler adopting Kenny and Steven.

♫

Axl may have left Lafayette behind but the old adage about not being able to take the city out of the boy was all too evident during the first few months of his arrival in LA. Whereas Izzy oozed a Keith Richards cool the local homegrown musicians both admired and longed to emulate, Axl's insecurities, coupled with a hair-trigger temper, meant people tended to give him a wide birth. Izzy had sensed from the get-go that Axl had the potential to be a "fucking great singer"; so much so, that he'd been willing to shrug off his friend's mercurial mood swings. Yet all his attempts to get Axl a gig would end in abject failure. That was, until the aforementioned Rapidfire took the plunge during the spring of 1983.

Axl was only with Rapidfire two months or so, but in that time they would come out on top in a battle of the bands competition staged at Gazzarri's, and recorded a demo featuring five original compositions: 'Ready to Rumble', 'The Prowler', 'All Night Long', 'On The Run', and 'Closure'. "We used to hang out at the Troubadour and Gazzarri's all the time and I just met him," guitarist Kevin Lawrence told www.maxim.com in November 2014. "We used to see each other around the club and started chatting."

Lawrence had been the singer prior to Axl's arrival but had hated singing and was desperate to bring in a frontman so that he could concentrate on the guitar. "Axl said he was a singer, and my first question was, 'Do you have a PA?' He said he did, and I said, 'Come on out and audition.' His PA never left our studio until he quit the band."

Axl was still plain old Bill Bailey/W Rose at the time, of course, but Lawrence says Axl had tentatively enquired if the band might consider a name change to A-X-L. Lawrence says Axl's

aspirations at the time he joined Rapidfire didn't extend much beyond being able to buy himself a pair of snakeskin boots. He also remembered Axl suffering a bout of stage fright when making his live debut and taking some time to loosen up.

Axl's last show with Rapidfire came in late May 1983, just three days after the band had recorded the demos – reportedly with Izzy in attendance. Again, Lawrence has cause to recall the occasion, if only for Axl's stage wear. "He arrived at the last minute with his white jacket dyed pink and his hair aqua-netted and straight out, like in 'Welcome to the Jungle'. I remember [our drummer], Chuck (Gordon), going, 'You're not going onstage like that!' I said to Axl, 'Let's do this gig and then kind of see how it goes but this isn't the vision that we have for this band.'"

Being dictated to – even in such a conciliatory manner – wasn't something that sat easily with Axl, of course, and as soon as the show was over he went backstage to inform Lawrence he was quitting the band. "He wanted to play with Izzy because they came out from Indiana," Lawrence explained. "We said best of luck to each other, and he invited me to his first Rose gig – before it was even Hollywood Rose. It was me, Chuck, and two waitresses in the whole Troubadour."

Not wishing to denigrate Rapidfire's talents in any way, had it not been for Axl's brief stint in the line-up it's unlikely anyone would remember the name – just one of a thousand bands that had come together on Sunset Strip; the mile-and-a-half stretch of Sunset Boulevard that serves as the petri dish of LA's underbelly. But that's how it was on the Strip during the mid-to-late Eighties. Bands formed, played, broke up on a near daily basis; the more talented musicians splintering off to form better bands that played a few bottom-of-the-rung dates at Gazzarri's, the Whisky, or the Troubadour, before either the singer or lead guitarist – or sometimes both – realised the futility in trying to polish a turd and jumped back aboard the musical merry-go-round.

Having turned his back on music at 25, Lawrence went on to make and lose a fortune in internet porn while the Rapidfire eight-track

demos lay collecting dust. In November 2014, however – after several years of legal wrangling with Axl's lawyers – Lawrence finally released the five tracks as the *Ready to Rumble* EP. He certainly hadn't been looking to cash in with the EP, he was just pissed off that other people were releasing product claiming to be the "first-ever Axl Rose recordings".

Lawrence was to suffer a fatal heart attack brought on by pneumonia in January 2016, aged just 51. His once-upon-a-while-ago association with Axl proved sufficient to ensure an obituary in several music mags – and rightly so, because electing to abandon the mic to concentrate on playing guitar serves as the first definitive link in the GN'R chain.

♫

Slash and Steven's fateful encounter in the playground at Laurel Elementary had come during the summer vacation prior to entering eighth grade (13 to 14-year-olds). At the time Steven was living out in the San Fernando Valley, which to Slash's mind – as indeed it was to most Angelenos – was almost as far removed from LA as either New York or Boston. Steven's wayward behaviour had driven Deanna to the point where she packed him off to live with her new in-laws in Hollywood, where he was to remain until reaching high school age. As luck would have it, he and Slash ended up attending the same school, Bancroft Junior High, owing to Slash having recently moved in with his grandmother at her new Hollywood condo.

Slash admits to being academically minded enough to at least pay attention in the classes that interested him (art, music and English), whereas Steven looked upon school as a chore, one that should be avoided whenever possible. As such, the two miscreants could usually be found wiling away their afternoons wandering up and down Sunset Boulevard bullshitting the breeze or panhandling loose change for the jukebox at their preferred hangout, Piece

O' Pizza. Even at 13, Steven seemed to have narrowed his ambitions down to having sex with as many foxy chicks as possible and playing in a happening rock band; the two goals going hand-in-hand presumably. With this in mind, he'd thrash away to his favourite Kiss, Queen, and Boston albums on the crappy Wal-Mart electric guitar and practice amp that he'd cajoled his grandmother into buying him. It was therefore inevitable that he'd invite his best buddy to help him realise his goals.

Though he'd grown up immersed in music, Slash says he'd never really stopped to consider which instruments were responsible for creating the sounds he heard either on the radio or on vinyl. With Steven "learning" guitar, it made sense for him to maybe try his hand at bass. It's strange to imagine someone who has come to be regarded as one of the greatest guitar players of the modern age not knowing the difference betwixt bass and electric guitars as a teenager. Yet this was evidenced by arriving for his first lesson at Fairfax Music School armed with a battered flamenco guitar (replete with one solitary nylon string) that his grandmother had fished from the back of a closet. And it's here that Robert Wolin takes a rightful bow. For imagine the loss the rock world might have suffered had Wolin – the teacher Slash was introduced to on first enquiring about taking bass lessons – assumed he was being made fun of and sent the youngster packing with a flea in his ear.

Slash remembers being blown away on hearing Van Halen for the first time at Steven's grandmother's, but it was watching Wolin playing along to the Stones' 'Brown Sugar' that was to set him on his path. "That's when I heard '*the sound*' . . . Whatever Robert was doing, that was *it*. I stared at Robert's guitar with total wonder. I started pointing at it. 'That's what I want to do,' I told him. '*That!*'"

Taking a line from Chuck Berry's 'Johnny B. Goode', Slash would indeed take to playing the guitar like he was ringing a bell. Refitting the flamenco with six strings took longer than Wolin might have anticipated but following the chord

GUNS N' ROSES

charts he'd sketched out Slash was soon playing along to his favourite songs – albeit in the most rudimentary of fashions. Like any prodigy, having to painstakingly go over the fundamentals – such as memorising the prerequisite major, minor and blues scales – proved frustrating, yet nonetheless provided the necessary grounding.

Flexi that changed history!

In another of those unanticipated life-enhancing moments, Slash was rummaging through a guitar store bargain bin when he happened upon what he has since described as his "Holy Grail". It was as if the dog-eared copy of *How to Play Rock Guitar* (replete with 45 rpm flexi-disc) had fallen to earth like his mum's now ex-boyfriend's screen character. "I took that thing home and devoured it," he reflected. "Once I was capable of mimicking the sounds on that little record, I was soon improvising on my own, and then I was beside myself. That book changed my life!"

Slash has the book still, locked away in some trunk in the attic. Despite several internet forays he's never found another copy, and the romantic in him has come to believe the book found him rather than the other way round.

Having borrowed $100 from his grandmother Slash bought himself a Les Paul copy; the readily identifiable solid-body shape epitomising the sound he hoped to make. Armed with the tools to go it alone he bid Wolin and Fairfax Music School a heartfelt fond farewell. Perfecting his guitar playing was now the only thing focusing his mind; better than BMX biking, better than booze, better than weed. Hell, it was even better than making out!

Though already an Aerosmith fan, it wasn't until hearing *Rocks* at some party or other that his epiphany was complete; the album's "dirty alley cat vibe" catching him completely unawares. "If lead guitar was the undiscovered voice that had resided within me, this was the record I'd waited my whole life to hear: the screaming vocals, dirty guitars, and relentless grooves are bluesy rock'n'roll as it is meant to be played."

While Axl was busy with Rapidfire, Izzy had struck up a mutual admiration with Tracy Ulrich, a hip and happening 17-year-old guitar player who'd recently taken to calling himself "Tracii Guns". Izzy had been hoping they might start a band together, but Tracii already had something going with a Fairfax High School buddy of his called Rob Gardner – a nascent LA Guns. Tracii, however, recognised Izzy's worth, and introduced him to Chris Weber, another Fairfax High alumnus. Izzy met with Chris the following night in the parking lot at the Rainbow Bar & Grill. The two hit it off and started jamming together the very next afternoon; a shared love of Aerosmith leading to their penning a clutch of songs influenced by the Boston-based quintet's most recent album, the previous year's *Rock in a Hard Place*.

Axl had served notice on Rapidfire specifically to work with Izzy, but having grown up sharing a zip code didn't mean dick to Weber. If Axl wanted in, then he was going to have to prove himself. This Axl duly did; being able to switch octaves with effortless ease leaving Weber mesmerised. Unlike Kevin Lawrence, Weber and Izzy raised no objection to Axl's suggestion they call their band A-X-L, even going so far as to daub the new moniker in three-foot-high letters on a wall running along Sunset Strip. They also countenanced Axl's mercurial mood swings, his walkouts and subsequent returns, and insistence on band name changes – first to Rose, then to the infinitely glitzier sounding Hollywood Rose.

"Our first gig was at Raji's in Hollywood," Izzy revealed on the *On Down The Road* fan page. "We realised that if you wanted to get a club gig, you had to say, 'Oh, man, we're huge in Orange County. We play these keggers, and they're massive. We can probably get 500 people.' Then seven people would show up, but we got to play."

Hollywood Rose have come to be regarded as a precursor to Guns N' Roses, if only because Axl, Izzy, Slash, and Steven Adler all featured in the line-up at various stages during the band's initial 12-month or so tenure; the link being indelibly cemented by a five-track demo recorded sometime during 1984 that contains the nuclei of three GN'R songs – 'Anything Goes', 'Reckless Life', and 'Shadow of Your Love'.

'Anything Goes' would appear on *Appetite for Destruction*, while 'Reckless Life' appeared on both the *Live?!*@ Like a Suicide* EP and *GN'R Lies*. 'Shadow of Your Love', a mainstay of early GN'R sets, was recorded during the *Appetite* sessions – with Steven subsequently expressing his disappointment over the song failing to make the album's final cut – but was destined to remain tucked away in the Geffen vaults until finally being released as a digital download in May 2018 as a taster single for *Appetite for Destruction: Locked n' Loaded Edition*.

Hollywood Rose were beginning to get noticed when Izzy upped and quit to join London, the now-legendary Sunset Strip

feeder band that can happily boast its whole proving somewhat lesser than its individual parts. Indeed, London are credited in Penelope Spheeris' 1988 film, *The Decline of Western Civilization Part II: The Metal Years*, as a "rock star training academy". Aside from Izzy, London provided a grounding for a host of soon-to-be-fuckin' famous rockers, notably Nikki Sixx (Mötley Crüe), Fred Coury (Cinderella) and Blackie Lawless (W.A.S.P.)

London had been ploughing a forlorn rut on and off since 1978 and founding guitarist Lizzie Grey was busy recruiting fresh blood in the hope of finding favour amid the resurgent West Hollywood glam metal scene. Izzy was quick to realise his mistake, but such was the fluidity of the scene that Axl had dissolved Hollywood Rose after agreeing to join LA Guns. Axl would soon give backword to Tracii before sloping off to reform Hollywood Rose with Izzy. While there was no danger of the music ever stopping, and no shortage of chairs, the frenetic chopping and changing must have proved confusing to those watching from the side-lines.

♫

Slash, meantime, formed his first proper band, Tidus Sloan, with a couple of his Fairfax High School peers – Adam Greenberg and Ron Schneider on drums and bass respectively. As the trio never got around to recruiting a singer they played instrumental versions of early songs from some of their favourite bands: Deep Purple, Black Sabbath, Rush, Led Zeppelin, Stones etc. It was at Fairfax High that Slash had first encountered Tracii Guns, who was rocking out with his own school outfit, Pyrhus; his green-eyed envy over the latter owning a genuine Les Paul rather than a third-rate copy serving to kickstart an internecine rivalry that would last throughout their time at Fairfax High and beyond.

GUNS N' ROSES

Upon leaving school, or upon being asked to leave school, to be more precise, Slash took a variety of jobs, one of the more interesting ones coming at the Hollywood Music Store which was located across the street from Cherokee Studios where several of the artists he would end up either sharing a stage with or guest on their albums had recorded: Aerosmith, Alice Cooper, Michael Jackson, and Mötley Crüe. It was also where Bowie had recorded *Station to Station* while with Slash's mum, of course.

Slash was hoping being in the heart of the action, so to speak, would lead to bigger and better things than playing keg parties with Tidus Sloan. He would also comb the Musicians Wanted ads in *The Recycler* each week hoping to find one that wasn't the usual "shredder-seeks-shredder-to-shred-together" dross. One ad that did catch his eye was that of a singer and guitarist seeking a "non-bearded or moustachioed guitarist in the Aerosmith and Hanoi Rocks vein". Slash duly called the number accompanying the ad and arrangements were made to meet later that day at the Laurel Canyon address the guitarist had given him.

The guitarist's voice had sounded vaguely familiar, but it wouldn't be until arriving at the guesthouse his potential new bandmates were currently renting that the mists parted. It was the same guy – the one oozing Johnny Thunders cool with the groovy name to match – that had sought him out at the Music Store a few weeks back to compliment him on a throwaway sketch he'd made of Aerosmith. Upon discovering Izzy was a fellow guitar player, Slash had invited him to swing by his place later that same evening. Izzy had brought a cassette tape of his band. The recording quality was pitiable, but through the static din Slash heard an intriguing high-pitched squeal that he'd initially assumed to be a technical flaw in the tape . . . except that it was in key.

The guesthouse was so small there was barely enough room to breathe; the only light emanating from the TV in the corner. Yet it was sufficient for Slash to catch a first glimpse of Axl. Axl happened to be on the phone when Slash arrived and had merely nodded an acknowledgement while continuing his conversation. Slash's chat with Izzy had proved somewhat stilted, and he'd come away again assuming his "non-bearded or moustachioed look" had fallen short of their expectations. The drive home was tinged with disappointment as Izzy and Axl had certainly met with his criteria of how a rock band should look . . . but the stars weren't quite yet ready to align.

Steven was back on the Hollywood scene now. He'd wasted no time in letting it be known that he'd abandoned the guitar in favour of learning the drums so that he and Slash might make good on their dream in starting a band together. Slash, however, was still struggling to take his friend seriously – especially when Steven began showing up at Tidus Sloan rehearsals and openly dissing Adam Greenberg's abilities. Indeed, Slash's reticence extended to skilfully avoiding all discussion about getting something together even after his bringing the curtain down on Tidus Sloan.

Steven would prove relentless, however; his endless puppy-dog pestering gradually wearing down Slash's resolve to the point where he agreed to drive over to the public park on Pico Boulevard where his friend had taken to practicing. The park was in complete darkness by the time he parked up beside Steven's car, but all he'd had to do was follow the double-bass beat. Steven had strategically set his drums up at a section of the park's walking/jogging path so that he was backlit by the distant floodlights. It was a surreal sight, seeing Steven pounding away oblivious to everything with his tousled blond locks bouncing in conjunction with the rhythm. Though unconvinced of his friend's abilities, Slash was nonetheless sold.

There were those in Slash's close circle of friends that would have seen starting out from scratch with an untried drummer as a backward stride. Yet Slash says he wasn't unduly fazed as whatever Steven may have lacked in terms of musical proficiency he more than made up for with always knowing what was going down on the Strip. Upon learning Lizzie Grey's London were auditioning for a drummer and guitarist (to replace the recently departed Izzy), Slash and Steven readily threw their hats into the ring. They got the gig and spent the best part of a week rehearsing with the reconstituted London working up a set from the band's sizeable canon. Nothing ever came of Grey's latest rehash, but Steven had at least proved himself capable of holding down a beat.

Rather than sit around awaiting another opportunity to join a band, Slash and Steven opted for grabbing the bull by the horns and striking out on their own. They settled on the name Road Crew and placed an ad in *The*

Recycler classifieds seeking a bass player; the logic being snagging a bass player meant they would have better luck in finding the right frontman when the time came. As Slash and Steven had anticipated, name-checking Aerosmith and Alice Cooper in the ad had resulted in a certain level of interest. One guy, however, had stood out from the others. Recently arrived in LA from his native Seattle, this one had sounded like he had the walk to match the talk. He also had a cool-sounding name.

"As far as I could tell, there was really no discernible rock scene in Los Angeles in the fall of 1984 - only the palpable hangover of a once-thriving punk movement, a thriving but really bad heavy-metal scene, and something called 'cow punk'. This was basically punk-rock dudes in plaid shirts trying to play Patsy Cline songs with their fat girlfriends singing."

DUFF

PART TWO

HUNGRY FOR SOMETHIN'

Twenty-year-old Michael "Duff" McKagan did indeed possess the stride to match the cut of his cocksure jibe. He could play guitar and drums as well as bass, and by his own estimation, had tried his hand in over 30 Seattle-based bands before deciding to expand his horizons. Being the youngest of eight children had given him more latitude than his elder siblings while growing up. His parents might have been closer in age to his classmates' grandparents but having a dad that had served during World War II, and who was now working as a fireman, coming to pick him up at the end of the school day more than compensated for any discomfiture he may have felt.

McKagan senior certainly didn't see age as a setback. With the Cascades mountain range (stretching from southern British Columbia, through Washington and Oregon and into northern California) practically on their doorstep, he thought nothing of taking Duff and his older brother Matt on back-packing trips up into the Alpine Lakes region to hunt and fish and camp under the stars. Within such settings, Duff naturally viewed his hunter/provider dad as being nigh-on omnipotent, but the illusion was to be shattered when he arrived home from school one day to find his hero in bed with a next-door neighbour – the mother of his best friend.

The anguish of catching his dad in the act left him feeling somehow responsible for the ensuing family break-up. When the panic attacks over the part he may or may not have played in his role model dad fleeing the family home started to kick in he began self-medicating, first with alcohol and then with drugs. A near-death experience while water-skiing during a subsequent summer vacation was to also to shape his formative thinking; the "feeling of warmth and bliss" that had washed over him as he lost consciousness removing any fear of death he might have been harbouring, if only subconsciously. "I felt a sense of exceptionalism after that," he revealed in his 2011 autobiography, *It's So Easy (And Other Lies)*. "But I also now operated under the assumption that I would die young – that this had just been a preview of a death that would come sooner rather than later, and definitely by thirty."

Rock'n'roll had served as a backdrop in the McKagan household for as long as Duff could remember, with several of his older siblings playing one musical instrument or another. His brother Bruce had advanced to a level where he was playing occasional bar-room gigs, and Duff would eagerly await his return to listen to another tale that reinforced his romantic image of what it must be like to hit the road, guitar in hand. Bruce also gave Duff his first lessons on bass; both being left-handed only proving problematic once the elder sibling moved out, taking his guitars with him. Having been born with an ear for music meant learning any song came naturally to Duff. He'd as yet no idea how to go about constructing a self-penned song and imagined years of painstaking practice ahead of him before he reached such a level. Hearing The Stooges' *Raw Power* for the first time would soon wash away any such preconceived notions, however.

Punk rock might have been considered old hat in some circles by 1978, but it was still fresh and exciting to the 14-year-old Duff's formative mind. He and best buddy, Andy Fortier, would think nothing of hotwiring a car to get them to an appointed punk party in some remote part of town. Indeed, if anything, their devil-may-care attitude served to heighten the euphoria. What had started out as a simple means to an end, however, quickly escalated to the point where tales of their nefarious escapades began appearing in the local newspapers. Unlike Axl some 2,000 miles away in Lafayette, Duff had yet to come under the local cops' radar. But it was surely only a matter of time before he heard the wail of sirens or the dreaded knock at the door. Thankfully, Duff was steered away from his criminal path when Chris Utting – whom Duff describes as "an older punkish kid with a mohawk calling himself Chris Crass – approached him to play bass in a new progressive punk band he was putting together called Thankless Dogs. Crass had already recruited Mike Refuzor (aka Mike Lambert), a guitarist of some renown who was already regarded as something of a punk legend in and around Seattle.

It also happened that Crass was on the lookout for a drummer, so Duff put Andy's name forward so that he wouldn't have to enter the lion's den alone. To Duff's astonishment, Andy got the gig. Both adopted a suitable punk *nom de guerre* – Duff "Nico Tine" McKagan, and Andy "Andy Freeze" Fortier. Aside from playing in a band with a bona fide musician like

Refuzor, Duff received what he describes as a "crash-course on how to act cool in a situation that was completely beyond the scope of my experience."

Refuzor was to prove a great mentor for Duff and with the guitarist's encouragement he took his first tentative stab at song-writing. He was understandably nervous when presenting his "little opus" to the others, but the song 'The Fake' – was well received. Indeed, it was so well received that it's one of the three songs the band recorded at Seattle's original rock shop – American Music Recording on Fremont Avenue – along with 'School Jerks' and 'The Loser'. By this juncture, however, Refuzor had gone off to form The Refuzors, and Thankless Dogs had undergone a name change to The Vains. "Looking back, we were very young at the time the record was cut," Utting told *nwmusicarchives.com*. "I think it turned out so well it really scared us. We couldn't handle that, so we broke up."

Utting describes 'The Fake' as an up-tempo, spontaneous rocker concerned with a "phony person", Duff and the rest of the band presumably knew from the Seattle punk scene. (*The Loser EP* was subsequently released via the No Threes label in April 1981.)

Duff made his live debut with The Vains on a three-band bill during the summer of 1979 at a local community centre. He and Fortier had kerbed their more daring criminal exploits yet were happy to pilfer a couple of dozen milk crates from the back of a grocery store and covered them with plywood to serve as a makeshift stage. The show attracted around 90 to 100 people and as The Vains took to the stage Duff was overwhelmed with the sensation that this was his destiny.

He remembered little about the show itself other than it being a moment of perfection. "Suddenly, all I wanted to do was play music," he reflected. "Day and night. But not everyone wanted to rehearse, or at least not as much as I did, so I tried to stay in multiple bands, so I always had people to play with. I started practising multiple instruments, too, so I could fill any position a band had open: *guitar, drums, bass, whatever, I'll join!"*

It wasn't long after the Vains show that Duff was introduced to Kim Warnick, lead singer with another of Seattle's leading punk bands, The Fastbacks. During an ad hoc jam, Warnick mentioned that The Fastbacks were looking for a drummer as the one they had – Kurt Bloch – was far better on guitar than he was behind the drums. Despite being five years younger than Kim and the other Fastbacks, Duff immediately put himself forward for the drumming gig. And what's more, he got it. (He played on The Fastbacks' 1981 single, 'It's Your Birthday'.)

Duff was still playing with The Fastbacks when he put The Fartz together with Paul Solger, another buddy from the local scene. The Fartz were an off-the-cuff outfit with an equally throwaway name, and it wasn't until they evolved into Ten Minute Warning that any measure of success was achieved; their slower, heavier sound reputedly paving the way for grunge. "By then a lot of us in the [Seattle] punk scene were getting fed up with paint-by-numbers hardcore," Duff explained. "Ten Minute Warning's solution was to slow things way down from hard-core speeds and add a sludgy, heavy psychedelic element. Black Flag's singer, Henry Rollins, told us we sounded like a punk rock version of Hawkwind. We took this as high praise. We were getting better and better."

It would prove a hard slog, but by 1984 Ten Minute Warning were being lauded as the Pacific Northwest's premier punk act, commanding $250 to $300 per headline show. They were also making a name for themselves elsewhere touring with D.O.A., Dead Kennedys, and their ultimate heroes, Black Flag.

Another of Duff's musical heroes was Sid Vicious, the ex-Sex Pistol that had OD'd on heroin in early February 1979 aged just 21, while awaiting trial for the murder of his girlfriend Nancy Spungen; his emulation going so far as to include a padlock and chain about his neck. Vicious' tragic fate hadn't served as

a warning – ten minute, or otherwise – among Duff's punk peers, however, as heroin was now the drug de jour on the Seattle scene. Solger would soon end up getting caught up in the vicious cycle of needing to score so that he could get straight to raise the cash to score again. By the middle of 1984 he was so strung out that Duff could see little point in continuing with the band.

Realising that remaining in Seattle might end up proving detrimental both to his health and musical aspirations, Duff's initial plan was to make for New York. Limited funds, coupled with having established plenty of punk contacts and crash pads all the way down the West Coast as far as San Francisco, made making for LA a more practical option. Besides, the climate in LA was infinitely more agreeable, and with his brother Matt already there studying to be a music teacher at Cal State University in Northridge, he would have someone to turn to should his plans hit the skids for any reason.

Sensing guitarists were two-a-penny in LA he decided the best way to get a gig – and a foothold on the scene – would be to make bass his main instrument. He hadn't played bass since quitting The Vains but had recently started experimenting again playing a Yamaha guitar through a crazy Peavey head and acoustic 2x15 cabinet in search of a sound that he could use as his signature. He'd sold his Marshall combo amp to fund his venture but decided it prudent to take his B.C. Rich Seagull guitar just in case. With $360 in cash, and a solid reference from the owner of the Lake Union Cafe where he'd been working as a sous chef in his pocket, he climbed behind the wheel of his '71 Ford Maverick and set off in search of his dreams.

He kept on driving till he reached San Francisco, the intention being to crash at a punk squat overnight before continuing on to LA. Having played in Ten Minute Warning had given him plenty of kudos on the Bay Area punk scene, however, so his plans ended up going slightly awry. There was also a girl in the equation, of course. By the time he did resume

GUNS N' ROSES

his journey a week or so later his kitty had dwindled to just sixty bucks.

The situation wasn't yet desperate, but close enough for concern. Matt McKagan was paying his way through school working as a cook at a Black Angus steakhouse, and Duff was hoping his brother might be able to pull a string or two. Getting the directions to the Black Angus from Matt, he drove straight over to the steakhouse and started his first shift as a prep chef that same night. The only downside was Northridge's location out in the Valley some 25 miles from West Hollywood, the epicentre of LA's music scene and therefore the fulcrum of Duff's ambitions. Schlepping to and from Hollywood in search of a gig wasn't really an option, and Duff was to spend many a night in the Hollywood Hills curled up on the back of his car.

Duff had little interest in looking to join a punk band as he might well have extended his stay in San Francisco. To his way of thinking hardcore punk was on the wane, and it was up to those such as himself to steer punk in a new and exciting direction, creating the next paradigm. He thought his luck was in on espying Slash's *Recycler* ad as anyone with a name like "Slash" had to be operating on a similar wavelength.

♫

Slash and Steven had arranged to meet their prospective new bassist at Canter's, a 24-hour deli on North Fairfax that was owned by the family of Slash's closest confidant, Marc.

Slash had first encountered Marc Canter back in Third Street Elementary, though by his own admission the two didn't become friends until he'd tried stealing the latter's bicycle in fifth grade. "When I barely had money to eat or even buy myself guitar strings Marc was there for me," Slash explained. "He'd front me the cash to take care of whatever needed to be done. I paid him back once I was able,

once Guns got signed. But I never forgot that Canter was there for me when I was down and out."

Canter's friendship with Slash meant he was perfectly placed to document the rise of Guns N' Roses, for a time serving as the band's official photographer. As Slash says, he readily supported the band paying for fliers, ads, demos, etc, as well as providing food and friendship. Many of Canter's photos appear in the artwork for *Appetite for Destruction* and *Guns N' Roses: Live Era 87-93*. His 2008, *Reckless Road: Guns N' Roses and The Making of Appetite for Destruction*, would scoop the Independent Publisher Award for best pop culture book.

Slash and Steven had their girlfriends in tow and were housed in a corner booth of Cantor's sharing an illicit bottle of vodka when Duff idled through the door. Slash says the four of them had been debating what Duff might look like. They'd been anticipating your everyday rocker, not some "bone-skinny, six-foot-plus guy with short spiked blond hair... wearing a Sid Vicious-style chain and padlock around his neck, combat boots – and a red and black leather trench coat in spite of the 75-degree weather." Slash gave Steven a sly kick under the table, while both elbowed their girlfriends to choke off any chuckling.

Duff had mentioned he'd be wearing his floor-length "pimp coat" during his phone call with Slash. The anarchy symbol he'd daubed on the back with red paint shortly after forming The Fartz was blacked out with Sharpie marker but still faintly visible. His initial impression of Slash and Steven was equally memorable. "I walked in, looked at the first booth on the left, and saw all this fucking hair," he recounted. "Somehow, I had expected these guys to look like Social Distortion. Of course, with my short Day-Glo blue hair and long coat, I must have looked like a Martian to them. Both parties were a little surprised and curious when we first met face-to-face."

Canter's Deli is located on Fairfax Avenue within LA's "Miracle Mile District". With its Art Deco décor and trademark autumn leaves ceiling, Canter's Deli was soon attracting Hollywood's showbiz elite. The Kibbitz Room cocktail lounge would prove the preferred late-night hangout for LA's rock and counter-cultural fraternity. One can picture the nascent Guns N' Roses huddled together in one of the booths wondering where their next meal might come from, little realising that in a few short years their names would stand alongside those of Marilyn Monroe, Elizabeth Taylor, Sydney Poitier, John Travolta, and Shelly Winters to name but a few of Canter's celebrity diners.

Slash's squeeze, Yvonne, was curious about Duff's sexuality and had leaned across the table to ask him outright if he was gay. With the ice now well and truly broken, they all piled into one of the upstairs bathrooms and celebrated Duff's induction into Road Crew. From Canter's, the five made their way back to Slash's mum's place where he was temporarily living at the time. Duff was still unsure what he was letting himself in for but says watching Slash strumming on an acoustic guitar as a "holy shit" moment: "He was 19 years old and playing like a really smooth old blues guy. He played with so much age; there was so much depth to his musicality. I was kinda stunned."

The trio started rehearsing together at an hourly-rate rehearsal space at the corner of Highland and Selma. The creativity was soon flowing freer than the whisky and wine Steven was throwing down his throat at any

given opportunity; the main riff that would subsequently feature in 'Rocket Queen' being just one of several promising song ideas the trio came up with. Steven says he sensed immediately that Duff was a rock star in the making from the moment he'd stepped through the deli door. "I thought he was totally right for the look we were after," he explained. "We hit it off right away, right down to the bands we liked, and just as important, the bands we didn't."

Slash believes that if they'd have found the right singer then Road Crew would have been a "band that was worth something". As it was, however, Steven's acting as if they'd already made it was soon grating on Slash's nerves. Slash came to the conclusion that nothing was likely to come of anything with Steven acting the way he was, going so far as to completely sever his ties with him for a while. Duff, however, has a different take on the demise of the short-lived

Road Crew. He felt he was taking a backward step; that he'd regressed to playing in a high school band. Having learned his chops playing with "countless professional musicians" in bands too numerous to mention back in Seattle, he hadn't moved all the way down to LA to "play with people who were still trying to figure their shit out."

Adopting a tone he might use when calling time on a relationship, Duff says he told Slash and Steven he didn't want to make music with them anymore but would still like to be friends. Slash and Steven were okay with this. A few weeks later they invited him to tag along to The Troubadour to catch Tracii Guns' new outfit LA Guns, who may or may not have featured Axl on vocals that night, depending on who you ask.

♫

Mötley Crüe's breakthrough second album, *Shout at The Devil*, had propelled them beyond the insular West Hollywood scene; so much so that frontman Vince Neil being charged with vehicular manslaughter after causing an accident that resulted in the death of Hanoi Rocks' drummer, Nicholas "Razzle" Dingley, failed to deflect their upward trajectory.

There were plenty of West Hollywood bands vying to emulate the Crüe's success, and of these, LA Guns were the only one deemed worthy of taking a shot at the title. Slash knew all about LA Guns, of course, owing to his ongoing rivalry with Tracii Guns. But even if Hollywood Rose were as yet still an unknown quantity – despite having already heard the band through his encounter with Izzy at the Hollywood Music Store – Slash still failed to join the dots when Steven returned from a Hollywood Rose show raving about the "high-pitched singer, a guy who could tear the roof off."

The mechanics of the human memory are such that no matter how many people witness the same events, each will remember them differently as the unfolding events are inevitably coloured by variations in the individuals' attention and emotional state. The passage of time is also a key factor, of course, and given the years of substance abuse Slash, Steven, and Duff would each go through, it's little wonder their versions of the same events are so startlingly diametric. As such, Slash remembers it not being until accompanying Steven to Gazzarri's to see Hollywood Rose that he finally connected the screech he'd heard on the crappy tape to the guy standing onstage. Regardless of which band Axl happened to be fronting, from the moment he let rip his first guttural shriek Slash knew instantly that he was seeing "hands down the best singer in Hollywood at the time."

Slash wasn't overly impressed with Hollywood Rose as a whole, but Axl's onstage interaction with Izzy was to leave a lasting impression. "Those two friends from Lafayette, Indiana, had an ominous presence about them. Izzy kept doing knee slides all over the stage and Axl screamed his fucking heart out – their performance was blistering. Axl's voice drew me in immediately; it was so versatile, and underneath his impossibly high-pitched shrieking, the bluesy natural rhythm he had was riveting."

> ## "Slash kind of made a noncommittal grunt, which you got to understand in Slash-speak is a very positive response."

It's more than likely that Slash and Steven would have given Duff the heads up as to which Sunset Strip bands – other than LA Guns – were worth making the effort to check out. Whether they mentioned Hollywood Rose to Duff is a

matter of conjecture, but Duff was at least familiar with Izzy – from both turning up at the door of a girl they'd both believed to be their date for that evening. Instead of feigning some macho posturing, the potentially embarrassing situation was quickly shrugged aside owing to their instantly recognising a kindred spirit. With the girl forgotten, the conversation turned to music; each name-checking the bands they most held dear. Duff says how Izzy had reminded him of "some of the cooler figures" he'd known back in Seattle. Espying Izzy loitering by a payphone in a hotel lobby close to the roach-infested apartment block on Orchid Street where he was now living, he'd idled over to say hello.

It transpired that Izzy had moved in across the street. Duff had only been living in the area a couple of weeks himself, but he knew enough to know the alley directly behind Izzy's new abode was considered a no-go area during even daylight hours. Having watched some of his closest friends back in Seattle get themselves sucked into heroin, Duff readily recognised the same tell-tale signs in Izzy. What he wouldn't learn until sometime later, however, was that Izzy had chosen his new dwelling with specific intent as it allowed him to peddle heroin from his back window free from prying eyes.

♫

Slash was still plotting his next step when Steven landed the drum stool in Hollywood Rose. He was no doubt envious of his buddy playing with the best singer on the scene, but within a couple of weeks Steven joining the band, Chris Weber was suddenly out. Steven readily put Slash's name forward as Weber's replacement. "I went back to the apartment and I told Slash, 'Dude, these guys are great, they're totally original, very cool, and they want to meet you,'" Steven reflected. "Slash kind of made a noncommittal grunt, which you got to understand in Slash-speak is a very positive response."

Slash accompanied Steven over to Izzy's place where he was properly introduced to Axl and also met with Hollywood Rose's bassist, Steve Darrow. Steven still hadn't said anything about the reason for Weber's sudden departure and he himself had no particular urge to pry. Steven remembers Slash borrowing Izzy's guitar at some point during the course of the evening and "tore off some cool lead stuff" – just enough to impress without showing off.   There was no formal offer for Slash to join Hollywood Rose, but Axl had decided he would make a perfect foil for Izzy's playing style. Axl had neglected to say as much to Izzy, however, and midway through their first get-together he casually unslung his guitar and disappeared out of the door. There was an awkward pause before Steven hit the toms and they resumed playing. It wouldn't be last time Izzy was to take a powder in the GN'R story, of course. It seemed Axl had neglected to inform Izzy of his decision to sack Weber. Slash, himself, was in the dark about Tracii Guns having auditioned for Hollywood Rose – or indeed, the latter guitarist's continued attempts to poach Axl and Izzy for LA Guns. Amid all the intrigue, Hollywood Rose had shows booked at Madame Wong's East and The Troubadour. With Izzy back in the saddle, the band moved into new rehearsal facilities at Shamrock Studios on Santa Monica Boulevard.

The Troubadour show would prove Hollywood Rose's final curtain call, however. The band went on late, the crowd was totally disinterested, the sound was awful, and things went rapidly south when Axl vented his frustrations by hitting a heckler over the head with a bottle. As with Izzy's disappearing acts, Axl's onstage temper tantrums were also to prove a recurring theme. Slash was already having second thoughts, and the bottle incident settled the argument. As soon as the band came offstage he announced his decision, grabbed up his guitar, and headed out the door. Hollywood Rose split soon thereafter, and Tracii Guns finally got Axl and Izzy. Slash temporarily joined Black Sheep, a rite-of-passage band in the London vein. His one and only gig with

GUNS N' ROSES

Black Sheep was at the Country Club out in the Valley. Slash later heard that Axl had been in the crowd that night.

Slash was still rehearsing on and off with Black Sheep when Poison's lead guitarist, Matt Smith, called to say he was quitting the band and moving back to his native Pennsylvania with his pregnant wife. Poison were beginning to make a name for themselves on the Strip, and though their poodle-pomp was the polar opposite of the hard, bluesy rock Slash envisioned playing, he allowed Smith to twist his arm into attending an audition.

Slash says he "nailed" the three songs he'd been asked to learn and so wasn't too surprised to be called back for a second audition. To be informed that his attire on the day – jeans, T-shirt and fringed moccasins – didn't meet with his potential new band's requirements did catch him unawares, however. Upon subsequently seeing C.C. Deville coming through the door sporting a sparkly white leather jacket with his hair dyed platinum blond and sporting full make up (including frosted pink lipstick), Slash knew Poison had their guy.

The myriad of strands that makes up the fabric of the Guns N' Roses story were slowly but surely enmeshing. Axl was fronting LA Guns but being in a band bearing any name other than his own went against the grain and inevitably proved too much of a cross to bear. To everyone's astonishm ..., proceeded to convince Tracii, along with LA Guns' drummer Rob Gardner, to reunite with Izzy and Steve Darrow in a temporarily reconstituted Hollywood Rose for a New Year's Eve show at the Dancing Waters Club, a one-time gay bar in neighbouring San Pedro. It being New Year's Eve had more or less guaranteed a full house, but Axl and Tracii took heart from the crowd's enthusiastic reaction and decided to let things run into the coming year, which in effect brought about the dissolution of LA Guns.

Steve Darrow would give back word soon into 1985 so Tracii brought in Ole Beich, the Danish-born bass player in the now defunct LA Guns.

How the band was named.

Speaking about his time with Guns N' Roses with *gnrcentral.com* in January 2018, Tracii Guns explained how the band's name came about:

"Izzy [was living] at my house, and he had Hollywood Rose with Axl – that was their band. I never played in Hollywood Rose. I had my high school band and I was really looking for a cool name. I had a girlfriend that had been calling me 'Mr Guns' [and] one day me and Izzy were sitting in the living room of my house and I said, 'L.A. Guns' and I made this Cheap Trick-looking logo on a blank album cover. I show it to Izzy and go, 'What do you think of this for a band name?' And he goes, 'That's great.' So that's been my band name ever since.

"So anyways, we had a little manager guy at the time and he hated our singer

Mike Jagosz, so we fired him. So then I asked Axl to join L.A. Guns and he was in the band for about six, seven months, and then the same manager ended up hating Axl and he wanted to fire him. We're all living together at this point, and Axl and I sat down and went, 'What are we going to do?' So we both said, 'Fuck that', and came up with the name Guns N' Roses which was going to be just a record label that we'd put singles out on. Sadly that idea only lasted for about ten minutes and then we decided to keep L.A. Guns going, add Izzy, and call it Guns N' Roses. And that's the whole story. And then I lasted for about seven or eight months in that, and then Axl and I got into an extraordinary fight – and we had never argued ever in the past few years before. That fight stemmed from a girl named Michelle Young (of 'My Michelle' fame] not being put on a guest list at three in the afternoon before even soundcheck, and we did two shows after that argument and then I left. It just wasn't fun anymore. I was probably 19 then and I thought, 'great band, and I love these guys, but they're not worth the headaches.' Even at that age I didn't want to deal with it."

But now it was Tracii's turn to baulk at playing in a band that didn't bear his name – which was hardly surprising given Hollywood Rose now had three LA Gunners in the line-up. A compromise was soon reached, however, which saw both egos salved to mutual satisfaction. The band's new name would be Guns N' Roses. (Though other names supposedly touted for a time were Heads of Amazon and AIDS.)

Guns N' Roses made their debut at The Troubadour on March 26, 1985, the set-list featuring 'Think About You', 'Anything Goes', 'Move to the City', 'Shadow of Your Love', and 'Don't Cry', as well as souped-up versions of the Stones' 'Jumping Jack Flash' and Elvis's 'Heartbreak Hotel'. A clutch of other LA shows were set to follow, but things were thrown into confusion following Ole Beich's sacking. Speaking about his brief tenure in the band many years later, Beich said he was dismissed because he chose to go check out a band rather than show for a rehearsal, which in turn forced the cancellation of a show at Radio City in Anaheim set for April 11.

Duff was aware of recent happenings owing to Axl now residing on Orchid Street, and as he'd nothing else cooking he readily agreed when Izzy approached him about the now-vacant bass slot in Guns N' Roses. Duff had caught LA Guns at The Troubadour, but Axl letting rip with another of his soon-to-be-trademark banshee shrieks during his first rehearsal with the band had him gawping in wide-eyed wonder. "It was like nothing I had ever heard," he recalled. "There were two voices coming out at once! There's a name for that in musicology (overtone singing), but all I knew in that instant was that this dude was different and powerful and fucking serious. He hadn't yet entirely harnessed his voice – he was more unique than great at that point – but it was clear he hadn't moved out to Hollywood from Indiana for the weather. He was here to stake a claim and show the whole fucking world what he had."

Duff was soon regretting his decision, however. To his way of thinking, Tracii and Rob were out-and-out metalheads and that simply wasn't his bag. He decided to persevere, but his heart wasn't really in

GUNS N' ROSES

it and he took the Ole Beich way out by skipping a rehearsal. Sure enough, Axl's call wasn't long in coming. Instead of hurling a stream of invective down the phone as Duff had anticipated, however, Axl asked him to come to the next rehearsal – going so far as to say "please".

When Axl asked Duff to explain his reservations at the next rehearsal, the latter saw little point in holding back. Aside from their obvious metal leanings, Duff doubted Tracii and Rob's commitment to the GN'R cause. He wanted to be in a band with a Three Musketeers' "all for one and one for all" mentality; a band whose members understood the sacrifices required to get where they needed to be and were prepared to make those sacrifices without question. He knew Axl and Izzy were of such ilk, but serious question marks hung over both Tracii and Rob. Realising there was only one way to find out, Duff called on his West Coast contacts and arranged a bare-bones tour taking in punk venues such as the Mabuhay Gardens in San Francisco, and the 13th Precinct in Portland before culminating with a final date opening for The Fastbacks at the recently opened Gorilla Gardens in Seattle.

It would mean throwing caution to the wind, roughing it on friends' floors, playing for gas money, and hopefully having enough left over for ramen noodles and a six-pack of beer.

As Duff had expected, Tracii and Rob proved less than enthusiastic about the idea; their mind set being why risk a leap of faith when they could stay put in LA playing the West Hollywood circuit. Such "big fish/little pond" thinking was total anathema to Duff. He certainly hadn't come to LA to play it safe. Fortunately, Axl and Izzy shared his viewpoint, and so when Rob and Tracii quit, Duff didn't spare either so much as a parting glance. Besides, he still had Slash's phone number.

Slash, at the time, was still holding down the job Axl had got for him at Tower Records – a conciliatory gesture on the singer's part for sleeping with Slash's now ex-girlfriend, Yvonne. Though free to choose which records to air over Tower's inhouse sound system, Slash was totally at a loose end music-wise; Izzy recently swinging by to drop off some flyers for a forthcoming Guns N' Roses show merely heightening his frustrations.

Slash readily admits to not knowing the blow-by-blow events that led to being invited

to join Guns N' Roses as much of what went down was happening behind the scenes. He knew from the West Hollywood grapevine that Duff had replaced Ole Beich on bass, however, and rumours were now circulating about Tracii Guns and Rob Gardner having quit the band; said rumours were soon confirmed when Axl arrived at Tower to ask Slash if he fancied getting together with Izzy to see if their playing styles complemented each other's on Guns' new material.

Slash agreed to hook up with Izzy, but only after some contemplative thinking on his part. He liked Izzy but knew that he and Axl were joined at the hip. Anyone coming into the band would have to get along with both of them. It wasn't that he didn't like Axl, they got along well enough. There was simply no getting away from their innate personality differences. The way he saw it, pretending those differences didn't exist would only see them manifest into something far more damaging somewhere further down the line. He doubted anyone knew the real Axl – not even Izzy. But he'd seen for himself during the brief time Axl had crashed at his mum's house that he was a powder keg with an indeterminate fuse.

The first song Slash and Izzy worked on together was 'Don't Cry', the haunting power ballad that would be released as the lead single from the *Use Your Illusion* albums in September 1991 (the song would feature on both albums albeit with alternate lyrics). The song was already a staple of Guns N' Roses' live set, but Slash's guitar parts gave the song added dynamic.

Guns N' Roses were a full complement again, but the scenesters on the Strip were most likely taking bets as to who would be the next to get caught in the fallout of Axl's ever-changing moods. Slash's version of events has Rob Gardner still in the band at the time of his joining, but whatever the reality, by the time Guns N' Roses hit the road for the "Hell Tour" – as their West Coast foray would come to be known – it was with the classic *Appetite for Destruction* line-up. "It wasn't even something I had to think about," Steven reflected. "I loved playing in a band and I loved rock'n'roll so much that it was a no-brainer: 'Where's the gig? Siberia? Okay, I'm there.'"

Wild abandon and streetwise composure are encompassed by the music of the savvy and sexy Guns N' Roses. Rising from the Hollywood underground, the band has confidence, raw power and charisma. Not every band currently playing the circuit can claim the authenticity of surviving the streets. A power based in the hard knocks depths of reality let the music of the band exude confidence in themselves and their music.

GN'R MISSION STATEMENT

PART THREE

KICKIN' UP SOME DUST

The confidence, raw power and charisma was pretty much in evidence from the moment Axl, Izzy, Duff, Slash and Steven got together for the first of three rehearsals intended to allow the new arrivals to get a feel for the clutch of songs making up Guns N' Roses' sparse repertoire; the chemistry betwixt the five proving immediate, thunderous, and soulful. The vibe was also a playful one as Duff hid one of Steven's bass drums, and a couple of other pieces of kit he and the rest of the band deemed irrelevant. Slash says losing the second bass drum was for the good of the band. "We bullied him into being a straight-ahead, 4/4 rock-and-roll drummer, which complimented and easily locked in with Duff's bass style, while allowing Izzy and me the freedom to mesh blues-driven rock 'n' roll with the neurotic edge of first-generation punk. Not to mention what Axl's lyrics and delivery brought to it."

Two days after a warm-up "bottom-of-the-bill" show at The Troubadour on Thursday, June 6, the band hit the I-5 in their buddy Danny's Buick LeSabre. With Danny, and another friend called Joe-Joe who was also happy to share in the sense of adventure, following behind in a U-Haul trailer housing the gear. The plan now was to drive straight up to Seattle, play the Gorilla Gardens, then stop off at the 13th Precinct and the Fab Mab on the return leg. All being well, they would arrive in the Emerald City sometime late Sunday afternoon, allowing them a couple of days to kickback before playing the Gorilla Gardens on the Wednesday.

But of course, things didn't go according to plan. In fact, the wheels came off – both in the metaphorical and literal sense - when the LeSabre packed up near Bakersfield some 100 miles outside of LA. The band had 37 dollars collectively and a thousand miles of road ahead of them but returning to LA wasn't an option. Leaving Danny and Joe-Joe to await the arrival of a tow-truck, the band (with Slash, Izzy, and Duff clutching their guitars) hit the hardtop in the hope some saintly Samaritan would take pity on them – a tall enough order for any five guys, let alone a scruff-ass rock 'n' roll band.

A Samaritan of sorts would indeed eventually materialise - an amphetamine-freak that was happy to take them as far as Medford, Oregon in exchange for their cash. Upon arrival in Medford, Duff called a friend in LA to see if there for an update on Danny's LeSabre. He was told a replacement part had been ordered in San Francisco but would take a couple of days in reaching Danny and JoJo in Bakersfield. Duff's next call was to Kim Warnick to explain the situation and ask if they might borrow The Fastbacks' gear for the Gorilla Gardens. Having received assurances from Warnick, Duff and the others set off walking. It seemed their luck was in when a Mexican farmworker offered to

33

take them as far as Eugene – some 167 miles closer to their destination. The farmworker's Datsun pickup couldn't cope with their combined weight, however, and they were soon treading tarmac again. They ended up walking through the night, stopping off in an onion field for sustenance.

They were so exhausted by this juncture they were barely aware of passing cars, but two women finally took pity on them and carried them as far as Portland; their munificence extending to stopping off at a gas station to buy the guys sandwiches and beer. While at the station, Duff called his pal Donner in Seattle to see if he might be able to arrange bus tickets from Portland. Donner, who'd already met Slash and Steven while visiting with Duff in LA, said he'd drive to Portland and pick them up himself. When they finally arrived in Seattle, Donner and the rest of Duff's old gang made the band welcome, readily sharing their booze and drugs.

> ## "We'd partied, we'd played, we'd survived, we'd endured, and we racked up a lifetime's worth of stories in just two weeks."

Guns would prove sloppy on the night but they'd at least made the show. When booking the show, Duff had managed to cajole the Gorilla Gardens' owners to guarantee a $200 fee, which could now be used to cover the cost of Danny and Jo-Jo paying for the part and resuming their journey with the band's gear. The owner refused to honour his side of the bargain, however, as only a dozen or so paying punters had come through the door. Axl was said to be beside himself, raging

about how they had "gone through hell" to get there – and inadvertently giving the tour its enduring name. Duff was equally pissed off and suggested they torch the venue. He and Axl threw some lighted matches into a garbage can filled with paper towelling before fleeing outside to watch the blaze. Nothing happened, which was just as well seeing as the cops wouldn't have had too much trouble in tracking them down.

The realisation wouldn't come overnight, but all five band members have since acknowledged the Seattle trip cementing them as a band. "Our commitments were tested on that journey," Slash reflected. "We'd partied, we'd played, we'd survived, we'd endured, and we racked up a lifetime's worth of stories in just two weeks."

♫

Marc Canter had taken some shots of Guns onstage at The Troubadour for the band to use as promotional head shots at the Gorilla Gardens and the other intended dates on the ill-feted Hell tour. Upon their return to LA, they once again called upon Canter to take more some more shots to use to book shows and print up as flyers. It was at his family's deli where he snapped Guns' now iconic first publicity photo. "The look on that photo basically shows the hunger in their eyes," says Canter. "They know that they're a band to be reckoned with, that they're here to fuck up Los Angeles, and show them, you know, this is the way to do it."

Canter's benevolence would also be called upon for the balloon payments the band needed to pre-buy tickets for shows at the Whisky, Troubadour, and other established rock venues in the city. To counter the risk of being left out-of-pocket, the clubs devised a "pay to play" policy whereby bands were required to buy a certain number of tickets at an agreed price in advance. This meant the clubs made their money before a note was played regardless of whether the bands managed to recoup their outlay. The key to ensuring said outlay was recovered lay in bands establishing mailing lists to let people know where and when they would be playing. As soon as Guns were playing regularly on the LA circuit they set about building their own phone and mailing list. The preferred method was to send a couple of their stripper friends out into the audience; the premise being that no red-bloodied male was likely to refuse a scantily-clad beauty's request for his phone number and home address.

Betwixt shows, the band knuckled down to serious rehearsals at Nicky Beat's in Frogtown (a.k.a. the Elysian Valley) in central LA. Beat, a jobbing drummer, was living in a small warehouse near the corner of Gilroy and Ripple Streets euphemistically known as the "Love Palace" that doubled as a rehearsal studio. The $6-per-hour fees seriously ate into whatever money the band were making on the circuit, however. Having to set up and tear down their gear to make way for the next band whenever they used the studio was also proving a pain in the ass so the decision was made to find a place they could call their own and rock out to their hearts' content. Cost obviously dictated which areas the band could carry out their search. They eventually found something that not only met with their budgetary requirements but was also just a short walk from Sunset Strip.

Situated half a block north of Sunset on Gardner lay an opening of a dead-end alleyway. Halfway down the garbage-strewn alley was a block of a half dozen or so decrepit, breeze-block garage-like 10 x 14 self-storage spaces. There was no air-conditioning, or heating, but electricity was on tap so long as they met the $400 monthly rental. There was no kitchen, of course, but Slash brought in a hibachi grill so they could cook up hamburger meat. Gravy and biscuits could be procured at nearby Denny's dinner for $1.25. Another cheap and cheerful food source came via an all-you-can-eat-for-a-dollar buffet a West Hollywood gay club. And should things get truly desperate, they could always join the line at the nearby Salvation Army Mission for a free Saturday hand-out. Liquid sustenance came courtesy of the infamous Night Train fortified wine, which not only got them off their gourds for a buck and a quarter but would also provide the theme and title for a new song.

A night raid on a local construction site provided enough two-by-fours and plywood to construct a rudimentary loft, which could serve as a sleeping space should the need arise - as it invariably would. The floor area was solely for making music. "If you were to walk in the door everything in the room would be to your left," Duff explained. "First there was my bass amp, then Izzy's Marshall half stack, then Steven's drums, and then Slash's guitar rig. This is also how we would set up onstage for each and every gig until Izzy left in 1991."

Guns N' Roses weren't the first band to see the advantages of using the Gardner Street hidey-hole as a rehearsal place, however. The space directly to their right was being used The Wild, whose line-up included Dizzy Reed on keyboards.

♫

There was no PA at Gardner Street and Axl would usually have to scream himself hoarse to make himself heard above the din. Yet it was here at the "Hell House", as the space would soon be dubbed, that Guns coalesced as a unit; spending every available hour honing their repertoire and shaping ideas into songs. Izzy's "Think About You" was worked up, as was "Back Off Bitch", a song Axl had penned with Paul Tobias (Another old Lafayette buddy who was set to feature large in Slash's departure from Guns N' Roses a decade or so on).

Axl also pressed Slash to play a riff he remembered from when he was crashing at Ola's place. After much head-scratching and noodling Slash finally hit on the riff, Steven came up with a beat, while Izzy moved things along with some chugging chords. But it was Duff's wild, rumbling bass line that was to serve as the glue that binds "Welcome to the Jungle", as GN'R's calling card was to be called. Slash says the song was completed in around three hours, the arrangement being virtually the same as it appears on *Appetite for Destruction*.

Another of Izzy's ideas was quickly worked up into 'Out Ta Get Me', the song taking even less time to arrange than "Welcome to the Jungle" according to Slash. "Izzy showed up with the riff and the basic idea for the song and the second he played it, the notes hit my ear and inspired me. That one happened so quickly. I think that even the most complicated section – the dual guitar parts – was written in under twenty minutes."

The band's reputation for hard partying – both individually and collectively – coupled with the Hell House's away-from-prying-eyes location, soon established it as the go-to place after the clubs closed down for the evening. On any given night dozens of people would thread their way through the alley to continue the revelry till dawn. The girls came either to hang-out or make-out with the guys in the band; guys came hoping to take up the overspill, while the drug dealers came to tout their wares.

With such goings on going down on a nightly or near-nightly basis, Hell House's anonymous location couldn't possibly remain a secret for long. The West Hollywood Sherriff's Department was soon attuned to rumours of the nocturnal debauchery supposedly taking place in their own backyard and would spring surprise raids to check everyone's IDs. Reflecting on this period in the band's early history in his autobiography, Duff took the line that the sheriffs went out of their way to make a nuisance of themselves, and that the "supposed complaints from girls were probably just ruses that were held over our heads to scare us – a retaliatory response to their "getting an earful from parents of kids who showed up late and wasted after a night in our backyard."

One of the "supposed complaints" Duff alludes to wouldn't turn out to be a scare tactic, however. When the parents of a 15-year-old girl arrived at the West Hollywood Sheriff's Department to press charges of statutory rape against two of the band – to wit Axl and Slash - the LAPD descended in force on Hell House with the girl in tow to identify her assailants.

Axl would subsequently boast that the cops had failed to find him as he was hiding behind some equipment making out with another girl, which, given the size of the storage space, seems mere bravado. Slash had made himself scarce, but Izzy, Duff, and Steven, along with everyone else that happened to be there, was lined up in the alleyway outside. The police went away again empty-handed but not before warning the rest of the band that Axl and Slash should turn themselves in sooner rather than later.

Given the seedy seriousness of the charge it's perhaps understandable that the band's collective memory about the incident remains somewhat ambiguous. While careful not to mention the girl's age, Axl would tell the *LA Weekly* about how "this hippie chick" coming into the band's rehearsal space and "fucking with our equipment trying to break stuff . . . so eventually she wound up running down Sunset naked, all dingy, and didn't even know her own name." What happened in the interim between her wandering into the rehearsal space and running naked along Sunset Strip in obvious distress, Axl neglected to say.

Slash's "hazy" version of events has the girl in question having consensual sex with Axl before losing her mind and freaking out – possibly as whatever drugs she'd taken began to wear off. Axl had tried getting the girl to leave, and Slash says he tried to "help mediate the situation" without much success.

The girl was obviously in a highly-agitated state, so any attempt to grab her by the arms could have been easily misconstrued. Though why Axl and Slash allowed a naked 15-year-old girl to run off into the night without making any attempt to give chase was worthy of a criminal charge in itself – regardless of what occurred.

With the possibility of a mandatory five-year jail sentence hanging over them, Slash and Axl went into hiding. Slash moved in with Steven at the latter's new girlfriend's apartment which was within walking distance of Gardner Street yet far enough away to risk capture – unless someone gave him up, of course. Axl reportedly fled to neighbouring Orange County and holed up with some girl he knew, but other reports have him living on the lam in West Hollywood. Needless to say, the band cancelled the shows they had lined up and didn't take any further bookings.

It was a fraught situation – and not only for Axl and Slash. Guns N' Roses were rising above the dross and making a name for themselves and the cops grabbing either Axl or Slash would in effect bring about the end of the band. In desperation, Slash reached out to one of the few people he felt the band could trust – their occasional promoter, Vicky Hamilton.

Hamilton, who was 27 at the time, had started out working as a cocktail waitress but was now working as a booking agent for Silver Lining Entertainment. She'd watched from the sidelines as LA Guns and Hollywood Rose slowly morphed into Guns N' Roses and had immediately offered her services to the band. She'd never imagined that "making myself available" would include harbouring a fugitive Axl. "I had started booking gigs for them and I was interested in managing them," she told the *Daily Mail* in April 2015. "At that point they had moved into a rehearsal hall just off the Sunset Strip. It was a little hole-in-the-wall type place. Over where they were rehearsing they had built this loft and about three people could sleep there. Apparently, they were having bonfires at night in the parking lot and doing drugs and stuff. One night Slash called me up and said, 'Can Axl come and sleep on your couch for a couple of days?' I said, 'Why?' and he said, 'Oh, the police are looking for him - something to do with a girl.' I started thinking 'Oh God I'll be harbouring a fugitive', but then I just said, 'OK yeah, sure.'"

Axl duly arrived at Hamilton's one-bedroom apartment - which she was already sharing with her friend, Jennifer – under cover of darkness, clutching a garbage bag and tiny suitcase containing all his worldly possessions. He swore faithfully to Hamilton that while he'd had sex with the girl he hadn't raped her. "He said it was consensual, but he'd thrown her out of the studio and locked her out without her clothes and she was mad. He went to court for it months later, but the charges were dropped."

The charges were indeed dropped owing to a lack of hard evidence. Slash was made to sweat as his court date loomed ever larger, however, while Axl reportedly attended at least one court hearing. One might have expected Axl and Slash's uncomfortably close brush with the law to dampen the band's wayward antics – if only in the short term. History, of course, tells us otherwise. Indeed, if anything the incident gave them a cachet that separated them from every other band operating out of the Strip; their "real-deal rock 'n' roll desperado" image propelling Guns N' Roses to heights few unsigned bands could hope to attain. They would still play the LA circuit for some time to come, but their shows were sold out well in in advance – regardless of whether they were headlining or not.

Reflecting on the band's time at Gardner Street for Danny Sugarman's 1992 tome, *The Days of Guns N' Roses: Appetite for Destruction*, Axl playfully alluded to the rape charge incident by saying how the band "could get away with whatever we wanted, except when the cops came," before going on to add that if anyone caused a problem they'd be "escorted out". His definition of "escort" being that they would drag said miscreant out "by their hair down the alley, naked."

What was supposed to be a couple of days of Axl sleeping on Hamilton's sofa would end up stretching to six months or so. Before long she would have other house guests to contend with. "The rest of the band had to move in because they were staying at the rehearsal space and

the cops were trying to question them about the rape so they all moved in - except for Duff who was living with his girlfriend," Vicky said in the same *Daily Mail* interview. "I wasn't their manager up until this point but that kind of cemented the deal seeing as I was harbouring the 'fugitive'."

Hamilton had worked with Mötley Crüe so was no stranger to the unseemly side of the rock 'n' roll world, but the Gunners' antics still took her by surprise. "It was insane! I came home one day, and Jennifer's dog, Babe, was hiding in the bath tub shaking because of all the crap that was going on. I guess someone had ramped the amps up full blast. The dog was freaked out. The table was always littered with drugs paraphernalia [and] cigarette burns. The bathroom was the worst with black-blue hair dye all over the walls from Izzy and Slash. There was some unidentifiable slime on the bathtub. I would take a bag in the shower as I didn't want to stand there.

"Jack (Daniel's) with them and smoked pot, but they knew that I wasn't a heroin or coke enthusiast. They went up on the roof to do that. Girls would come at night. They would do zip up their sleeping bags together to make double ones to fit the girls in. Me and Jennifer would barricade the doors, so they couldn't get in. In the daytime I tried to barricade because they were always stealing my T-shirts. The cops beat open my door a bunch of times. I'd wake up to a cop flashing his flashlight in my face. It was a crazy, crazy time."

It was indeed a crazy, crazy time, but to paraphrase the 1974 Bachman-Turner Overdrive song, no one had seen nothing yet . . .

♪

Guns N' Roses were as yet still unsigned but with their star in ascendency the sharks came a circling. Kim Fowley, best known for producing novelty and cult pop singles during the 1960s, as well as for mismanaging The Runaways a

decade later, was the first to enter the fray. Fowley's colourful, yet chequered past usually preceded him wherever he went. Duff was already familiar with his reputation from the tales Joan Jett had shared when The Fastbacks had opened for the one-time Runaways singer. Sensing the band's suspicion as to his motives, Fowley tried a different tack by inviting them to a breakfast meeting at Denny's diner to discuss his buying the publishing rights to three songs including "Welcome to the Jungle". He'd apparently brought along a contract and a traveller's cheque for $10,000. Vicky Hamilton, however, recalls Fowley arriving at her door with a contract and a cheque for $7,500. She says that Axl had been amenable to Fowley's proposal, and might well have signed the rights over had she not stepped in to persuade him otherwise.

Regardless of which version holds true, either amount was more money than any of the band had seen in their lives before. However, as it was Fowley doing the chasing, instead of their doing pestering as had been the case thus far, the band sensed holding onto the publishing rights to their songs might be the more sensible option; their suspicions ultimately being confirmed when Fowley subsequently upped his offer to $50,000.

The industry interest in Guns N' Roses was gathering pace at a dizzying speed. Although her dealings with Mötley Crüe and Poison had left her with the shitty end of the stick, Hamilton believed her loyalty, largesse – which extended to her taking a daytime job at The Roxy to help make ends meet as the band were literally "bleeding me dry" – coupled with the hard work she'd put in to get them to the point they were now at would be rewarded with a managerial deal once they were signed. Witnessing Fowley's determination to grab a slice of GN'R's publishing rights, however, triggered her into getting something a little more concrete than a verbal handshake from Slash. She paid a visit to a music biz lawyer of some renown called Peter Paterno. Paterno

Part Three: KICKIN' UP SOME DUST

♫

was used to overseeing first-time deals and handed Hamilton a standard draft contract for herself and the band to sign. The band, however, didn't appear to be in any hurry to sign – at least not until Hamilton threatened them with immediate eviction. A follow-up meeting was duly arranged with Paterno, but within days of the meeting Paterno called to say that he would be handling the band's legal negotiations and as such, he could no longer represent her in the matter.

Hamilton was understandably furious. Her losing out on Mötley Crüe and Poison had left her with egg on her face. If she allowed Guns N' Roses to slip through her fingers she might as well pack up and catch the next Greyhound bus heading back to West Virginia. The band told Hamilton she had nothing to fear, however, and that they would take care of her. By her own admission, she was "too naïve to realise that I was being played" and so continued accompanying the band to meetings with various labels.

When reflecting on the band's dealings with Hamilton, Slash said that up to this juncture they'd been reluctant to sign with anybody. Her bringing Paterno into the mix had given them something other than appointing a manager or securing a record deal to think about. Money hadn't really featured large in their thinking up until now, as they'd never had enough where it might prove an issue. Fowley's approach over the publishing rights changed everything. Suddenly, arguments were breaking out as to who wrote the respective parts in the songs. They each had a different take on how certain songs had come about; the more hot-tempered members of the band – namely Axl and Steven – proving less amenable. With Paterno's guidance they eventually formulated a partnership agreement whereby future publishing royalties were to be split across the board. However, what was a sound and sensible resolution was to prove the first chink in the band's all-for-one-and-all-for-one-gang mentally.

Duff says the first label to express interest in the band was Restless Records, a sub-division of Enigma Records (who in turn were owned by Warner Bros) that primarily specialised in metal, punk and alternative and operated out of El Segundo in Santa Monica Bay. Enigma was launched in 1980 as a division of Greenworld Distribution, and already had an impressive and diverse roster of acts such as The Cramps, Pere Ubu, Berlin, Hüsker Dü, Motörhead, and Red Hot Chili Peppers. The label's first release had been Mötley Crüe's *Too Fast for Love*. Though initially released on the Crüe's own Leathür Records imprint, it was manufactured, marketed and distributed by Enigma.

> ## If she allowed Guns N' Roses to slip through her fingers she might as well pack up and catch the next Greyhound bus heading back to West Virginia.

At the meeting, Enigma tabled a pressing and distribution deal with $30,000 towards recording costs, while talking the band though each step of the process and answering their many questions. Though impressed with Enigma's honesty, Guns came away again without signing. Their reasoning being that if one record label was keen to take them on, then it stood to reason others would show their hands soon enough. And so it was to prove . . .

The major record labels were long-accustomed to going against each other in bidding wars,

 41

GUNS N' ROSES

and as such each had come to believe it was simply a case of offering more money than the competition. Guns N' Roses were no different from any other band in that they wanted to get the best deal. Yet whereas most bands arrive at the negotiation table with dollar signs in their eyes, Guns remained aloof until finally sitting down with a label that not only understood them, but one that wouldn't try to neuter their sound for wider commercial appeal. And with each A&R chief picking up the tab at ever-more-fancy restaurants, there were worse ways to while away a couple of hours. "We'd roll into these nice restaurants and order these extravagant liquid lunches then sit there and just play the game," Slash reflected. "The only thing we'd agree on was that we needed to meet again for lunch to discuss things further before we agreed on anything."

Chrysalis steamrollered in with a $750,000 bid without having actually seen the band play live. What happened next would go down in West Hollywood folklore. The band's meeting with the label's head, Ron Fair, had been arranged by Chrysalis exec, Susan Collins. The meeting was coming to an end when Axl leaned across to Collins, casually informing her the band would sign with Chrysalis but only if she was willing to run naked down Sunset Boulevard.

Vicky Hamilton came away from the Chrysalis meeting doubting very much that a woman in Collins' position would risk getting arrested on a public lewdness charge (which carried a one-to-three-month jail sentence) simply to sign the band. Espying upwards of a dozen A&R reps jostling for shoulder room while awaiting the arrival onstage of Guns N' Roses at The Troubadour on February 28 brought about a rethink, however.

Geffen's new A&R head, Tom "Zoots" Zutaut, was at The Troubadour that night at the bidding of his good friend Joseph Brooks, the one-time record store owner that was now a hip and influential DJ at KROQ. While working at Electra Records, Zutaut

had cajoled his bosses into signing Mötley Crüe; his suggesting they record Brownsville Station's 1973 hit, 'Smokin' in the Boys Room', providing Nikki Sixx and Co. with their first *Billboard* 100 Top 3 smash. There would be occasions when Guns N' Roses pushed Zutaut to the point where he'd wished Susan Collins had taken one for the Chrysalis team. A listen to the demo of 'Welcome to the Jungle' Brooks played him had proved sufficient to come along to The Troubadour. Hearing "Jungle" live was enough to convince him that in the right hands Guns had the potential to be the biggest band in the world. He stuck around to hear the next song – 'Nightrain' – before heading for the exit; careful to make sure to dismiss Guns within earshot of one or two of his competitors en route. He was determined to sign Guns N' Roses to Geffen come hell or high water; his first move coming with inviting the band over to his place the day after the Troubadour show. According to Duff, Zutaut tabled a $250,000 advance, while assuring them they would enjoy total artistic freedom at Geffen – an incidental inducement being the label's recent acquisition of Aerosmith.

In a 2005 letter to the *New York Times*, Zutaut said how Axl was "one of the only artists I ever worked with who was never motivated by money." Though impressed by Zutaut's heartfelt pitch, the half million bucks' shortfall to what Chrysalis were offering wasn't to be sniffed at. Another meeting was scheduled for several days hence, at the end of which Axl, without going into specifics, told Zutaut they would sign with Geffen if he could match the Chrysalis deal and have a $75,000 cheque (A ten per cent advance of the band's $750,000 asking price) ready by the following evening (Friday) at 6 p.m.

Zutaut returned to Geffen's offices in Santa Monica and presented his case to the label's president, Eddie Rosenblatt. Though respectful of Zutaut's savvy having elevated Mötley Crüe to multi-platinum-selling status, he couldn't possibly sanction his request. Beneath Zutaut's

cherubic exterior lay a steely determination, however. Knowing that David Geffen had built up two labels acting on similar gut feeling hunches, he intuitively asked for a meeting the man himself. Geffen is said to have burst out laughing when Zutaut had reiterated his belief that Guns N' Roses were set to become the biggest band in the world. He nonetheless inked a cheque for $75,000.

Zutaut was understandably elated and called Axl to give him the news. It was only then that he'd discovered the motivation behind Axl's insisting on having the $75,000 check by the close of business. The idea of a high-powered female executive stripping off and parading herself along Sunset Boulevard was totally out of leftfield, but this was LA, and stranger things had happened. Fortunately for Zutaut, the 6 p.m. deadline came and went without Collins exposing so much as a shapely ankle, and later that same evening Axl, Slash, Duff, Izzy, and Steven swung by his office to cement the deal in true West Hollywood style.

Guns N' Roses officially became a Geffen act on Wednesday, March 26, 1986. Two days later they staged two celebratory shows at The Roxy. Vicky Hamilton had booked the shows several weeks earlier, both intended as label showcases. The days of showcasing were now at an end. Should anyone be unaware of this the band placed the following full-page ad in all the local music papers: "Geffen recording artists Guns N' Roses, live at the Roxy".

In his memoir, Steven cites Hamilton's entering Guns N' Roses' orbit as being a seismic step in moving the band "closer to our dream". Now that the dream had been realised, however, Hamilton found history was indeed repeating itself. The band even had the gall to seek her help in cashing the $75,000 advance cheque (Of which each member came away with $7,500 "spending money"). "The guys were running around town buying clothes, getting tattoos, buying musical equipment, all the while partying to the extreme," she later bemoaned. "I was broke, sitting in my destroyed apartment

not sure how I was going to pay that month's rent, or buy groceries."

Hamilton wasn't exaggerating when she says Guns N' Roses were "partying to the extreme", either. The days of bumming drinks were also at an end. Now it was drinks on the house with a couple of chasers on the side. Duff was already drinking heavily; so much so that Axl would soon start introducing him onstage as "Duff 'King of Beers' McKagan". The bassist readily admits he'd already lost his footing on the slippery slope to alcoholism by the time of the Geffen signing but had assumed he'd be able to address the problem at some later date. More often than not, Slash was happy to match Duff drink for drink, but now that he was relatively flush with cash he sought to feed another habit. He'd dabbled in the past, but as a certain song goes, the little was getter more and more. The influx of cash allowed Steven and Izzy to up their own respective habits.

In the lead up to the signing Axl had invited Hamilton out to the Rainbow. Over dinner he'd proceeded to share his vision for Guns N' Roses. He saw the band becoming as big as, or maybe even bigger than Queen or Elton John. But for that to happen, the band were going to need a "real heavy hitter" manager; one with proven experience beyond LA's cosy confines. Axl had then sought to temper her obvious disappointment by saying he and the rest of the band weren't going to forget what she had done for them. Not only were they going to pay her back, she could also expect a juicy bonus. Axl's promises were to ring hollow, however, and it seems Kim Fowley ultimately got his revenge on Hamilton over her dissuading Axl from signing over the rights to "Welcome to the Jungle" by playing devil's advocate while the band were contemplating whether to make good on their promises by installing her as their official manager.

Speaking with *www.legendaryrockinterviews. com* in April 2012, Steven said how it was Fowley that had suggested to the band that Hamilton was "too pretty" to be a manager, and therefore wouldn't be taken seriously. "While Fowley might not have been that big of an influence personally on Axl he was an influence as far as what he had accomplished in the business," he explained. "Axl agreed with Kim, and I didn't. I knew that [Vicky] was great and she still is.

"It was beyond ridiculous to say that a woman couldn't have impact on our careers, because as I knew full well that Teresa Ensenat (Geffen A&R exec) and Vicky Hamilton were every bit as important as Tom Zutaut to our success. Axl was all worried about having women involved in our careers when two of the three main people involved in us making it were women! It made no fucking sense to me that he couldn't see that while some women were crazy as fuck, some of them are freakin' geniuses. Vicky Hamilton is not only crafty, but smart as a whip, and knew better than anyone how to guide our career."

When Guns N' Roses were inducted into the Rock and Roll Hall of Fame in April 2014, Steven, Duff, and Slash would publicly thank Hamilton for her largely unsung efforts; the latter going so far as to say how she'd "tried to manage us with all her heart and soul." It was something of a volte face on Slash's part. While penning his memoir he said how it was "obvious to everyone in our camp that Vicky wasn't going to cut it as a manager once our operation increased in scale."

As a means of softening the blow Zutaut offered Hamilton a job as an A&R scout at Geffen. She was still working for the label when, in 1989, she launched a $1 million lawsuit against the band. The suit was eventually settled out of court for $30,000; half being paid by the band, the other half coming from Geffen.

Guns N' Roses had been the talk of LA for several months, but their signing with Geffen brought the band wider exposure. With their coming from the same West Hollywood gutter as Mötley Crüe, coupled with their being signed by Zutaut, the national music press was curious to see if lightning could indeed strike twice.

♫

Zutaut knew beyond question that Guns N' Roses were capable of becoming the biggest band in the world. In his mind's eye it was as clear as the 45-foot-high steel sign up on Mount Lee overlooking Hollywood. Had it been his money that had snagged the band's signatures he'd have considered the soundest of investments. But it wasn't his cash, of course, and while had every sympathy for Vicky Hamilton's plight, he was relieved the band had come to the decision to pass her over on their own. If they hadn't done so, he knew he'd have had to take her to one side as there was no way his bosses at Geffen would have entrusted their $750,000 acquisition to a relative novice.

Guns N' Roses' already riotous reputation was such that appointing the right manager was probably the most crucial decision of his career to date, and Zutaut was also under no illusion that he'd be clearing out his desk should he get it wrong. His initial choice was Aerosmith's co-manager Tim Collins. Axl and the rest of the band were already buzzing about labelmates with their heroes and sharing the same management would have surely been the cherry on the cake. Collins agreed to meet the band and came away again with his suspicions confirmed – that at least one member of the band was heavily into heroin. With Aerosmith's self-styled "Toxic Twins", Steven Tyler and Joe Perry, having finally gotten clean after years of substance abuse, there was every chance that Geffen would make good on their promise to resurrect the band's career. Bringing Guns N' Roses into the same sphere of operations simply wasn't worth the risk.

Next on Zutaut's list was Iron Maiden's no-nonsense, Cambridge-educated co-manager, Rod Smallwood. Smallwood had been looking after Maiden's affairs since 1982 and was no stranger to the West Hollywood scene. He'd also been aware of the vibe surrounding Guns N' Roses, yet while recognising the band's potential he too decided to pass. It eventually began to dawn on Zutaut that if Guns N' Roses were to rival Mötley Crüe, it made sense to sound out those that had first-hand experience of working with the latter act. And he already had such a person on speed-dial.

The fee-spirited, New Zealand-born Alan Niven was 33 at the time of Zutaut's call. He'd grown up in the UK following the family's move from his native Wellington aged four. Preferring to head out into the wider world in search of accommodating ladies and good pot to the military career his strict disciplinarian father had already mapped out for him, Niven had headed for the bright lights of London and soon landed a job working for Caroline Distribution, a subsidiary of Richard Branson's Virgin Records. Whilst with Caroline he'd moved to Sweden, and it was there that he received a tantalising offer from Greenworld Distribution to come and work for them out of their Torrance offices.

Niven had still been finding his feet at Greenworld when he was handed a Mötley Crüe demo tape. Speaking with www.legendaryrockinterviews.com in April 2012, Niven said how the early Crüe were mindful of Arthur Brown and Alice Cooper - "American rock 'n' roll vaudeville - the sizzle of the spectacle and the fascination of the outrage." He'd been writing songs since his public school days, and one of the songs on the tape had grabbed his attention. "As far as I was concerned, 'Piece of Your Action' was a fair enough statement and a rockin' track – enough to get me to persuade (Greenworld partners) Mark Wesley and Steve Boudreau that they should sign the band and do whatever it took."

Wesley and Boudreau were in agreement and Niven brokered the deal that had enabled Mötley Crüe to release their debut album, *Too Fast for Love*, via Leathür Records in November 1981. (The resulting advance from the deal reportedly saving Greenworld from impending bankruptcy and saving over 30 jobs)

"The record itself, as has been said, is a glorious train-wreck of an album," Niven continued, "not great playing but great attitude. And that was Mötley then. The Flock of Duran Haircuts business considered them a joke, but believe me, in those early days, the little girls understood. Professional things got organised once we had them signed over to Elektra, which Tom Zutaut and I effected."

Niven and Zutaut had met at the 1982 NAMM (National Association of Music Merchants) convention. Zutaut was working as a junior talent scout at Elektra at the time and had been drawn to Niven's booth on seeing Mötley Crüe posters lining the walls. The two had struck up a conversation, quickly becoming friends, which in turn had led to their effecting the deal that saw the Crüe sign with Elektra. Indeed, it was only because of their friendship that Niven agreed to meet with Zutaut to hear the latter's proposition about his managing Guns N' Roses via his management company, Stravinsky Brothers Inc.

It would take a lot of arm-twisting on Zutaut's part because Niven was already managing Great White, an LA-based quartet that had shown initial promise but had been foundering on the reef of anti-climax prior to his taking them under his wing. Indeed, it was Niven that had suggested the name-change from Dante Fox to Great White. After a monumental struggle, Niven had got Great White a one-off album deal with Columbia Records, and then persuaded the label to re-sign the band even though their eponymous debut had stalled at a desultory # 144 on the *Billboard* chart. "It took me a year and a half and a complete re-invention of the band," he told *www.legendaryrockinterviews. com.* "No more wannabe Halen Priest. (Mark) Kendall is a truly great blues rock guitar player, most under-rated for his playing, and Jack (Russell) had a voice that could embrace that idiom wonderfully ... so I got Jack to hear 'Face The Day' (a minor 1980 hit for Aussie rock outfit The Angels) and I used that as a bridging template to get to a better place." It was Niven self-financing and self-promoting Great White's follow-up album, *Shot In The Dark*, which took the band to that "better place".

Speaking in 2016, Niven explained his anxiety over taking the GN'R reins. "The only plan that suggested itself was to hope for the best. I'm looking at GN'R and going, 'I don't expect this band to be anything more than a really great underground band.' It wasn't going to be a radio-friendly band and it had so much attitude and was so raw. I knew it was going to be a lot of hard work."

According to Niven, his appointment was Zutaut's "last desperate management throw" as Eddie Rosenblatt was already making noises about dropping Guns N' Roses from the label. Unbeknown to him, on agreeing to manage the band he'd had just three months to turn things around or Guns would have been toast. Niven would indeed turn things around . . . and then some. Slash's initial impression of Niven was his thriving on Guns' reckless energy to get them over "the initial hump" that had stalled the band from becoming a professional entity. Izzy has gone on record hailing Niven as the "sixth, silent member" of Guns N' Roses. For Axl, however, the ice would never quite thaw – despite Niven arriving at the band's new Hollywood HQ (a house in Laughlin Park in the decidedly more upmarket Los Feliz area) loaded down with gifts, namely several bottles of Jack Daniels, a couple of hardcore porn mags and a large pizza.

It was as if Axl set out to test Niven's mettle as, following the latter's appointment, the singer failed to show for Guns N' Roses' first show (opening for Alice Cooper at the Arlington Theatre in Santa Barbara). It was the first occasion Guns would be sharing the bill with a named act. Niven decided the occasion was deserving of the band arriving at the venue in style and hired a Lincoln sedan. When Axl announced he'd be making his own way to the show Niven thought nothing of it. Axl would later insist he arrived at the theatre just as the band was going out onstage. Niven begs to differ, however, claiming they saw neither hide nor hair of Axl despite leaving passes at the door. With ten minutes to showtime Niven gave up the ghost and headed for the dressing room. The rest of the band tried to shy out of going on without Axl, but Niven knew if he capitulated at this early stage he might as well walk away from the band. He told them in no uncertain terms they were booked to play and that they would be going on regardless of who took on singing duties.

The buzz surrounding Guns ensured a healthy turnout for their set – even if seeing Izzy and Duff fumbling their way through songs Axl had made his own left many in the crowd wondering what was going on. Niven says this was the moment Slash, Izzy, Steven and Duff won his affections for soldiering on in a ridiculous situation. "From that moment my commitment was even more clearly to the band, to the whole, rather than one prima donna fronting it." Unfortunately for Niven, the prima donna was calling the shots and didn't particularly care if anyone got hurt in the crossfire.

Whatever else Guns were accused of, Zutaut could at least take heart from the band's work ethic. Soon after signing the group, Zutaut booked a session at Sound City Studios out in Van Nuys. Set amid rows of crumbling dilapidated warehouses, Sound City is now hailed as America's "greatest

unsung recording studio". With Nazareth's guitarist, Manny Charlton, overseeing the session, the band laid down some 27 songs, including most of the tracks that make up *Appetite for Destruction*, as well as a number that were held back for the *Use Your Illusion* albums. Niven might not have shared Zutaut's belief that Guns N' Roses could be the biggest band in the world, but he nonetheless shared his friend's conviction that, if harnessed properly, then they were capable of selling a lot of records.

The Geffen contract didn't extend to recording costs so with the band having set aside $250,000 from their advance to record their debut album, they were somewhat limited in their options. According to Duff, the band had wanted Mutt Lange to produce the album owing to the latter's work on AC/DC's 1980 album *Back in Black*, but Lange had insisted on a $400,000 fee and a cut of the royalties. Kiss rhythm guitarist, Paul Stanley, was another early candidate that talked himself out of the gig over his insistence on adding double-kick drums to Steven's stripped-down kit.

Zutaut suggested Spencer Proffer, the Munich-born singer/songwriter that had turned his hand to producing with the likes of W.A.S.P., Heart, Cheap Trick, and Vanilla Fudge out of Pasha Music House, the recording studio he'd designed and built with the studio's in-house engineer, Larry Brown. The band would get as far as recording a clutch of demos with Proffer including a new ballad called 'Sweet Child O' Mine' that Axl had penned as an ode to his latest squeeze, Erin Everly, daughter of Don Everly.

'Sweet Child O' Mine' would give Guns N' Roses their one and only US # 1, and in turn help propel sales of *Appetite for Destruction* into the troposphere. Had Slash had his way; however, the song would never have seen the light of day. Rather than run through the formulaic scales while practising, Slash preferred to conjure up unorthodox fingerings of simple melodies. He was amusing himself with one of his more carnivalesque melodies (with half-step-down D#-G#-C#-F#-A#-D# tuning) when Izzy jumped in with the appropriate chords. Duff and Steven got in on the act and before Slash knew what was happening "my little guitar exercise had become something else".

Despite coming up with various ideas, most notably the "Where do we go? Where do we go now?" dramatic breakdown towards the end of 'Sweet Child O' Mine', it was felt that Proffer wasn't the right producer for the band and so the search continued. The band eventually settled on Mike Clink, an engineer-turned-producer who had cut his teeth working out of the Record Plant under Ron Nevison. Clink's first co-production credit came with Survivor's 'Eye of the Tiger' which had, of course, proved a worldwide hit owing to Sylvester Stallone requisitioning it as the theme song for *Rocky III*. He'd since worked with Whitesnake, Triumph and UFO. "Clink loved GN'R and had seen us live a few times," Duff revealed. "He said he would come down and record us for nothing and convince us with his recording. He did a playback and said, 'This is how I think your record should sound.' And it was basically us live. And I immediately thought, *That's exactly right*."

"We do have a fuck-you attitude, but our goal is to break down as many barriers as we can. I mean we want to break down the barriers in people's minds too."

AXL

PART FOUR

GETTIN NOTHIN' FOR NOTHIN'

Mike Clink had booked Guns into Rumbo Recorders; an adobe-walled 10,000sq ft three-room studio in Canoga Park, built by Daryl Dragon of Seventies husband and wife singing duo Captain & Tennille. Canoga Park is located in the Valley some 20 miles north-west of Hollywood, and Zutaut and Clink were no doubt both hoping that putting some distance betwixt the band and their bad habits would prove beneficial for all concerned. Despite trashing the apartment Clink rented for them, Slash insists when it came to recording the album he and the rest of the band "were pretty much together". Yet Clink would be forced to call Zutaut to warn him the pre-production sessions were going down the tube owing to Slash's near-constant no-shows. Indeed, Slash's dope habit was such that playing guitar was coming in a very sorry second to getting high with Izzy and Steven. Duff's drinking was also drifting beyond the pale. Axl, though sober, spent much of his time holed up in his room with Erin.

Zutaut, knowing both his job and reputation were on the line should Guns fail to deliver, tore into the band; going so far as to threatening to wash his hands of them unless they started getting their act together. His broadside proved sufficient to shock the band from their torpor. With the basic tracks intended for the debut album being laid down to Clink's satisfaction, Geffen's legal team got to work on finalising the band's 62-page contract.

While the band were holed up with Clink at Rumbo, Alan Niven set to work on the "live" GN'R recording Axl had promised onstage at the Troubadour back in July. The end product, a 12-inch, four-track EP titled *Live?!*@ Like a Suicide*, was far from "live", however. The tracks were untouched demos of Aerosmith's 'Mama Kin', Rose Tattoo's 'Nice Boys', coupled with their own compositions 'Move to the City' and 'Reckless Life', while the crowd noise was lifted from a recording of a recent Texxas Jam rock festival staged over the July 4 weekend in Houston. (The inclusion of a stadium crowd being more of an in-joke rather than any deliberate attempt at deception as Guns N' Roses were still playing clubs at the time.) *Live?!*@ Like a Suicide* was released via the band's one-off UZI Suicide label on December 15, 1986. Any lingering doubts about Guns N' Roses' upward trajectory were soon dispelled with all 10,000 copies of the EP snapped up within days of going on release.

Although Geffen pressed the EP, the records themselves were distributed via an independent company called Important, as per Niven's agreement with Eddie Rosenblatt. There was method to Niven's perceived madness, for when he next showed up at the bemused Rosenblatt's offices with a cheque for $42,000, it was to hammer out another deal that would see the EP cash going towards financing Guns N' Roses first

49

GUNS N' ROSES

overseas trip – a three-show stint at London's legendary Marquee Club.

Few venues could set a musician's pulse racing quite like the Marquee and Guns N' Roses were no different. The Marquee had started out during the late Fifties in the basement of the Academy Cinema on nearby Oxford Street, so it wasn't until relocating to Wardour Street in 1964 that its reputation first began to take root. Over the next quarter century every major rock act or artist of note would play there. Indeed, it could be argued that a band couldn't claim to have "made it" until treading the Marquee's boards. Slash was the only member of the band to have visited London, and the memories of those childhood jaunts with his dad were hazy at best. Duff had played a couple of shows in Vancouver, while Axl, Izzy, and Steven had never before had cause to venture outside of the US.

There were no fanfares when Guns N' Roses flew into Heathrow the day prior to their opening June 19 show. However, thanks to *Sounds* and *Time Out* having both carried features on the band in recent weeks there was a groundswell of interest among London's heavy metal and hard rock fraternity. Geffen's UK offices had moved into gear the moment they heard about the impending trip and rush-released 'It's So Easy'/'Mr Brownstone' as a limited-edition double A-side single. There was zero hope of getting either track any daytime radio airplay, but the music press pounced on the record, if only for it serving as a taster for the much-vaunted forthcoming debut album.

♫

The Marquee was an established haunt of the NWOBHM (New Wave of British Heavy Metal) bands, with Iron Maiden firmly entrenched at the movement's vanguard. The vast majority of the Marquee's lager-fuelled Friday night crowd at the opening GN'R show were therefore most likely sporting Maiden, Motörhead, Ozzy and AC/DC T-shirts. Def Leppard would also have been well represented given the phenomenal worldwide success of the Sheffield-based outfit's most recent album, *Pyromania*. Hanoi Rocks had always received a rapturous welcome when visiting the UK, but Mötley Crüe had as yet failed to cast much of a shadow. If Guns N' Roses thought they were in for an easy ride simply because many of their musical inspirations hailed from Britain they were in for a rude awakening.

Encouraged by the reception they received on emerging from the dressing room door out onto the stage, the band thundered into 'Reckless Life'; Steven pounding away with his surfer locks bouncing in tandem with the beat, Izzy and Duff driving the rhythm while Slash blister-riffed away with his face hidden behind a mop of corkscrew curls and trademark top hat. When the song came to a close, however, Axl barely had time to declare how great it was "to be in fucking England, finally" when a hail of spit, beer, beer cans, and plastic glasses began raining down on the stage. Of course, Axl's grousing only resulted in repeat barrages. It was a clichéd baptism of fire that all visiting bands could expect, but Guns blinked first and came away scorched.

It wasn't the first time Guns N' Roses had faced an antagonistic crowd but when starting out playing bottom-of-the-bill at the Troubadour or the Whisky they'd at least been able to count on their friends to shout down the hecklers. No one needed telling they'd sucked on the night, but the *NME* and *Sounds* were all too happy to point as much out in their stinging rebukes; the latter paper's Andy Ross (aka Andy Hurt) going so far as to describe Axl's singing as being akin to "a hamster with its balls trapped in a door. 'Squeak, squeak, squeak...'"

Axl was furious and arrived at *Sounds*' offices in Mornington Crescent – with the rest of the band in tow – spoiling for a fight. Ross was nowhere to be seen, however. Paul Elliott, another of *Sounds*' writers, had visited the band at their rented apartments in Kensington soon after their arrival in London, having also

interviewed Guns in LA some three months earlier. Recognising at least one sympathetic face, the band ambled over to say hello. Axl brought the small talk to an end by enquiring as to Ross's whereabouts. With the mood he was in, it's likely he'd have camped out in the office until Ross showed his face had the paper's editor not told Elliott to get rid of the interlopers. There was only one surefire way of ensuring the band left peaceably, of course, and that was to suggest a liquid lunch. Before leaving, however, Axl left a note for Ross with one of the secretaries. The note simply read: "You're a dead man."

If Guns N' Roses thought they were in for an easy ride simply because many of their musical inspirations hailed from Britain they were in for a rude awakening.

During his visit to LA to interview Guns N' Roses, Elliott caught the band play the Whisky a Go Go. He'd come away again in two minds. "They sounded good and looked great," he recounted for www.loudersound.com in May 2017. "The songs they played from the new album – 'Welcome to the Jungle', 'It's So Easy', 'Nightrain' – pissed all over anything that Mötley Crüe or Poison had ever come up with. Axl, certainly, had the aura of a star in the making. But still, I wasn't sure about Guns N' Roses.

"I'd heard their EP, *Live Like A Suicide*, and it was pretty good, but in the photo on the EP's sleeve Guns N' Roses looked like any one of a thousand LA hair metal bands. Tougher than Poison, maybe. But that wasn't saying much.

They trashed other LA bands and said they were different, better. But every rock band said that. Until I heard the album, the jury was out." Said jury wouldn't be out for long, however . . .

Elliott had set up the interview at his hotel, the Park Sunset, the day after the Whisky show. While there Slash whipped a Walkman from his jacket pocket, placed the headphones over Elliott's ears, cranked the volume up to max, and pushed the play button. "What I heard was a rough mix of a song from the album: a song called 'It's So Easy'," Elliott recounted. "It was electrifying; the riff just slammed into me. It had the punk rock fury of the Sex Pistols mixed with the swagger of Rocks-era Aerosmith. It was mean and dirty, really nasty stuff. Axl sang the verses in a low sneer, full of venom. And just when it seemed like this song couldn't get any better, Axl snarled, 'Why don't you just … FUCK OFF!' I simply couldn't believe what I'd just heard. This one song was a hundred times better than anything on the EP. And if the rest of the album was as good as this, Guns N' Roses weren't just the best band in LA – they were the best band in the world."

Guns' lacklustre Marquee debut had left the band feeling deflated. The mood within the camp was lightened somewhat, however, by the arrival of Slash's bass-playing booze buddy, Todd Crew, in tow with Axl's short story-writer friend, Del James; the two having blown the dust from the Eurorail passes Todd's parents had presented him upon graduating college a couple or three years earlier. According to Duff, Del and Todd had rocked up at the Marquee while the band were giving a Guns N' Roses twist to Dylan's 'Knockin' on Heaven's Door' for the first time during soundcheck.

Following three days of solid rehearsing and hard partying, the band arrived back at the Marquee on Monday, June 22, in determined mood. They didn't disappoint. The third and final show six days later – by which time they'd also worked AC/DC's 'Whole Lotta Rosie' into the set – proved beyond doubt that Guns N' Roses were a world removed from the LA hair metal bands that had passed through London previously. "We were [now] seen as something else," Slash reflected, "which was what we'd been saying all along. Finally, it felt like we'd been justified."

Guns N' Roses returned to LA with an added spring in their cowboy-booted step, secure in the knowledge that with London conquered the rest of the UK was now there for the taking. Niven was set to accompany Tom Zutaut to New York for the New Music Seminar, as well as to meet with the band's new booking agents, ICM. As Slash had designed Guns' destined-to-be-iconic logo of two guns intertwined with roses and a human skull, he elected to accompany them. Upon discovering his new girlfriend, porn actress Lois Ayers, would be in the Big Apple making what he describes as "feature performances" at several Times Square strip clubs, the guitarist altered his schedule accordingly.

Slash was holed up with Ayers at the Mitford Plaza on Eighth Avenue when they were roused from their slumber by an early morning call to say Todd Crew was in reception. Slash was understandably surprised as Crew had said nothing about coming to New York. The explanation wasn't long in coming. Since returning from his London jaunt, Crew had been dumped both by his band, Jetboy, and his long-term girlfriend. Despite the early hour, Crew was already so out of it that he could barely stand. The sensible thing to do would have been to leave Crew to sleep off his drink, but Slash didn't want to leave his friend alone so decided to take him along to all his meetings little caring what any of the suits might say.

It was to prove a taxing experience, but once the meetings were over Slash suggested they head into Central Park so that Crew could grab a couple of hours shuteye. They'd no sooner entered the park when they happened upon three mutual musician acquaintances that also happened to be visiting New York. The talk quickly turned to their grabbing a cab to the East Village to score some heroin. Crew was all for it, but Slash was trying to stay clean

and instead suggested they grab a bottle of something from a liquor store and find a shady tree to sit under. They ended up in a bar where the conversation once again turned to scoring some heroin. Slash says there was simply no stopping Crew by this point, and once their LA acquaintances returned with the dope the five then made their way to the apartment of Plasmatics' bassist, Chosei Funahara. Upon their arrival, Slash tried the dope. Satisfied that it wasn't too potent, he cooked up a hit for himself and Crew. They remained at Funahara's place for a couple of hours and having made arrangements to meet up with the LA trio later on at the Mitford Plaza to finish off the heroin, Slash and Crew took their leave. They bought a crate of beer and whiled away a couple of hours watching *Jaws 3-D* at a Times Square cinema before returning to the hotel for the pre-arranged rendezvous.

At some point during the evening Crew slipped into unconsciousness. Slash remains convinced the dope they'd scored that day was of low-grade strength, and that one of their "friends" must have slipped Crew a hit of something stronger. Sensing Crew had OD'd, the trio bolted from the room leaving Slash to revive his friend any way he could. He dragged the hapless Crew into the en suite bathroom, dumped him in the tub and doused him with cold water, all the while shaking and slapping him about the face until he eventually came around. He then put Crew to bed before calling a couple of mutual friends back in LA to explain the situation. There was little the friends could do, of course, but talking about it was helping calm Slash down.

Slash's next call was to the only person he says he felt he knew well enough in New York to confide in – a girl called Shelley that worked at ICM. He was still on the phone when he noticed Crew wasn't breathing. He dashed across the room and started slapping and shaking his friend even more vigorously than before, but to no avail. In desperation he called 911 before sinking to the carpet with the unconscious Crew cradled in his arms. By the time the paramedics arrived – some 40 minutes later in Slash's estimation – Crew was beyond all earthly help. He was just 21 years old.

Slash was questioned by police for several hours before being released into Alan Niven's care. By the time they arrived back in LA, however, the accusations and finger-pointing had already started.

♫

Appetite for Destruction was released worldwide on July 21, 1987; the album taking its name from a Robert Williams painting depicting a *robotic* rapist about to meet his retribution at the many hands of a metal avenger while rapist's teenage victim lies slumped on the pavement. Axl had apparently happened upon a print of the painting while perusing the art galleries on Melrose Avenue. Speaking about his body of work in 1997, Williams said how his paintings were designed to trap rather than entertain; to hold you before them while you try to rationalise what elements of the picture are making you stand there.

Instead of viewing the image as an interpretation of the karmic retribution, the buyers at Walmart and other major US retailers saw only a bruised and battered girl with her blouse ripped open and her panties about her knees. Steven says that Geffen were content to run with the artwork as the ensuing controversy provided an opportunity to "grab a little [or] maybe a lot of extra press". However, with more and more retail stores across America refusing to stock the album, the offending image was moved to the inside sleeve on all future pressings. The new front cover featured an image – lifted from a painting that a friend had done during their Hell House days – depicting all five band members as cartoon-esque skulls on a cross set against a black background. (The same image that was soon to adorn Axl's right forearm.)

Despite a slew of excellent reviews, *Appetite*

for Destruction wasn't selling anywhere near the number of albums anyone at Geffen had anticipated. And with David Geffen having expressed his displeasure upon hearing the finished album, Zutaut couldn't be sure if his next visit to the office might well prove his last. On a brighter note, The Cult's Ian Astbury had been in the crowd at the first of the Marquee shows. He was impressed enough by what he'd seen to have his management invite Guns N' Roses to open for The Cult on the forthcoming North American leg of a world tour in support of their most recent album, *Electric*.

Aside from cementing inter-band relationships, however, Guns' going out on the road with The Cult did little other than allow them the chance to iron out the rough edges of their stage act. Duff cites *Appetite*'s Canadian release date being held back several weeks as the reason for their playing to near-empty stadiums over the border, yet the situation hardly changed once they crossed back onto US soil. "It probably made us more entertaining because we were so loose around the edges," Slash reflected. "We showed up with no experience; just the clothes on our back, the gear on the stage, and a handful of songs to play for people who had never heard of us."

Zutaut believed his luck was about to change for the better when Tim Collins proved amenable to having Guns N' Roses open for Aerosmith on a clutch of European dates to promote their second Geffen album, *Permanent Vacation*. It was a win/win situation as both bands were Geffen acts, whose musical styles suited the other perfectly. Guns were thrilled at the prospect of playing overseas with a band they held in such high esteem. When Collins decided to scrap the European dates in favour of an extensive US tour to capitalise on *Permanent Vacation*'s assault on the *Billboard* chart en route to multi-platinum-selling success (the album eventually peaking at # 11), Zutaut was dancing for joy. His victory jig would prove short-lived, however, as Collins had also had a

GUNS N' ROSES

rethink about Guns N' Roses. It had only taken a phone call to his opposite number in The Cult camp to learn of Guns' offstage proclivities while out on the road. With *Permanent Vacation* showing a true return to form for Aerosmith, letting his charges within bargepole distance of the Gunners risked ruining all the hard work that had gone into getting and keeping Tyler and Co clean.

Appetite for Destruction was in danger of becoming a millstone about Zutaut's neck. There were already those at Geffen questioning the label's $750,000 outlay on Guns N' Roses, and the higher the rejuvenated Aerosmith's star rose, the more likely the decision would be reached to cut their losses with Guns. If that were to happen, Zutaut's own star would be tarnished beyond redemption.

The cancellation of the Aerosmith European dates had also left Alan Niven reaching for the Valium. Keeping Guns N' Roses out on the road was the only viable means of promoting *Appetite*. To date, the album had shifted somewhere in the region of 7,000 units; a far cry from the half-a-million records he'd believed the band capable of selling under the right stewardship. Yet here he was, a year into taking over the reins, and the band were facing the very real possibility of being written off as a tax loss. The most galling thing was that it wasn't the band's fault. *Appetite for Destruction* was a great album. It just wasn't reaching its target audience. Deciding on one last roll of the dice, Niven called John Jackson, the London-based promoter that had booked the Marquee dates. Jackson had seen with his own eyes how Guns N' Roses had wrenched victory from the maw of disaster. At the final Marquee show Guns had left the crowd baying for more. With the right marketing there was no reason they couldn't bring about a similar reaction elsewhere in England – especially if a few select European dates were booked prior to their arriving in England to allow Guns to hit the ground running.

The first stop-off on Guns N' Roses' five-date UK tour came at Newcastle City Hall on October 4, 1987; the other dates being Nottingham (Oct 5), Manchester (Oct 6), Bristol (Oct 7), and London (Oct 8). Accompanying the band on their latest European venture was their newly installed tour manager, Doug Goldstein. Upon graduating from North Arizona University, where he'd studied law, Goldstein (who was 26 at the time) had started out working events security before being appointed chief security recruiter for the 1984 Olympics in LA. Since then he'd handled security for the likes of Van Halen, David Lee Roth, and Black Sabbath.

Guns had arrived in the UK on the back of three sell-out European shows in Hamburg, Düsseldorf and Amsterdam, yet advance ticket sales for the British dates were sluggish at best. Sales of *Appetite* were proving lethargic in the UK – especially outside of London. But this was hardly surprising given MTV's ongoing reluctance to air the promo video to 'Welcome to the Jungle' outside of the fag-end of its midnight to 6am "graveyard shift".

It was at the Manchester Apollo show that *Kerrang!*'s Mick Wall, who would go on to pen several books on Guns N' Roses, first encountered the band. Wall was taken aback when Axl thanked him for *Kerrang!* having championed Guns N' Roses over the past few months – even if his co-writer, Howard Johnson, had taken a swipe at the band when reviewing *Appetite* by saying many of the tunes sounded like "second-hand Aerosmith riffs". He'd heard all the rumours surrounding the band's offstage profligacy, of course, and now he was witnessing it first-hand. He came away from the Apollo knowing that it was no longer a question of Guns N' Roses living up to the hype, but rather whether certain members would live long enough to enjoy the success that surely awaited them.

The final date at London's Hammersmith Odeon was to prove the clearest indicator to date that Guns N' Roses were coming to prominence as only a fraction of the 3,200 tickets remained on

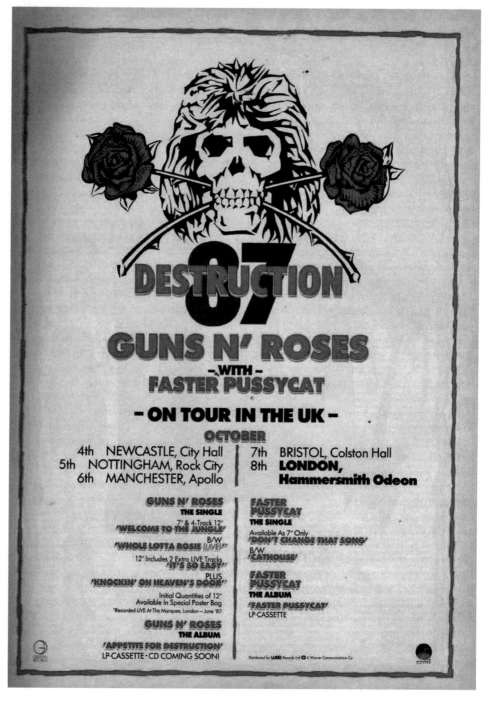

GUNS N' ROSES

sale come showtime. And what a show it proved! With Sid Vicious' 'My Way' ringing around the semi-darkened gloom, the band came charging out and launched into 'It's So Easy'; Axl screeching out the lyrics sporting the straight-hair/bandana look that would soon become his trademark. 'Knockin' on Heaven's Door' and 'Whole Lotta Rosie' both featured in the 15-song set; the first being dedicated to Todd Crew, the latter bringing the show to a climactic finale. Probably the standout moment of the night, however, came with 'Rocket Queen' being extended to a free-for-all jam with Duff providing additional percussion and Axl riffing along on bass at one point.

From London, Guns N' Roses flew to New York where they were scheduled to appear on MTV's Headbangers Ball, as well as play a few East Coast headline dates in Boston, Baltimore, Philadelphia and New York, where they played the Ritz on October 23. They also put in an acoustic set at CBGBs' Record Canteen (located further along the block from the iconic punk club) on October 30. *Appetite* was still stuttering in the lower reaches of the *Billboard* 200, yet only two tracks from the album – 'You're Crazy' and 'Mr Brownstone' – featured in the acoustic set. Instead, the 100 or so lucky punters were treated to first-time airings of 'Patience', 'Used to Love Her', and the highly contentious 'One in a Million'.

Rolling Stone was on hand to review the acoustic show, yet somewhat unbelievably neglected to make any mention of the latter song's inflammatory lyric in which Axl wilfully denigrates blacks and homosexuals – especially seeing as Slash was of mixed race, and David Geffen was openly gay. Owing to Guns N' Roses still being a club act at the time, coupled with the limited number of times the band played 'One in a Million' live, the controversy surrounding the song's lyrical content could well have escaped public censor had Axl not subsequently elected to bring shit and fan together by insisting 'One in a Million' be included on the *GN'R Lies* album.

Meantime, Guns N' Roses were invited to take over from Whitesnake midway through the North American leg of Mötley Crüe's *Girls, Girls, Girls*

world tour. 'Here I Go Again', the lead single from Whitesnake's latest – eponymously titled – studio album, had scored a surprise US # 1, and the single's success had in turn propelled the album to # 2 on the *Billboard* chart so it didn't come as much of a shock when the British rockers shied off the tour to play some headline shows of their own. It was surely a magnanimous gesture on Mötley Crüe's part as Guns N' Roses were such obvious pretenders to their throne. Instead of using the tour as a means of putting their would-be usurpers in their place, however, the headliners extended every courtesy, occasionally allowing Guns to travel to shows in their private jet.

As perhaps was to be expected given the Crüe's penchant for syringes and binges it was excess all areas away from the stage, with Slash readily admitting to his shamelessly shadowing Nikki Sixx around with a rolled-up $20 at the ready. In what was surely a portent of things to come, Axl was arrested midway through a show at The Omni Arena in Atlanta for attacking an overzealous security guard. With Axl being questioned backstage, one of the roadies was pressganged into taking centre stage while Slash played extended solos to pad out what remained of their 45-minute set.

Tom Zutaut and Alan Niven had obviously been all too aware of such an eventuality when calling in favours to get Guns onto the Crüe tour, but they did so knowing the potential rewards far outweighed the risks. Unlike The Cult tour, the crowds flocking to see Mötley Crüe were very much Guns N' Roses' target audience. This was soon evidenced as, slowly but surely, *Appetite* began creeping up the *Billboard* chart.

Following on from the Crüe tour, Guns were set to hook up with Alice Cooper, who was touring his new album, *Raise Your Fist and Yell*. The timing of the Crüe and Cooper tours couldn't have served Zutaut and Niven's wishes better had they penned the itinerary. Guns being in the public eye in the run up to Christmas ensured *Appetite* found its way onto many a Santa wish list. Indeed, by year's end the album would be hovering just outside the US Top 50 with sales approaching the 250,000 mark.

1987 had proved one hell of a year for Guns N' Roses. They'd recorded and released their debut album, toured extensively in the US, had played dates in the UK as well as mainland Europe, and were set to bring the year to a climatic finale with four consecutive headline "homecoming" shows at Perkins Palace in Pasadena from December 26-30.

Unbeknown to the band, however, Cooper's father was terminally ill. The tour had rolled into Madison, Wisconsin on December 19 when the inevitable sadly came to pass. With the gig cancelled, Guns were left to amuse themselves any way they could. Steven allowed his frustrations to get the better of him in one of the bars and – by his own estimation – got "terminally shit-faced" knocking back some 20 kamikaze shots (vodka, triple sec and lime juice) one after the other.

Reflecting on that night in his book, Steven admits he "became pretty damn obnoxious", and ended up being tossed out on his ear by the doormen. In a rage he punched a metal light covering and ended up breaking the little finger of his right hand. Slash maintains that Steven's whole hand was busted up, but either way, there was no chance of his hand healing in time for the Perkins Palace shows. Cinderella's Fred Coury was recruited as a temporary stand-in for the four Perkins Palace shows, but it still rankled Steven that the shows went ahead instead of being put back until his hand had healed. "There was no talk of postponing anything until I knitted up," he seethed. "They just went out and got someone else to fill in. I swear, if it was anybody else in the band, they would never have gotten a replacement – no way in hell!" Despite having known Steven the longest out of the band, there would be little forthcoming from Slash in the way of compassion for his friend. As far as he was concerned, Steven had "gotten too drunk and done something stupid. He fucked up [and] had to deal with the consequences."

Steven was obviously out of action, but the sudden curtailment of the Alice Cooper tour gave the rest of the band some unanticipated free time. Slash's English girlfriend, Sally McLaughlin, had joined him midway through the Cooper dates. He was giving her a guided tour of Sunset Strip when they happened upon Steven and Nikki Sixx at The Cathouse (which had recently relocated from N. La Cienega to North Highland). Slash and Steven had booked adjoining suites at the Franklin Plaza hotel and at some point during the evening Steven and Sixx headed back to the hotel to shoot up with some dope procured by their drug buddy, Robbin Crosby, the guitarist in Ratt. (In June 2002, Crosby would die from a heroin overdose and pneumonia with complications from AIDS.)

Steven's version of events has Sixx – and presumably Crosby – calling on him and Slash at the Franklin. And that Crosby's drug connection had arrived soon thereafter. Whatever the sordid scenario, Sixx OD'd and most likely would have died had McLaughlin not called 911. The attending paramedics managed to wrench Sixx back from oblivion with an adrenaline shot to the heart. After the paramedics had taken the Crüe bassist off to hospital, the cops arrived with their questions. Slash was so drunk he'd had to be dragged through to Steven's room for the interrogation. "[Nikki's] management came down later and yelled at me as a horrible influence, but the truth was that I was seventy-five percent oblivious to what was going on," he revealed in Sixx's harrowing 2007 memoir, *Heroin Diaries: A Year in the Life of a Shattered Rock Star*. (Sixx would subsequently immortalise his near-death escapade in 'Kickstart my Heart'.)

Fred Coury would again be called upon for a Guns show in early January 1988 supporting Great White at the Santa Monica Civic Auditorium. Once Steven had proved he was back to his fighting best at The Cathouse later that same month Guns returned to Rumbo Studios for an acoustic recording session. The tracks recorded were 'Used to Love Her', 'One in a Million', 'Patience', and a slowed-down version of 'You're Crazy'. With the exception of 'Patience', the other tracks were viewed as potential B-sides. Geffen were also dropping none-too-subtle hints about a follow-up album. Zutaut, however, still believed *Appetite* would surpass the million mark if Geffen would only throw their not inconsiderable weight behind the album. He also thought 'Sweet Child O' Mine' a definite Number One single, but his was a lone voice at Geffen HQ. Eddie Rosenblatt certainly wasn't listening to Zutaut's entreaties and continued pushing Niven for a new Guns N' Roses album.

Zutaut was determined to stick to his guns in every sense, however. Just as he had when looking to sign Guns, he sidestepped Rosenblatt and pleaded his case directly to David Geffen. Whether it was Zutaut's earnest pleas, or simply because he'd once babysat Slash, Geffen agreed to call in a favour from his good friend Tom Freston, the chief executive at MTV, to see about getting the 'Welcome to the Jungle' video some airplay. Freston begrudgingly agreed, but not before imposing a caveat – the video would be screened just once at 3am EST; midnight over on the West Coast.

On the surface this might not appear much of an improvement on the intermittent graveyard airings 'Welcome to the Jungle' had received at the time of the single's release. But Freston had agreed to air the video over a weekend and 3 a.m. is the time when Guns N' Roses East Coast target audience would have most likely just arrived home after the clubs closed, while no self-respecting Sunset Stripper ventured out till after midnight. Zutaut's gamble paid off as within minutes of the airing the switchboard at MTV's New York Offices lit up like the advertising hoardings at nearby Times Square.

MTV's filming the band live at The Ritz in New York on February 2 served to further underpin the buzz surrounding Guns N' Roses. The station had initially contacted Alan Niven about filming Great White at The Ritz for an MTV Special as their third album, *Once Bitten*, was

fast-approaching platinum status in the US. Niven readily agreed, on the proviso that Guns opened for Great White and would feature in the show. Come the day of the show, Niven had elected to flip the billing so that Guns followed Great White. Both bands were onstage the same length of time, so it wasn't a question of Great White losing face by going on first, it was just that Niven sensed Guns would steal the show. While Great White put in a blinding performance, there was only one band's name on everyone's lips.

The Ritz show was the first time Guns N' Roses had performed in front of television cameras. They open their truncated 11-song set with 'It's So Easy'; the beshaded Axl effortlessly working the stage, looking every inch a rock star in the making. At the end of 'Welcome to the Jungle' Axl takes time out to introduce the rest of the band. On arriving at Slash, he playfully goes into schlock-horror soliloquy about the guitarist going through the world he did not create as though it was of his own making. "Half man, half beast. I'm not sure what it is, but whatever it is, it's weird and it's pissed off, and it calls itself 'Slash'."

Slash was indeed pissed off, pissed off by Axl's theatrics. The singer's Elizabeth Taylor-esque tantrums were already worthy of his idol Elton John, but his hinting that he wouldn't go out unless Doug Goldstein went out into the crowd to find a bandana to his liking to replace the one he'd misplaced was bordering on absurdity.

Axl's onstage antics were also becoming a concern, as he thought nothing of storming off if something or someone offended him. Things would come to a head ten days on from the Ritz date at the second of two headline shows at Phoenix's Celebrity Theatre in Phoenix. Axl had refused to go back out for the encore the previous evening but come the afternoon of the second show he barricaded himself in his hotel room with Erin, refusing all entreaties to open the door. To buy some time, Niven sent the support act, T.S.O.L. (True Sounds of Liberty), back out onstage. The Californian punk-metal quintet were happy to oblige and ran through the rest of their canon. Axl still wasn't for budging, however, and with T.S.O.L. reduced to playing Beatles songs Niven was left with little choice but to go out and tell the crowd that Guns N' Roses wouldn't be playing owing to a medical emergency. The emergency services would indeed be summoned to the theatre, but only to quell the rioting that spilled out onto the parking lot.

When the rest of the band arrived back at the hotel they headed straight for Axl's room where Steven, the only member of the band seemingly immune to Axl's mood swings, shouted through the door that he was fired. Axl calmly shouted back that they were too late as he was quitting the band. He then made good on his word by calling a cab to take him and Erin to the airport. For a time everyone held their breath, but thankfully Axl backed down. In the interim, however, AC/DC's management retracted their invitation for Guns to open for the Aussie rockers on the North American leg of their Blow Up Your Video world tour in support of the album of the same name.

Appetite for Destruction was finally beginning to make waves yet Guns N' Roses were still treading water, headlining their own club dates while playing support in arenas and stadiums; the latest second fiddle forays coming with opening for Iron Maiden on the North American leg of the British metal act's *Seventh Son of a Seventh Son* world tour.

Hearing they would be traversing the same ground they'd covered supporting The Cult several months previously didn't go down well with the band – if only because they considered their blues-tinged rock the polar opposite to Maiden's Spinal Tap-esque heavy metal. Or as Duff pointedly observed: "We didn't write songs about elves and demons." Indeed, his opinion was such that he returned to LA a few dates into the tour to marry his girlfriend, Mandy Brix (having called upon Cult bassist Haggis to fulfil his duties). Nor did Duff shed many tears when

Guns were subsequently forced to pull out of the tour altogether owing to Axl experiencing problems with his throat.

Prior to heading out with Iron Maiden, the band – with various friends and their girlfriends in attendance – had recorded a promo video for 'Sweet Child O' Mine', which Geffen had earmarked for the follow-up single to 'Welcome to the Jungle'; the idea being that releasing the most radio-friendly track from *Appetite* as a single might drive sales of the album beyond the 500,000 high-water mark that Alan Niven had originally envisaged. Whatever Niven had envisioned for Guns when taking the reins he certainly hadn't anticipated the album topping the *Billboard* chart; the cherry on the cake coming with their being out touring with Aerosmith at the time.

Appetite was sitting pretty atop the *Billboard* chart one year on from its release date, having already gone platinum at the beginning of April. The album still being on the chart some 12 months on was a remarkable achievement in itself, but Tom Zutaut's assertion that "Sweet Child O' Mine" was the song that would carry the album to number one had indeed transpired. "It happened very fast for us," Slash reflected. "Thanks to MTV's chronic rotation of 'Sweet Child O' Mine', within a few weeks of the single's release in early June it hit number one and we became the most popular band in the nation."

Duff remembers being backstage at one of the venues when someone from Geffen arrived with the news that *Appetite* was at Number One. There was a cake, but surprisingly little in the way of celebration. It was too much for the band to take in. Here they were with the number one-selling album in the country opening for a band whose album, *Permanent Vacation*, was languishing outside the Top 50 – even if it was Aerosmith. Indeed, the realisation wouldn't sink in until the writer covering the tour for *Rolling Stone* changed tack in focusing their attentions on the support act. "After a few days of watching the crowd's reaction and seeing us

GUNS N' ROSES

play live the magazine opted to put us on the cover instead," Slash continued. "By the end of the tour we were absolutely fucking huge." And yet the Aerosmith tour almost didn't come to pass, as with less than a week to go before the opening show at the Poplar Creek Music Theatre in Hoffman Estates, Illinois, Axl had called Niven insisting he cancel the tour.

The way Niven saw it, Guns N' Roses had signed onto the Aerosmith tour, and he wasn't about to let one spoil it for the others. Grabbing up a pair of dice he'd brought back from a recent trip to Las Vegas, he gave Axl the "weight of the odds" before rolling what was undoubtedly the biggest call of his managerial career to date. That wasn't to say Axl would give a flying fuck what number Niven threw, but fortunately for all concerned the bluff worked and Axl showed up at the hotel on the morning of the opening show. Axl still had to have the last word, however, and informed Niven that if he was anywhere near the venue come showtime he wouldn't go onstage. Niven reportedly ended up missing the first three weeks of the tour, but it was a small price to pay to see Guns N' Roses live to fight another day.

There can be little arguing that while Guns were a great band, and *Appetite for Destruction* one of the greatest albums of all time, the band owed much of their success to MTV's putting the promo video for 'Sweet Child O' Mine' on heavy rotation through the summer of 1988. With 'Paradise City' already being earmarked as the next single to be lifted from *Appetite*, the band were filmed playing the song at Giants Stadium in East Rutherford, New Jersey, both at the soundcheck as well as during the set. The idea was to shoot the band performing the song at that year's Monsters of Rock festival at Donington Park raceway in Castle Donington on August 20 and splice the footage for a high-voltage performance video.

Being invited onto the Monsters of Rock bill was the clearest indication yet of how far Guns N' Roses' stock had risen of late. "This was the kind of thing you heard about other bands

playing," Duff revealed. "Big bands, household names, not grubby kids a year or two removed from living in a back-alley storage space and treating their venereal diseases with fucking fish food."

the band owed much of their success to MTV's putting the promo video for 'Sweet Child O' Mine' on heavy rotation through the summer of 1988.

Monsters of Rock was in its eighth year. The "household name big bands" that Duff alluded to included Rainbow, Status Quo, AC/DC, Van Halen, Mötley Crüe, ZZ Top and Bon Jovi. Iron Maiden would be headlining this year with Guns N' Roses taking their place in a support bill alongside Kiss, David Lee Roth, Megadeth and Helloween. It was a day the band would never forget . . . but for all the wrong reasons.

The festival line-up had been compiled while *Appetite* was still hovering around the # 50 mark on the *Billboard* chart, and thoughts of 'Sweet Child O' Mine' being released as a single didn't exist anywhere outside of Tom Zutaut's imagination. As such, they went on second after Helloween. Though only 2pm when Guns arrived onstage, their burgeoning reputation was enough to guarantee that a sizeable number of the estimated 107,000 crowd were already inside the raceway at the appointed hour. Despite it being the height of summer, however, the weather was appalling and worsened as the day went on. An ominous portent of the tragedy yet to unfold came with gusting winds bringing one of giant video screens mounted high up at the sides of the stage crashing to the ground during Helloween's performance.

The swirling rain that had plagued the German speed-metal act's set had mercifully stopped by the time Guns took to the stage, but the near-continual downpour had turned the sloping ground towards the front of the stage into a mud bath; the quagmire rapidly worsening as thousands of fans rushed toward the stage in unison as the band thundered into 'It's So Easy'. Duff sensed danger from the get-go, but during the third number, 'You're Crazy', it seemed as if the 50,000-strong crowd had taken temporary leave of their senses. Axl had been yelling for those towards the rear of the crowd to move back but in the excitement his pleas fell on deaf ears. The band stopped playing to allow the hapless festival security to fish a few bedraggled fans out of the scrum, but the slippery slam-dancing continued the moment they started playing again.

Shooting footage for the 'Paradise City' promo video was the least of anyone's considerations. From his elevated position Duff could see what was happening – "kids piled on top of other kids, horizontally in the mud". He sensed some of those kids were hurt, but readily admits fear got the better of him when contemplating whether to jump into the crowd to help. Axl brought the show to another, more prolonged halt while security waded in to untangle the writhing, mud-coated leather and denim-clad limbs as best they could.

The set continued with 'Welcome to the Jungle', which, in hindsight, wasn't the most sensible option – though the less frenetic 'Patience' that followed allowed a temporary respite. The final number, 'Sweet Child O' Mine', seemed an irreverent afterthought; as though the crowd and organisers had realised something serious was amiss but weren't quite ready to acknowledge as much. Before taking his leave Axl had beseeched, "Don't kill yourselves". For two fans – 20-year-old

Landon Siggers and Alan Dick, who was two years younger – Axl's counsel came too late.

When compiling his report, Mick Upton, the head of security for festival promoters Aimcarve, said that he saw a surge that stopped suddenly with a crowd collapse at the centre of the audience some 15 yards from the front of the stage. "It was immediately obvious that this was a serious situation as about 50 people were involved. I sent a four-man team into the crowd to assess the problem and sent a message to the singer with Guns N' Roses to stop the show. He immediately did this, and then used the stage PA to calm the crowd and advise them of the problem."

According to Upton, he and his advance team were helping those fans unfortunate enough to have ended up at the bottom of the melee when Guns, assuming the incident had been contained, resumed playing. "Suddenly, the whole crowd around us erupted," he continued. "A large section of the crowd, and two of our own security team, collapsed in front of us. I witnessed 30 to 35 bodies that suddenly piled up in front of me, covered in mud."

Those fans pressing from the rear had also thought the situation had been contained and renewed their surge to the front – some of them crowd-surfing over Upton and his team while they continued feverishly pulling the injured out of the mud. Most of the injuries appeared superficial. For a heartbeat, Upton thought disaster had been averted, but as they removed what they took to be the last casualties, two lifeless bodies lay face down in the mud, almost to the point of being covered over. It was obvious to all that both boys were dead. Indeed, Siggers was so badly disfigured that identification was only possible owing to the scorpion and tiger tattoos on his arms. A verdict of accidental death would be recorded at the subsequent inquest.

"Money was never a thing any of us understood because we didn't have any. We had long been comfortable with subsistence living. Now we had a hit record. I remember the first cheque I received from that: we each got $80,000. It was an incomprehensible amount of money. It might as well have been a billion dollars."

DUFF

PART FIVE

TO MAKE IT, WE WON'T FAKE IT

There is still much debate among GN'R purists as to whether *GN'R Lies* counts as an album or an EP owing to its consisting of eight tracks with a running time just scraping beyond the half-hour mark. Originally titled *Lies! The Sex, the Drugs, the Violence, the Shocking Truth,* the snappier-sounding *GN'R Lies* was released at the end of November 1988 packaged in a satirical tabloid newspaper-style sleeve tongue-in-cheekily parodying the plethora of tales about the band's supposed debauched behaviour.

Reports also vary as to how *GN'R Lies* came about. One version has Geffen being keen to release product to further boost Guns N' Roses' profile, while Doug Goldstein claims to have come up with the idea in response to Axl's reaction on being approached by an irate teenage fan outside the Pine Knob Music Theatre in Detroit a few days prior to the fateful Monsters of Rock appearance. The fan in question was apparently in tears because bootleggers were asking – and getting – upwards of $500 for copies of the *Live?!*@ Like A Suicide EP*. Axl had duly called a meeting between himself, Goldstein, and Slash to look at ways of beating the bootleggers. It was at the meeting that Goldstein mooted the idea of reissuing *Live?!*@ Like A Suicide* with the acoustic numbers the band had recorded earlier in the year with Mike Clink at Rumbo Studios.

Such was the groundswell of interest in all things GN'R, that *GN'R Lies* was soon soaring up the *Billboard* chart. *Appetite* had been toppled from its lofty perch by the time of the new record's release and was slowly slipping out of the Top Ten. The interest generated by *GN'R Lies* would enable *Appetite* to briefly reclaim the top spot at the beginning of February 1989.

GN'R Lies would go Top Five, but chart placings soon became a secondary consideration because of Axl's insistence on including 'One in a Million' in the track listing. Slash objected to certain lines in the song for obvious reasons, as did Duff whose brother-in-law was black. Steven and Izzy had also pleaded with Axl to consider the shitstorm that was sure to descend, but conciliation didn't appear to feature in the W. Axl Rose lexicon. David Geffen had arranged for Guns N' Roses to appear at a charity show in New York in benefit of AIDS research but owing to the mounting protest in the wake of the release they would be dropped from the bill.

In hindsight, it's hard to believe no one at Geffen recognised the elephant in the room. Including 'One in a Million" on *GN'R Lies* was utter folly, and it's incomprehensible that the label's legal eagles thought having Axl pen an apology incorporated into the artwork might somehow avert the PR disaster looming on the horizon:

GUNS N' ROSES

"Ever been unjustly hassled by
someone with a gun and
and a badge? Been to a gas
station or a convenience store
and treated like you don't
belong here by an individual
who barely speaks English?
Hopefully not, but have you
ever been attacked by a
homosexual? Had some so-
called religionist try to con you
out of your hard-earned cash?
This song is very simple. My
apologies to those who may
take offence."

If Axl had asked the crowd at any of the US
shows Guns N' Roses had played to date if
they or anyone dear to them had ever been
"unjustly hassled by the cops ("Someone with
a gun and badge") he would have no doubt
received a thunderous cheer. Questioning
the ethnicity of the average gas station
employee or convenience store owner, or
denigrating homosexuality, however, would
surely have caused consternation amongst
any audience outside of the Deep South.
When penning his memoir, Duff said how
art often gets misconstrued by the beholder,
and that although he'd "stood by his original
interpretation of the song and of Axl's
intentions," he'd nonetheless felt uneasy about
this particular misinterpretation. The rest of
the band were already referring to Axl as the
"Ayatollah" by now because of his "my way
or highway" stance, so it's doubtful if making
a collective stand to force Axl into replacing
the offending lines would have carried much
import. Would he have dared adopt the same
myopic stance had Geffen insisted the song be
removed from GN'R Lies?

In an article about 'One in a Million' on www.
loudersound.com in May 2108, Classic Rock
magazine's Scott Rowley questioned Geffen's

motives: "It's a shit song. They could've lost
that one easy and no one would've mourned.
How did the record company let that go? Not
by accident – you can't tell me that no one
was listening to those lyrics and it just slipped
through. So you've got to ask: was it just a
cynical stab at getting controversy?"

Alan Niven was one of the few people who
saw nothing gratuitous in Axl's intentions, but
rather than allow the band's achievements
get lost in the gathering storm clouds of
controversy, he hastily rescheduled five
headline dates of Japan that had been held
over from the summer and tagged on four
Australasian dates, three in Australia and one
in the New Zealand capital, Auckland.

The band had resumed their commitments
on the Permanent Vacation tour and had also
performed at Survival of the Fittest 1988 in
Irving, Texas, on September 17 alongside
Iggy Pop, Ziggy Marley, The Smithereens and
headliners INXS (whom Axl declared from
onstage to be the "biggest group of fags I've
ever met") in a near-somnambulistic state; the
fear of another crowd stampede whenever they
walked out onstage only ever a heartbeat away.

Guns N' Roses had traversed the USA and
Canada several times over, had visited the UK
on three occasions, and had also dipped a toe
into West Germany and Holland, but Japan
was an experience to savour – or at least it
would have been had they remained sober long
enough to take stock of their surroundings.
Indeed, Slash's recollections of the trip centre
around "sticky rice, sake, and Jack Daniel's".

Japan's zero tolerance drugs policy is
renowned around the globe and both Niven
and Goldstein made sure to hammer home
what would happen to anyone foolish enough
to try and smuggle dope into Japan. When
The Specials toured Japan for the first time
in August 1980 they'd been lucky enough to
score some weed from a Japanese Rasta. This,
however, was a rare exception to the rule as
Paul McCartney had found to his cost at Narita
Airport a few months earlier. Izzy had gotten so

strung out in the lead-up to the tour that rather than spend the ten-hour flight fretting about where his next fix might come from, he popped several slow-release Valium at LAX. He was still unconscious when the band landed and had to be carried through customs. Upon finally resurfacing in his room at the Roppongi Prince Hotel many hours later, he'd no idea where he was or how he'd gotten there. His confusion was such that he refused to believe they were in Tokyo until Steven playfully offered to give him a blow job should he look out the window and see a single blond head of hair.

Mr Udo, the legendary local promoter that would be looking after Guns N' Roses throughout their stay in Japan, had already experienced the headiness of West Hollywood excess first-hand the previous December during Mötley Crüe's first visit to his country. Slash, Duff, Steven, and Izzy were rarely sober away from the stage, but none had thought to cause havoc on a bullet train by blindsiding any of their fellow passengers with an empty Jack Daniel's bottle, or playfully insult a police inspector safe in the knowledge that any cock-in-mouth jibes would be safely lost in translation. Indeed, Mr Udo was so pleased at the band's behaviour and the respect they'd shown him and the representatives from their Japanese record label that he presented each member with an expensive camera as a memento of their inaugural visit. Neglecting to declare the cameras would cause one or two problems upon re-entering the US in Hawaii, but the band were too exhausted to care.

Guns N' Roses had been on the road for some 18 months. Yet although the demands of excessive touring had begun to exact a toll – both physically and mentally – with sales of *Appetite* soaring towards the five million mark and *GN'R Lies* having gone Top 5, no one was complaining.

When Guns N' Roses returned to LA at the end of 1988, Mötley Crüe were holed up with Bob Rock at Little Mountain Sound Studios in Vancouver recording *Dr Feelgood*, the album that would score them their first US number one. In the interim, however, Guns were the undisputed cocks of the West Hollywood walk. They'd been mobbed for autographs at LAX, but as with every other returning hero they'd quickly come to realise how anonymity is so undervalued – once you lose it there's no going back. Steven might have been relishing every moment of his newfound fame but the rest of the band were somewhat more hesitant. Duff now found popping out to the local store to buy a pack of smokes or a six-pack of beer no longer possible without being hounded at every turn. The sizeable royalty cheques that were now rolling in might have given him hitherto unknown financial security, yet the world he knew was shrinking to the point where he felt like an exotic bird trapped within a gilded cage.

Axl bought himself a twelfth-floor condominium at the plush Shoreham Towers situated just off Sunset, as well as a sizeable plot of land in Wisconsin for as yet unspecified intentions. The rest of the band would also end up buying homes, cars and saddling themselves with other material trappings, but in doing so they lost the of-the-street mentality that had melded them together and brought them this far; the self-imposed isolation of their respective ivory towers unwittingly tugging lose a thread that would irrevocably unravel the band from within. Drugs and booze had always been an ever-present within the band – some members guiltier than others – but with money to burn and the devil happy to oblige idle hands, Slash, Izzy and Steven slipped deeper into their respective habits while Duff drowned his marital woes in alcohol.

At the end of January, with The Eagles' Don Henley mysteriously filling in for Steven, Guns performed 'Patience' at the 1989 American Music Awards at the Shrine Auditorium in LA. Neither Slash nor Duff thought to mention their

♫

drummer's absence during the AMA appearance in their respective tomes, but Steven has never been one to hold back. He says that it was in the run-up to the AMAs that Alan Niven had suggested he look at going into rehab. As with all addicts, he thought he was in control but trusted Niven's judgement to the point where he agreed that maybe he could use a "little tidying up". It wasn't until he came out of rehab that he learned of the band's appearance at the AMAs. "I was completely blindsided by this," he reflected. "I can't begin to describe the feeling of betrayal. Nobody in our organisation ever mentioned anything about the AMAs to me."

Steven does at least admit he was already on the downward spiral that would lead to being sacked – even if he only admits to being "partly" at fault in his downfall. "Like the broken finger incident, I'm sure I'd done my fair share to irritate them. I ticked them off just enough to have made them feel indifferent about insisting I be kept in the loop."

With 'Patience' earmarked as the follow-up single to 'Paradise City', Guns N' Roses took over the recently closed Ambassador Hotel on Wilshire Boulevard to record footage for the accompanying promo video. Following its April release, 'Patience' would score Guns N' Roses their third Top Five *Billboard* hit single. (The video shoot was the first time all five members of the band had been in the same room since coming off the road at the end of the previous year.)

Only six months had passed since the release of *GN'R Lies* but the band agreed the EP was nothing more than a stopgap betwixt *Appetite* and the follow-up studio album. Several new songs were already taking shape. One of these was 'Civil War'. On being presented with an instrumental that Slash had been working on sporadically, Axl and Duff had set about trading ideas for lyrics. "Basically it was a riff that we would do at sound-checks," Duff told *Rockline*'s Bob Coburn in September 1993. "I went in a peace march when I was a little kid, with my mom. I was like four years old. For Martin Luther

King. And that's when: 'Did you wear the black arm band when they shot the man who said, "Peace could last forever"?' It's just true-life experiences, really."

Izzy had come up with 'You Ain't the First', 'Double Talkin' Jive', as well as the framework for '14 Years', and 'Dust N' Bones, while Axl had penned 'The Garden' and 'Yesterdays' with West Arkeen and Del James. With the creativity flowing, the decision was made for the band to relocate to Chicago to start working on the as yet unnamed second Guns N' Roses album for real. Or to be more succinct, Axl made the decision for them.

♫

Duff says the move to Chicago was in part to try and "recapture the hothouse effect" that living cheek by jowl at Gardner Street had played in forging the songs making up *Appetite*. But another factor in his and Axl's thinking was to put some distance between Slash, Izzy, and Steven and their respective drug connections. Indeed, the two had met up on several occasions to discuss their concerns about what "Mr Brownstone" was doing to the band. "All we could do was hope they would find it in themselves to pull back and get into the swing of things as far as the band was concerned," he reflected. "We never thought of rehab or interventions back then."

Slash was all for getting back into the swing of things as the inherent emptiness that comes with achieving one's wildest dreams had slowly been eating away at him. He already had more money than he knew what to do with, and the royalty cheques were getting bigger and bigger. Money had never proved a motivating factor in his thinking. He'd always been a jeans, boots, and T-shirt guy, and that wasn't likely to change regardless of the ever-bigger royalty cheques dropping through his door. All he wanted to do was play guitar and the sooner the new Guns album was in the can, the sooner they could get back out on the road. He remembers Axl and Izzy wanting to record the new album in Indiana. Duff, however, believed Axl opted for Chicago so that he could be closer to his roots; that he was harbouring "the last vestige of a romantic notion" of one day returning to Indiana the conquering hero to lead something resembling a normal life. Normalcy isn't a word one usually associates with Guns N' Roses, but Axl was perhaps leading the more regular life than anyone else in the band. This largely stemmed from an overriding desire to keep Erin happy, of course. She'd grown up witnessing her father's struggles with substance abuse, so while Axl still liked a drink on occasion, the days of getting blindsided on Nightrain wine were now a thing of the past.

Steven, Duff and Slash were the first to arrive in the Windy City; the latter having already sorted out the living and rehearsal arrangements via a reconnaissance mission with Doug Goldstein. The band, along with their small retinue, would be staying in two apartments situated above a family-run Italian restaurant off Clark Street, one of Chicago's main north-south thoroughfares. Rehearsals were to be carried out in a vacant theatre situated above the Cabaret Metro rock club. Steven remembers the theatre having a state-of-the-art PA and a grand piano (which may or may not have been to Axl's specifications). The piano largely went to waste as Axl didn't show until a week or so prior to the three-month rental lease at the theatre expired. Rather than accompany Slash, Duff, and Steven on the flight to Chicago, Axl had remained in LA with Erin. Their relationship had run into turbulence of late, mostly due to Axl's volatile mood swings, and he was desperate to smooth things out.

While Slash, Duff and Steven were wondering when their singer and rhythm guitarist might deign to put in an appearance at Cabaret Metro, Axl flew to New York to make a cameo appearance in the promo video to former Hanoi Rocks frontman Michael Monroe's debut solo single, 'Dead, Jail, or Rock 'n' roll'.

He then headed upstate to make a guest appearance with Tom Petty at the New York State Fairgrounds in Syracuse, duetting with Petty on 'Free Fallin'', the impending lead single from the latter's new album, *Full Moon Fever*, and Dylan's 'Knockin' on Heaven's Door', which was a staple in the Guns N' Roses set. It would have been a relatively short hop from Syracuse to Chicago, but Axl returned to LA before finally heading out for Chicago in a rented truck. Owing to the attendant pitstops, it took him two weeks to cover the 2,000-odd mile road trip. And even when he did finally appear, Axl – according to Steven's clouded recollections – refused all entreaties about putting lyrics to the few song ideas Slash, Duff and Steven had worked on betwixt marathon booze sessions and working their way through a seemingly inexhaustible line of obliging females. Indeed, the only song he was prepared to work on was 'November Rain', a ballad he'd been toying with since his days in LA Guns, as Tracii Guns reflected: "When we were doing that EP for LA Guns, like '83? He was playing 'November Rain' – and it was called 'November Rain' – you know, on piano. Way back then, it was the only thing he knew how to play, but it was his. He'd go, 'Someday this song is gonna be really cool.' And I'd go, 'It's cool now.' 'But it's not done,' he used to say. And, like, anytime we'd be at a hotel or anywhere, there'd be a piano; he'd just kinda play that music. And I'd go, 'When are you gonna finish that already?' And he'd go, 'I don't know what to do with it.'"

Slash most likely had a suggestion or two as to what Axl could do with 'November Rain', as symphonic ballads were far removed from where he envisioned taking Guns N' Roses. As with everything else of late, however, Axl's vote was the only one that appeared to carry any weight. Slash also shares Steven's stance about the Chicago trip being a wasted opportunity. Duff counters their claims, however, saying that even with just the three of them they were "like a locomotive" working on song ideas. Axl also took the view that the four of them had "been on a

GUNS N' ROSES

roll" following his arrival in Chicago. Speaking about the trip shortly after the band had returned to LA, Axl admitted to his late show causing some consternation but denied having insisted on their working solely on 'November Rain'. "I was, like, just into fuckin' everybody's music – getting into Slash's stuff, getting into Duff's stuff. Our timing schedules were all weird and we kept showing up at different times. But when I would show up, I'm like, okay, let's do this, let's do that, let's do this of yours, Slash. Okay, now let's go to this one and Steven needs to do this . . . And then they decided I was a dictator, right?"

Though less remarked upon at the time, Izzy's total no-show in Chicago was to have long-term repercussions on the future of Guns N' Roses. Towards the end of August the guitarist was arrested at Phoenix's Sky Harbor airport for urinating in the aisle of the first-class section of the aeroplane ferrying him from LA to Indianapolis. He'd also proved abusive to the harried stewardess that had dared to remonstrate with him for sparking up in the no-smoking section. Izzy was so strung out on coke and heroin by now that he had no recollection of the unsavoury and shameful episode when he woke up in jail sometime the following day. In hindsight, however, it could be argued that it was his refusal to wait his turn at the toilet on the plane that ultimately saved his life.

Several years earlier, Ozzy Osbourne had famously been banned from performing in San Antonio ever again after being caught pissing on the Alamo Cenotaph. Had Izzy chose to relieve himself in front of his fellow passengers once the plane had touched down in Indianapolis he probably would have suffered a similar fate in being banned from ever performing in his home state's capital. However, because the incident happened in mid-air – coupled with a prior arrest for possession of marijuana – the authorities placed Izzy on 12-month probation during which time he would be subjected to random urine tests.

Slash, though hardly in a position to throw stones himself, says Izzy was "pretty fuckin' far gone". Prior to the Chicago trip, the band had convened for a rehearsal at Izzy's place out in the Valley. It was obvious to all that while Izzy could still function musically, he was off the grid in every other respect. Such was his cocaine-induced paranoia that he'd covered the windows of his apartment in tin foil to thwart the government's radio spy waves. He no longer answered the door other than by a prearranged coded knock, and reportedly screened all incoming phone calls with a Geiger counter; his distrust stretching to walking around with a cashier's cheque for $750,000 tucked into one of his socks rather than entrust it to a bank.

> ## Izzy's total no-show in Chicago was to have long-term repercussions on the future of Guns N' Roses.

Steven and Slash were still kidding themselves they were taking the lead while dancing with 'Mr. Brownstone', but should Izzy test positive for heroin, cocaine or even marijuana within the next calendar year, he could expect serious jail time. He returned to LA knowing the party was over. "That was my wake up call," he later reflected. "That was the point where I said, 'This has got to fucking stop!' I didn't wanna wind up dead, or worse, in prison."

Duff says that Izzy – or "Whizzy" as he and the rest of the band had taken to calling him – did show his face in Chicago but had hightailed it out of Dodge again before the day was out. The abundance of powders and potions littering the apartments the band were renting were already making him anxious when Axl got into

 70

a fight with some girl Duff, Slash, and Steven had befriended during their stay and ended up trashing the furniture. That was it for Izzy. Adios, amigos; goodbye. Duff believes this was the moment when Izzy realised his days in Guns N' Roses were numbered. "He (Izzy) would still send in riffs and ideas for *Use Your Illusion*, but his day-to-day involvement with the band pretty much ended that day."

Izzy would find himself the centre of unwarranted attention a few weeks later at that year's Video Music Awards. 'Sweet Child O' Mine' had come out top dog in the Best Heavy Metal/Hard Rock Video category and, aside from picking up the award in person, Axl and Izzy joined Tom Petty onstage for a run-through of 'Free Fallin'', which was racing up the *Billboard* chart, before bringing the show to a close with a souped-up version of 'Heartbreak Hotel'. Izzy was making his way backstage after the performance when Mötley Crüe frontman, Vince Neil, sprung out of the shadows and punched him in the mouth, splitting his lip. Neil would subsequently claim the punch was payback for Izzy supposedly hitting on his second wife, a former mud wrestler called Sharise.

There are always two sides to every story, of course, and either Izzy had hit on Sharise or vice-versa; either way, Neil had to be seen to do something to save face. Izzy had too much shit to deal with to get into a fight with Neil but Axl gave chase threatening to tear the Crüe singer limb from limb. When Neil suddenly wheeled round with "fists pumping with blood", Axl suddenly lost his appetite for confrontation, instead telling Neil to "stay the fuck away from my band" before retracing his steps.

It was all handbags at five paces and as Izzy was happy to let things lie that really should have been the end of the matter. Axl, however, allowed his antipathy towards Neil to fester.

Guns N' Roses were already one of the most talked about bands on the planet but their profile would be cranked up another couple of notches on being offered to open for the Rolling Stones on the North American leg of their impending Steel Wheels/Urban Jungle World Tour. Jagger and Richard had set aside their own long-standing squabbles for the greater good and the Stones were heading out on the road again after a seven-year hiatus in support of their latest studio album, *Steel Wheels*. All five Gunners were huge Stones fans, of course, yet that didn't necessarily translate to accepting the invitation. After all, *Appetite* had recently reclaimed the number one slot on the *Billboard* chart and was on its way to accruing sales of 10 million, so there was little need to prostate themselves at the Stones' altar.

Though showing little sign of calling time on their nigh-on six decade long career at the time of writing, the Stones were already regarded as a "heritage act" by the time of the Steel Wheels/Urban Jungle Tour. And while *Steel Wheels* would go Top 3 in both the US and the UK, the overall 5.5 million worldwide sales the album would accrue failed to match the "stopgap" *GN'R Lies* – let alone *Appetite for Destruction*.

The offer, when it was officially made via Metallica and Def Leppard management duo Cliff Bernstein and Peter Mensch, was for $50,000 per show. Jagger's thriftiness was legendary within the entertainment world but $50,000 per show for a band of GN'R's stature was an insult. Alan Niven pretty much treated it as an insult – even though his tenure as GN'R's manager might well have ended then and there had his bluff rebounded and the Stones turned their attentions elsewhere.

Brian Jones had most likely been in the Stones the last time anyone had dared refuse one of their entreaties, so the news that Niven had rebuffed Jagger and Co a second time would even have the nationals sniffing out a story. The improved proposal was for Guns to appear at each of the Stones' four shows at the 77,000-capacity LA Coliseum for a flat fee of

GUNS N' ROSES

$500,000. While speaking with *Rolling Stone*'s Rob Tannenbaum backstage at the Pine Knob Music Theatre in Clarkston, Missouri in August 1988, Slash had opined that Jagger "should have died after *Some Girls*, when he was still cool". He would nonetheless have crawled the length of the Staples Centre over broken glass for an opportunity to share the same stage with the Stones. Niven's mantra, however, was to ensure his acts always got top billing and if, or when, this wasn't possible, he would settle for getting top dollar. Therefore, if the Stones still wanted Guns N' Roses to open for them at the Coliseum then it was going to cost them a cool million. Jagger was said to be apoplectic, yet nonetheless acquiesced.

Holding the Stones over a barrel was to prove a two-pronged masterstroke on Niven's part. Firstly, the four Coliseum dates would see Guns N' Roses pull in almost as much cash had he agreed to Jagger's opening offer of $50,000 per show for the whole tour once the usual touring costs they would incur were factored into the equation. Secondly, while Izzy was taking his first tentative steps towards sobriety, Slash and Steven were in no fit state to undertake any tour – let alone one opening for the Stones.

One might have expected the Coliseum dates to galvanise Guns into action yet, according to Duff's reflections, Slash and Steven showed no sign of cleaning up. He even has Izzy slipping back into his old ways. "Sometimes those guys put their drug use in front of band practice," he bemoaned. "One or the other often showed up late or left early from rehearsal – if they showed up at all. But we never talked about the problem. We were never any good at communication, especially when that meant confrontation. If we had developed those skills then, the story of GN'R might have been very different."

Hindsight, as the saying goes, is 20/20 and Duff was reflecting on that period some 20 years hence. But would the GN'R story really have turned out any different had he, Slash and Steven followed Izzy's lead in knocking the booze, coke, and heroin into the bleachers? Steven might well have stayed in the band a while longer but his relationship with Axl was already strained to bursting and would have led to a parting of the ways at some juncture in the not-too-distant future. The music would have still been kick-ass fantastic, and Guns N' Roses might well have gone on to surpass the success of *Use Your Illusion I & II* but rehashing their days of hedonistic wild abandon during interviews so as to remain cool outa school would have got boring really quickly. It was one thing for Glimmer Twins Mick and Keith to reminisce about "breaking the butterfly on the wheel", or their "Toxic" counterparts Steven Tyler and Joe Perry to share their septum-deviating war stories as they'd survived into their forties (or fast-approaching the "big 40" in Perry's case). Slash, Duff and Steven were still in their mid-to-late twenties and had a whole lot more debauched living to do.

♫

$1 million for four nights work is good business in any strata, but accepting the Stones' dollar would ultimately end up biting them in the ass. Living Colour, an all-black trio whose debut album *Vivid* had gone Top 10 on the US chart earlier in the year, had been booked as the official opening act on the North American leg of the Stones tour. With their London-born guitarist, Vernon Reid, being the founder of the Black Rock Coalition – a New York-based artists' collective dedicated to promoting the creative freedom of black musicians – it was inevitable the controversy surrounding 'One in a Million' would come to the fore.

The day prior to the opening Coliseum date, Reid participated in a radio interview/phone-in. On being asked by a caller to comment on 'One in a Million' he said that while he liked Guns N' Roses he "took exception to some of the words and sentiments in that particular song". Come showtime, Reid had repeated his thoughts about

'One in a Million' during Living Colour's set and had received a near-standing ovation from the crowd. It was now game on as far as Axl was concerned and he readily delivered on cue. Living Colour were making their way offstage when Axl squared up to Reid. "I heard on the radio that you guys got a problem with some of the things I got to say," he challenged before brazenly adding that he'd never thought of "you guys as niggers". It was as laudable as it was risible. It was at this point that either Alan Niven or Doug Goldstein rushed across to intervene, excusing Axl's behaviour because he was "from Indiana and doesn't know any different". In *The Days of Guns N' Roses: Appetite for Destruction*, Danny Sugarman questions whether Axl heard his behaviour being thus excused. Given what we know of Axl's temper it's unlikely he heard the exchange or Guns N' Roses would surely have been looking for new management.

With the media having ramped up the Coliseum dates as a "young guns versus the old guard" scenario there was nary an empty seat in the house when Guns took to the stage. Axl, however, wasn't yet finished in regard to his rights under the First Amendment. He said

he was "sick of all this publicity" surrounding 'One in a Million', before proceeding to tell the hushed crowd he wasn't a "fuckin' racist", that "not all black men are niggers", but that if someone is "acting like a nigger", then he was going to call it as he saw it. It was the same for "fuckin' faggots", and if anyone still saw him as a racist, well they could "shove it up their ass". They were his words, or at least his interpretation of them, so what did it matter whether they were "delivered sung or spoken?"

It was time to get on with the music. Well, not quite, as Axl had something else he wanted to get off his chest. As the opening song, 'It's So Easy', came to a close, Axl launched into another harangue – one much closer to home. "I just want to say . . . I hate to do this onstage," he announced while Slash, Izzy, and Duff twiddled with their plectrums and Steven glanced about him, "but I tried it every other way. And unless certain people in this band start getting their shit together, this is going to be the last Guns N' Roses show you will ever see."

A low rumble of perplexed murmuring rippled around the Coliseum as the crowd struggled to absorb what Axl was implying. "I'm sick of too

GUNS N' ROSES

many people in this organisation dancing with Mr Goddamn Brownstone." Cue the song . . .

Axl had in fact called Izzy earlier in the day to say he was quitting the band. It wasn't the first time he'd threatened to walk away so Izzy didn't take the latest threat too seriously. Several days earlier at the Park Plaza Hotel, during a low-key warm-up for the Coliseum dates (billed as a *RIP* magazine party) Axl had told Izzy he didn't want to play with the Stones. Again, Izzy hadn't put much stock in Axl's outburst – if only because the Stones were one of Axl's favourite bands and how could he pass up the chance to share a stage with his idols? However, as the afternoon crept into early evening with no sign of Axl, the anxiety within the GN'R dressing room began to mount. Alan Niven, however, had no intention of letting Axl dictate the order of play on this day of all days.

Calling a favour from the Stones' production chief, Brian Ahern, Niven was put in touch with someone within the LAPD. Minutes later, a patrol car was winging its way through traffic towards Shoreham Towers and an unsuspecting Axl. The question still remains, however, whether Axl would have stayed home with Erin had his "black and white" escort not arrived. Duff was furious that Axl had chosen to air the band's dirtiest laundry in public, while Steven thought his outburst "way over the top"; subsequently likening the idea of disbanding Guns N' Roses over drug abuse akin to "grounding a bird for flying".

Whether Axl was grandstanding or speaking out of genuine concern that one or more of the band would end up in a body bag, his stratagem had the desired effect. When Guns took to the Coliseum stage the following night, Slash (mischievously sporting a Betty Ford Clinic T-shirt) ambled up to the mic and entered into a monologue about Elvis, Janis, Jim Morrison, John Bonham being just a few

of the rock'n'roll icons who had died because of their respective drug intake. "There has been a lot written about this band and drugs," he continued. "A lot of it is bullshit. A lot of it is true. Last night you almost saw the last Guns N' Roses gig." He then spoke about coming to the Coliseum to see the likes of Aerosmith, Van Halen and, of course, the Stones, and dreaming about one day being on that very stage before admitting that he'd fulfilled his teenage wish yet had been too stoned to take in the experience. "No one in this band advocates the use of heroin," he added somewhat disingenuously, given that his dealer had an access all areas pass and was most likely chuckling to himself while watching on from the wings. "That's not what it's all about and we're not going to be one of those weak bands that falls apart over it."

For now at least . . .

♫

What only a handful of people were aware of at the time was that Slash had only agreed to bite the bullet onstage at the LA Coliseum because of Alan Niven issuing an ultimatum earlier in the day. Calling from Axl's apartment, Niven told Slash he was to set aside his own feelings in the matter and apologise unreservedly to Axl. Prior to slipping off to the bedroom to make the call, Niven, along with Goldstein, had suffered another of Axl's rants in which he'd griped about Steven, griped about Duff, and had even took a couple of sideswipes at Izzy. The main target for his ire, however, was Slash; his vitriol stretching to his threatening to never set foot onstage with the guitarist again – regardless of the consequences his actions would bring about once the Coliseum promoters launched their lawsuits.

Setting Slash's drug proclivities aside, he could – and should – have called Axl's bluff. Guns N' Roses had played shows with

 74

Fred Coury filling in for Steven, Cult bassist Haggis had stepped in for Duff on the Iron Maiden tour, while Gilby Clarke would prove a more-then-capable replacement for Izzy. But Guns N' Roses could never really be Guns N' Roses without Axl and Slash – as has since been proved. Slash would acknowledge during a subsequent interview with VH1 that while he'd been totally strung out during the opening Coliseum show, Axl's onstage rant was "probably one of the things that made me hate Axl more than anything."

The bruhaha surrounding 'One in a Million', coupled with Axl's opening night onstage rants, had made the remaining Coliseum dates the hottest tickets in town – something Mick Jagger certainly wasn't slow to realise. When the Stones announced a special pay-per-view show at Convention Hall in Atlantic City, New Jersey on December 19, Axl and Izzy were invited to join the Stones onstage. What's more, the GN'R duo was allowed to choose which number they'd like to perform. After much debate they decided upon 'Salt of the Earth' (the closing track on side two of *Beggars Banquet*). For two dyed-in-the-wool Stones fans, the invite was surely the ultimate

bucket-lister – especially on learning the Stones had never actually performed 'Salt of the Earth' live.

Axl's laissez-faire attitude towards punctuality was already a gnawing bone of contention within the GN'R camp, but Alan Niven couldn't believe his ears when the singer casually instructed him to get word to the Stones camp that he'd be at soundcheck an hour or so later than scheduled. Whereas his own band was expected to suffer in silence, however, Keith Richards wasted little time in ripping into Izzy over Axl's tardiness. Niven, in turn, would find himself in Axl's crosshairs for refusing to make the call to Convention Hall; his churlishness stretching to banning Niven from the venue.

That Axl would think nothing of keeping the Rolling Stones waiting till he deigned to put in an appearance speaks volumes about his mindset at the time. Jagger and Richards were – and still are – two of the most easily recognised people on the planet, but the Stones were already trading on their former glories whereas Guns N' Roses were the hippest, most happening band on the planet.

"I never thought this could happen to me. It was always the five of us united, an inseparable team. But the Guns N' Roses machine had become massive, and I could feel it shoving me aside. I couldn't stand the idea of being pushed out of the band. I desperately didn't want this to end, and I honestly thought I had done nothing to deserve having it taken away from me. I just did what we were all doing, living the rock star life."

STEVEN

P A R T   S I X

LOOK AT THE LIVES WE'RE LEADING

In early 1990, Guns N' Roses headed into the studio with Mike Clink to record 'Civil War' for the *Nobody's Child: Romanian Angel Appeal* charity compilation album. The album, in aid of Romanian orphans following the collapse of Nicolae Ceau escu's Communist regime, was organised by Olivia Harrison (wife of George), who'd created the Romanian Angel Appeal Foundation alongside Yoko Ono, Linda McCartney and Barbara Bach. It was a noble gesture for an equally principled cause, and yet charity would prove in short supply when Steven fell ill after taking an opiate blocker his doctor had given him to help him in his quest to kick heroin.

Steven is still adamant to this day that the opiate blocker his doctor prescribed should only be administered once the patient is fully detoxed. As Steven still had heroin in his system the effects of the pill left him feeling worse than ever. Yet, despite what he was going through, he says, the rest of band were supposedly unsympathetic to his plight. Slash, however, counters Steven's claims saying that while everyone in the band was allowed to fuck up on occasion, they did so knowing they would be expected to deal with the attendant repercussions. Izzy was completely clean, of course, and Slash says he also had the wherewithal to pull back from the brink once he realised his drug intake had progressed

beyond what he describes as "recreational consumption". Steven, however, "didn't have all his faculties and couldn't maintain a line between his excesses and his productivity."

Steven had hankered for the sex, drugs and rock'n'roll lifestyle since first picking up a pair of drumsticks, but there can be little argument that over the past 12 months the line betwixt excess and productivity had become blurred. One can almost sense Slash and Duff squirming as they reflected on the period leading up to Steven's sacking because of their own offstage antics – their inebriated state at the recent American Music Awards an obvious case in point – yet both insist that, unlike Steven, they made sure they maintained a professional attitude when it came to Guns N' Roses. Duff was used to him and Steven laying down their respective parts in the studio efficiently and effectively. By the time the band came to record 'Civil War', however, Steven's drumming had become "erratic". So much so, that he and Clink were forced to patch together the drum track from dozens of inadequate takes; a task that proved laborious and time-consuming in the pre-digital editing age.

The personnel might still be the same, but by the spring of 1990 Guns N' Roses were no longer the same band that had recorded *Appetite for Destruction*. The songs making up the debut album were representative of where

GUNS N' ROSES

they were – both as individuals and as a band –when they'd first started out. Songs that hadn't made it onto *Appetite*, such as 'You Could Be Mine', 'Back Off Bitch', and 'Don't Cry' were earmarked for the new album, but no one was looking to make *Appetite for Destruction II*. A clear indicator of where Axl was looking to take Guns musically came with his insistence that Dizzy Reed be brought in as a hired gun.

♫

Izzy was keeping his distance from Steven for obvious reasons, but Slash and Duff were initially willing to try to help their friend. Specialists such as Bob Timmons, the renowned rehab guru who had helped Mötley Crüe clean up their act, were called upon, but all attempts to drag Steven back from the abyss were to prove futile. Steven's input was minimal during the songwriting process so it wasn't until the band headed into the studio to record 'Civil War' for the *Nobody's Child* album that the true extent of the deterioration in his playing became noticeable . . . painfully so. Slash goes so far as to say that when they'd begun rehearsing the new material in earnest Steven had proved "utterly useless" – either fading out of the proper time signature mid-song or losing himself completely. "He was just incapable of locking in with Duff and me like he used to do. It was pretty dire; something had to be done."

Addiction is a cancer that eats away at the individual's willpower. Many addicts want to get clean but lack the resolve to stay the course.

Axl saw no reason for mollycoddling their drugged-up drummer and the "something" that was decided upon – primarily at the singer's behest – came with having Steven sign an agreement that effectively saw him forfeiting his rights as an equal partner in Guns N' Roses. In essence, the agreement gave him a 30-day probation period to get himself cleaned up.

Steven says he was still so ill from the effects of the opiate blocker that he could barely read what was written on the pages he was being asked to sign – reportedly at the offices of A&M Records on North La Brea Avenue. "I thought I was agreeing not to party and not screw up on any band-related activities for the next four weeks," he revealed. "If I fucked up, they would fine me $2,000. I thought, 'What the hell, no problem. The band doesn't even have anything scheduled during the next month. And even so, what's two grand?' I signed everything. I just wanted to get out of there, go home, and lie down."

Had Steven been compos mentis he would have realised the terms of the agreement stated that he was to be paid $2,000 for his contribution to Guns N' Roses, and that he'd naively signed away his rights and future royalties. Slash remembers the contract stipulating Steven would be fined should he show up high for rehearsals, and that if he did so three times then he would be fired. Whatever the contractual legalese, it was only Slash's having the greater self-discipline that had saved him from the dark path Steven now found himself on.

Speaking about the Steven situation with *Kerrang!*, Izzy admitted that Steven was "definitely out of the band" for an undisclosed period of time but was keen to stress that he hadn't necessarily been fired. During this time, the band had supposedly worked with Adam Maples (drummer with the San Franciscan hard rock outfit, Sea Hags), as well as ex-Pretender Martin Chambers, before Steven did "the Guns N' Roses thing and got his shit together". According to Izzy, Steven found his game – if only temporarily. "It worked, and he did it," he enthused. "He plays the songs better than any of 'em, just bad-assed. And he's GN'R. And so if he doesn't blow it, we're going to try the album with him, and the tour and, you know, we've worked out a contract with him. It's worked out. It's finally back on and we're hoping it continues. It's only been a few days so far. It's only been since Thursday last week, and he's doing great. We're all just hoping it continues."

Guns N' Roses put the new album on hold after receiving an offer to appear at Farm Aid IV at the Hoosier Dome in Indianapolis in early April. Any lingering hopes Slash and the others had of their playing such a high-profile show (Farm Aid was broadcast live on local television channels) might motivate Steven into keeping his shit wired evaporated into the ether when he misjudged his run-up to the drum riser, which, Slash recalled as being "a pretty big platform" that was harder to miss. "I assume he was planning on landing next to his kit, but his depth perception and reflexes were clearly impaired, so he ended up landing about four feet short."

Steven still feels he was "suffering under an unfair double standard" and cites Axl's tumbling from the stage during the opening Stones Coliseum show as an example. Axl had simply got carried away with the performance and the fall hadn't bruised much other than his ego. Steven, alas, injured his ankle which further affected his playing, and in turn, the band's performance.

Slash has since mooted that Axl didn't like Steven – if only for his guileless honesty when it came to voicing his opinions. He, Duff, and Izzy had come to understand that confronting Axl about his tardiness, stage tantrums, or whatever else might be irking them about their singer's behaviour was always counterproductive, whereas Steven called it as he saw it. If Axl, or indeed anyone else in the band, was being a dick then he had no problem in saying so. Though Steven's frankness offended what Slash describes as Axl's "hyperemotional sensitivity", he believes Axl never really gave Steven the credit he deserved for the musicality he brought to Guns N' Roses.

It was Axl who had vetoed Steven's receiving a

fifth equal share of band royalties. To his mind, Steven wasn't making an equal contribution to the songwriting and demanded five per cent of the drummer's share on top of his own 20 per cent. Little wonder Steven was happy to get on Axl's case whenever the situation warranted it. And shame on Slash, Duff and Izzy if this was indeed the case. Alan Niven, however, has gone on record saying Steven was "paid composer royalties that he didn't deserve" as a "courtesy" bestowed upon him by the rest of the band.

"The policy was that while one was a member of the band one would benefit from all moneys being shared – one for all and all for one," Niven said in a January 2019 gnrcentral interview. "If you left the band, and were not a writer, then the privilege ended. This method was used by lots of bands – the idea being to prevent arguments over money destroying band chemistry. Van Halen, for example, did the same. No one enforced this on anyone in the band – it was accepted and understood well before [Doug] Goldstein was employed as tour manager. It was their decision, including Axl. I considered that the band bent and made a gift to Axl that he received a larger share. If anyone actually deserved a larger share it was Izzy."

♫

Addiction is a cancer that eats away at the individual's willpower. Many addicts want to get clean but lack the resolve to stay the course. It should be recognised as an illness and treated as such. When all is said and done, of course, Steven was his own man and there was little arm-twisting while applying the tourniquet. As Joe Strummer points out while talking about Topper Headon's sacking in The Clash documentary *Westway to the World*, heroin is a drug more suited to horn players than drummers simply because it robs them of their energy. And as the apocryphal saying goes: any band is only as good as its drummer.

GUNS N' ROSES

Speaking about Steven's dismissal with MTV during the summer of 1990, Axl said how he and the rest of the band had given their wayward drummer every ultimatum. "We had Steven sign a contract saying that if he went back to drugs he was out. He couldn't leave his drugs . . . and other things had happened involved with Steven... that Steven is basically someone I used to know. It makes me feel bad, but there's other things beside the band that he was involved in with his drugs that's been very dangerous and scary, and I want nothing to do with him."

Speaking with *Musician* magazine towards the end of the year, Slash said that he'd at least attempted to stay in touch with Steven. "I'd pop into his house every now and then to see how he was doing. I stuck with him, as you'd do for a loved one. And then he started getting on my case, saying, 'I've heard you guys are all on heroin and what's the difference, blah blah blah . . .' And finally I couldn't talk to him anymore. I'd take him out to dinner and it would turn into this huge fight, to the point where I couldn't take it. So now I don't see him anymore. I call his doctor and I think about him a lot. And I worry. 'Cause it's a scary thing. And he was my best friend for a long time."

The next time Slash saw his one-time best friend was in front of a judge. Whether Steven received his fair share of the composer royalties – or "mechanicals" as they're known within the music industry – in July 1991 the drummer launched a lawsuit (rumoured to be $2 million) against his one-time comrades-in-arms.

At the time of launching his lawsuit, Steven issued the following press release through his lawyers:

"They told me I had a drug problem, well, who the fuck were they to tell me that? A couple alcoholics and heroin users? Did they take some time in between fucking strippers to decide they were going to throw me out of the band? Doug Goldstein took me to have an opiate blocker, which made me very sick. I told them that I felt sick and couldn't record. Slash told me we had to, because we couldn't waste the money. I said, 'Money? What about the money we wasted last year (referring to the 1989 Chicago rehearsal/recording sessions) when Izzy was cleaning himself up, and Axl was nowhere to be found? Why was it okay for those guys to waste the money, but not me [in order to] get well?' So anyway, they bring me into the studio and I feel like shit. It took me forever to get the song ['Civil War'] right, and they got frustrated with me. So next thing I know, Doug has a stack of papers in front of me that I could never fucking read because they were about five inches thick! He's telling me 'sign here, sign there' and telling me I was signing an agreement saying I was on 'probation', meaning I was going to detox in time to record, or else. But it turns out, those papers weren't really giving me that chance. So I don't hear a fucking thing from anyone for a while, then I got these notices saying, 'You're out of the band'. Through my lawyers, I discovered that the 'probation' papers that Doug had me sign were actually the rights to my partnership and all my royalties, which I was unknowingly signing away! They completely screwed me out of everything, these guys, [who were] my friends, my family. It hurt more than anything. My royalties were from playing, writing, and [use of] my image such as T-shirts and shit.

When we recorded [*Appetite For Destruction*], Slash came up with this system where whoever wrote got credit. But then when it came time to actually divide them up, suddenly everybody was getting credit but me. I mean, Izzy wrote the song 'Think About You' by himself before we started playing it, yet Slash, Duff, and Axl were also going to be receiving royalties for it, since they supposedly 'added to it'. I said, 'Well what about me? Did I add nothing?' I mean Izzy wrote the fucking song, I thought that's how the writing credits were determined, but the other guys were getting credit for something they didn't write, and I wasn't. Same thing for all the other songs. Axl would get credit for songs such as 'Brownstone' [written by Slash and Izzy] and 'It's So Easy' [written by Duff and West Arkeen], even though he didn't write anything on them, and the other guys [who didn't write also got credit] too. So why not me? So Axl gave me a portion of his [to compensate for not being included], and my name was put beside the rest of theirs [in the writing credits] and that was that. But now they've screwed me out of those royalties and my other ones too. Two fucking albums that I played on are still selling and they're collecting money from them, and I'm not. Guns N' Roses T shirts with my face on them are still selling, and they're collecting money from them, and I'm not. That's what they did to me; people I thought were my friends took it all away and said goodbye as if I never existed. Fuck that! That's why I sue them, and I'm confident the jury will see it my way."

"The fact that Steven sued and benefitted was not appropriate or just," Niven said in the same January 2019 gnrcentral interview. "He'd received composing monies he did not have a legal right to. What is more Doug had indeed kept him alive. According to Doug, Adler's own attorney stated at deposition that Goldstein should have let him die of an overdose. We all worked hard to keep everyone alive. Slash even went turkey in my spare bedroom – I cleaned the vomit from his mouth and counted out the Valium. The problem is that once you go to a jury it is generally understood the case becomes basically a beauty pageant – who does the jury like? They didn't like Rose and Goldstein."

A settlement would be agreed upon in September 1993 prior to the case going before a Superior Court jury. Steven was reportedly awarded $2.5 million – $2.3 million from the band, $150,000 from Alan Niven, and $50,000 from Doug Goldstein.

Speaking with the GN'R Central podcast in January 2019, Goldstein insists the suit personally cost him $500,000. "We settled on the courtroom steps, which means we didn't wait for the jury to come back," he explained. "When you do that, they do what's called a jury debriefing. So my attorney, god rest his soul, Howard King, got to go first and the jury foreman stood up and said, 'The only question we have is: Is your client married?' My lawyer said, 'I don't understand the relevance.' He said, 'This guy didn't do anything wrong, we want him to marry our daughters. All he did was try to save the guy's life.' Then [Alan] Niven's attorney came up, and they were going to crucify Niven because he was at the helm of it. The band didn't know, the band was following the lead of the manager and the attorney. Literally, all I was doing was taking Steven to different rehabs and trying to get him clean."

Alan Niven, however, vehemently disputes Goldstein's claims. "The case was not settled on the steps of the court. It was settled immediately before the jury retired, after two weeks of hearings in front of the judge.

"Adler's attorneys offered a settlement of $375,000 after approximately one week of the case being heard [as] they were concerned they were losing the case," he continued. "Goldstein and Rose rejected the offer. Thereafter Goldstein and Rose took the stand. At the conclusion of the case I had lunch with the entire jury. They informed me they thought Goldstein was a phony and were amused at his crocodile tears on the stand. They disliked Axl intensely, who seemed medicated and thus cold ... these two shifted the case into Adler's favour."

Niven also scoffs at Goldstein's assertion the case cost him $500,000. "Goldstein was covered by a litigation insurance – that also protected the band – I had put that in place. His claim of paying $500,000 is bullshit."

Niven says the settlement order was in fact "$2,750,000" – the majority of which was fronted by the band and Goldstein. "I was tapped for a relatively modest $175,000," he says. "I further paid over $300,000 in legal fees out of my own pocket – at the mercy of the actions of Rose and Goldstein."

Steven admits he was so strung out that his mum was actually the one to instigate legal proceedings against her son's erstwhile band and management. Indeed, he readily admits that when it came to taking the stand he would first pay a visit to the bathroom and have a hit

from the stash he kept in his pants. As a result, he ended up delaying the proceedings on more than one occasion – a daily occurrence that didn't go unnoticed by Slash.

One of the more unsavoury episodes surrounding Steven's departure from Guns N' Roses was his supposedly giving Erin Everly a "speedball" – a mix of cocaine and heroin. All that anyone knew at the time of the incident was that Erin was rushed to the emergency room after nearly OD'ing on the speedball. Axl, who, by this time had married Erin, later confided to Del James that Erin had been found "naked" and rushed to the nearest emergency room where she'd spent the night in intensive care "because her heart had stopped thanks to Steven."

Steven's version has it that he'd been jamming in his tool shed, which he'd recently had remodelled into a small recording studio with Hanoi Rocks guitarist, Andy McCoy, when the latter's wife Laura arrived with Erin, who was in an obvious state of distress and could barely stand. From what Steven could ascertain, Erin and Axl had had a fight and Laura had given Erin an undisclosed number of Valium to calm her down. Laura then allegedly asked Steven to give Erin "something" to bring her round. Steven could see Erin was "starting to go out" and in his panic he called 911. The attending paramedics had duly checked Erin's vital signs and pumped her stomach before whisking her off to the nearest emergency room.

Steven readily admits there was no love lost between him and Laura McCoy, but would the latter have gone so far as to lie to Axl about Steven having given Erin a potentially lethal heroin and cocaine cocktail? "I would never shoot heroin or any drug, into Erin," he reflected. "I always adored her, and probably helped to save her life day, but it didn't mean shit."

According to Steven, it was subsequently confirmed that Erin had traces of heroin in her system. When Axl told the press about how Steven was responsible, Guns N' Roses' profile was such that no one had any reason to believe otherwise. With Axl being Erin's next of kin, the doctors would have informed him as to what drug(s) Erin had ingested.

In the aforementioned 1992 interview with Del James, Axl said how he'd not only kept himself from doing Steven serious harm, but that he'd also stopped members of Erin's family from killing him. By the time of the interview, Axl and Erin were divorced, of course. Shortly after the band's Farm Aid IV appearance Axl had supposedly turned up at Erin's door at 4am threatening to kill himself if she didn't marry him that very night. The two then made a moonlight drive through the desert to Las Vegas and tied the knot at Cupid's Inn a few hours later. Once word was out about the wedding, those closest to the couple most likely began placing bets as to how long the marriage might last. Taking their vows certainly didn't assuage the fiery side of their relationship as within a month Axl had filed for divorce. He soon changed his mind again, but the writing was on the wall for all to see.

In an attempt to move forward with the relationship, Axl bought a sumptuous house for him and Erin high up in the Hollywood Hills. The two spent every available hour redesigning and furnishing their love nest, but yet another blazing row put paid to Axl's plans. According to Erin's deposition at the divorce hearing in January 1991, Axl flew into such a rage that he spray-painted an image of a gravestone on the garage door underneath which he wrote: "Erin Rose: RIP Sweet Child O' Die. Slut. You Were One Of Many. Nothing Special."

Axl did indeed call Steven in a rage threatening to kill him, and Steven readily admits to being worried enough by the threat to flee his house that same night and hole up in Palm Springs for an extended period of time.

Penning his memoir wouldn't exorcise certain of Steven's ghosts. "I built up a family and I thought they had my back like I had theirs," he railed during a June 2012 interview with www.*musicradar.com*. "So it was crushing for me when all of a sudden I was alone. I had nobody,

it was hard. They say there is safety in numbers and all of a sudden those numbers threw me out. I thought, 'What did I do?' It was hurtful. It was totally unexpected. All of a sudden the family thing turned into little cliques. Duff and Slash would hang out, Izzy would disappear, Axl – god knows what he was doing. I was hanging out with the crew guys. Then the crew guys, if they were seen hanging out with me, they would get a reprimand. It was terrible.

"It also pissed me off with those guys, I was doing drugs with them. Rick Allen lost his arm, his brothers didn't throw him out, they found a way. They didn't give me a chance, it was just one afternoon, all of a sudden, 'You're out.' In eight hours my life changed."

Those same eight hours would also forever change the dynamic of Guns N' Roses.

♬

The singer in a known band seldom gets involved in the recruitment process until the hopeful auditionees have been whittled down to the final two or three most promising candidates. As such, the task of finding Steven's replacement fell to Slash, Izzy, and Duff. Guns N' Roses played largely straightforward 4/4 blues-tinged rock rhythms with a few fancy time changes. How hard could it be to find a drummer that ticked the necessary boxes? It wasn't as if Guns were just starting out! After several frustrating and ultimately fruitless days, the realisation finally dawned that a drummer's personal feel for the song is just as important as the bassline or guitar riff – if not more so.

After months and months of relative inactivity, Slash, Axl, Duff, and Izzy had amassed an incredible 25-30 new songs. They were straining at the leash, and it was only Steven's inability to perform that had held them back. Now, his mere absence was stymying the momentum. Slash was becoming increasingly worried that without a full complement Guns might slip back into turgid inactivity that had almost rent them

GUNS N' ROSES

ROCKseat

STEVEN ADLER & TOMMY LEE
So satisfy your lust.
too much can't be enough
I'll introduce myself today

asunder. He was equally concerned as to what he might do with – and to – himself should the band start to drift apart.

At some point during the malaise, however, Slash remembered being impressed by the no-nonsense, hard-hitting style of The Cult's drummer while catching one of their recent Sonic Temple Tour dates at the Universal Amphitheatre at the beginning of April.

Californian-born Matt Sorum was 29 years old when Slash made the call inviting him to an audition. The realisation of wanting to be a drummer came while watching The Beatles making their third and final appearance on *The Ed Sullivan Show* in September 1965. He was only four at the time, of course, so suddenly announcing that he wanted to be just like Ringo when he grew up probably didn't provoke much of a reaction from his parents. Yet one of his older brothers must have sensed something in the seemingly throwaway comment as a few days later he presented Matt with a copy of *A Hard Day's Night*.

Matt and his family were living in Long Beach (a city within the Greater Los Angeles area) at the time. Life within the Sorum household was in stark contrast to their idyllic surroundings, however, and Matt's parents would soon separate. Matt was too young to understand why his dad was leaving and was even more confused when the principal at the junior high school where both his parents worked as teachers moved in soon thereafter. His first drum kit, a Tiger Junior – or a "Tigger Tiger" as they were known – arrived that Christmas, and he would drive everyone crazy bashing away for hours on end in emulation of his beak-nosed Beatles hero.

Following his mum's remarrying, the family moved to Mission Viejo, a "master-planned community" set within the Saddleback Valley in neighbouring Orange County. His dad's leaving home had proved distressing enough for Matt, and now he had to wave goodbye to the only life he knew. Such upheaval would prove stressful for any six-year-old but having to live with his

hot-tempered and quick-fisted step-father served to compound Matt's misery.

Watching Ringo Starr on *The Ed Sullivan Show* had provided the spark for Matt's drumming aspirations, but it was seeing Kiss playing at the Long Beach Arena circa May 1975 that spring that set the fire a-raging. By his own admission, he wasn't much of a Kiss fan and had tagged along with a friend. But Peter Criss's rudimentary playing during his spotlight drum solo brought the "Eureka" realisation that his own playing was on a par with – if not better than – what he was witnessing onstage.

He was already playing in the Silverado Continuation High School orchestra when he started his first band (Liquid Earth), but it was only upon joining Prophecy – a blues-rock trio making a splash on the Orange County live circuit – that he began to believe he might be able to make a living as a rock drummer. With little or no interest in continuing his education, he dropped out of school. He also left home, moving into a house in Newport Beach with some like-minded friends. By 1979 he was sofa-hopping in West Hollywood, eking out a living playing in a variety of here today, gone tomorrow bands; the most notable being Y Kant Tori Read, with a then relatively unknown Tori Amos.

Matt's "break" came with passing an audition to replace Les Warner in The Cult, who were set to go out supporting Metallica on the US leg of the latter act's Damaged Justice tour in support of the . . . *And Justice for All* album. It was when the tour rolled into New York that Matt got to meet Axl and Izzy for the first time.

Axl and Izzy were in town supposedly seeking inspiration for what was to become the *Use Your Illusion* albums. Axl had invited Ian Astbury along with the rest of The Cult to join them for a night's fun and frolics in the East Village. Having spent several hours at The Scrap Bar, the party moved onto The Loft where, among other things, Matt joined Ian, Axl, Izzy and The Cult's bassist, Jamie Stewart, in an impromptu jam.

GUNS N' ROSES

Matt also remembers seeing Slash and Duff at the Sonic Temple Tour date at the Universal Amphitheatre. He was standing by the stairwell leading up to the stage talking with his girlfriend when he was distracted by a sudden commotion. Several of the venue's security were hurriedly opening the gates in the outdoor section of the backstage area. A limo came idling into the area and had no sooner pulled up when Duff and Slash emerged from the back with four scantily clad girls and ambled through to the VIP area. It was a rock star moment to remember, yet little could Matt have known that within a matter of weeks he'd be recreating such moments with Duff and Slash.

Ian Astbury and Billy Duffy were hardly saints when it came to living the excess all areas rock'n'roll life, of course, and once the Sonic Temple Tour was over Matt was so worn out that he ended up with pneumonia. He went to stay with his mum in Mission Viejo, and it was there – while laid out in bed – that Mike Clink called out of the blue telling him he could expect another call from a known band that were in urgent need of a drummer.

Matt says he wasn't invited to join Guns N' Roses *per se*, but rather asked to help out with the recording of the new album as Steven would supposedly be returning to duty at some unspecified date in the future. "Steven was going through a lot of personal stuff," he told *www.musicradar.com* in June 2012. "I was temporarily there, but as time progressed – maybe a couple of weeks into the session – Slash pulled me aside and said it didn't look as if Steven was coming back and asked if I'd like to join the band. Here I was in an already successful band that I was very happy with, but to be offered that gig at the time was the highest level you can imagine. If you compare it to what's out there now, I don't think there's anyone that can compare to that level.

"The Cult was a straight-ahead rock'n'roll band; a little more behind the beat. But the groove was more Phil Rudd than punk rock. When I joined Guns N' Roses it was more of a

punk rock attitude mixed with the rock'n'roll. My playing was not meat and potatoes but that kind of style, laying it right down the middle. It was a little more of a garage band with a loose feel to it. With Guns N' Roses it was more haphazard, Slash might be pulling away and I had to pull the reins in. I had a different feel to Steven. The thing about drummers is that we're all different. Guys can try to emulate John Bonham until the cows come home but it isn't going to happen."

Neither Slash nor Duff make any mention of the invitation to Matt extending solely to studio work in their respective tomes, but the latter recognised the enormity of the task facing their new drummer. "We had 27 songs to record, and some of them – like 'November Rain', 'Coma' and 'Locomotive' – were epic in length. Matt had to learn all the songs in rehearsals and make charts for the recording sessions."

As with everything else in GN'R world, the solving of one problem merely gave rise to a host of others.

Izzy had become so estranged from things of late that he wasn't even consulted about Matt, and only met his new drummer once at rehearsals. Izzy got on well enough with Matt, but that didn't stop him from saying how he would have preferred to continue working with Steven during a 1992 interview – by which time he'd joined Steven on the ex-GN'R members list. "The first time I realised what Steve did for the band was when he broke his hand in Michigan. We had Fred Coury come in from Cinderella for the Houston show. Fred played technically good and steady, but the songs sounded just awful. They were written with Steve playing the drums and his sense of swing was the push and pull that give the songs their feel. When that was gone, it was just . . . unbelievable, weird. Nothing worked."

Matt proved up to the challenge and within no time the majority of the basic tracks had been recorded. But of course, it wasn't only in the studio that Matt tried to keep pace with his new bandmates, as Duff explained. "Between the volume of work, the volume of booze, and the pressure of recording with a band that was being treated as the biggest thing in town, Matt hit a wall. With three songs to go, he disappeared."

Duff left untold messages begging Matt to come into the studio to record the remaining three songs, but his entreaties remained unanswered. He even resorted to offering to buy Matt a stash of drugs, but again there was no response. As Matt was renting Duff's old place on Laurel Terrace, the bassist decided to pop round there – if only to satisfy himself that Matt hadn't met with an accident.

Duff arrived to find the door unlocked and, knowing the layout of the house, he set off in search of Matt calling out his name as he went should Matt or whoever else might be in there think he was an intruder. The bedroom had a walk-in closet and on hearing noises coming from within he tentatively opened the door. He found Mat sitting cowering in the darkness, hiding away from the world with a huge pile of coke his only company.

Matt would be able to pull himself together, however, and the remaining three songs were soon in the can. But as with everything else in GN'R world, the solving of one problem merely gave rise to a host of others. Whereas the royalty percentages on *Appetite* or *GN'R Lies* had been split equally, Duff says he now sensed a seismic shift in how things were going to be in regard to the new album, referring to developing subplots among the other band members, the management, and even Geffen Records. Indeed, the subterfuge reached the point where he "looked around at how fame and a little bit of power had affected the guys I'd been in the trenches with."

The success of *Appetite* alone had seen the trenches replaced with cosy condominiums and out-of-the-way houses up in the Hollywood Hills. Barring any major investment fuck-ups Duff was financially set for life and he'd no need to worry about ever reliving the hand-to-mouth existence of Hell House. But fighting for leg and elbow room in the trenches was what he missed most about playing in a band. Yet those days were already a distant memory.

With the basic tracks finished, Slash went into the studio to lay down his guitar parts. Again, the work rate was prodigious with all the parts completed within a month or so. Now it was Axl's turn to work his magic. And that's the point when the recording process stalled. Slash had begrudgingly acquiesced to Axl's insistence that Dizzy Reed be brought into the band, and now the direction he'd envisioned for the new album while laying down his guitar parts was going off on a tangent. "Everything hit a brick wall when it came to doing the synthesiser stuff," he bemoaned. "I never agreed with doing the synthesiser stuff anyway." Though readily admitting some of Dizzy's work was "brilliant", Slash nonetheless decries it as being the beginning of the end for Guns N' Roses. "That was the beginning of the whole taking for ever. It was like a lot of the days were not working, some days it was working, and most of the record was finished. It didn't really need all the rest of it. That was the biggest disappointment for me."

If Slash was so upset in how the new album was taking shape he had plenty of opportunities to voice his concerns in the studio. He, Duff, and Izzy could have made a stand against Axl's intention to pepper the new album with grandiose power ballads. To Slash's mind, Guns N' Roses had made their name as a hard-rocking combo and while there was perhaps room on the new album for 'November Rain', if Axl was so desperate to get 'Estranged', 'Don't Cry', 'So Fine' et al onto vinyl he should maybe have looked at making a solo record.

GUNS N' ROSES

Duff found recording 'November Rain' "torturous". He also felt the song wasn't in keeping with Guns N' Roses. Izzy knew Axl well enough to know any objections to their wasting countless hours of studio time on 'November Rain' would be so much wasted breath and distanced himself from the mounting tension by moving back to Indiana.

When push came to shove, Slash, Duff, and Izzy would always be willing to compromise whereas Axl rarely took anyone else's viewpoint into consideration – especially when it came to his lyrics. There were those at Geffen, and indeed one or two within GN'R's inner circle, telling Axl at every turn that he was the star and everyone else in the band was replaceable. Axl would use such sycophantic whisperings as leverage in his dealings with Slash, Izzy and Duff. He'd also come to believe that while Guns N' Roses as a whole was greater than the sum of its individual parts, some parts were more vital than others.

Reflecting on the situation surrounding the recording of the *Use Your Illusion* albums, Slash admitted that he, Duff and Izzy should have refused Axl's every whim. "It wouldn't have been any fun [and] I don't think it would have been very productive. But, all things considered, what we ended up doing was going along with a lot of stuff just in order to continue on, which built a monster."

♫

Guns N' Roses had amassed some 40 tracks. These were then pared down to 30 or so, but with the running time still coming in at over two-and-a-half-hours the question remained as to how best to market them. They could follow in the footsteps of George Harrison, PiL, and The Clash in releasing the whole caboodle as a triple album, make further parings to fit a double album, or pick the 12 most standout tracks for a single

killer album that might well surpass the sales of *Appetite* (then estimated at somewhere between 10 and 11 million copies).

Slash says that while his preference was to "choose the 12 best and hone them down to perfection," Axl was equally keen to get all the songs out on a double album – if only because he didn't want to sit on the songs as several had already been held over from *Appetite*. Tom Zutaut was also favourable to the idea of releasing a double album with the possibility of a mini album of cover versions or a standard single album consisting of the tracks deemed surplus to requirements for the mooted double. Alan Niven had been growing increasingly concerned about a double album, however; his anxiety stemming from the potential adverse reaction among fans to the retail cost of a double CD. By his reckoning, the double CD would retail at around $30 – a sizeable outlay for the average blue-collar GN'R fan.

From a sales point of view, *Appetite for Destruction* was always going to be a monumentally tough act to follow, but Niven believed that releasing the new material as two separate albums would at least give them a fighting chance. During a meeting with Eddie Rosenblatt he estimated they might sell upwards of four million of each single album, which would at least secure Top 10 placings on the *Billboard* chart as well as in the UK and elsewhere about the world. An added factor to his aversion to releasing a double CD was that the band would receive a better royalty rate in releasing two separate albums. Axl readily bought into the proposal of releasing two single albums; not so much because of the more favourable royalty rate, but rather because he wanted to see Guns N' Roses make history by having the albums enter the *Billboard* chart at # 1 and # 2.

As with *Appetite*, Axl found the title for the new albums through his growing appreciation of art. This time round it was the work of a 29-year-old Estonian-American painter/ sculptor called Mark Kostabi that had fired the singer's imagination. Kostabi's Use Your Illusion painting was adapted from Raphael's *The School of Athens*, which can be found in the rooms now known as the Stanze di Raffaello, in the Apostolic Palace in the Vatican. Upon graduating from Californian State University, Kostabi had relocated to New York and soon established himself among the city's East Village art community.

Unlike Robert Williams' painting, *The School of Athens* fresco was in the public domain. Axl could have either offered Kostabi a nominal fee for the use of his work or had Slash or Del James put their artistic skills to use in coming up with near-identical imagery. Instead, he agreed to the artist's $85,000 asking price – much to Alan Niven's amusement. Indeed, he would admit to always having a smile on his face whenever he thought of Axl handing over so much money when he could have had Del James paint similar backgrounds and cut out the image Kostabi had lifted from the fresco.

Working on the marketing to the *Use Your Illusion* albums was to prove Niven's final act as the manager of Guns N' Roses. His and Axl's working relationship had been fraught from the off, but whether his chuckling at Axl's handing over $85,000 for an image he could have picked up for free played any part in his downfall is anyone's guess. According to reports in the media, Axl reportedly refused to finish laying down his vocals on the new albums unless Niven was relieved of his duties.

Axl's high-handed actions supposedly went against the wishes of some of the band, yet Slash says he didn't put up much protest because of an inappropriate comment Niven supposedly made about his then girlfriend and future wife, Renée, at his house. While he could no longer remember the comment word for word, it was "creepy enough" to bring the evening to an embarrassingly early end.

Reflecting on Niven's departure, Slash says he sees that juncture as the moment that precipitated the downfall of Guns N' Roses. He also had his concerns about Doug Goldstein stepping into Niven's shoes. "I saw Doug coming," he revealed. "He'd made a place for himself in Axl's life, and once Axl had made his feelings about Alan clear, I don't think it's a coincidence that Doug was right there to pick up the reins. He had been strategically moving up the ladder from the beginning. He was like an ambush predator. His divide-and-conquer techniques were instrumental in achieving our end."

"The first solo I did was at Rock in Rio in front of 145,000 people, and I didn't even know about it until on the way to the gig. Axl said he needed to take a break in the middle of the show for his voice and I should do a solo. I'd just joined the band, it was my first show, I'm not going to say no! So I was like, 'Okay, fuck! I'm going to do a solo.' Now I'd probably be like, 'Fuck, I don't know man, let me work on that a bit!'

MATT

PART SEVEN

CONFUSING YOUR ILLUSIONS

On January 20, 1991, Guns N' Roses made the first of two headline appearances at Rock in Rio II (Billy Idol and Faith No More were also on the bill). It was the band's first live outing since Farm Aid IV the previous April. It was also the first time they'd taken to a stage with Matt Sorum and Dizzy Reed. With an estimated 180,000 people packed inside the Maracanã Stadium, it was by far the largest crowd the band had ever played to. Duff remembers Rio de Janeiro being "on fire" for Guns N' Roses, with the fans chanting themselves hoarse beforehand and singing along to every word. The *Use Your Illusion* albums were still some eight months away from release so it's doubtful the crowd would have known the lyrics to the opening song, 'Pretty Tied Up', or the other as yet unreleased songs included in the set: 'Double Talkin' Jive', 'You Could Be Mine', 'Dead Horse', and 'Estranged'. ('Bad Apples' received its first public airing at the second show on January 23). But there's no disputing Brazilians being as passionate about their music as they are their football and the stadium was bouncing from the get-go.

When reflecting on the Rock in Rio II shows Duff says that instead of marking the "triumphant beginning of a new phase in the history of the band", he felt Guns had changed from a band into a "travelling extravaganza in which we each just played a more or less independent role." Aside from Dizzy Reed, the travelling extravaganza also featured a second keyboard player in Teddy "Zig Zag" Andreadis, a trio of female backing singers, and a horn section. Yet despite the influx of personnel, Duff couldn't shake the nagging feeling that something felt "terribly wrong".

Duff's drinking was already prodigious but the Rio shows marked the beginning of a three-year headlong descent into a booze and drug hell – "the darkest days of my life" – with Slash and Matt all too happy to ride shotgun. Axl still liked to party but in the lead-up to live performances he would imbibe sparingly for fear of damaging his voice. Izzy was merely going through the motions, already pondering a life away from Guns N' Roses.

Guns N' Roses always appeared destined for greatness, yet there's no denying the soar-away success of *Appetite for Destruction* propelled them to stadium headline status far sooner than anyone anticipated. It could be argued Slash, Duff, and Izzy – as well as Matt – were initially daunted at playing to five and six-figure crowds. Axl, however, was in his element. Indeed, he'd probably been dreaming of performing to a sea of flickering cigarette lighters since first taking piano lessons.

Axl has talked about wanting Guns N' Roses to keep their trademark aggressive hard-rock edge yet would browbeat Bob Clearmountain

GUNS N' ROSES

into neutering the very thing that made Guns the band they were. "They (the mixes) had no vitality or punch," Alan Niven reflected. "They were overworked. There was no spontaneity. There was nothing vital in them whatsoever."

Niven and Tom Zutaut playfully contemplated allowing Axl to hoist himself with his own petard before reason kicked in. Instead, the Clearmountain mixes were scrapped and renowned British producer Bill Price was called upon to work a similar wizardry to that he'd applied on the Sex Pistols' *Never Mind the Bollocks*, and The Clash's *London Calling*. The *Use Your Illusion* albums nonetheless represent a turning point in the band's sound. As with any artist of note, Axl was keen for Guns to expand their repertoire to incorporate all kinds of music. And it wasn't as if his penchant for penning syrupy power ballads wasn't already known to the band. He and Izzy had written 'Don't Cry' (originally entitled 'Don't You Cry Tonight') shortly after his relocating to LA.

It was at Rock in Rio that Axl's "Ayatollah" mandates went into overdrive. Any journalists wishing to interview the band were informed they would need to sign a written agreement that essentially meant their forfeiting all control over their own work. Failure to comply with the document's wording would result in a $200,000 damages claim. Whether said claims would stand up in court was rendered a moot point as all the major media refused to play ball. The contract would subsequently be revised to omit the $200,000 penalty, but the battle line betwixt Axl and the media had been drawn.

Defending his actions during an interview with *Rolling Stone* in April 1992, Axl said he was simply trying to cut down on the band's exposure. "There is such a thing as overexposure. We were also trying to weed out the assholes from the people who were gonna be cool. You know, if you were willing to put your ass on the line and sign the damn thing, then we pretty much figured you weren't gonna try and screw us. There were people who agreed to sign it and then we told them they didn't have to.

"I want the real story," he continued. "I never wanted 'Steven Adler's on vacation.' I wanted 'Steven Adler's in a fucking rehab!' I wanted the reality. I've always been more into the reality of the situations, because that's what I wanted to read about the band. I can see where it would look like we just wanted everything to be right about us. But it was also trying to find a way to work with certain metal magazines. There are a lot of kids who collect those, and we'd rather they have real stories than bullshit stories."

> ## As with any artist of note, Axl was keen for Guns to expand their repertoire to incorporate all kinds of music.

Alan Niven and Doug Goldstein began preparing the Use Your Illusion World Tour while Guns N' Roses were in Rumbo Studios recording the new album(s). By the time the contractual i's had been dotted and the t's crossed, the tour itinerary consisted of 209 shows, taking in 27 countries across four continents. It was set to be the longest tour in rock history; a feat that will surely never be surpassed. In hindsight, however, it's easy to see it was an undertaking beyond human endurance. By the time the tour climaxed in the Argentinian capital, Buenos Aires, in June 1993, Guns N' Roses had ceased to exist in all but name.

In preparation for the mammoth tour, three warm-up shows were staged in San Francisco, LA and New York. The first two shows passed without a hitch, but during the final "live rehearsal" as Axl joking referred to these shows, he tumbled from one of the monitors, badly injuring his left ankle. The tour's opening date in East Troy, Wisconsin was but a week away and it was a real hearts-in-mouths moment. Thanks to the boffins behind the scenes at sports shoe giants, New Balance, however, Axl was able to take to the Alpine Valley Music Theatre stage in a specially crafted space-age boot.

The band arrived in Brazil for the Rock in Rio shows in a Boeing 747 leased from the MGM Grand Hotel in Las Vegas. Aside from the arrangement allowing the band to cherry-pick the best-looking stewardesses to cater to their every onboard mile-high whim, the 747 came equipped with a fully stocked bar that ran half the length of the plane, with bolted down tables and seats fanning out from the bar to create what Duff describes as a "party room". Each of the staterooms – which were the strict reserve of the band members – was fitted with a fold-out bed, dresser, and TV.

The band were so impressed with the plane's interior luxury that a deal was struck with the casino to lease the plane for the entire tour. "It was a great crash pad," Slash reflected. "And it was the best way to get from country to country because you took off and landed on your own schedule and you circumvented the standard entry procedure." Another added bonus came with a similar waiving of standard custom procedures such as luggage searches. Izzy, however, would be travelling separately so as to avoid falling back into habits of old.

Being able to bypass all the usual airport bruhaha allowed the band to arrive at their hotels and venues in ample time. Yet as early as the third show – at the Deer Creek Music Centre in Noblesville, Indiana – they were an hour or so late in taking to the stage. Axl actually had the gall to bawl-out the "nameless, faceless bureaucrats" of his home state over their imposing a curfew that required all outdoor public gatherings to be concluded by 10.30pm, when he was the only one at fault. Keeping the crowd waiting would quickly become the norm. Yet instead of confronting Axl over his boorish behaviour, Slash, Duff, and Matt chose to ramp up their booze and drug intake – if only to help drown out the boos and catcalls emanating from the restless crowds. Izzy being Izzy, mooted the idea to Slash and Duff that they should perhaps learn a killer cover song to cover for Axl, but neither had seemed particularly interested.

"We never aired what was bothering us about one another," says Duff. "Nobody ever stated outright to Axl how much we resented going on late or having him stop shows." Nobody was telling Slash, Duff, and Matt that their boozing and cocaine-bingeing was becoming a cause for concern, either. "We were all kept separate and that is the way we began to like it," Duff continued. "We each had our own security guards [and] our own 24-hour limos picking us up planeside and taking us to the hotel and anywhere else we wished to go. We rode separately to and from the gigs. We had separate dressing rooms. A sense of band unity was evident only when we were onstage. Otherwise it was every man for himself."

Axl brought the show at the Spectrum in Philadelphia (June 13) to a halt on seeing the tour photographer, Robert John, being set upon by someone in the crowd. He then waited until John's assailant had been ejected by the venue's security before continuing. Seeing as John happened to be a close friend of the band, Axl's actions were perhaps justified. The same couldn't be said when Axl again took matters into his own hands in Maryland Heights, St. Louis, some three weeks later, however.

♫

Guns N' Roses were set to play two shows over consecutive evenings at the 20,000-capacity Riverport Amphitheatre. They were about an hour and a half into the opening night's set when Axl spotted a member of the audience not-so-furtively filming the show with a video camera. He shouted for the venue's security to deal with the situation. When security failed to do so he launched himself at the bootlegger. "When he (Axl) jumped down it was great," Slash reflected. "We kept playing that

GUNS N' ROSES

suspenseful riff that starts off 'Rocket Queen', and I thought the whole moment was killer."

When Axl clambered back up onto the stage – without the video camera – he announced he was going home because of the "lame-ass security" before hurling the mic to the stage in disgust and storming off to his dressing room with Doug Goldstein in tow. Slash and the rest of the band continued playing for several minutes before retreating to the wings, unsure as to what to do.

From what can be ascertained, the guy with the video camera was either the leader of the Saddle Tramps (a local biker gang of questionable repute), or one of the venue's security staff who had taken the night off to watch the show. Either way, the security staff that were on duty proved reluctant to intervene. What makes the situation even more comical is that Goldstein had eight security guys working independently of the venue's security and none of them thought to act.

Axl had cut his knee in the melee but supposedly intended to go back out and resume the show after he'd tended to the wound. Because the dressing rooms were located deep within the bowels of the arena, however, a full-scale riot had erupted by the time Axl reached the stage area. Goldstein says he tried remonstrating with the chief of police to allow the band back onstage to quell the unrest, only to be shouted down by the promoter. By the time order was forcibly restored, the rioters had made off with anything that wasn't nailed down – including much of the band's backline – while leaving an estimated $250,000 worth of damage in their debris-strewn wake.

The following night's show was cancelled and Guns N' Roses were banned from playing St Louis again. The loss of the band's backline also forced the two subsequent shows in Tinley Park, Illinois, and Bonner Springs, Kansas, to be cancelled.

According to local press reports every available police officer within the St Louis area were despatched to the Amphitheatre in full

body armour. By the time the Cap-Stun had dissipated, some 60 fans were being treated by paramedics. The following day, the promoters, Contemporary Productions – in conjunction with the venue owners – filed lawsuits against Guns N' Roses. The St Louis authorities would subsequently issue a warrant for Axl's arrest on no fewer than five misdemeanour charges: four of "misdemeanour assault" and one of "property damage". Said arrest came some 12 months later at JFK Airport after the St Louis County authorities issued fugitive warrants seeking Axl's arrest. Axl would be the second Gunner to be arrested at an airport but by then, of course, Izzy wouldn't be around to share the joke.

Izzy officially "left" Guns N' Roses in November 1991; his final live appearance coming at London's Wembley Stadium on August 31; the final date of the first European leg of the Use Your Illusion Tour. The guitarist had in fact dropped the bombshell within a week of their coming off the road at the end of the North American leg. Axl and Slash are said to have offered the gig to Jane's Addiction guitarist, Dave Navarro, only for Izzy to have a change of heart. However, as Guns were gearing up for the European leg Izzy had a serious rethink about his future. What finally tipped Izzy over the edge was Axl's issuing him with a contract that basically demoted him to second-string status similar to that of Dizzy Reed and Matt Sorum. Izzy was outraged. He'd been with Guns N' Roses since before they even became Guns N' Roses. In jump blues parlance, he'd first set the GN'R train-a-rollin'. Indeed, had he not had the cajones to head for LA there wouldn't have been a Guns N' Roses. "I was like 'Fuck you! I'll go play the Whisky," Izzy recounted. While he may not have intended it as another "fuck you" to Axl, Izzy rehired Alan Niven as his manager.

Reflecting on Izzy's departure in the aforementioned April 1992 *Rolling Stone* interview, Axl said his "personal belief" was that Izzy had never truly wanted Guns N' Roses to make it as big as they did. "There were responsibilities that Izzy didn't want to deal with.

94

He didn't want to work at the standards that Slash and I set for ourselves. Getting Izzy to work on his own songs on this record was like pulling teeth. When Izzy had 'em on a four-track, they were done. I mean, I like tapes like that, but we'd just get destroyed if we came out with a garage tape. People want a high-quality album. And it was really hard to get Izzy to do that, even on his own material. Izzy's songs were on the record because I wanted them on the record, not because Izzy gave a shit either way. If people think I don't respect Izzy or acknowledge his talent, they're sadly mistaken. He was my friend. I haven't always been right. Sometimes I've been massively wrong, and Izzy's been the one to help steer me back to the things that were right."

Axl then went on to mention Izzy's absence in the promo video for 'Don't Cry'. Instead of reporting for duty Izzy had sent a "really short, cold letter saying, 'This changes, this changes, and maybe I'll tour in January.'" Izzy's demands were never going to be met, but Axl says he spent hours on the phone begging and pleading with Izzy to stay in the band.

As for the contract demoting Izzy to a hired hand, Axl said this was done because Izzy was no longer pulling his share of the GN'R load. "If he was going to do like the old Izzy did he wasn't going to make as much money. It was like, 'You're not giving an equal share.' Slash and I were having to do too much work to keep the attention and the energy up in the crowd. You're onstage going, 'This is really hard.' I'm into it and I'm doing it, but that guy just gets to stand there."

Needless to say, Izzy's hooking up with Alan Niven had left a bad taste in Axl's throat. "I don't need Alan Niven knowing jack shit about Guns N' Roses," he seethed. "Everybody has a lot of good and bad, and with Alan, I just got sick of his fucking combo platter. It's like, if you're involved with these people, we can't talk to you."

♫

Following Izzy's departure, Guns N' Roses returned their attentions to Dave Navarro – despite the latter being a lead guitarist rather than a rhythm player. Slash had fruitlessly tried pointing out the problems of having two lead guitarists but Axl was insistent that Navarro was their guy and had Slash set up a rehearsal/audition. When Navarro stood them up for the fourth time, Slash put a line through Navarro's name and began racking his brain for the name of the guitarist he'd caught playing in a band called Candy that had supported Hollywood Rose at Madam Wong's (East or West), whose laidback style was not dissimilar to that of Izzy. That was seven years ago, of course, so Slash had his work cut out.

> ## "Sometimes I've been massively wrong, and Izzy's been the one to help steer me back to the things that were right."

Gilby Clarke, who like Steven Adler, hailed from Cleveland, was playing with another low-rent LA outfit called Kill For Thrills when Slash came a-calling. Gilby, aged 29, had been playing guitar since he was ten years old. In his teens he worked at a music store for a year to enable him to save up the money for a Gibson Les Paul. He hadn't had the Les Paul long when an opportunist thief made off with it. "When it was stolen I was shattered," Gilby told online magazine, *The Seeker*, in September 2017. His obvious despair stemming from wanting to make playing guitar his life. "I wanted to do music as a career from day one," he continued. "I was never in a cover band. I went straight to writing songs and playing original gigs when I was 16."

At the time of Gilby's replacing Geoff Siegel in Candy they were being "helped" by Kim Fowley who had expressed an interest in Guns N' Roses. "Candy was already a band that was out and playing shows and doing fairly well but the guitar wasn't working out," Gilby explained in an interview with www.rocknworld.com. "So I answered an ad in the paper. The ad said: 'Guitarist wanted, Bowie and T.Rex influences'. So I called it and got the gig and Kim was already involved in the band so I went over and met him. At that time I had had more studio experience, believe it or not, even being younger than everybody in the band. So when I came in, the first demos we did with myself and the band, I actually produced those demos too. So it was kinda fun. Kim and I just sort of really clicked. Kim also was really helpful with a lot of us guys. None of us really had jobs back then, you know. We were just young guys in bands. And he always had jobs for us. I used to do a lot of session work for Kim."

Giving up grubbing for gigs on the West Hollywood circuit in favour of going on tour with the biggest band in the world was a no-brainer for Gilby. Slash's intuition about Gilby was to prove bang on the money. His laid-back playing style was perfectly suited to Guns N' Roses, and nor was he fazed at having just two weeks to learn upwards of 60 songs. He was still working the sound at Club Lingerie when Slash called him out of the blue asking him to swing by Guns' rehearsal space for a jam. "I came and played with him the first day, and he [said to] come down the next day, and I did that three days in a row," he explained. "And then he goes, 'All right, you've got the gig. Learn the whole catalogue. We'll see you next week.'"

"He came in for an audition and just nailed it," Slash recounted. Once Gilby had learned the songs he auditioned with the band. "It was a strange moment," Slash continued. "Izzy's departure happened so quietly with no fanfare, and no media awareness. It was such a major change within the band, but to the outside world it was a non-event."

Speaking with www.ultimate-guitar.com in 2018, Alan Niven revealed how he was holidaying in Switzerland when Izzy called to say he was quitting Guns N' Roses. "He (Izzy) came up on my cellphone and I'm going like, 'What the hell is Izzy calling me for?' He told me that he had enough and wanted to quit. That set off alarm bells. I knew that they had some dates coming in because that was one of the last things I did for GN'R. Izzy left three months after I did and of course Gilby had an unenviable task of having to slip on Izzy's boots and get in there and be a replacement."

Izzy's departure from Guns N' Roses was far from a non-event and the media may well have made more of the story had it not been for the *Use Your Illusion* albums slamming onto the *Billboard* chart at # 1 and #2 following their release on September 17, 1991. (*UYI II* narrowly pipping its twin to the coveted top slot.)

Gilby's relaxed attitude was such that he didn't mind being left to his own devices while learning Guns' entire back catalogue. "Because the band knew all the songs the last thing they want to do is sit around and go to rehearsal with me," he reasoned. "They were over it, so I had to do my own homework. I sat there for a full week learning all those songs, and the last day I called Dizzy because I was having a hard time trying to figure out what to play on 'Estranged'. I couldn't figure it out. Dizzy goes, 'Oh, here's a music book.' I went, 'There's a music book? I just spent a week with my ear grinded to the records.' I didn't even think about it; that I could have just picked up the chord charts."

Gilby was also under no illusion as to what he was getting into. "I knew that Izzy was such a big part of the band. I wasn't trying to replace Izzy – I was trying to find my place in the band; have my own voice, play guitar the way I play guitar. I just said, 'I'm going to be myself – they either like me or they don't.' But they were happy – they never ever said anything to me, like, 'Wear this on stage,' or 'Do this,' or 'Don't do that.' Duff made a suggestion in the beginning because I was playing a little ahead of the beat, and he goes, 'You gotta relax, man. Just lay back.' It really helped me lock into their music of just kind of relaxing and staying behind the beat.

Gilby made his GN'R debut at the Worcester Spectrum in Worcester, Massachusetts on December 5, 1991; the Spectrum's 14,800 capacity proving a significant jump from the crowds he was used to. Going onstage with the biggest band in the world, in front of the largest crowd he'd ever faced, was daunting enough but just as the band were about to go on Slash pulled Gilby to one side. "Slash came up to me and said, 'You know before 'Patience' Izzy always did a little something; it's a solo, what are you gonna do?'" Gilby told *Kerrang!* in May 1994. "I gotta tell you, I didn't even think of anything but I had done 'Wild Horses' acoustic a couple of times. So it was just my idea to do that and it just kinda clicked with the guys, they liked it. You know. And everybody knew it so they sang and played along. There was a point actually where I switched, I did 'Happiness is a Warm Gun' a couple of times, but it didn't work very good, so I just stopped with that."

If anything, the *Use Your Illusion* albums engendered even greater interest in Guns N' Roses. The clamour for tickets was such that the tour was now set to stretch midway into 1993. With Guns earning an average gross of $600,000 from ticket sales per each show they should have been rivalling the Rolling Stones in the money-making stakes. What only a select number of people knew at the time the UYI tour got under way the previous May, however, was that Guns N' Roses were on the brink of financial meltdown.

Aside from the additional musicians and back-up singers that were accompanying the band on the road, some 230 crew were needed to operate two colossal identical stages that leapfrogged one another from city to city. These costs had long-since been factored into the ticket pricing, of course. What dumped Guns N' Roses into the red were the endless penalty fines the band were having to pay out

to venues and promoters for going on late and breaking predesignated curfews. Then there were the seemingly no-expense-spared on-the-road extravagances (organised by Axl's sister, Amy, and half-brother, Stuart) such as yacht excursions, go-kart rallies, and the private hire of fashionable restaurants. As laughable as it sounds, it would take two years of UYI shows just to break even. "It was all senseless spending," Slash reflected. "Doug approved one crazy idea after another to fill our free time at our expense. With the exception of Axl, the band wouldn't have cared if none of it ever happened. We were more than capable of entertaining ourselves in any global locale on a shoestring budget."

A psychiatrist and professional psychic had also been added to the payroll at Axl's instruction. The psychiatrist was a stunning Victoria Principal lookalike called Suzi London (who features in the 'Don't Cry' promo video). The psychic, a dumpy, diminutive middle-aged Asian lady by the name of Sharon Maynard.

Much has been made of Maynard's behind-the-scenes influence over Axl that was to extend way beyond the UYI tour. She and her husband, Elliott (both of whom receive a "thank you" in the *Use Your Illusion* liner notes) ran a non-profit organisation based in Sedona, Arizona, called Arcos Cielos Corp. Through her Japanese cultural background, Maynard claimed to be skilled in bridging Eastern and Western viewpoints, which she integrated into programmes for new ways of thinking and effective action. She also reportedly held an ARCT (Associate of the Royal Conservatory of Toronto) diploma from the Toronto Royal Conservatory of Music, but Axl was infinitely more interested in Maynard's supposed aptitude for channelling past lives than her appreciation of a catchy piano piece.

The rest of the band and crew dubbed Maynard "Yoda" after the goblin-like mystic from the *Star Wars* franchise. But no one was laughing when Axl – at Maynard's behest – had everyone sign confidentiality agreements

GUNS N' ROSES

forbidding them from commenting publicly on any aspect of the tour without Axl's express permission – regardless of where they stood in the GN'R food chain.

Following on from a second round of US dates and three sell-out shows at the Tokyo Dome, Guns N' Roses arrived in London for the Freddie Mercury Tribute Concert at Wembley Stadium on Easter Monday, April 20, 1992. (The flamboyant Freddie having died the previous November due to complications from AIDS.) Guns were just one of a host of stellar names coming together to give Freddie a fitting send-off. Guns were set to play a three-song set – 'Paradise City', 'Only Women Bleed', and 'Knockin' on Heaven's Door', but owing to technical problems earlier in the show, Alice Cooper's 1975 hit had to be sidelined. Slash would also join Brian May, Roger Taylor, John Deacon, and guest vocalist Joe Elliott from Def Leppard for a rendition of 'Tie Your Mother Down', while Axl duetted with Elton John on 'Bohemian Rhapsody'.

Upon the band's return to LA, Slash and Lars Ulrich staged a press conference at the Gaslight to announce a Guns N' Roses/Metallica joint headline US stadium tour (with Faith No More opening on the majority of the dates). The mouth-watering 26-date tour would get under way in Washington D.C on July 17.

♫

In terms of making music, Guns N' Roses could do no wrong but constantly being out on the road was playing havoc with their respective love lives. Slash's relationship with Renee had floundered owing to his infidelity during the tour's second US leg; Renee's learning of her beau's philandering from someone on the GN'R team serving to lay to waste the age-old what-happens-on-tour-stays-on-tour ethos (though the couple would subsequently get back together and end up tying the knot). Axl's 12-month relationship with supermodel Stephanie Seymour was also coming under strain owing to disquieting rumours

that she'd been spotted out and about with her old flame, Warren Beatty. Matters would come to a head in Paris where Guns were set to perform a special pay-per-view show at the 58,000-capacity Hippodrome de Vincennes, with Jeff Beck, Lenny Kravitz, and Aerosmith's Steve Tyler and Joe Perry all being flown in to add some more pizazz to the televised extravaganza. Beck would pull out at the eleventh hour, claiming to have developed tinnitus as a result of the loudness of Slash's guitar at the previous afternoon's rehearsals. Kravitz, Tyler and Perry fulfilled their respective guest slots, however; Kravitz joining the Gunners onstage for a storming run-through of 'Always on the Run' (the debut single from Kravitz's album, *Mama Said*, on which Slash had penned the music), while Tyler and Perry added a certain *je ne sais quoi* to 'Train Kept A-Rollin'' and 'Mama Kin' during the extended encore.

It's Stephanie, of course, who plays the bride to Axl's groom in the overblown $1.5 million promo video to 'November Rain'. Promoted as the follow-on to 'Don't Cry' in the Meat Loaf/*Bat Out of Hell*-esque trilogy that would be completed later in the year with 'Estranged', the video to 'November Rain' was loosely based on a short story called *Without You,* written by Del James who in turn took his inspiration from Axl's doomed romance with Erin. A sure case of art imitating life if ever there was one. Axl would – not entirely in jest, it has to be said – claim he and Stephanie were married for real as the Italian priest conducting the celluloid ceremony was an actual priest rather than a jobbing actor.

The band had a couple of days off before the next scheduled show at Manchester City's Maine Road football ground on the Tuesday, and Axl had been hoping Stephanie would be flying over from LA to help him take in the sights of the French capital. Axl is said to have gotten himself so worked up over Stephanie that on the Sunday evening a doctor was summoned to the band's hotel. The doctor's diagnosis was that Axl was suffering from "complete physical exhaustion" and recommended he take 36 hours complete rest – which would force the postponement of the Manchester show.

Taking the doctor's advice to the letter, Axl remained in Paris while the rest of the band and their sizeable tour entourage travelled onto London in preparation for Guns N' Roses' forthcoming Wembley date. Come the day of the show, Axl was back to his belligerent best and proved as much by insisting he be flown by helicopter from the band's hotel – the Conrad in St James – to Wembley Stadium despite repeated assurances from those in the know that there would be nowhere for the chopper to land. As a result, Axl ended up disembarking from the helicopter further away from the Twin Towers than when he set off and had to continue to the stadium by road. Despite this latest show of foolhardiness, Guns N' Roses took to the stage at the appointed hour. Axl would revert to type when it came to the rearranged Manchester show, however. For reasons that are unlikely to ever come to light he wilfully kept the capacity crowd wilting in the heat for over two hours after Faith No More had departed the stage.

A retribution of sorts would be meted out at Heathrow Airport a few days later when an overzealous security guard singled Axl out for a grilling as to his travel plans while conducting a painstaking search of his entire luggage. It must have seemed to Axl that Heathrow's security had a private vendetta against him as he'd suffered similar harassment on arrival at the airport for the Freddie Mercury Tribute concert back in April. On that occasion he'd stayed his tongue, but upon arrival in Würzburg where the tour was set to continue, he instructed Geffen's publicity team to issue a press statement in which he aired his grievances. Having stressed that he didn't expect to be treated any different to everybody else either arriving or departing from Heathrow he ended his tirade by taking sarcastic swipe at the unnamed jobsworth for purposely singling him out in order to have a story with which to regale his friends over a beer.

Several of the remaining European dates ended up either cancelled or postponed to a later date, while those that did go ahead suffered from the band's by now customary late arrival onstage. In Lisbon it seemed as though history was set to repeat itself. It was exactly 12 months to the day since the St Louis riot, and Guns N' Roses were playing to a packed house at the Estádio José Alvalade. The band was yet again late coming onstage and the crowd expressed their displeasure by pelting the stage with plastic water bottles – not all of them empty. One dimwit, however, took his frustrations too far in hurling a homemade pipe bomb up onto the stage. Axl, perhaps understandably, hurled the mic down and stormed off. Doug Goldstein hurriedly ordered the band's security to keep them onstage. Thankfully, Goldstein was able to coax Axl back out to continue with the show on this occasion.

The final European show in Madrid had to be cancelled owing to unforeseen problems with the venue's construction. Rather than head for home with the rest of the tour entourage, Axl and Stephanie instead returned to San Remo, the picturesque Italian Riviera city that had served as a base earlier in the tour. The couple flew into JFK on the Monday before the opening GN'R/Metallica show five days hence. They had no sooner cleared customs when Axl was promptly arrested on the outstanding fugitive warrant. When he went up before a judge in Clayton, Missouri, two days later, Axl would plead not guilty to all five counts. A court date was set for October 13, and Axl was released on a $100,000 bond. (He would subsequently be found guilty on all five counts. Instead of the five-year jail term the local prosecutor had been pushing for, Axl would be placed on two years' probation and ordered to donate $50,000 to local community groups.)

In the run-up to the opening GN'R/Metallica show at the Robert F. Kennedy Memorial Stadium on June 17, the Metallica camp called for an inter-band meeting to express their concerns over Guns' ongoing failure to get onstage at the appointed hour. "Metallica was not a band to pull that kind of shit at all," Slash sagely observed. "They wisely opted to play first so as to avoid being pulled down by our bullshit. They were macho in their work ethic and dedicated to their fans."

Reflecting on the tour with *Metal Hammer* in May 2017, former Metallica bassist, Jason Newsted, spoke of the "lessons his band learned" from being on the road with Guns N' Roses. "We chose to play first because we wanted to play on time. We deliver. If we're going on at 8.01, we're on at 8.01. That's the way it's always been. That's why Metallica's still touring now and crushing everybody and selling more records. They played after us, whenever they decided to come on stage – 30 minutes late, an hour late, two hours late, whatever the time 'homeboy' decided to come on.

"They showed me what I don't ever want to become," he continued. "What I would not do. Antics, pissing away of money, disrespecting people that work for you, looking down on people who look up to you. [The] worst thing you can do – especially in this business. I saw them do that a lot, and I didn't like it. Some of the stories – jokey, funny-ass stories – those guys pulling stuff that was just not okay. As a band they were powerful for about three-and-a-half years, and really had their sharp teeth. After that, everything fell apart."

Newsted's comment about the "pissing away of money" relates to the lavishly themed backstage parties Guns N' Roses laid on after each and every show during the tour. With Stuart and Amy Bailey seemingly operating with a blank cheque mandate, the parties grew ever more ostentatious. One night it would be "Greek night" with greased-up muscle-bound male models carrying silver platters laden with roasted pigs, while another night would be "Sixties night"; the backstage area mocked up to resemble the Tate/La Bianca murders. Both bands were receiving the same bumper pay-cheques after each show. But whereas Metallica banked their cash, Guns pissed away up to 80 per cent of their earnings either on the theme parties or late fees.

The shows weren't without their talking points, either. During the Gunners' performance at the Giants Stadium in East Rutherford, Axl was struck in the genitals by a well-aimed cigarette lighter and had to vacate the stage in agony leaving Duff to take over on vocals. Axl returned soon thereafter, even making a joke about "being hit in the dick by a Bic". Rather less amusing – at least from the fans' point of view – was the postponing of the three following shows in Boston, South Carolina, and Minneapolis owing to Axl sustaining severe damage to his vocal chords.

> ## "They wisely opted to play first so as to avoid being pulled down by our bullshit. They were macho in their work ethic and dedicated to their fans."

Axl's sore throat and swollen gonads were to pale into insignificance compared with the injuries that would befall Metallica frontman, James Hetfield, at Montreal's Stade Du Parc Olympique on August 8. Owing to a misunderstanding as to the positioning of the onstage pyrotechnics, Hetfield suffered severe burns to his left arm, which not only brought Metallica's set to an immediate halt but also led to the following seven shows being rescheduled. Instead of going on early and playing an extended set so as to compensate the crowd, Axl brought Guns' set to a premature close claiming he couldn't hear himself through the monitors. Before retiring, he informed the disgruntled crowd they would be entitled to a full refund. The offer failed to pacify some 2,000 fans who proceeded to vent their frustrations by running amok outside the stadium.

According to Slash, the final date of the GN'R/Metallica tour at the Kingdome in Duff's native Seattle on October 6 was to have also brought the Use Your Illusion Tour to a climactic finale. Yet by the time of the show the tour had been extended to include a nine-date tour of South America, and return visits to Japan, Australasia, the US, and Europe.

Guns N' Roses were afforded a break from their ongoing tour commitments after being asked to perform 'November Rain' live onstage at MTV's annual Video Music Awards which was being staged at UCLA's Pauley Pavilion in LA's Westwood Village. Guns N' Roses weren't in line for an award directly but the 'November Rain' video had scooped two awards – Best Art Direction in a Video and Best Cinematography in a Video. Axl was said to be particularly excited as Elton John would be accompanying them on piano (Elton would also be performing 'The One', the lead single from his most recent album of the same name.) Other guest performances included Def Leppard, Bryan Adams, Pearl Jam, The Black Crowes, Eric Clapton, and Nirvana.

Axl was a huge Nirvana fan and had originally offered them the opening act slot on the ongoing GN'R/Metallica tour only for Kurt Cobain to refuse. Nirvana were booked to get the proceedings under way performing 'Lithium', the third single taken from their ground-breaking *Nevermind* album. They would also be picking up the much-coveted Video of the Year award for 'Smells Like Teen Spirit' – the song MTV had been desperately keen for Nirvana to perform. The network had initially given Cobain and Co. carte blanche to perform any song they wanted. However, when Nirvana announced they would be performing 'Rape Me' (which would remain

unreleased until December 1993), the show's producers stepped in for obvious reasons. A compromise was reached but come showtime the brazen trio started playing 'Rape Me' and only segued into 'Lithium' moments before the panicked organisers were about to cut to a commercial break.

Cobain would later say they'd done it to give MTV "a little heart palpitation". It was the sort of cocky snook to the corpulent corporate suits running MTV that a pre-Geffen-signed Guns N' Roses might have once pulled. However, while Axl might have believed Guns and Nirvana were of similar rock'n'roll outlaw chic, the two bands were polar opposites as the bloated Spinal Tap-esque excesses of the Use Your Illusion Tour so painfully laid bare.

Nirvana were simply the latest Young Turks to come bulling out the gate brimming with ideas and impatient for change. Cobain's suicide in April 1994 would bring Nirvana to a shotgun stop, otherwise they too would have surely been assimilated into the system. For no matter what you throw at capitalism, it will absorb it and sell it back to the masses.

Cobain also reportedly spat on the keys of the piano he believed Axl would be playing during Guns' performance. It was an unsavoury episode, but there was to be further shenanigans in the wake of Guns' performance. Axl was making his way to his band's trailer with Stephanie when Cobain's wife, Courtney Love, jumped out of her seat holding the couple's baby daughter Frances Bean in her outstretched arms and mockingly asked if Axl would be the "godfather to our child". Axl strode over to where Cobain and Love were seated with their entourage. Jabbing a finger into Cobain's face for added emphasis, Axl told him, "Shut your bitch up or I'm taking you down to the pavement!" It was a risible reaction that played directly into Love's hands as she'd so obviously intended. All that was left was for Cobain to deliver the knockout. Feigning indignation, he glared at Love for several seconds before telling her, "*Shut up, bitch!*" On cue, their entourage burst into renewed guffaws. Stephanie attempted to lighten the darkening mood by enquiring of Love if she were a model. "No," Love spat back, her tone dripping with disdain. "Are you a brain surgeon?"

There would be further fireworks outside Nirvana's trailer with Duff and Nirvana's Krist Novoselic, squaring up. The two bassists might well have come to blows had cooler heads not prevailed.

♫

The next leg of the newly extended Use Your Illusion Tour got under way with a show in the Venezuelan capital Caracas in front of 45,000 ecstatic fans – the biggest show ever staged in Venezuela to date. The show itself passed without incident but Venezuela would be thrown into turmoil by a military coup – the second to occur that year – within hours of the band's departure. The coup would ultimately fail but in the ensuing chaos one of the cargo planes ferrying GN'R's gear was left stranded on the tarmac along with several understandably nervous crew members. As a result, the next two scheduled shows in the Colombian capital of Bogota (over the consecutive evenings of November 28 and 29) were rolled into one as the missing gear wouldn't arrive at the El Campin Stadium until 7 pm on the Saturday. Disaster struck when torrential rains brought the stage roof and lighting rig crashing to the ground. While an ever-increasing number of fans occupied themselves erecting makeshift encampments in the car park, the crew selflessly worked through the night rejigging the surviving lights.

While rolling the two shows into one seemed a logical solution on paper, it didn't quite translate to reality as hundreds of irate ticket-holders were left stranded outside the venue come showtime. As a result, sporadic fighting broke out and riot police had to be brought in to restore order.

Next up was a sell-out show in Santiago at the Chilean national football stadium. The day following the show reports appeared in the local media claiming Axl had been drunk onstage and that a quantity of drugs was found in the band's hotel. Doug Goldstein responded by staging a press conference at which he steadfastly denied both allegations. While it was true officers from the CDI (Chilean Department of Investigation) had paid a late-night visit to the hotel, they had left again empty-handed. From Chile the band made the relatively short jump to neighbouring Argentina for two back-to-back shows in Buenos Aires over December 5 and 6, before heading for São Paulo, Brazil. The opening show at the Estacionamento Do Anhembi went ahead despite torrential downpours throughout. However, with the deluge showing no sign of abating, the local officials insisted on cancelling the following night's show. Following the final show at the Autódromo Internacional Nelson Piquet on December 13, the band returned to LA for an extended Holiday season.

The break was to prove far from festive for Axl, however. He'd recently purchased a dream home for himself, Stephanie, and Stephanie's son Dylan. The four-acre, Mediterranean-style   complex was situated atop a steep hill overlooking Malibu and came replete with all the usual fixings: manicured grounds, swimming pool, and floodlit tennis court. Stephanie had arranged a Christmas dinner/party for a select number of friends. According to Stephanie's sworn declaration in the legal action she subsequently took against Axl, they gotten into "a verbal argument" which had ended with Axl announcing there wasn't going to be a party. Stephanie couldn't be sure whether Axl would calm down in the interim so didn't bother calling to inform their friends as to what was occurring. The party did indeed go ahead in a fashion as Axl was still in a foul mood; going so far as to get abusive at Stephanie's mother when she tried reasoning with him.

This was a mere dress rehearsal for what was to occur once their friends had departed. Again, according to Stephanie's deposition, Axl started "yelling and swearing" before knocking some empty wine bottles to the kitchen floor and smashing the glass. He then grabbed her by the throat and dragged her barefoot across the broken glass while repeatedly hitting and kicking her. Axl would subsequently claim his actions had been retaliatory after Stephanie grabbed him by the balls. It may well have been six of one and half a dozen of the other but one thing was certain; however. The relationship was over.

Axl could at least throw himself into his work, and there were worse ways of starting the year than playing three sell-out shows to ecstatic crowds at the futuristic Tokyo Dome. He'd insisted on having his support team and assorted suck-ups accompany him on the latest leg, but Teddy Andreadis, along with the horn section and backing singers, had been deemed surplus to requirements. In their stead, the band introduced an intimate mid-set acoustic jamboree with the band gathered around a coffee table. The occasions allowed Gilby to take centre stage with 'Dead Flowers', yet while three of the four acoustic tracks from GN'R Lies were among those played, 'One in a Million' unsurprisingly remained locked away.

After the opening Tokyo Dome date, the band and their entourage descended upon the Lexington Queen – or the "Lex" as the preferred Reppongi district watering hole was colloquially known – for the customary after-show shenanigans. Ronnie Wood happened to be in town playing a solo show and invited Guns to his own Lex after-show; the bonhomie extending to Wood agreeing to join Guns N' Roses onstage for an extended version of 'Knockin' on Heaven's Door' at the third final Dome show the following evening.

There would be a two-week break before Guns' next outing at Sydney's Eastern Creek Raceway, which at the time was the largest musical event ever staged in Australia. Another record was set two nights later with Guns smashing the existing national attendance record at Melbourne's Calder Park Raceway. Then it was onto Auckland, where the night prior to the show at the Mount Smart Stadium

GUNS N' ROSES

was spent at a plush restaurant overlooking the harbour celebrating Duff's birthday. The show itself fell on Axl's birthday, and midway through the set he was presented with an enormous candle-lit cake while Slash and the rest of the band led the audience in a heart-warming rendition of 'Happy Birthday'.

The next tour leg saw Guns N' Roses take yet another trawl across the US. The opening couple of shows largely went according to script, but several subsequent dates would have to be cancelled owing to adverse weather conditions. Inclement weather could be waved away as an act of God but it was the act of an idiot that curtailed the April 3 show in Sacramento. Guns were some 90 minutes into the set when a plastic water bottle (filled with piss, according to Slash) launched from the crowd during 'November Rain' smacked Duff square on the forehead sending him crashing to the floor. All Duff remembered of the incident was catching sight of the bottle careening off Matt's floor tom before "everything went black".

Axl was responsible for the cancellation of the April 14 show in Atlanta simply because it was the same venue (Omni Coliseum) where he'd been arrested onstage six years earlier during the Mötley Crüe tour for taking security measures into his own hands.

The tour appeared to be back on track when Gilby broke his left wrist after falling off his motorbike during a practice run for a celebrity race in support of the TJ Martell Foundation. The race was undoubtedly in aid of a worthy cause but Gilby's injury forced the cancellation of the remaining four US dates. The penultimate leg – Europe (again) – was set to commence with a couple of shows in Russia in a little over a fortnight's time and it was touch and go whether Gilby's wrist would heal in time. Desperate to avoid cancelling more dates, Axl called in a favour from an old friend.

Two Russian dates would have to be cancelled owing to the ongoing constitutional crisis that was engulfing Russian politics. With a dreadlocked Izzy temporarily returned to the fold

Guns flew on to Tel Aviv a few days in advance of the May 22 show at the Hayarkon Park Arena so as to allow Izzy time to familiarise himself with the set. Following shows in Athens and Istanbul, Izzy took his leave with two consecutive evenings at the National Bowl in Milton Keynes. While Izzy enjoyed getting to do a spot of sightseeing in Tel Aviv, Athens, and Istanbul – places he'd never before visited – there was a déjà vu feel about everything else. "It was really bizarre," he later recounted. "It was like playing with zombies. It was just horrible."

For the next six weeks or so, the "zombies" lurched across Europe playing various sports stadiums in Austria, Holland, Scandinavia, Switzerland, and Germany, before arriving in Barcelona on July 5. Duff says that by this stage he and the rest of band might only convene for the shows themselves. With the last of the Italian dates in Cava de' Tirreni having been cancelled, he and his new wife Linda, had idled in Ibiza before heading for the Catalonian capital. It was approaching showtime at the Estadi Olímpic Lluís Companys when Duff received word that Doug Goldstein wanted to see him and Slash. Upon their arrival at the "vibe room" each was handed legal documentation by one of Goldstein's underlings that effectively gave Axl the right to continue to play as Guns N' Roses in the eventuality of either Slash or Duff leaving. Though their status as shareholders in Guns N' Roses wouldn't be affected, Axl alone would control the name once they signed the agreement.

While Goldstein watched on, the underling launched into a tirade about Duff and Slash's being in poor shape because of their booze and drug intake, and that signing the name over to Axl would at least spare years of legal wrangling in the courts should either of them die. It was also implied that Axl wouldn't go onstage should the agreements remain unsigned. Rather than risk another riot should Axl live up to his threat, Duff and Slash begrudgingly signed the agreements. A decision both would come to regret.

While Doug Goldstein was renegotiating the band's contract with Geffen, Axl had insisted on a clause being inserted giving him full legal control over the name "Guns N' Roses" as protection for himself as he'd come up with the name. "It had more to do with management than the band as our then manager (Alan Niven) was always trying to convince someone they should fire me," he explained on GN'R's online forum in 2008. "As I had stopped speaking with him, he sensed his days were numbered and was bending any ear he could, along with attempting to sell our renegotiation out for a personal payday from Geffen."

Axl then went on stress that the clause wasn't hidden away in legalese as everyone who was asked to sign off on the clause had had to initial the relevant section to show they were in full acknowledgment. "At the time, I didn't know or think about brand names or corporate value etc. All I knew is that I came in with the name and from day one everyone had agreed to it being mine should we break up, and now it was in writing."

Axl's reasoning appears straightforward enough but his refusal to go onstage in Barcelona should Duff and Slash refuse to sign the agreement was tantamount to coercion. The plot was to thicken, however. During a

December 2008 interview with *Rolling Stone*, Axl claimed the whole contractual clause saga was nothing more than "fallacy and fantasy" on Duff and Slash's part. "Not one single solitary thread of truth to it," he said. "Had that been the case I would have been cremated years ago legally, [they] could've cleaned me out for the name and damages. It's called under duress with extenuating circumstances."

"Duress with extenuating circumstances" seemed to be the price of being in Guns N' Roses, but Slash and Duff appeared willing to soldier on . . . for the time being at least.

Having taken their European bow at the Palais Omnisports de Paris-Bercy in Paris on July 13, it was straight to Buenos Aires for two final shows at the 70,000-capacity Estadio River Plate. Guns' return to the Argentinian capital was marred somewhat when 50 officers from the city's narcotics division descended en masse at the band's hotel in search of drugs following a supposed tip-off. The search yielded nothing of interest. Nor did a search of the band's equipment at the stadium prior to the opening Friday night show. Saturday's show was being broadcast live on TV in Argentina as well as neighbouring Paraguay, so for once the proceedings got under way on schedule – 9.30pm.

"What made dealing with Axl so maddening was the fact that he and I were also in agreement on a lot of things. One of the points of contention between Slash and Axl was a batch of songs Slash brought to the table. Axl thought it was Southern rock – not Guns N' Roses material. I backed Axl."

DUFF

PART EIGHT

THERE'S NO LOGIC HERE TODAY

The Use Your Illusion Tour was the longest tour in the history of rock'n'roll, yet within a month of Guns' returning to LA Duff had put a band together and hit the road again in support of his debut album *Believe In Me* (which Geffen released at the end of September 1993. Upon discovering Duff was heading over to Europe to promote *Believe In Me*, Axl thought his friend had taken leave of his senses and called him up to say as much). In a repeat of Guns' UYI tour warm-up dates, Duff played three showcase shows in LA, San Francisco, and New York, before heading over the Atlantic to serve as support on the European leg of The Scorpions' Face the Heat Tour. He'd recorded rough demos of his songs in a variety of studios during the Use Your Illusion Tour, before corralling Slash, Matt, Gilby, West Arkeen, Teddy Andreadis, Sebastian Bach, Lenny Kravitz and Jeff Beck to help record the songs for real. Slash had been equally industrious during the tour, getting together with Matt and Gilby to work on a clutch of the new songs he'd written. He'd been writing for the fun of it so wasn't overly downhearted when Axl dismissed the demos out of hand.

Geffen were all too happy to entertain overtures about solo side-projects from the individual band members, but Guns N' Roses was the label's overriding priority. Two years had passed since the release of the UYI albums and Eddie Rosenblatt was already leaning on Doug Goldstein to get the band into the studio to start

work on a new album. In the interim, however, Geffen would release an album of cover versions from the *UYI* recording sessions that had initially been mooted as possible themed EPs.

If it can be said that the *Use Your Illusion* albums capture Guns N' Roses at the height of their creativity, then *The Spaghetti Incident?* surely serves as the band's nadir. There are the odd noteworthy exceptions - Johnny Thunders' 'You Can't Put Your Arms Around a Memory' (which Axl reportedly insisted Duff leave off of *Believe in Me*) , The Dead Boys' 'Ain't it Fun', and The Skyliners' 'Since I Don't Have You' – but the rest of the covers should have been the reserve of soundcheck and rehearsal room mess-abouts.

Calling the album *The Spaghetti Incident?* was an in-joke referring to Steven Adler's lawsuit. While Guns were in Chicago three years earlier, Steven had used "spaghetti" as the codeword for his cocaine stash that he'd kept in a butter dish in one of the refrigerators. When Steven's lawyer asked him to explain "the spaghetti incident" in court, Duff had burst out laughing at the sheer absurdity of it all.

The album's insipid artwork – a bowl of tinned spaghetti – showed a distinct lack of imagination from a marketing point of view, yet nonetheless appears to contain another in-joke. What could be construed as a barcode printed at the bottom of the sleeve is in fact a cypher consisting of symbols from a 408-symbol cryptogram the Zodiac – a serial killer operating in Northern California during the late Sixties to the early Seventies whose identity remains unknown – used in a series of letters sent to three newspapers – the *Vallejo Times Herald*, the *San Francisco Chronicle*, and *The San Francisco Examiner* – in August 1969 that supposedly revealed his identity. The GN'R cypher simply reads "fuck 'em all".

Axl was used to courting controversy – indeed, there were those within the band's inner-circle who believed he thrived on it. According to the track-listing, Fear's 'I Don't Care About You' brings *The Spaghetti Incident?* to a close. Axl had a trick up his sleeve, however, by including Charles Manson's 'Look at Your Game, Girl' as an uncredited bonus track. Doug Goldstein says Manson's pre-'Helter Skelter' acoustic ditty wasn't listed on advance tapes sent out to reviewers as Axl had wanted the song to "speak for itself". The song's inclusion had plenty of others speaking out, none more vociferously than David Geffen. In response to *The New York Times*' pointing out that Manson could earn up to $60,000 for every million copies of *The Spaghetti Incident?* that were sold, Geffen,

who'd known two of the Manson Family's victims, said he thought Manson's earning money from "the fame he derived committing one of the most horrific crimes of the 20th century" as "unthinkable. He also castigated Axl for failing to stop and think about the public backlash Guns N' Roses – and Geffen Records – would now face. Geffen's comments smack of disingenuity, however. As with 'One in a Million', it beggars belief *The Spaghetti Incident?* went from inception to pressing without anyone at the label bringing the inclusion of 'Look at Your Game, Girl' to the attention of Eddie Rosenblatt or even Geffen himself.

The band initially considered removing 'Look at Your Game, Girl' from the album before ultimately deciding to donate all the royalties from the song to Bartek Frykowski, the son of Manson victim Wojciech Frykowski.

Axl would spuriously claim he'd believed 'Look at Your Game, Girl' was penned by Beach Boy, Dennis Wilson – despite his near-whispered "Thanks, Chas" at the song's finale. With the controversy showing little sign of abating, Axl issued the following statement via the March 1994 issue of *Q* Magazine:

It's come to my attention that some people have taken offence to a particular song, 'Look At Your Game, Girl', on our new album *The Spaghetti Incident?* What it all boils down to is this: *The Spaghetti Incident?* is 13 historical and musical gems that may have been overlooked. For instance, 'New Rose' was one of The Damned's main songs but for whatever reason a lot of the world didn't hear it. In Indiana, I was ridiculed and physically attacked for my musical tastes, tastes that I never made any effort to hide. I thought it would be interesting for the so-called mainstream and the people who were against this material when I was a teenager to actually hear these songs. Maybe they'll hear something they like, and more importantly, maybe they'll go and find the originals better, including 'Look At Your Game, Girl'. The reason we didn't list that song on our album is we wanted to downplay it. We don't give any credit to Charles Manson on the album; it's like a hidden bonus track. It's my opinion that the media are enjoying making a big deal out of Guns N' Roses covering a song that Charles Manson recorded, but if another band had recorded that song, it probably wouldn't have been of interest. The media need their "bad guys" to guarantee some ratings, so they use Manson's name coupled with mine to promote their news programmes. However, when I do something positive, like contribute to charity, it's hard to get the news to pick up on those stories. The media is an interesting beast.

Why did I choose to cover that particular song?

Oddly enough, one of the things we do up at my house is have "Name That Artist" contests where we play obscure songs and everyone tries to name the artist. My brother Stuart found 'Look At Your Game, Girl' at a large record chain and, needless to say, he won that round. Personally, I liked the lyrics and the melody of the song. Hearing it shocked me and I thought there might be other people who would like to hear it.

I like the words because, to me, it's about a woman who has thrown things away. She thinks she's gaining love but basically she's gaining sadness. It was very fitting for a personal situation I happened to be in. The song talks about how the girl is insane and playing a mad game. I felt that it was ironic that such a song was recorded by Charles Manson, someone who should know the inner intricacies of madness.

Manson is a dark part of American culture and history. He's the subject of fear and fascination through books, movies, and the interviews he's done. Most people hadn't heard anything Charles Manson recorded.

A lot of people can say I wear the "Charlie Don't Surf" T-shirt for shock value, but I've worn that shirt for the past year on tour, all over the world. Yes, I was trying to make a statement. I wore the T-shirt because a lot of people enjoy playing me as the bad guy and the crazy. Sorry, I'm not that guy. I'm nothing like him. That's what I'm saying. There's a real difference in morals, values and ethics between Manson and myself and that is "Thou shalt not kill", which I don't. I'm by no means a Manson expert or anything, but the things he's done are something I don't believe in. He's a sick individual. Look at Manson and then look at me. We're not the same. Plus, I like the black humour of the "Charlie Don't Surf" line for the movie *Apocalypse Now*.

I think people think I'm crazy because I believe in telling the truth. I'll admit sometimes I don't do a perfect job of it, but my efforts are true.

GUNS N' ROSES

It is my understanding that the song was written by Dennis Wilson. To what extent Charles Manson is involved in the publishing, I'm not aware. However, I am donating all my personal profits from having that song on our album to a charity, an environmental group to help protect wildlife and our oceans. In our video for 'Estranged', which will be the last video for the *Use Your Illusion* albums, we used dolphins, and this is my way of giving something back to the dolphin, which are endangered and threatened with extinction.
Unfortunately I Don't Surf Either.

Duff's decision to accompany The Scorpions across Europe had as much to do with keeping himself busy as it did promoting *Believe in Me*. He'd managed to kick his sizeable coke intake during the latter stages of the Use Your Illusion tour, but feared he'd slip back into old habits once his LA-based drug connections got wind he was back in town. Though he'd switched from vodka to red wine, his drinking was totally off the chart and he was soon getting through a case of wine a day simply to keep functioning. Like every other alcoholic in denial, Duff believed he was still in control. He'd only recently turned 30 yet looked nearer to 50; the blank-eyed, booze-bloated face in the mirror barely recognisable from the fresh-faced kid that had left Seattle less than a decade earlier.

When a forthcoming solo tour of Australia was cancelled Duff flew to Seattle where he'd recently purchased a home on Lake Washington. As luck would have it he found himself booked on the same flight as Kurt Cobain. The MTV Awards spat from two years earlier was long forgotten and the two ended up sitting next to each other. Certain subjects were tacitly left off the menu, however – as though each recognised their own private nightmare in the other's haunted stare. Several days later, Duff would receive a call from Doug Goldstein saying Cobain had shot himself at his own lakeside bolthole. The man *Time* Magazine had billed as being the "John Lennon of the Swinging Northwest" was just 27 years old.

Cobain and Courtney Love often signed hotel registers as either "Sid and Nancy" or "Mr and Mrs Beverley" (Sid's mum's married name was Beverley). Duff had also worshipped the doomed Sex Pistol, of course. On May 10, on what would have been Sid's thirty-seventh birthday, Duff woke with indescribable pains coursing through his body and he might well have put a shotgun to his head had there been one close to hand. His already enflamed pancreas had swollen to the point of bursting and he too would have ended up in a Seattle mortuary with a tag on his toe had a childhood friend not fortuitously happened by to say hello.

Duff was given two shots of Demerol en route to the Northwest Hospital and Medical Centre but the synthetic opioid didn't touch the pain. These were followed up with a shot of morphine upon arrival at the hospital, but if anything, the pain was intensifying, which was hardly surprising given that the digestive enzymes leaking from his burst pancreas were dissolving his insides. Immediate surgery to repair the tear was Duff's only hope. But even if the operation proved successful he faced a lifetime of dialysis treatment. His time in hospital was spent on morphine and Librium drips, one to alleviate the pain, the other to ease him along the first steps on the long-winding road to sobriety.

Duff had always believed he would be dead by the time he was 30, having lived fast and leaving a relatively good-looking corpse behind. Yet while the surgery saved him from the dialysis, his life as he'd known it was over. So was his marriage to Linda, but he'd come through one divorce without too many mental scars. With the doctors' warnings that his next drink might well prove his last rattling around his head like so many ice cubes, Duff returned to his lakeside home to ponder his future.

Guns N' Roses were in as fragile a state as their bassist. The band of brothers solidarity had long since fragmented, perhaps irrevocably; the tragedy of it all being Goldstein and the other "yes" men surrounding Axl being largely to blame for the backstabbing duplicity. Axl had called Duff during his stay in the hospital and was also the only band member to visit him in Seattle. They talked long and hard about Guns' disjointed state. The challenge facing the band was to figure out what musical direction they should take on the new studio album.

Although Duff continued talking to Axl on a daily basis about the mooted new GN'R album after the latter had returned to LA, he had rather more immediate concerns – how to while away the endless days without succumbing to temptation. He started going out on his old mountain bike to help stave off the dreaded DTs (Delirium tremens) but soon found he was enjoying testing his endurance. His insides were on fire again, but this time the pain proved invigorating. Upon his return to LA he bought a new mountain bike and registered for a long-distance cross-country bike race in Big Bear – albeit in the "beginners' category".

♫

Slash might not have been privy to Duff and Axl's musings about the musical direction the new Guns album should take, but he'd been busy writing new material since coming off the road. Axl would once again deem Slash's efforts unworthy of a Guns N' Roses record, but rather than risk another argument he instead turned to Geffen to finance his own solo project.

Reflecting on this period with www.musicradar.com in June 2012, Matt spoke of the pressure the band was under to write a new Guns record. "Axl's thing was to outdo the last thing and we'd just done a three-year tour in massive stadiums and done epic videos. Me and Slash wrote a bunch of songs and gave them to Axl and he didn't like them. Those songs turned into Slash's Snakepit."

> ## *"We should have stuck together, it wasn't the time for solo records. You don't see Metallica running around doing solo records."*

"In retrospect that was probably the beginning of the end [for Guns N' Roses]. We should have rallied as a band and figured out how to get the songs better instead of jumping out on our own. In Axl's defence he was probably right. We should have stuck together, it wasn't the time for solo records. You don't see Metallica running around doing solo records. Has Bono or the Edge made a solo record? No."

Aside from Matt, Gilby, Dizzy and Teddy Andreadis were also happy to contribute. Duff's recuperation was going well enough but he wasn't yet ready to start playing again. Instead, Slash called upon Alice in Chains' bassist, Mike Inez, and Jellyfish' frontman Eric Dover before heading into the studio with Mike Clink. *It's 5 O'Clock Somewhere* was released on Valentine's Day 1995, but the love Slash felt for his debut solo offering wouldn't extend much beyond the studio door. Tom Zutaut reportedly went so far as to call the album "abysmal". The album would stall at # 70 on the *Billboard* chart but shifted in excess of one million copies worldwide.

GUNS N' ROSES

When Duff and Slash signed away their respective rights to the Guns N' Roses name in Barcelona the previous July, they had done so because they were both tired of the attendant hassle that came with going against Axl. It wasn't until the band reconvened at The Complex studios to record a version of the Rolling Stones' 'Sympathy for the Devil', which was set to be included on the soundtrack to the film adaptation of Anna Rice's *Interview With The Vampire* starring Tom Cruise and Brad Pitt, that the duo realised their reduced roles within Ayatollah Axl's new fiefdom. Without bothering to consult either of them, Axl had decided not to renew Gilby's contract and instead brought in Paul Tobias to play on the song. Slash was initially "open to the idea" of working with Tobias . . . at least until the latter arrived for the session. "He had no personality whatsoever and no particular guitar style or sound that I could identify with," he said of Tobias. "He was, without a doubt, the least interesting, most bland guy holding a guitar that I'd ever met. I tried working with him but it went nowhere."

Doug Goldstein has since insisted that Axl had been "open" to Slash and Duff bringing in a replacement of their choosing. His version of events has Ozzy Osbourne's preferred axeman of choice, Zakk Wylde, being in the frame to replace Gilby, and that Slash had stubbornly refused to share solos with Wylde or indeed anyone else. He believes that had Slash proved more amenable to what Axl was trying to do then Guns N' Roses could have continued on a forward momentum. Whatever the scenario, Slash felt he'd no option but to take Axl to one side and lay out his objections towards Tobias so that there couldn't be any misunderstanding. Unsurprisingly, his reasoning was brushed aside.

It was Tom Zutaut's idea to have Guns N' Roses cover 'Sympathy for the Devil', his logic being that as the band wouldn't be touring to promote *The Spaghetti Incident?*, covering the Stones' classic for *Interview With The Vampire* would at least keep them in the public eye. Slash was familiar with Anne Rice's books and so came away from a private screening of *Interview With The Vampire* somewhat underwhelmed by director Neil Jordan's interpretation of the 1976 best-selling novel – if only because he couldn't imagine Tom Cruise or Brad Pitt playing the lead roles; his disillusion stretching to calling Cruise and telling him to have the producers license the Stones' original. Conversely, Axl came away from a separate screening having loved the film and insisting they cover the song.

Despite his misgivings about *Interview With The Vampire*, Slash was content to proceed with the project as it got the band working together again – something that had been appearing increasingly unlikely of late. Yet while he, Duff, and Matt all reported for duty, Axl failed to put in a solitary appearance; his wilful disregard for anyone's time but his own resulting in what Slash describes as a "very uninspired" instrumental track. Imagine his astonishment on receiving word from Axl – albeit via a flunky – that he should re-record his guitar part so that it sounded more in keeping with Keith Richards' original.

Slash couldn't see the point in copying Keith's part note for note – especially if they were trying to give 'Sympathy For The Devil' a GN'R twist. When word came back that Axl was refusing to lay down his vocal unless he did as he was told, Slash once again swallowed his pride for the greater good of the band. On listening to a DAT (Digital Audio Tape) of the finished song, Slash was horrified to find Axl had had Tobias double over his solo note-for-note. Slash had bent over backwards to appease Axl, but enough was enough. Washing his hands of the whole thing, he took Slash's Snakepit out on the road. Little wonder then, "Sympathy For The Devil" is the guitarist's least favourite GN'R track - "the sound of a band breaking up" as he succinctly put it.

"As a 30-year-old millionaire, how do I admit to somebody that I don't know what the fuck I'm doing?"

For the first time in years Slash was free to play without constraint, but the fun wasn't set to last. The band were going down a storm in Japan, and he was set to book a tour of Australia when he was summarily ordered to return to LA as Axl had announced he was ready to begin work on the new Guns N' Roses album and so anything he, Duff, or Matt might be doing was of secondary importance. With Geffen having made it clear that they were no longer willing to provide tour support for Slash's Snakepit, he headed home knowing in his heart of hearts there was going to be no new GN'R album.

Duff had recently taken up kick-boxing as part of his new health regime. He'd also enrolled on a basic finance course at Santa Monica Community College so as to get some understanding of the stack of GN'R financial statements that had been gathering dust in his basement. "I couldn't make sense of it," he said in a March 2011 interview with *Fortune* Magazine. "I didn't know how much we had made or lost on the [Use Your Illusion] tour. As a 30-year-old millionaire, how do I admit to somebody that I don't know what the fuck I'm doing?"

While Slash was out on the road with Slash's Snakepit, Duff received a call from Matt (who was now also newly sober) in early March 1995 asking if he was interested in playing rhythm guitar alongside himself and Teddy Andreadis at the opening of the Hardrock Hotel in Las Vegas. Billed as "Wayne Neutron", the ad hoc "house band" performed a set of covers including Jimi Hendrix's 'Manic Depression' and 'Hey Joe' (both with Seal on vocals), Johnny Kidd & the Pirates' 'Shakin' All Over' and Billy Idol's 'Rebel Yell' (with Idol), the Sex Pistols/Professionals' 'Black Leather' (with Steve

Jones), and The Stooges' 'Raw Power' (with Iggy and Jones sharing the vocals). Duran Duran were also performing on the night and following a couple of conversations with John Taylor, the Neurotic Outsiders were born.

The Neurotic Outsiders made their live debut several weeks later at The Viper Room on Sunset Boulevard. The black-fronted club, partly owned by Johnny Depp, had opened to much fanfare two years earlier and was now regarded as the in-place by Hollywood's movers and shakers; its shady allure made all the more appealing following River Phoenix's suffering a fatal drug overdose during the early hours of October 31, 1993. Although the likes of Iggy and Billy Idol could still be teased into getting up for the odd number, the line-up consisted of Duff, Matt, Jones, and Taylor. The star-studded audience were again treated to a set brimming with covers – the Sex Pistols' 'Pretty Vacant', the Stooges' 'No Fun', Roxy Music's 'Virginia Plain', and The Clash's 'Janie Jones'. "The whole thing was totally casual," Duff reflected. "Our live shows were nothing more than punk-rock parties, a couple of dudes playing loads of cover songs – Clash, Pistols, Damned, Stooges – with lots of our friends jumping onstage to join us for a song or two."

Buoyed by favourable reviews, the quartet embarked on a mini-tour of the Eastern Seaboard with shows in New York, Philadelphia, Boston, and Washington D.C; their sets now peppered with original compositions such as 'Nasty Ho', 'Jerk', 'Feelings are Good', and 'Revolution'. The interest in the "supergroup" was such that a bidding war broke out among the major labels, with Madonna's newly incorporated Maverick label (a subsidiary of Warner Bros) proving the winner after tabling a whopping million-dollar advance.

The Neurotic Outsiders consisted of four friends that had each left an indelible mark in music who were content to run with things so long as people continued turning up to watch the game. It was never set to last, however – especially with the reconstituted Sex Pistols about to embark on their Filthy Lucre reunion world tour.

GUNS N' ROSES

It was now 11 years and counting since Guns N' Roses had burst onto the West Hollywood scene and much had changed within the rock world during that time. Grunge was on the wane, having never really recovered from Kurt Cobain's untimely demise, and America's teenage misfits and miscreants were now attuned to the steel-edged industrial rock espoused by Nine Inch Nails, Marilyn Manson and Ministry. These same misfits could be forgiven for only identifying Guns N' Roses from seeing their videos aired on MTV or VH1. Axl dug this, of course. Chasing the zeitgeist was a young man's game and here he was pushing 40. He was still keen to take Guns N' Roses to the next level, however. He was equally anxious that Guns avail themselves of the latest technology and set about ordering in banks of state-of-the-art equipment. He would also hire a full-time computer techie to teach him how to get the biggest bang for his buck.

Entering The Complex and seeing row upon row of synthesisers and an "arsenal of Pro Tools" reminded Slash of working on Michael Jackson's *Dangerous* album. It wasn't that he had any objection to using Pro Tools just so long as everyone was pulling in the same direction. It quickly became obvious to all that Axl was operating to his own agenda, however. Even when Axl did deign to put in an appearance it would be late into the evening and he was only willing to work on certain ideas.

For Slash and Duff it was "shades of Chicago". With the tension in the studio becoming ever more insufferable Slash finally snapped. Rather than risk getting into a situation where he and Axl would end up taking pot shots at each other via the press, he called Doug Goldstein, said he was quitting the band, and put the receiver down before the latter had a chance to respond. Axl, or at least a part of him, would have been hoping Slash would have a rethink. Upon discovering Slash had said how he and Axl were "deliberating over the future of our relationship" during an online interview a few weeks later, he flew into a rage and rushed off the following fax to MTV:

"LIVE!!!! From "Burning Hills", California...

Due to overwhelming enthusiasm, and that "DIVE IN AND FIND THE MONKEY" attitude....
#1. There will NOT be a Guns N' Roses tour.
#2. There will NOT be an official Guns N' Roses web site.
#3. There will NOT be any NEW Guns N' Roses videos.
#4. There will NOT be any new Guns N' Roses involved merchandise (sic).
#5. There will NOT be a Guns N' Roses Fan Club.
#6. There will be a new Guns N' Roses 12-song-minimum recording with three original "B" sides.
NOTE: If all goes well this will be immediately repeated.
#7. However*******Slash will not be involved in any new Guns N' Roses endeavors? (sic) as far has not been musically involved with Guns N' Roses since April 1994 with the exception of a BRIEF feel period with Zakk Wylde and a 2 week initial period with Guns N' Roses in the late fall of '95. He (Slash) has been "OFFICIALLY and LEGALLY" outside of the Guns N' Roses Partnership since December 31, 1995.

GUNS N' ROSES

Speaking about the split on the official GN'R website in 2002, Axl's feelings towards Slash had far from mellowed. "Originally I intended to do more of an *Appetite*-style recording so I opted for what I thought would or should've made the band and especially Slash very happy," he explained. "[But] it seemed to me that anytime we got close to something that would work, it wasn't out of opinion (sic) that Slash would go, 'Hey, it doesn't work', but it was nixed simply because it did work. In other words, 'Whoa, wait a minute. That actually might be successful, we can't do that."

For Duff, the news – official or otherwise – of Slash's departure barely registered. "It wasn't as if Guns was active," he reflected. "He (Slash) left behind an empty studio being paid for by an entity that itself barely existed."

Though not quite ready to call time on Guns himself, Duff knew the day was coming. It was merely a case of when. "The music was going in a direction that was completely indulgent to his friend (Tobias)," he told *Classic Rock* in January 2002. "Another factor is this guy that Axl brought in and told us, 'This is our new guitar player' . . . There was no democracy there. And that's when Slash really started going, 'Fuck this. What, this is his band now? Or something?' It was ridiculous."

Slash's replacement in Guns N' Roses was Robin Finck, a 26-year-old guitar for hire that had played with several low-rent bands in his native Atlanta before coming to the fore as a touring guitarist with Nine Inch Nails. Matt had brought Finck to Axl's attention, believing Finck's style would complement Slash's playing. He was still clinging to the hope that Slash might yet be tempted back. Axl's retort was that Finck would make a "great *replacement*" for Slash. Finck was initially brought in as a hired hand before being offered a two-year contract making him a full member of Guns N' Roses in August 1997.(*For full bio see Gunsology.*)

There was tragic news for everyone with a GN'R connection when West Arkeen was found dead in his apartment towards the end of May 1997. His death was ruled an "accidental opiate overdose", but Duff believes there was more to it as Arkeen's body was "riddled with track marks and fresh bruises". The apartment had also been ransacked, with the thieves – most likely West's drug buddies – making off with all his musical equipment along with the tapes containing demos of all his songs.

Other than Arkeen's funeral, life in Guns N' Roses idled on with nothing of consequence going on. When Axl brazenly announced he was firing Matt, however, Duff knew his own day of reckoning had finally arrived. Ironically, it had been a disparaging remark Tobias made in the studio about having caught Slash's Snakepit performing on the *David Letterman Show* the previous evening that had rubbed Matt up the wrong way. Matt had let rip at Tobias, telling him to shut the fuck up because he "couldn't hold a candle" to Slash. Axl had leapt to Tobias's defence but Matt refused to back down. He told Axl he was smoking crack if he thought the band was still Guns N' Roses without Slash. The argument raged for another 20 minutes or so before Axl casually asked Matt if he was quitting. When Matt replied in the negative, Axl told him he was fired.

Matt strode out of the studio and was halfway to his car when Tobias came charging after him, telling him to come back in and apologise. But Matt's mind was set. He was working with his Maverick labelmates Candlebox at the time and the Seattle-based band were living at his house. On hearing the news, his bemused houseguests told him to expect Axl's call. Matt had had occasional dust-ups with Axl in the past, but this time he knew it was different. Sure enough, a few weeks later a letter from Axl's lawyers landed in his mailbox.

Duff had turned his life around 180-degrees by this juncture. He was married again, about to become a father, and had never been happier. Slash's leaving had cut deeply, but Axl's firing Matt for standing up and saying what had needed saying went beyond the pale.

In his memoir Duff says that having broken the news to his "good friend and business partner" over dinner they'd shaken hands and gone their separate ways. Speaking elsewhere, however, he said he told Axl that Guns N' Roses had become a dictatorship and he was no longer prepared to play under such conditions.

Despite trashing the apartment Clink rented for them, when it came to recording the album the band "were pretty much together".

Slash

GN'R ALBUMS

APPETITE FOR DESTRUCTION

US, Geffen Records, July 21, 1987.
Highest chart position: US No 1; UK No 1

*Welcome to the Jungle / It's So Easy / Nightrain /
Out Ta Get Me / Mr. Brownstone / Paradise City / My
Michelle / Think About You / Sweet / Child O' Mine /
You're Crazy / Anything Goes / Rocket Queen*

As with every other band or solo artist's
debut album, the track-listing on Appetite For
Destruction was Guns N' Roses' early live show
set to vinyl. The majority of the recording was
completed at Rumbo Studios, a 10,000 square-
foot, three-room facility located in Canoga Park
in the San Fernando Valley. Guns had been
signed to Geffen Records some 12 months
before work began on the debut album. One
reason for this was finding the right producer;
someone that could harness the chaotic energy
of a Guns N' Roses live show yet make the
album appeal beyond the band's fanbase.

Having approached the likes of Paul Stanley,
Bob Ezrin, and Nikki Sixx, Tom Zutaut (head of
A&R at Geffen) turned to Baltimore-born Mike
Clink, who at the time was perhaps best known
for his working alongside "soft rock" producer
Ron Nevison at the Record Plant in New York.

Aside from being cheaper to hire than the
more central-based LA studios, Zutaut's
overriding decision to book Guns N' Roses into
Rumbo was to get the band away from Sunset
Strip and its attendant nocturnal delights.
It was also believed that having the band
living under the same roof would prove more
productive. Taking Axl and Co. out of LA proved
far easier than getting LA out of their system,
of course. But after some initial high jinks the
band knuckled down to the work in hand. Clink
would enforce a "no drugs" policy, but as long
as the band's drinking didn't interfere with the
recording he was happy to turn a blind eye.
He'd initially intended recording each of the 12
tracks live and to keep overdubs to an absolute
minimum. Axl's demanding endless retakes
damn near drove him to drink.

Axl's strive for perfection wouldn't be Clink's
only headache during the recording process,
however. Slash had hocked his favourite guitar
to feed his heroin habit and was unhappy with
how his other guitars sounded on the finished
mixes. Alan Niven came to the rescue by taking
Slash guitar shopping before booking time at
Take One Studios so that he could redo his
guitar parts.

Appetite For Destruction opens with 'Welcome
to the Jungle'; the song the band already
regarded as their clarion call to arms. During a
1988 interview with Hit Parader magazine, Axl
explained how he'd penned the lyric in Seattle

GUNS N' ROSES

during the fabled "Hell Tour" of June 1985. Having been raised in a relative backwater such as Lafayette, Indiana, he was striving to differentiate betwixt a city such as Seattle and the sprawling metropolis that was Los Angeles. "[Seattle's] a big city, but at the same time it's still a small city, and the things that you're gonna learn. It seemed a lot more rural up there. I just wrote how LA looked to me. If someone comes to town and they want to find something, they can find whatever they want."

The inspiration behind the song's opening salvo comes from an earlier incident when Axl ran away to New York with an unnamed companion. With money in short supply, the two were bunking down in a fenced-in schoolyard in Queens when a homeless black guy stumbled upon them. "Do you know where you are?" he asked menacingly. "You're in the jungle, baby; you're gonna die . . ."

It was MTV's relenting to pressure from David Geffen and airing the promo video to 'Welcome to the Jungle' that kickstarted the album's slow-burning climb to the top of the Billboard chart and sales of 30 million and counting.

'It's So Easy', which Axl has since referred to as the band's "Ya-ya, hippie song" was one of the first songs Guns N' Roses wrote while living at the Hell House. The band was still eking out a hand-to-mouth existence, but being the most talked about band in West Hollywood made it easier to connive groupies into tending to their every need. The promo video, filmed at The Cathouse, would remain locked away in the vault until the release of the Appetite For Destruction: Locked n' Loaded box set, owing to Axl's insisting Erin Everly mimic certain scenes from Pulp Fiction that involve "the Gimp".

'Nightrain' is Guns N' Roses' paean to the cheap, gut-rot fortified wine that was affordable to bums, hobos, and rock'n'roll bands on the rise. Slash and Izzy came up with the initial riff before Axl and Duff knocked it into its more recognisable shape. When introducing the song at the SDSU Open Air Theatre in San Diego on

September 4, 1987, Axl said from the stage: "I got a tip. If you ain't got no money, and you wanna get fucked up, you find these liquor stores that the winos hit up, you know? And right beside Thunderbird, you'll find a bottle of Nightrain. That'll fuck up you twice as bad as that Thunderbird and it's only a buck and a quarter. If you drink a quart, I don't care how bad you are, you're gonna black out."

'Out Ta Get Me', another of Axl's autobiographical offerings that for a time served as an early GN'R set opener, rails against the Lafayette authorities that had given him such a hard time. But given his charge sheet, it's little wonder the cops were out to cuff his ass. Given its overt references to heroin abuse, 'Mr. Brownstone', is another ditty that would surely have had the morality-mongers at the RIAA (Recording Industry Association of America) petitioning Congress.

'Paradise City', which in old money, brings side one of Appetite For Destruction to a close, is undoubtedly one of the most recognisable songs in the Guns N' Roses canon. Slash first came up with the tell-tale G/C/D/F/C/G riff while he and Steven were ploughing a lone furrow in Road Crew, little imagining that he'd be playing it in packed stadiums about the globe.

Side Two opens with 'My Michelle', arguably the best GN'R song never released as a single. Axl penned the lyric as an homage of sorts to Michelle Young, an old high school acquaintance of Slash and Steven's that had since befriended the band. She and Axl were en route to a concert one evening when Elton John's 'Your Song' came on the radio. Michelle innocently remarked how nice it would be if someone wrote a song about her. Axl needed no further bidding. Instead of penning a saccharine-sweet ode, however, he delivered an honest, true-to-life vignette of Michelle's then troubled, drug-addled existence. "At the time, I didn't care because I was so fucked up," Michelle told Classic Rock in 2005. "But what it says is all true: my dad does distribute porno films and my mom did die [of a drug overdose]."

'Think About You' is probably the only "filler" on an otherwise "thriller". Indeed, the song had been dropped from the band's set-list by the end of 1987 (though it was resurrected in 2001 and regularly featured on the Chinese Democracy Tour). It was originally assumed that Axl wrote the song about Erin Everly. Yet Tracii Guns insists the lyric is about a girl called Monique Lewis, who all the band apparently dated.

> **'Michelle innocently remarked how nice it would be if someone wrote a song about her. Axl needed no further bidding.'**

'Sweet Child O' Mine' was most definitely written about Erin Everly. The song that gave Guns N' Roses their one and only Billboard Hot 100 No. 1 started out as little more than a string-skipping exercise – or "circus riff" – that Slash favoured to limber up his fingers before getting down to more serious fretwork. And that's the way things would have stayed had Izzy not jumped in with some accompanying chords. Aside from being an ode to the then love of his life (and soon-to-be wife), Axl's heartfelt lyric also contains autobiographical references to the mental and physical abuse he suffered at the hands of his stepfather as a child. The accompanying promo video, which was designed to capture the band in a relaxed mood with their girlfriends and anyone else in attendance free to grab up a camera, was filmed at LA's Huntingdon Park Ballroom.

The rather self-explanatory 'You're Crazy' was written soon after Guns signed with Geffen. The song originally started out as a ballad – see GN'R Lies – but would soon be transformed into the souped-up version that appears on Appetite. 'Anything Goes' was the only song Axl and Izzy carried over from Hollywood Rose, when it was better known as 'My Way Your Way'.

'Rocket Queen', the album's rabble-rousing finale, relates to Barbie von Grief, another female LA scenester said to be close to Axl during Guns N' Roses' early days (she's listed in the album's liner notes as Barbie 'Rocket Queen' von Grief). Barbie and her one-time roommate, Pamela Manning, had apparently started a band with the intention of calling themselves Rocket Queen.

'Rocket Queen' has earned a unique place in the pantheon of rock for being the only song to feature a recorded sex act within the mix. Legend has it that Steven's then girlfriend, Adriana Smith, rocked up to the studio looking to pick a fight with Steven. Axl was no fan of Steven's, and on sensing Smith was up for some fun, made his pitch. The engineer miked up the floor of the vocal booth, dimmed the lights, hit the red button and vacated the room leaving Axl and Smith to get on with it. According to Smith, it was a bit awkward, as Axl wanted serious passion, which was hard to deliver under the circumstances. She would later say how the incident had "weighed on her soul", as all she'd gotten out of it was a bottle of Jack Daniel's and a certain degree of infamy.

In 1999, while racking up untold hours of studio time recording Chinese Democracy, Axl had his revolving door of musicians re-record Appetite with a view to releasing it at some future date. Nothing came of the idea, of course, but in 2018 – by which time Axl and Slash had settled their differences and reunited under the GN'R banner - Appetite For Destruction: Locked N' Loaded hit the shops.

GUNS N' ROSES

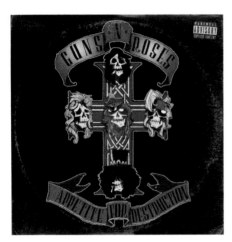

Appetite For Destruction: Locked N' Loaded

Released: June 2018.

Disc One: Appetite For Destruction
Welcome to the Jungle / It's So Easy / Nightrain / Out Ta Get Me / Mr. Brownstone / Paradise City / My Michelle / Think About You / Sweet Child O' Mine / You're Crazy / Anything Goes / Rocket Queen

Disc Two: B-Sides N' EPs
Reckless Life (Live) / Nice Boys (Live) / Move to the City (Live) / Mama Kin (Live) / Shadow of Your Love / You're Crazy (Acoustic version) / Patience / Used to Love Her / You're Crazy / It's So Easy (Live at the Marquee Club London June 1987) / Knockin' on Heaven's Door (Live at the Marquee Club / London June 1987) / Whole Lotta Rosie (Live at the Marquee Club London June 1987)

Disc Three: 1986 Sound City Session
Welcome to the Jungle / Nightrain / Out Ta Get Me / Paradise City / My Michelle / Think / About You / You're Crazy / Anything Goes / Rocket Queen / Shadow of Your Love /Heartbreak Hotel / Jumpin' Jack Flash

Disc Four: 1986 Sound City Session N' More
Shadow of Your Love / Move to the City / Ain't / Goin' Down No More (Instrumental version) / The Plague / Nice Boys / Back off Bitch / Reckless Life / Mama Kin / New Work Tune / November Rain (Piano version) / Move to the City (Acoustic version) / You're Crazy (Acoustic version) / November Rain (Acoustic version) / Jumpin' Jack Flash (Acoustic version) / Move to the City (1988 Acoustic version)

Disc Five (Blu-ray)
Welcome to the Jungle / It's So Easy / Nightrain / Out Ta Get Me / Mr. Brownstone / Paradise City / My Michelle / Think About You / Sweet / Child O' Mine / You're Crazy / Anything Goes / Rocket Queen / Shadow of Your Love / Patience / Used to Love Her / You're Crazy / Move to the City (1988 Acoustic version) / Welcome to the Jungle (Promo video) / Sweet Child O' Mine (Promo video / Paradise City (Promo video) / Patience (Promo video) / It's So Easy (Promo video) (Previously unreleased)

GN'R Lies

US, Geffen Records, November 29, 1988.
Highest Chart Position: US No 5; UK No 1

Reckless Life / Nice Boys / Move to the City / Mama Kin / Patience / Used to Love Her / You're Crazy / One in a Million

Though officially an EP, GN'R Lies was generally regarded as an album at the time of its release. Appetite For Destruction was still riding high in many charts around the world, but Geffen were keen to keep Guns in the public eye while the band was in the studio working up song ideas for the follow-up studio album. As well as the four tracks making up the much sought after Live?!*@ Like a Suicide EP, and the acoustic version of 'You're Crazy', Lies features three brand new acoustic numbers penned by the band in a single afternoon at Rumbo Studios ("One of those magical rock'n'roll history moments," as Mike Clink would later recall).

There are two schools of thought surrounding the lyric to 'Patience'. One is that it's yet another of Axl's outpourings about his strained relationship with Erin Everly, while the other is that it's Izzy's ode to his ex-girlfriend Angela Nicoletti (who would subsequently marry Hanoi Rocks' Andy McCoy).

'Patience' was released as a single and scored Guns a Top 10 hit both in the US and the UK. The promo video, one of several GN'R videos directed by Nigel Dick, was filmed on Valentine's Day 1988 at the recently closed Ambassador Hotel (the scene of Robert Kennedy's slaying in June 1968), with other scenes shot at the Record Plant. Though Steven Adler appears in the video he doesn't play on the recorded track.

'Used to Love Her' was a playful ditty that would come back to haunt the band some 15 years on when it was cited as evidence in the Florida vs. Justin Barber murder trial. The prosecuting counsel suggested it was Barber's listening to 'Used to Love Her' (the track was found among deleted files on the hard drive of the finance lawyer's computer) to commit uxoricide (the slaying of one's wife). Barber was ultimately found guilty and sentenced to life imprisonment. The publicity surrounding 'Used to Love Her' being used as evidence in a murder trial pales into insignificance compared to the bruhaha surrounding the album's final track, however.

'One in a Million' was surely another let's-get-out-the-acoustics-and-have-a-fuck-about throwaway that would most likely have soon been discarded had Geffen not pressed the band for new product. The band did actually play 'One in a Million' live during an acoustic performance at the CBGBs Record Canteen in New York in October 1987. But with *Appetite* still struggling in the lower reaches of the *Billboard* chart at the time, the show attracted no media coverage to speak of.

John Lennon had written 'Woman is the Nigger of the World', but ex-Beatles could pretty much get away with anything – especially in the early Seventies. In response to accusations of homophobia, Axl initially stated that he was "pro-heterosexual" and that he wasn't against homosexuals "as long as it's not hurting anybody else and they're not forcing it upon me." He subsequently softened his stance by pointing out that several of his musical icons, such as Freddie Mercury and Elton John – not to mention Geffen head, David Geffen – were either bisexual or gay.

> ## "This song is very simple and extremely generic or generalized, my apologies to those who may take offense."

Both Duff and Slash would try persuading Axl to drop 'One in a Million' from *Lies*. Duff's brother was married to a black woman, while Slash was himself half black. Speaking with *Rolling Stone* in February 1991, Slash said he hadn't thought it very cool when Axl first played him the song. He then went on to add that while he didn't regret recording 'One in a Million', he regretted what the band subsequently went through because of "the way people have perceived our personal feelings".

Geffen must have anticipated a backlash over 'One in a Million' as the cover of the *GN'R Lies*, which was designed as a mock-tabloid newspaper front page, contains an advance apology on Axl's behalf: "This song is very simple and extremely generic or generalized, my apologies to those who may take offense."

GUNS N' ROSES

Use Your Illusion I

US, Geffen Records, September 17, 1991.
Highest chart position: US No 1; UK No 1

Right Next Door to Hell / Dust N' Bones / Live and Let Die / Don't Cry (Original) / Perfect Crime / You Ain't the First / Bad Obsession / Back Off Bitch / Double Talkin' Jive / November Rain / The Garden / Garden of Eden / Don't Damn Me / Bad Apples / Dead Horse Coma

Use Your Illusion II

US, Geffen Records, September 17, 1991.
Highest Chart Position: US No 1; UK No 1

Civil War / 14 Years / Yesterdays / Knockin' on Heaven's Door / Get in the Ring / Shotgun Blues Breakdown / Pretty Tied Up / Locomotive / So Fine / Estranged / You Could Be Mine / Don't Cry

(Alt. Lyrics) / My World

Appetite for Destruction and *GN'R Lies* selling in excess of 15 million albums worldwide had propelled Guns into rock's elite pantheon by the time the band knuckled down to writing new material for what would become the *Use Your Illusion* double albums. Even getting the band in the same room together would prove problematic as the royalties pouring in from the sales of *Appetite* and *Lies* – and their attendant singles – meant they'd long-since abandoned the Hell House in favour of Hollywood Hills condos. Steven had initially been involved in the song-writing process but by the time it came to recording the albums his spiralling drug problems had forced the band to dispense with his services. His replacement, The Cult's Matt Sorum, would have just three weeks or so to familiarise himself with some 30 songs.

Rumours were rife around the time of Steven's departure that Guns N' Roses were on the point of splitting up. For a band that prided itself on its live shows – with the exception of the odd awards ceremony or guest appearance – between December 1988 and January 1991 they played just four live dates (all four coming with supporting the Rolling Stones at the LA Memorial Coliseum in October 1989).

It was also reported that the delay betwixt *Appetite* and the *UYI* albums was due to the band suffering from collective writer's block. This wasn't strictly true, however, as they already had the bare bones of several new songs: 'You Could Be Mine' (which was carried over from the *Appetite* recording sessions), 'Civil War', 'Estranged', 'Pretty Tied Up', 'Dust N' Bones', and 'November Rain'. While Guns N' Roses' trademark aggressive hard-rock style was still in evidence on songs such as

'Right Next Door to Hell', 'Perfect Crime', and 'Back Off Bitch', the *Use Your Illusion* albums would see the band demonstrate their musicality – especially with Axl's piano-led power ballads.

In order to get the creative juices flowing, the band decided to convene in Chicago. Things didn't quite go according to script, of course. Axl elected to make the 2000-mile journey by car, and by the time he finally showed up Slash, Duff, and Steven had been partying hard for so long they were past caring. Izzy, suspecting nothing was likely to get done amid the coke-fuelled chaos, lit out of Chicago again without bothering to say hello.

With Steven having been shown the door and Slash and Izzy having kicked their respective habits into touch, Guns were firing on all cylinders on reconvening much closer to home at A&M Studios in West Hollywood at the end of September 1990. Mike Clink's itinerary had called for the sessions to begin at noon but as with most rock musicians Guns N' Roses lived a vampire-like existence, preferring to operate during the hours of darkness.

The suits at Geffen were delighted with Guns' prolific output at A&M but were rather less enthused at Axl's insistence that all the recorded material be released simultaneously. Several alternate permutations were put forward, but Axl argued the songs represented a particular period in Guns N' Roses' history and might well lose all relevance and meaning if they were released piecemeal.

Use Your Illusion I is generally considered to be the angry "ying" to its sister album's bluesier "yang". The discussion still rages on GN'R web forums as to the merits of a truncated single *UYI* album, with fans arguing over which songs should be included. (The author, while appreciating the band's work ethic, happens to be in agreement that a single *UYI* album would today be regarded as a contender for "Greatest Rock Album of All

Time". His choices: 'Civil War'/'Yesterdays'/ '14 Years'/ 'Right Next Door to Hell'/ 'You Could Be Mine' / 'Don't Cry' / 'Breakdown' / 'November Rain' / 'Knockin' on Heaven's Door' / 'Live and Let Die'/ 'Estranged'/ 'The Garden').

In August 1998, Geffen would issue a single album version of *Use Your Illusion*. This, however, was a US-only release and was primarily sold at Walmart and Kmart – the two major retail outlets that had refused to stock the original *UYI* albums due to explicit lyrics.

Geffen's primary concern was getting the albums into the record stores before Guns N' Roses hit the road in support of the albums. Realising the project was woefully behind schedule, Bill Price (best known for his work on the Sex Pistols' *Never Mind the Bollocks* and The Clash's *London Calling*) was brought in to work alongside Clink. Tom Zutaut had originally wanted the band to record *Appetite* in London with Price. Negotiations were said to have been well under way before David Geffen's insistence the album be recorded in LA put the kybosh on things, as Price had other long-standing commitments.

Despite their love of both the Sex Pistols and The Clash, Guns N' Roses were unsure as to whether Price was the man for the job. To prove his worth, Price selected 'Right Next Door to Hell' and set about making a heavily compressed mix of the upfront-in-your-face rocker's backing track before then adding Axl's screeching vocal. Both Guns and Geffen were delighted with the results and Price returned to London to pack a larger suitcase.

With ongoing support from Clink and in-house engineer Jim Mitchell, Price began beavering his way through the 20 tracks already down on tape. Guns N' Roses were midway through the first US leg of the mammoth Use Your Illusion Tour, so Clink booked studio time in whatever city the band happened to be in to work on the remaining tracks. These were then duly Fed-Exed to Price back in LA.

GUNS N' ROSES

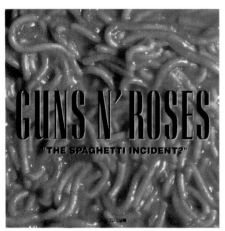

The Spaghetti Incident?

US, Geffen Records, November 23, 1993.
Highest chart position: US No 4; UK No 2

Since I Don't Have You / New Rose / Down on the Farm / Human Being / Raw Power / Ain't It Fun / Buick Makane (Big Dumb Sex) / Hair of the Dog / Attitude / Black Leather / You Can't Put Your Arms Around A Memory / I Don't Care About You / Look at Your Game, Girl

The unwritten rule regarding cover versions is that the band or solo artist strives to make the song their own – and if possible, improve on the original. Guns N' Roses undoubtedly ticked both boxes with their versions of Wings' 'Live and Let Die' and Dylan's 'Knockin' on Heaven's Door' that appear on *UYI I* and *UYI II* respectively. The same, alas, can't be said of the majority of the offerings on *The Spaghetti Incident?*. While the deliberations on how to package the *UYI* albums were ongoing, someone at Geffen mooted the idea of including an EP of covers. (By the time the idea was expanded to a full album consisting entirely of songs, Izzy had long-since quit the band and been replaced by Gilby Clarke.)

Guns N' Roses were now not only the "most dangerous band on the planet", they were also arguably the biggest (or at least worthy of toppling the Stones from their perch). During the two-and-a-half years Guns N' Roses were criss-crossing the globe promoting the *UYI* albums there'd been a seismic shift on the rock scene. Grunge was what was happening now, with Nirvana receiving the kudos Guns had once enjoyed.

Nirvana were signed to Geffen subsidiary DGC Records (David Geffen Company). The Seattle-based trio's third album, *In Utero*, would debut at # 1 on the *Billboard* chart following its September 1993 release. Guns N' Roses didn't have to prove anything to anybody, of course, but repeating the phenomenal success of *Appetite*, *Lies*, and the *UYI* albums was always going to be a tall order. Maybe an impossible one. Instead of allowing the band to recharge their batteries before heading into the studio to work on whatever song ideas they might have come up with while out on the road, however, Geffen allowed greed to get the better of them as releasing what was little more than a third-rate punk/glam karaoke album was utter folly.

The album's opening track, 'Since I Don't Have You', was originally a 1958 *Billboard* hit for Pittsburgh doo-woppers The Skyliners. Subsequently it was recorded by a plethora of artists including the Four Seasons, Manfred Mann, Barbara Streisand, and Don McLean.

The Damned's 1976 classic, 'New Rose' needs no introduction but was nonetheless a strange choice for a Guns N' Roses makeover – even the band must have known they were on a hiding to nothing in trying to improve on the original. (Though Duff gives his all on vocals.) The UK Subs' 'Down on the Farm' is another mediocre offering – one made even more execrable by Axl adopting a risible Dick Van Dyke "Mockney Poppins" accent. It's perplexing enough trying to reason why Guns N' Roses would think to cover a UK Subs song, let alone one of their more obscure numbers (from the band's 1982 *Endangered*

Species). With Duff being a massive New York Dolls/Johnny Thunders fan, it was perhaps inevitable that both would feature – the Dolls' 'Human Being' (from their second and final album, *Too Much Too Soon*), and Thunders' 'You Can't Put Your Arms Around a Memory' (from the latter's 1978 debut solo, *So Alone* – again sung by Duff). Stiv Bators, another punk fatality, is commemorated with the Dead Boys' 'Ain't It Fun', from the New York quartet's 1978 album, *We Have Come for Your Children,* and features Hanoi Rocks' Michael Monroe sharing vocal duties with Axl. (During the *Spaghetti* sessions, Guns recorded an instrumental version of Hanoi Rocks' 'Beer and a Cigarette'. The vocals were not recorded, however, as Guns were reportedly loath to allow Andy McCoy to earn royalties.)

'Buick Makane' from T-Rex's 1972 *Slider* album (original spelling 'Buick McCane') which segues into Soundgarden's 'Big Dumb Sex', and Nazareth's 'Hair of the Dog' (the title track from the Scottish rockers' 1975 album) were both chosen by Slash. Duff's punk rock roots again come to the fore with The Misfits' 'Attitude', while Guns' version of 'Raw Power', the title track from The Stooges' 1973 album of the same name, is probably the standout highlight on the album.

No punk/glam tribute album could be complete without a Sex Pistols track. Rather than copy Megadeth in covering one of the Pistols' classics, Guns instead opted for 'Black Leather'. Steve Jones and Paul Cook penned 'Black Leather' for the soundtrack to *The Great Rock 'N' Roll Swindle* but it has since come to be viewed as a song by The Professionals (Jones' and Cook's first post-Pistols project). Soon after *The Spaghetti Incident?*'s release, Slash bumped into Jones at a mutual friend's wedding. Jones was naturally curious as to whether Guns' version was better than The Runaways' 1978 offering (from the album *And Now . . . The Runaways*). Imagine the ex-Pistol's bemusement on being informed by Slash that in his opinion Guns' version was better than the original.

According to the official track-listing, Fear's 'I Don't Care About You' (from the LA punksters' 1982 debut album, *The Record*) brings *The Spaghetti Incident?* to a close. There is a hidden track, however: Charles Manson's 'Look at Your Game, Girl', from the cult leader's 1970 album, *Lie: The Love and Terror Cult.*

Axl's sporting a T-shirt bearing Manson's image onstage was one thing but recording one of his songs brought another publicity backlash. Axl would shamefacedly offer to make amends by donating royalties from the song to the son of one of the Manson Family's victims.

Chinese Democracy

US, Geffen Records, November 23, 2008. Highest chart position: US No 4; UK No 2

Chinese Democracy / Shackler's Revenge / Better / Street of Dreams / If the World / There Was a Time / Catcher in the Rye / Scraped / Riad N' the Bedouins / Sorry / I.R.S. / Madagascar / This I Love / Prostitute

With the possible exception of Axl W. Rose, there was no way *Chinese Democracy* was ever going to live up to expectations. Indeed, again with the possible exception of Axl, everybody else with a vested interest in the

 129

GUNS N' ROSES

album had all but given up the ghost of seeing it go to press. In essence, *Chinese Democracy* had long-since come to be regarded as a white elephant dutifully trailing behind Axl from studio to studio as he burned his way through an estimated $13 million, little caring who picked up the tab.

Guns N' Roses had gotten together to trade ideas for potential new songs in the summer of 1994, but Duff's recollections have everyone "so stoned at that point that nothing got finished". When reflecting on that period in the band's turbulent history, Axl said that Guns N' Roses needed the "collaboration of the band as a whole to write the best songs," and that it was certain members not giving their all that led to the new material being scrapped. The truth probably sits somewhere in between, of course.

Duff and Slash had each written an album's worth of hard rockin' songs while out on the Use Your Illusion Tour, but Axl had rejected them out of hand – the material being deemed unworthy of a Guns N' Roses album. The *UYI* albums had taken Guns to another level in terms of musical dexterity, so to go back to their roots was anathema to Axl. To his way of thinking, this was a field well furrowed and he'd no intention of hitching up the plough. He wanted to deliver the best possible album – a "masterpiece" that would surpass the *UYI* albums. Axl's determination is to be applauded as every artist should strive to better themselves. It was just unfortunate his obduracy had now reached the point where no one – not even Slash or Duff – could make themselves heard. It could, of course, be argued that *Chinese Democracy* is an Axl Rose solo album in all but name.

Axl's "masterpiece" was met with generally positive reviews when it finally emerged into daylight in November 2008. While it has several decent tracks, however, the album as a whole is somewhat underwhelming.

It's not so much the absence of Slash's fretwork or Duff's melodic basslines that consigns *Chinese Democracy* to mediocrity, but rather Axl's blinkered obsession in tinkering with every song until their original promise was buried beneath layer upon layer of superfluous gloop. *Blender* magazine's Jon Dolan hit the nail firmly on the head in opining: "These aren't songs, they're suites, energetic and skittering and unpredictable hard rock hydras cut with miasmic industrial grind, stadium rattling metal solos, electronic drift and hip-hop churn."

Of the 14 songs on *Chinese Democracy*, 'Street of Dreams', a lilting, piano-led quasi-ballad is easily the stand-out track, while 'Better', 'Madagascar', 'There Was a Time' and 'Chinese Democracy' show hints of how great the album might have been had there been anyone within hearing range with the wherewithal to tell Axl to step away from the console.

There's also no escaping that listening to *Chinese Democracy* leaves one feeling the album is somewhat bloated. There's only 14 songs, yet the album's running time stretches to 71 minutes – at least ten minutes of which – 'Sorry' and 'I.R.S', for example – perhaps should have been exorcised during the editing. The album is also heavily front-loaded, which unfortunately makes listening to the record in its entirety more of a chore.

Perhaps *Chinese Democracy*'s biggest failing – and the irony certainly isn't lost here – is that despite the album taking some 14 years to bring to fruition it still feels rushed in places – as though Axl finally reached the point where he feared for his sanity.

COMPILATIONS

Live Era '87-'93

US, Geffen Records, November 23, 1999.
Highest chart position: UK No 45; US No 45

Disc One:
Nightrain / Mr. Brownstone / It's So Easy / Welcome to the Jungle / Dust N' Bones / My Michelle / You're Crazy / Used to Love Her / Patience / It's Alright / November Rain

Disc Two:
Out Ta Get Me / Pretty Tied Up / Yesterdays / Move to the City / You Could Be Mine / Rocket Queen / Sweet Child O' Mine / Knockin' on Heaven's Door / Don't Cry / Estranged / Paradise City / Coma

Live Era '87 – '93 was the first official Guns N' Roses official release since The Spaghetti Incident? – which was coincidentally released on the same day back in 1993. The album would be certified gold by the RIAA for sales in excess of 500,000 (and at the time of writing has sold 2,730,000 copies worldwide). Live Era was intended as a testament to Guns' 'classic line-ups' onstage

heyday, which although only six years on, already seemed like a sepia-toned memory. With the exception of Dizzy Reed, Axl was no longer conversing with his one-time brothers-in-arms; his only interaction with Slash and Duff on Live Era coming via lawyers and other intermediaries. The insouciance surrounding the project would prove all-encompassing, alas, as the packaging – though primarily made up of the band's in-house early fliers - possessed little information as to where the 22 tracks originated. It was only some time later that the dates and venues were made available. As anticipated, the tracks are lifted from the Use Your Illusion Tour; the set-lists of which tended to include the majority of Appetite for Destruction. Indeed, only eight of the 22 tracks come from the UYI albums. Another surprise is the decision to include a cover of Black Sabbath's obscure "It's Alright", yet omit "Civil War" and "Live and Let Die"? Go figure.

The underlying tragedy here, of course, is Geffen's underlying motive for releasing Live Era '87 – '93 was simply as an easy means to offset the spiralling costs Axl was running up with Chinese Democracy. But with Axl and Slash having kissed and made up, there's every chance we might see a live album that captures vintage Guns N' Roses in all their Jack Daniel's and kerosene-soaked majesty when every show - at least according to the tagline on one of the band's early fliers reproduced in Live Era '87 – '93's accompanying booklet - was "A Rock N Roll Bash Where Everyone's Smashed".

GUNS N' ROSES

Greatest Hits

US, Geffen Records, March 23, 2004.
Highest chart position: UK No 1; US No 3

Welcome to the Jungle / Sweet Child O' Mine / Patience / Paradise City / Knockin' on Heaven's Door / Civil War / You Could Be Mine / Don't Cry (Original) / November Rain / Live and Let Die / Yesterdays / Ain't It Fun / Since I Don't Have You / Sympathy for the Devil

Whereas *Live Era '87-'93* had only really appealed to die-hard GN'R fans, the unimaginatively titled *Greatest Hits* proved the band's mainstream popularity remained as strong as ever. Indeed, despite a total lack of promotion, *Greatest Hits* sold in excess of three million copies worldwide within a month of going on sale. It's since gone on to sell over six million copies in the US and is one of the longest charting albums in the *Billboard* 200 era – being one of only seven albums to accrue 400 weeks on the chart. At the time of writing, *Greatest Hits* has sold 13,610,000 copies worldwide. None too shabby by anyone's standards.

The release was to prove a double-edged sword for Axl as well as Slash and Duff. With the warring parties going so far as to consider taking legal action over Interscope's decision to release a Guns N' Roses greatest hits package. Their reasons for doing so weren't too dissimilar, either.

Slash and Duff were putting the finishing touches to Velvet Revolver's debut album, *Contraband*, and didn't want the greatest hits release to steal their thunder – even if 'It's So Easy', 'Mr. Brownstone' and 'Used to Love Her' regularly featured in Velvet Revolver's sets. Axl, of course, was desperate to distance the new look Guns N' Roses from the band of old – even if the set-lists had changed little in the intervening years.

Axl's de facto manager, Merck Mercuriadis, was able to use his not-inconsiderable influence to cajole Interscope into holding back on the greatest hits package – but only on giving his iron-clad guarantee that *Chinese Democracy* would be completed and in the shops in time for the all-important Christmas market. Whether Axl made such assurances to Mercuriadis beforehand is up for conjecture, but the 2003 Holiday season came and went with *Chinese Democracy* still withering away on the festive bough.

'Despite a total lack of promotion, Greatest Hits sold in excess of three million copies worldwide within a month of going on sale.'

For Jimmy Iovine, Interscope's new CEO, this was to prove the final straw. Not only was the greatest hits album given the green light, but Interscope issued a letter via Mercuriadis Sanctuary Music Group (dated February 2, 2004) informing Axl that as *Chinese Democracy* had "exceeded all budgeted and approved recording costs by millions of dollars", it was now his obligation to fund the completion of the album rather than the label's.

Without going so far as to communicate with Axl, Slash and Duff went to some lengths assisting their one-time frontman in pressing on with the lawsuit to halt the album. The trio's combined efforts were to be in vain, however, as the suit was thrown out of court and the release of *Greatest Hits* proceeded as scheduled.

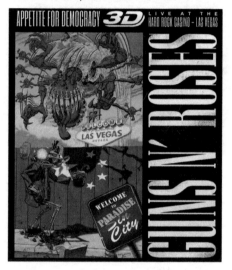

Appetite For Democracy 3D

US, Interscope/Universal, July 1, 2014.
Highest chart position: UK No 1; US No 3

Chinese Democracy / Welcome to the Jungle / It's So Easy / Mr. Brownstone / Estranged / Rocket Queen / Live and Let Die / This I Love / Better / Motivation / Catcher in the Rye / Street of Dreams / You Could Be Mine / Sweet Child O' Mine / Another Brick in the Wall Part 2 / November Rain / Objectify / Don't Cry / Civil War / The Seeker / Knockin' on Heaven's Door / Nightrain / Used to Love Her / Patience / Paradise City

If there's a common theme running through Guns N' Roses' timeline following on from Slash and Duff's respective departures, it's Axl's total lack of concern about keeping the fans waiting. If one excludes 'Oh My God' (from the *End of Days* soundtrack) some 17 years would pass before the release of original recordings. It also beggars belief that

Appetite For Democracy 3D was Guns' first live concert film since the *Use Your Illusion World Tour* videos since December 1992. When Guns N' Roses first exploded onto the West Hollywood scene in 1985 no one would have imagined the "most dangerous band in the world" one day playing the Vegas cabaret circuit taking to the stage with laser lighting, flash pots, and a bevy of scantily clad beauties performing either high-wire routines or pirouetting around stripper poles. Axl, of course, is the only survivor from Guns' hedonistic heyday, but Dizzy Reed has managed to stick around since the Use Your Illusion Tour.

As the title suggests, *Appetite for Democracy 3D* features an array of GN'R songs lifted from *Appetite For Destruction* and *Chinese Democracy* and can be viewed in 3D should this format take the viewer's fancy. The performance clocks in at over two-and-a-half hours and features all the classic songs one would expect to hear at a Guns N' Roses show. What is surprising is that 'Chinese Democracy' is preferred to 'Welcome to the Jungle' as a show-opener. Though 'Jungle' is next up, the spleen-venting vitriol that made the song so memorable has been replaced by a slick, workmanlike performance that sounds pretty much as though it's being played by . . . well, by a Las Vegas cabaret act. Axl's voice also strains to capture the *Appetite*-era venom, but this is perhaps to be expected from a guy in his fifties.

There are also a smattering of surprises thrown in, such as covers of Pink Floyd's 'Another Brick in the Wall, Part 2', and The Who's 'The Seeker'. Tommy Stinson leads the band – sans Axl – through 'Motivation', a Stooges-esque rocker from his 2004 solo album *Village Gorilla Head*, while Ron "Bumblefoot" Thal takes centre stage playing 'Objectify' from his eighth solo offering. Another highlight that isn't given the set-list credit it so richly deserves is a Reed piano solo that morphs into Led Zeppelin's 'No Quarter'.

GUNS N' ROSES

Axl is also no slouch on the ivories, of course, and no GN'R show would be complete without him crooning 'November Rain' – even if he's playing piano aboard a circular rig, which is suspended from the ceiling by cables and allows him to float out over the audience. The show-closing 'Paradise City' transcends into a free-for-all ten-minute jam replete with enormous confetti explosions and a frenetic light show.

Appetite For Democracy 3D undoubtedly has its critics, yet nonetheless scooped the award for Best 3D Music Entertainment Feature at the sixth annual International 3D & Advanced Imaging Society Awards in January 2015. It would also pip Elton John's *The Million Dollar Piano* to the top spot on the Music DVD chart.

SINGLES, EP'S & VIDEOS

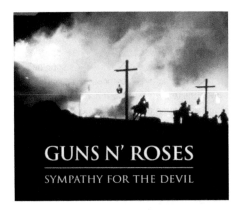

GUNS N' ROSES
SYMPATHY FOR THE DEVIL

'Sympathy for the Devil' / 'Escape to Paris' (by Elliot Goldenthal)

US, Geffen Records, December 13, 1994.
Highest chart position: UK No 9; US No 10

Promo singles

'Mr. Brownstone' (1988) (UK only)
'My Michelle' (1989)
'14 Years' (1991)
'Pretty Tied Up' (1992)
'So Fine' (1992)
'Dead Horse' (1993)
'Garden of Eden' (1993)
'Hair of the Dog' (1993)
'New Rose' (1993)
'Oh My God' (*End of Days* soundtrack) (1999)
'Better' (2008)
'Street of Dreams' (2009)
'Welcome to the Jungle' (1986 Sound City Session) (2018)
'Move to the City' (1988 Acoustic version) (2018)
'November Rain' (Piano version) (1986 Sound City Session) (2018)

EPs

1986
Live ?!@ Like a Suicide* (10,000 copies only)
Track-listing: Reckless Life/Nice Boys/Move to the City/Mama Kin

1988
Guns N' Roses (Live from the Jungle) (Japan only)
Track-listing: It's So Easy/Shadow of Your Love/ Move to the City/Knockin' on Heaven's Door/ Whole Lotta Rosie/Sweet Child O' Mine/

1993
The Civil War EP (GFSTD 43)
Track-listing: Civil War (Album version)/Garden of Eden (Album version)/Dead Horse (Album version)
Exclusive Interview with Slash
German version (GED 21810)
Track-listing: Civil War (Album version)/Garden of Eden (Album version)/Exclusive Interview with Slash
Japanese version (GEFDM-21794)
Track-listing: Civil War (LP version)/Don't Damn Me (Album version)/Back Off Bitch (Album version)/Exclusive Interview with Slash

Video albums

1992
Use Your Illusion World Tour - 1992 in Tokyo I
Track-listing: Introduction: "Tokyo! Banzai motherfuckers! From Hollywood . . . Guns N' Roses!/Nightrain/Mr. Brownstone/Live and Let Die/It's So Easy/Bad Obsession/Attitude/ Pretty Tied Up/Welcome to the Jungle/Don't Cry (Original)/Double Talkin' Jive/Civil War/Wild Horses/Patience/November Rain/Use Your Illusion World Tour - 1992 in Tokyo II
Track-listing: Introduction/You Could Be Mine/ Drum Solo & Guitar Solo/Theme from The Godfather/Sweet Child O' Mine/So Fine/Rocket Queen (w/ It Tastes Good, Don't It?)/Move to the City/Knockin' on Heaven's Door/Estranged/ Paradise City

1993
Don't Cry – Makin' F@*!ing Videos Part I
Track-listing: Don't Cry (Original)/Don't Cry (Alt. lyrics)/Don't Cry (Demo - 1985 Mystic Studio Sessions)
November Rain – Makin' F@*!ing Videos Part II
Track-listing: November Rain

1994
The Making of Estranged – Part IV of the Trilogy!!!
Track-listing: Estranged

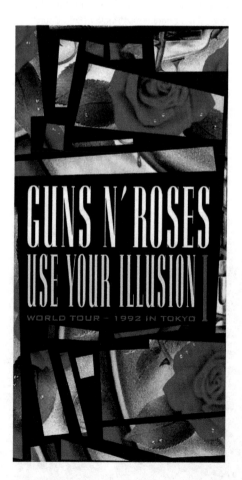

 135

GUNS N' ROSES

W. AXL ROSE

2004

Hollywood Rose: The Roots of Guns N' Roses
Track-listing: Killing Time (Original demo
version)/Anything Goes (Original demo version)/
Rocker (Original demo version)/Shadow of
Your Love (Original demo version)/Reckless
Life (Original demo version)/Killing Time (Gilby
Clarke remix)/Anything Goes (Gilby Clarke remix)/
Rocker (Gilby Clarke remix)/Shadow of Your Love
(Gilby Clarke remix)/Reckless Life (Gilby Clarke
remix)/Killing Time (Fred Coury remix)/Anything
Goes (Fred Coury remix)/Rocker (Fred Coury
remix)/Shadow of Your Love (Fred Coury remix)/
Reckless Life (Fred Coury remix)

2015

Radpidfire – Ready to Rumble EP
Track-listing: Ready To Rumble/All Night Long/
Prowler/On The Run/Closure

Guest appearances

*The Decline of Western Civilization Part II:
The Metal Years* – Original Motion Picture
Soundtrack by various artists ('Under My
Wheels' ft. Alice Cooper, Slash and Izzy Stradlin)
(1988)
The End of the Innocence – Don Henley ('I Will
Not Go Quietly') (1989)
Fire and Gasoline – Steve Jones ('I Did U No
Wrong') (1989)
Pawnshop Guitars – Gilby Clarke ('Dead
Flowers') (1994)
Anxious Disease – The Outpatience ('Anxious
Disease' ft. Slash) (1996)
Angel Down – Sebastian Bach ('Back in the
Saddle', '(Love Is) a Bitchslap', 'Stuck Inside')
(2007)

SLASH

Slash's Snakepit

It's 5 O'Clock Somewhere (1995)
Track-listing: Neither Can I/Dime Store Rock/
Beggars & Hangers-On/Good to Be Alive/What
Do You Want to Be/Monkey Chow/Soma City
Ward/Jizz da Pit/Lower/Take It Away/Doin' Fine/
Be the Ball/I Hate Everybody (But You)/Back and
Forth Again

Ain't Life Grand (2000)

Track-listing: Been There Lately/Just Like
Anything/Shine/Mean Bone/Back to the
Moment/Life's Sweet Drug/Serial Killer/The
Truth/Landslide/Ain't Life Grand/Speed Parade/
The Alien
(Japanese edition)
Bonus tracks: Rusted Heroes/Something About
Your Love

Velvet Revolver

Contraband (2004)
Track-listing: Sucker Train Blues/Do It for the
Kids/Big Machine/Illegal i Song/Spectacle/Fall to
Pieces/Headspace/Superhuman/Set Me Free/
You Got No Right/Slither/Dirty Little Thing/Loving

Singles from Contraband:

'Set Me Free' (Promo) (2003)
'Slither'/'Negative Creep' (2004) (3-track edition
also included live version of 'Bodies')
'Fall to Pieces'/'Surrender' (2004)
'Dirty Little Thing' (Promo) (2005)

'Come On, Come In' (Fantastic Four: The Album) (2005)

Libertad (2007)

Track-listing: Let It Roll/She Mine/Get Out the
Door/She Builds Quick Machines/The Last Fight/
Pills, Demons & Etc./American Man/Mary Mary/
Just Sixteen/Can't Get It Out of My Head/For
a Brother/Spay/Gravedancer (contains hidden
track Don't Drop That Dime from 4:40)
(Japanese edition)
Bonus track: Gas & a Dollar Laugh (contains
hidden track Don't Drop That Dime from 3:20)
Bonus feature: Re-Evolution: Making of Libertad
(making-of video)

Singles from Libertad:

'She Builds Quick Machines' (2007)
'The Last Fight' (2007)
'Get Out the Door' (2008)

Slash featuring Myles Kennedy & The Conspirators

Slash (2010)

Track-listing: Ghost/Crucify the Dead/Beautiful
Dangerous/Back from Cali/Promise/By the
Sword/Gotten/Doctor Alibi/Watch This*/I Hold
On/Nothing to Say**/Starlight/Saint Is a Sinner
Too/We're All Gonna Die
* Different countries list the track title as Watch This Dave.
** Nothing to Say and Chains and Shackles are
versions of the same song with alternate lyrics
and production.
(Japanese edition)
Bonus track: Sahara

Singles from Slash:

'Sahara' (2010)
'By the Sword' (2010)
'Ghost' (2010)
'Back from Cali' (2010)
'Beautiful Dangerous' (2010)
'Starlight' (2011)
'Gotten' (2012)

 137

GUNS N' ROSES

Apocalyptic Love (2012)
Track-listing: Apocalyptic Love/One Last Thrill/
Standing in the Sun/You're a Lie/No More Heroes/
Halo/We Will Roam/Anastasia/Not for Me/Bad
Rain/Hard & Fast/Far and Away/Shots Fired

Deluxe Edition
Bonus tracks: Carolina/Crazy Life

World on Fire (2014)
Track-listing: World on Fire/Shadow Life/
Automatic Overdrive/Wicked Stone/30 Years
to Life/Bent to Fly/Stone Blind/Too Far Gone/
Beneath the Savage Sun/Withered Delilah/
Battleground/Dirty Girl/Iris of the Storm/Avalon/
The Dissident/Safari Inn/The Unholy

Live at the Roxy 9.25.14 (2015)
Track-listing Disc One: Ghost/Nightrain/Halo/
Back from Cali/Stone Blind/You Could Be Mine/
Doctor Alibi/You're Crazy/Wicked Stone/30 Years
to Life/Rocket Queen
Track-listing Disc Two: Bent to Fly/Starlight/
You're a Lie/World on Fire/Anastasia/Sweet Child
O' Mine/Slither/Paradise City

DVD/Blu Ray Track-listing:
Ghost/Nightrain/Back from Cali/You Could Be
Mine/Rocket Queen/Bent to Fly/Starlight/You're a
Lie/World on Fire/Anastasia/Sweet Child O' Mine/
Slither/Paradise City
Bonus tracks: Stone Blind/You're Crazy/Wicked
Stone/30 Years to Life

Living the Dream (2018)

Track-listing: The Call Of The Wild/Serve You Right/My Antidote/Mind Your Manners/Lost Inside The Girl/Read Between The Lines/Slow Grind/The One You Loved Is Gone/Driving Rain/Sugar Cane/The Great Pretender/Boulevard Of Broken Hearts

Nothing Left to Fear (2013)

Track-listing: The Road to Stull/Cold Welcome/Lamb's Blood/One Choice, Two Fates/A Prayer/Dark Dreams/Sermon/The Tooth/Retrieval/Silent Secrets/Pain and Premonition Part 1/Pain and Premonition Part 2/Observations/The Secret Tower/Do Your Part/Don't Forget/A Flash and a Feeling/Abduction/Bleeding In/Urgency/Have Faith/The Decline/Trauma/The Blood Lust/Our Broken Home/Revelations/No Safety in Numbers/Childhood's End/The Fear/The Perfect Circle/Nothing Left to Fear/Welcome to Stull

Session recordings:

Lennie Kravitz – *Mama Said* – 'Always on the Run' (1991)
Alice Cooper – *Hey Stoopid* – 'Hey Stoopid' (1991)

Michael Jackson – *Dangerous* – 'Give In to Me' (1993)
Marta Sánchez – *Azabache* – 'Moja Mi Corazón' (1997)
Clown Posse – *The Great Milenko* – 'Halls of Illusions' (1997)
Paulina Rubio – *Ananda* – 'Nada Puede Cambiarme' (2007)
Daughtry – *Daughtry* – 'What I Want' (2007)
Clint Mansell – 'The Wrestler' (non-album single) (2009)
Global Sound – 'Hands Together' (non-album single) (2010)
Beth Hart – *My California* – 'Sister Heroine' (2010)
Edgar Winter – *Rebel Road* – 'Rebel Road' (2010)
Rihanna – *Rated R* – 'Rockstar 101' (2010)

The Fartz

You, we See You Crawling (1990)
Track-listing: Music Critics/Is This The Way?/Judgement Day/Dead Soldier/Resistance/People United/Police Force/Buried Alive/2525 (Exordium & Terminus)/Death Merchants

GUNS N' ROSES

DUFF MCKAGAN

Solo

Believe in Me (1993)
Track-listing: Believe in Me/I Love You/Man in the Meadow/(F@*ked Up) Beyond Belief/Could It Be U/Just Not There/Punk Rock Song/The Majority/10 Years/Swamp Song/Trouble/F@*k You/Lonely Tonite
Bonus tracks on 2009 Japanese reissue: Bambi/Cracked Actor

Singles from Believe in Me
'Believe in Me' / 'Bambi'/ 'Cracked Actor'

Promo singles from Believe in Me
'Punk Rock Song'
'Man in the Meadow'
'I Love You'

Beautiful Disease (Unreleased)
Track-listing: Seattlehead/Who's To Blame/Superman/Song For Beverly/Put You Back/Shinin' Down/Missing You/Hope/Holiday/Then And Now/Rain/Beautiful Disease/Mezz

'How to Be a Man' (non-album single) (2015)

10 Minute Warning (1998)
Track-listing: Swollen Rage/Buried/Face First/Mezz/Disconnected/Erthe/No More Time/Is This The Way?/Pictures

Velvet Revolver

Loaded

Episode 1999 Live (1999)
Track-listing: Sycophant/Shinin' Down/Seattle Head/Superman/Missing You/Then and Now/She's Got a Lot/Mezz/Ridin'/Home/Raw Power

Dark Days (2001)
Track-listing: 1. Seattle Head/Then & Now/Wrap My Arms/Dark Days/Want To/Misery/Criminal/Queen Jonasophina/Shallow/Superman/King of Downtown/Your Way

Wasted Heart EP (2008)
Track-listing: Sleaze Factory/No More/Executioner's Song/IOU/Wasted Heart

Sick (2009)
Track-listing: Sick/Sleaze Factory/Flatline/IOU/The Slide/Translucent/Mother's Day/I See Through You/Forgive Me/Bruce, Loaded/No Shame/Blind Date Girl/Wasted Heart/No More

The Taking (2011)
Track-listing: Lords of Abbadon/Executioner's Song/Dead Skin/We Win/Easier Lying/She's an Anchor/Indian Summer/Wrecking Ball/King of the World/Cocaine/Your Name/Follow Me to Hell

Neurotic Outsiders (1996)
Track-listing: Nasty Ho/Always Wrong/Angetina/Good News/Better Way/Feelings Are Good/Revolution/Jerk/Union/Janie Jones/Story of My Life/Six Feet Under

Singles from Neurotic Outsiders:
'Jerk' (1996)

EPs

Angelina (Japan only) (1997)
Track-listing: Angelina/Seattle Head/Spanish Ballrom/Planet Earth/Jerk

Walking Papers (2013)
Track-listing: Already Dead/The Whole World's Watching/Your Secret's Safe with Me/Red Envelopes/Leave Me in the Dark/The Butcher/Two Tickets and a Room/I'll Stick Around/Capital T/A Place Like This/Independence Day

WP2 (2018)
Track-listing: My Luck Pushed Back/Death on the Lips/Red & White/Somebody Else/Yours Completely/Hard to Look Away/Before You Arrived/Don't Owe Me Nothin'/This Is How It Ends/I Know You're Lying/Into the Truth/King Hooker/Right in Front of Me

Session recordings:
Iggy Pop - *Brick by Brick* – 'Home'/'Butt Town'/'Pussy Power'/'My Baby Wants to Rock and Roll' (1990)
Gilby Clarke - *Pawnshop Guitars* – 'Jail Guitar Doors' (1994)
Teddy Andreadis - *Innocent Loser* – 'Shotgun Shack' (1996)

The Outpatience – 'Anxious Disease' (1996)
Izzy Stradlin - *117°* all tracks except 'Memphis' and 'Good Enough' (1998); *Ride On* (1999)
Various - *Humanary Stew: A Tribute to Alice Cooper* – 'Elected' (1999)
The Racketeers - *Mad for the Racket* (2000)
Zilch – *Skyjin* – 'Give 'Em What You Got Given'/'Make the Motherfuckers Wake Up'/ 'Hide and Seek'/ 'Absolute Zeroes'
Mark Lanegan - *Field Songs* – 'Fix' (2001)
Izzy Stradlin - *River* (2001); *On Down the Road* (2002)
Burden Brothers - *Queen O' Spades* – 'Walk Away' (2002)
Alien Crime Syndicate - *XL from Coast to Coast* – 'Don't Go Breaking My Heart' (2002)
Mark Lanegan - *Bubblegum* – 'Strange Religion' (2004)
Izzy Stradlin - *Concrete* – 'Concrete' + two other unconfirmed tracks); *Wave of Heat* – seven unconfirmed tracks (2008)
Slash – *Slash* – 'Watch This' (2010)
Macy Gray - *The Sellout* – 'Kissed It' (2010)
Manic Street Preachers - *Postcards from a Young Man* – 'A Billion Balconies Facing the Sun' (2010)
Crosses - *EP 1* – 'This is a Trick' (2011); *Crosses* – 'This is a Trick' (2014)
Sebastian Bach - *Give 'Em Hell* (2014)
Various - *KEXP Presents* - *Raw Power : A Tribute to Iggy & The Stooges* (2015)

IZZY STRADLIN

Hollywood Rose

Izzy Stradlin and the Ju Ju Hounds (1992)
Track-listing: Somebody Knockin'/Pressure Drop/
Time Gone By/Shuffle It All/Bucket O' Trouble/
Train Tracks/How Will It Go/Cuttin' the Rug/Take a
Look at the Guy/Come on Now Inside/Morning Tea
(hidden bonus track, starts 4:26 into track 10)
(Japan issue only)
Track-listing: Bucket O' Trouble/Cuttin' The Rug/
Jivin' Sister Fanny/Time Gone By/Highway 49

117° (1998)
Track-listing: Ain't It a Bitch/Gotta Say/Memphis/
Old Hat/Bleedin/Parasite/Good Enough/117°/
Here Before You/Up Jumped the Devil/Grunt/

Freight Train/Methanol/Surf Roach
Japanese edition
Bonus tracks:
Crackin' Up (Live)
Pressure Drop (Live)

Ride On (1999)
Track-listing: Ride On/California/Spazed/Primitive
Man/Trance Mission/Needles/The Groper/Here
Comes the Rain/Hometown/Highway Zero

River (2001)
Track-listing: Jump In Now/Head On Out/River/
Far Below Me Now/What I Told You/Get Away/
Underground/Shall Walk/Run-In/Feelin' Alright

On Down the Road (2002)
Track-listing: You Betcha/Gone Dead Train/
Monkeys/On Down the Road/Sweet Caress/
Coke'n/Got Some News/Way to Go/Please Go
Home/Lot to Learn

Like A Dog (2005)
Track-listing: Bomb/Hammerhead/Snafu/Hell
Song/Rollin' On/Just Don't Know/Chop Away/Win
U Lose/On the Run/Like A Dog/Hidden Bonus
Track Miami (2007)
Track-listing: Tijuana/Buildings In The Sky/Let Go/
Junior's Song/Partly Cloudy/Waiting/Bombs Away/
Tough Check/Pick Up The Phone/Everythings
Alright/FSO Ragga (Not included on remix)

Fire, the Acoustic Album (2007)
Track-listing: I Don't Mind/Infrastruk/Listen/Airbus/
Fire/Seems to Me/Long Night/Box/Milo/Harp Song

Concrete (2008)
Track-listing: Ball/Circle/Easy/Concrete/
Drove/Ship/G.B./Knuckleheads/I Know/
Raggadubbacrete

Smoke (2009)
Track-listing: Nothing On Me/Too Hot/30k Up/
Dehydrated/Comfort Zone/Snow/I'm Breathing
In/Gotta Go/Driving Down/Smoke

GUNS N' ROSES

Wave of Heat (2010)
Track-listing: Beat Up/Old Tune/Rollin Rollin/
Gone/Difference/Waiting For My Ride/Job/Raven/
Way It Goes/Texas

Singles
'Shuffle it All' (1992)
'Pressure Drop' (1992)
'Been a Fix' (1992)

'Came Unglued' (1992)
'Can't Hear 'Em' (1992)
'Somebody Knockin'' (1993)
'Ain't It a Bitch' (1998)
'Do You Love Me?' (2004)
'Baby Rann' (2012)
'Walk´n Song' (2016)
'F. P. Money' (2016)
'To Being Alive' (2016)
'Call Me the Breeze' (2016)

STEVEN ADLER

GN'R Albums
Appetite For Destruction (1987)
GN'R Lies (1988)
Use Your Illusion II ('Civil War' only)

EPs
Live ?!*@ Like a Suicide (1986)
Live from the Jungle (1988)
The Civil War EP (1993; 'Civil War')

Live albums
Live Era '87 – '93 (1999)

Compilation albums
Greatest Hits (2004)

Singles
'It's So Easy' / 'Mr. Brownstone' (1987)
'Welcome to the Jungle' / 'Mr. Brownstone' (US)
'Whole Lotta Rosie' (Live) (1987)
'Sweet Child O' Mine' / 'It's So Easy' (live) (US)
'Out Ta Get Me' (UK) (1988)
'Paradise City' / 'Move to the City' (US) 'Used to Love Her' (UK (1988)
'Patience' / 'Rocket Queen' (LP version) (1989)
'Nightrain' / 'Reckless Life' (1989)
'Civil War' (1993)
'Shadow of Your Love' (2018)
Adler's Appetite

EPs
Adler's Appetite
Track-listing: Suicide/99/Empty/Hollywood/Little Dancer/Draw the Line (2005)
Alive
Track-listing: Alive/Stardog/Fading/Alive (Instrumental) (2012)
Singles from *Alive*: 'Alive' (2010), 'Stardog' (2010), 'Fading' (2010)

Albums
Back from the Dead (2012)
Track-listing: Back from the Dead/Own Worst Enemy/Another Version of the Truth/The One That You Hated/Good to Be Bad/Just Don't Ask/Blown Away/Waterfall/Habit/Your Diamonds/Dead Wrong
Singles from *Back from the Dead*:
'The One That You Hated' (2012)
'Good to Be Bad' (2012)

Session recordings
With Davy Vain
Fade ('Breakdown', 'Cindy', 'Can't Get Back') (1995)

With Slash
Slash ('Baby Can't Drive') (2010)

With Chip Z'Nuff
Adler Z'Nuff ('All Day and All Of The Night', 'The Pain Is All On You') (2010)

Strange Time (2015)

GUNS N' ROSES

MATT SORUM

DIZZY REED

GN'R Albums
Use Your Illusion I (1991)
Use Your Illusion II (1991)
The Spaghetti Incident? (1993)
Live Era '87 – '93 (1999)
Greatest Hits (2004)
Chinese Democracy (2008)

GN'R contributions and soundtracks
Nobody's Child: Romanian Angel Appeal (1990)
'Civil War'
Days of Thunder OST (1990)
'Knockin' On Heaven's Door'
Interview with the Vampire OST (1994)
'Sympathy for the Devil'
End of Days OST (1999)
'Oh My God'

Solo
Rock 'N Roll Ain't Easy (2018)
Track-listing: Rock 'Roll Ain't Easy/This Don't Look Like Vegas/Forgotten Cases/Cheers 2 R Oblivion/Crestfallen/Mystery in Exile/Reparations/Splendid Isolation/Mother Theresa/Fragile Water/I Celebrate/Understanding/Dirty Bomb
The Dead Daisies (2013)
Track-listing: It's Gonna Take Time/Lock 'N' Load/Washington/Yeah Yeah Yeah/Yesterday/Writing on the Wall/Miles in Front of Me/Bible Row/Man Overboard/Tomorrow/Can't Fight This Feeling/Talk to Me
Revolución (2015)
Track-listing: Mexico/Evil/Looking for the One/Empty Heart/Make the Best of It/Something I Said/Get up, Get Ready/With You and I/Sleep/My Time/Midnight Moses/Devil out of Time/Critical/Leave the Truth Behind/Last Night

Unfinished Business (2008)

Guest appearances
Coneheads soundtrack - Various Artists (1993)
Believe in Me - Duff McKagan (1993)
Pawnshop Guitars - Gilby Clarke (1994)
Wish Across The Land - The Merchants Of Venus (1994)
Live At 14 Below - Mick Taylor (1995)
Coastin' Home - Mick Taylor (1995)
It's Five O'Clock Somewhere – Slash's Snakepit (1995)
Playtime - Michael Zentner (1995)
Not What I Had Planned – Maissa (1996)
Copper Wires - Larry Norman (1996)
Steinway to Heaven - Various Artists (1997)
Electrovision - Doug Aldrich (2001)
Rock N' Roll Music - Col. Parker (2001)
Hammered - Motörhead (2002)
Ready to Go - Bang Tango (2004)
Village Gorilla Head - Tommy Stinson (2004)
Strangeland - Court Jester (2006)
Bare Bones - The Blessings (2006)
The Still Life - Various Artists (2007)
Gilby Clarke - Gilby Clarke (2007)
Backyard Babies - Backyard Babies (2008)
Spirit of Christmas - Northern Light Orchestra (2009)
One Man Mutiny - Tommy Stinson (2011)

GUNS N' ROSES

GILBY CLARKE

GN'R Albums

The Spaghetti Incident? (1993)
Live Era '87 – '93 (1999)
Greatest Hits (2004)

Solo

Pawnshop Guitars (1994)
Track-listing: Cure Me . . . Or Kill Me . . ./Black/
Tijuana Jail/Skin & Bones/Johanna's Chopper/
Let's Get Lost/Pawn Shop Guitars/Dead Flowers/
Jail Guitar Doors/Hunting Dogs/Shut Up
Japanese edition
Bonus track 'West of the Sunset'
Blooze EP (1995)
Track-listing: Tijuana Jail/Melting My Cold Heart/
Life's A Gas/He's A Whore/Skin & Bones
The Hangover (1997)
Track-listing: Wasn't Yesterday Great/It's Good
Enough for Rock N' Roll/Zip Gun/Higher/Mickey
Marmalade/Blue Grass Mosquito/Happiness Is
a Warm Gun/Hang on to Yourself/The Worst/
Captain Chaos/Punk Rock Pollution
Rubber (1998)
Track-listing: Kilroy Was Here/The Haunting/
Something's Wrong With You/Sorry I Can't Write
A Song About You/Mercedes Benz/The Hell's
Angels/Saturday Disaster/Trash/Technicolour
Stars/Superstar/Bourbon Street Blues/Frankie's
Planet
99 Live (1999)
Track-listing: Wasn't Yesterday Great/Monkey
Chow/Black/Kilroy Was Here/Motorcycle
Cowboys/Good Enough For Rock N' Roll/Cure Me
. . . Or Kill Me . . ./Tijuana Jail
Swag (2002)
Track-listing: Alien/Under the Gun/Crocodile
Tears/Broken Down Car/Margarita/I'm Nobody/
Judgment Day/Beware of the Dog/Heart of
Chrome/Warm Country Sun/Diamond Dogs
Gilby Clarke (2007)

Track-listing: Cure Me . . . Or Kill Me . . ./Tijuana
Jail/Skin & Bones/Alien/I'm Nobody/Judgement
Day/Motorcycle Cowboys/Wasn't Yesterday
Great/It's Good Enough for Rock N' Roll/Punk
Rock Pollution/Kilroy Was Here/Bourbon Street
Blues/Monkey Chow/Dropping Out/Can't Get
That Stuff/Black

Slash's Snakepit
It's 5 O'Clock Somewhere (1995)
Colonel Parker
Rock N Roll Music (2001)
Track-listing: Dropping Out/Can't Get That Stuff/
Harmony/All The Kings Horses/Blink Of An Eye/
Mother Mary's Son/Angel's Run/Pills/Mercedes
Benz/Pushing 40 Blooze/Down Home Cookin'/
Lord Only Knows
Nancy Sinatra
California Girl (2002)
Track-listing: How Are Things In California?/San
Fernando Valley/99 Miles From LA/California
Girls/Hello LA, Bye-Bye Birmingham/California
Dreamin'/Route 66/San Francisco/Do You Know
The Way To San Jose?/Hooray For Hollywood/
Saturday In The Park/California Man/ Hotel
California/Cuando Caliente El Sol/There's No
Place Like Home
Rock Star Supernova (2006)
Track-listing: It's On/Leave the Lights On/Be
Yourself (and 5 Other Clichés)/It's All Love/
Can't Bring Myself to Light This Fuse/Underdog/
Make No Mistake . . . This Is the Take/Headspin/
Valentine/Social Disgrace/The Dead Parade
Candy
Whatever Happened to Fun . . . (1985)
Track-listing: American Kix/Turn It Up Loud/
Whatever Happened To Fun . . ./Last Radio
Show/Kids In The City/Weekend Boy/First Time/
Electric Nights/Lonely Hearts
Teenage Neon Jungle (2003)
Track-listing: Intro/Whatever Happened to Fun
. . ./Stuff/First Time/Turn It Up Loud/Kids in the

City/The Girl I Love/Weekend Boy/Champagne/
She Loves You/Lonely Hearts/Electric Nights/
Number One/Daddy Is a Jet/Sound of a Broken
Heart/Turn It Up Loud '03/War Is Over/Crocodile
Tears/You Will Dance Again/The Return of the
X-Girlfriend/The Last Radio Show '03
Kills For Thrills
Commercial Suicide EP (1989)
Track-listing: Commercial Suicide/Silver Bullets/I
Wanna Be Your Kill/Danger/Pump It Up

Dynamite from Nightmareland (1990)
Track-listing: Motorcycle Cowboys/Commercial
Suicide/Brother's Eyes/Paisley Killers/
Something For The Suffering/Rockets/Wedding
Flowers/Ghosts And Monsters/My Addiction/
Misery Pills/Silver Bullets
The Loveless
A Tale of Gin and Salvation (1990) 'Wish I
Could Fly'

GUNS N' ROSES

ROBIN FINCK

GN' R Albums
Chinese Democracy

Nine Inch Nails
Further Down the Spiral (1995)
Track-listing: Piggy (Nothing Can Stop Me Now)/The Art of Self Destruction, Part One/Self Destruction, Part Two/The Downward Spiral (The Bottom)/Hurt (Quiet)/Eraser (Denial/At the Heart of It All/Eraser (Polite)/Self Destruction, Final/The Beauty of Being Numb/Erased, Over, Out
And All That Could have Been (2002)
Track-listing: Disc One: (Halo 17a) Terrible Lie/Sin/ March of the Pigs/Piggy/The Frail/The Wretched/ Gave Up/The Great Below/The Mark Has Been Made/Wish/Suck/Closer/Head Like a Hole/The Day the World Went Away/Starfuckers, Inc./Hurt/

Disc Two: Still (Halo 17b) Something I Can Never Have/Adrift and at Peace/The Fragile/ The Becoming/Gone, Still/The Day the World Went Away/And All That Could Have Been/The Persistence of Loss/Leaving Hope
The Downward Spiral (Deluxe Edition) (2004)
Track-listing: Mr. Self Destruct/Piggy/Heresy/ March of the Pigs/Closer/Ruiner/The Becoming/I Do Not Want This/Big Man with a Gun/A Warm Place/Eraser/Reptile/The Downward Spiral/Hurt
The Slip (2008)
Track-listing: 999,999/1,000,000/Letting You/ Discipline/Echoplex/Head Down/Lights in the Sky/Corona Radiata/The Four of Us Are Dying/ Demon Seed

TOMMY STINSON

GN' R Albums
Chinese Democracy
Appetite For Democracy 3D
'Oh My God' - *End of Days Soundtrack* (1999)

Solo

Village Gorilla Head (2004)
Track-listing: Without a View/Not a Moment Too Soon/Something's Wrong/Couldn't Wait/OK/Bite Your Tongue/Village Gorilla Head/Light of Day/Hey You/Motivation/Someday

One Man Mutiny (2011)
Track-listing: Don't Deserve You/It's A Drag/Meant To Be/All This Way For Nothing/Come To Hide/Seize The Moment/Zero To Stupid/Match Made In Hell/Destroy Me/One Man Mutiny

The Replacements

Sorry Ma, Forgot to Take Out the Trash (1981)
Track-listing: Takin' a Ride/Careless/Customer/Hangin' Downtown/Kick Your Door Down/Otto/I Bought a Headache/Rattlesnake/I Hate Music/Johnny's Gonna Die/Shiftless When Idle/More Cigarettes/Don't Ask Why/Somethin' to Dü/I'm in Trouble/Love You Till Friday/Shutup/Raised in the City

Singles from Sorry Ma, Forgot to Take Out the Trash
'I'm in Trouble'/ 'If Only You Were Lonely' (1981)

Stink (1982)
Track-listing: Kids Don't Follow/Fuck School/

Stuck in the Middle/God Damn Job/White and Lazy/Dope Smokin' Moron/Go/Gimme Noise
Hootenanny (1983)
Track-listing: Hootenanny/Run It/Color Me Impressed/Willpower/Take Me Down to the Hospital/Mr. Whirly/Mostly Stolen/Within Your Reach/Buck Hill/Lovelines/You Lose/Hayday/Treatment Bound

Let It Be (1984)
Track-listing: I Will Dare/Favorite Thing/We're Comin' Out/Tommy Gets His Tonsils Out/Androgynous/Black Diamond/Unsatisfied/Seen Your Video/Gary's Got a Boner/Sixteen Blue/Answering Machine

Singles from Let It Be
'I Will Dare'/'20th Century Boy'/'Hey Good Lookin'' (1984)

The Shit Hits the Fans (1985)
Track-listing: Lawdy Miss Clawdy/Ye Sleeping Knights of Jesus/Lovelines/I'll Be There/Sixteen Blue/Can't Hardly Wait/I Will Dare/Hear You Been to College/Saturday Night Special/Iron Man/Misty Mountain Hop/Heartbreaker/Can't Get Enough/Jailbreak/Breakdown/No More the Moon Shines on Lorena/Merry-Go-Round/Left in the Dark/Takin' Care of Business/I Will Follow/Jumpin' Jack Flash/Radio Free Europe/The New World/Let It Be

Tim (1985)
Track-listing: Hold My Life/I'll Buy/Kiss Me on the Bus/Dose of Thunder/Waitress in the Sky/Swingin Party/Bastards of Young/Lay It Down Clown/Left of the Dial/Little Mascara/Here Comes a Regular

GUNS N' ROSES

Singles from Tim
'Bastards of Young' (1985)
'Kiss Me on the Bus' (1985)

Boink!! (1986)
Track-listing: Color Me Impressed/White and Lazy/Within Your Reach/If Only You Were Lonely/ Kids Don't Follow/Nowhere Is My Home/Take Me Down to the Hospital/Go

Pleased to Meet Me (1987)
Track-listing: I.O.U./Alex Chilton/I Don't Know/ Nightclub Jitters/The Ledge/Never Mind/ Valentine/Shooting Dirty Pool/Red Red Wine/ Skyway/Can't Hardly Wait

Singles from Pleased to Meet Me
'Can't Hardly Wait' (1987)
'Alex Chilton'/'Election Day' (1987)
'The Ledge' (1987)
'Skyway' (1988)

Don't Tell a Soul (1989)
Track-listing: Talent Show/Back to Back/We'll Inherit the Earth/Achin' to Be/They're Blind/ Anywhere's Better Than Here/Asking Me Lies/I'll Be You/I Won't/Rock 'N' Roll Ghost/Darlin' One

Singles from Don't Tell a Soul
'I'll Be You'/'Date to Church' (1989)
'Back to Back' (1989)
'Achin' to Be' (1989)

All Shook Down (1990)
Track-listing: Merry Go Round/One Wink at a Time/Nobody/Bent Out of Shape/Sadly Beautiful/ Someone Take the Wheel/When It Began/All Shook Down/Attitude/Happy Town/Torture/My Little Problem/The Last

Singles from All Shook Up
'Merry Go Round' (promo)
'Someone Take the Wheel' (promo)
'When It Began' (promo)
'Happy Town' (promo)

2008 CD reissue bonus tracks: When It Began (Demo) Kissin' in Action (Demo) Someone Take the Wheel (Demo) Attitude (Demo) Happy Town (Demo) Tiny Paper Plane (Demo) Sadly Beautiful (Demo) My Little Problem (Alternate Version) Ought to Get Love/Satellite/Kissin' in Action

All for Nothing / Nothing for All (1997)
Track-listing (Disc one): Left of the Dial/Kiss Me on the Bus/Bastards of Young/Here Comes a Regular/Skyway/Alex Chilton/The Ledge/Can't Hardly Wait/I'll Be You/Achin' to Be/Talent Show/ Anywhere's Better Than Here/Merry Go Round/ Sadly Beautiful/Nobody/Someone Take the Wheel
(Disc Two): Can't Hardly Wait/Birthday Gal/Beer for Breakfast/Till We're Nude/Election Day/Jungle Rock/All He Wants to Do Is Fish/Date to Church/ Cruella De Ville/We Know the Night/Portland/Wake Up/Satellite/Like a Rolling Pin/Another Girl, Another Planet/Who Knows/All Shook Down/I Don't Know

Don't You Know Who I Think I Was? (2006)
Track-listing: Takin' a Ride/Shiftless When Idle/ Kids Don't Follow/Color Me Impressed/Within Your Reach/I Will Dare/Answering Machine/ Unsatisfied/Here Comes a Regular/Kiss Me on the Bus/Bastards of Young/Left of the Dial/Alex Chilton/Skyway/Can't Hardly Wait/Achin' to Be/I'll Be You/Merry Go Round/Message to the Boys/ Pool & Dive

For Sale: Live at Maxwell's 1986 (2013)
Track-listing (Disc one): Hayday/Color Me Impressed/Dose of Thunder/Fox on the Run/Hold My Life/I Will Dare/Favorite Thing/Unsatisfied/ Can't Hardly Wait/Tommy Gets His Tonsils Out/ Takin' a Ride/Bastards of Young/Kiss Me on the Bus/Black Diamond
(Disc Two): Johnny's Gonna Die/Otto/I'm in Trouble/Left of the Dial/God Damn Job/ Answering Machine/Waitress in the Sky/Take Me Down to the Hospital/Gary's Got a Boner/If Only You Were Lonely/Baby Strange/Hitchin' a Ride/ Nowhere Man/Go/Fuck School

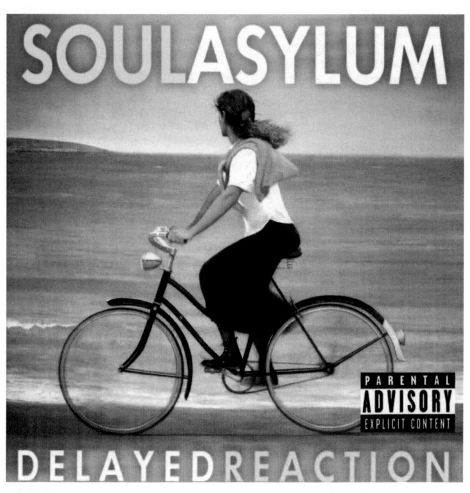

Stand-alone singles
'Cruella DeVille' (Stay Awake: Various
Interpretations of Music from Vintage Disney
Films) (1988)

Bash & Pop

Friday Night Is Killing Me (1993)
Track-listing (Disc one): Never Aim To Please/
Hang Ups/Loose Ends/One More Time/Tickled To
Tears/Nothing/Fast n' Hard/Friday Night (Is Killing
Me)/He Means It/Tiny Pieces/First Steps

(Disc two): Never Aim To Please (Demo)/
First Steps (Demo)/Hang Ups (Demo)/Tiny
Pieces (Demo)/Situation/Harboring A Fugitive/
Making Me Sick/Nothing (Alternate version)/
One More Time (Alternate version)/He Means
It (Alternate version)/Loose Ends (Alternate
version)/Hang Ups (Alternate version)/Tickled To
Tears (Alternate version)/Fast n' Hard (Alternate
version)/Friday Night (Is Killing Me) (Alternate
version)/Tiny Pieces (Alternate version)/Never
Aim To Please (Alternate version)/Speak Now Or
Forever Hold Your Peace

GUNS N' ROSES

Anything Could Happen (2017)
Track-listing: Not This Time/On the Rocks/
Anything Could Happen/Breathing Room/
Anybody Else/Can't Be Bothered/Bad News/
Never Wanted to Know/Anytime Soon/Unfuck
You/Jesus Loves You/Shortcut

Singles
'Too Late'/'Saturday' (2017)

Perfect

When Squirrels Play Chicken (1996)
Track-listing: Makes Me Happy/Sometimes/
Alternative Monkey/Miss Self-Esteem/
Don't Need To Know Where

Once, Twice, Three Times a Maybe (2004)
Track-listing: Better Days/Turn It Up/Little Drum/
Days A Week/Me/Catch 'em/Yap Yap/Making Of
An Asshole/Thing I Call My Life/Flap

Soul Asylum

The Silver Lining (2006)
Tommy was brought in to finish the album following
the death of Karl Mueller – tracks unknown

Delayed Reaction (2012)
Track-listing: Gravity/Into the Light/The Streets/
By the Way/Pipe Dream/Let's All Kill Each Other/
Cruel Intentions/The Juice/Take Manhattan/I
Should've Stayed in Bed

The Old 97's

Most Messed Up (2014)
Tracks: 'Intervention' and 'Most Messed Up'

Guest appearances
Clerks: Music from the Motion Picture – 'Making
Me Sick' - Various Artists (1994)
It's All about the Benjamins - Puff Daddy (1998)
Like a Butterfly 'cept Different - MOTH (2001)
Provisions, Fiction and Gear - MOTH (2002)
Catch and Release - Various Artists (2006)
Catch and Release - with BT (2006)
Unfurled - Bobot Adrenaline (2008)
Dumb Bomb - Bobot Adrenaline (2010)

BUCKETHEAD

GN' R Albums

Chinese Democracy (all tracks except 'Catcher in the Rye' and 'This I Love')

Solo

Bucketheadland (1992)
Track-listing: Park Theme/Interlude/Giant Robot Theme/Enter Guillatine/Giant Robot Vs. Guillatine/Bucketbots Jig/Enter Slipdisc/Bansheebot Vs. Buckethead/The Haunted Farm/Hook and Pole Gang/Cattle Prod/Phantom Monk/The Rack/Nosin'/Gorey Head Stump/Sterling Scapula/Skid's Looking Where/Steel Wedge/Wonka in Slaughter Zone/Nosin' Part 2/Diabolical Minds/Alice in Slaughterland/Bleeding Walls/Buddy on a Slab/Buddy in the Graveyard/Oh Jeez…/Funeral Time/Computer Master/Part 1/Part 2/Home Run Derby/Interlude/Main Theme/I Love My Parents
Disc Two (Remixes): Park Theme Extension/Guillatine Battle/Giant Robot Theme/Robot Dance/Virtual Reality/Bansheebot Bop/Baseball Buddy

Giant Robot (1994)
Track-listing: Doomride/Welcome to Bucketheadland/I Come in Peace/Buckethead's Toy Store/Want Some Slaw?/Warweb/Aquabot/Binge and Grab/Pure Imagination/Buckethead's Chamber of Horrors/Onions Unleashed/Chicken/I Love My Parents/Buckethead's TV Show/Robot Transmission/Pirate's Life for Me/Post Office Buddy/Star Wars/Last Train to Bucketheadland

The Day of the Robot (1996)
Track-listing: Destroyer: Speed Flux Quadrant/Inclusion/Exhaust Release/Flying Guillotine/Quantum Crash/Collision/Caution Drop

Colma (1998)
Track-listing: Whitewash/For Mom/Ghost (Part 1)/Hills of Eternity/Big Sur Moon/Machete/Wishing Well/Lone Sal Bug/Sanctum/Wondering/Watching the Boats with My Dad/Ghost (Part 2)/Colma

Monsters and Robots (1999)
Track-listing: Jump Man/Stick Pit/The Ballad of Buckethead/Sow Thistle/Revenge of the Double-Man/Night of the Slunk/Who Me?/Jowls/The Shape Vs. Buckethead/Stun Operator/Scapula/Nun Chuka Kata/Remote Viewer #13 (Japanese edition bonus track)

Somewhere Over the Slaughterhouse (2001)
Track-listing: Somewhere over the Slaughterhouse/Help Me/Pin Bones and Poultry/My Sheeetz/Day of the Ulcer/You Like Headcheese?/Burlap Curtain/You Like This Face?/Wires and Clips/Knockingun/Conveyor Belt Blues

Funeral Weaver (2002)
Track-listing: The Blind Centipede/Kurtz Temple/Covert/Death Card/R.I.P./Plans Within Plans/Eye In the Sky/Freezer Burns/Sky Drones/Operation Gateway/Bantam Rising/Combat Shadow/Azzim's Lectures/Channel Of Secrets/Comet Shower/The Worm Turns/Silhouettes Against the Sky/Sleeper Agents/Recreational Cryonics/The Blind Sniper (Fred Rogers)/Atlantis Found/The Spider's Web/Blue Crystal/Reaping the Whirlwind/The Hills Have Eyes/The Other Side Of Midnight/Sea the Hollow Man/Unsound Methods/Hall Of Records/Aluminum Clouds/Lost Threads/Killing

GUNS N' ROSES

Mask/Rattlesnake Hill/F-4 Phantom/Stub Pylons/ Armour Piercing Projectile/Stolen Identities/ The Shriek Of Revenge/5-Card Trick/Caretaker Of Memory/The Kingdom Of Nie/Kangaroo Kranes/High Seat With the Devil/Jessy/From the Foxholes/(F.L.I.P.)/Frozen Head/Who Is the Enemy/Nappler Radar

Bermuda Triangle (2002)
Track-listing: Intro/Davy Jones Locker/Flight 19/ Mausoleum Door/Sea of Expanding Shapes/The Triangle (Part I): Extrakd/Bionic Fog/Forbidden Zone/Telegraph Land of the Crispies/Pullin' the Heavy/Phantom Lights/Jabbar on Alcatrazz Avenue/BEESTRO Fowler/Splintered Triplet[9]/ Whatevas/Sucked Under/Isle of Dead/The Triangle (Part II)/911

Electric Tears (2002)
Track-listing: All in the Waiting/Sketches of Spain/Padmasana/Mustang/The Way to Heaven/ Baptism of Solitude/Kansas Storm/Datura/ Mantaray/Witches on the Heath/Angel Monster/ Electric Tears/Spell of the Gypsies

Bucketheadland 2 (2003)
Track-listing: Welcome/Slaughter Zone Entrance/ The Cobra's Hood/Transportation Options/ Machete Mirage/Slaughter Buddies Outside the Revenge Wedge/We Cannot Guarantee Bodily Harm/John Merrick - Elephant Man Bones Explosion/Taxidermy Tots/Bloody Rainbow Spiraling Sherbert Scoop/Can You Get Past Albert?/Vladimir Pockets' Incredible Bloated Slunk Show/The Ballad of the Inside-Out Face/ The Battery Cage Brawls (Cage Announcer: The Ghost of Abraham Lincoln; Winner Has to Eat His Way Out)/Ferris Wheel Apology/Can You Help Me?/Grimm's Sponsorship/Realistic Coop Replica/Frozen Brains Tell No Tales/Rooster Landing (1st Movement) / Lime Time (2nd Movement)/Two Pints/Health & Safety Advisory/ Digger's Den/One-Way Ticket to Grab Bag Alley/ Fun for You/Carpal Tunnel Tomb Torker/Today's

Schedule/The Corpse Plower/Unemployment Blues/Slaughter Zone Exit

Island of Lost Minds (2004)
Track-listing: Island of Lost Minds/Shock Therapy Side Show/Dream Darts/Vacuum Tube Implant/ Skull Scrape/Ice Pick Through Eyes/Four-sided Triangle/Korova Binge Bar/Bruised Eye Sockets/ Mud Of The Gutter/The Cuckoo Parade/Viravax/ Lobotomizer

Population Override (2004)
Track-listing: Unrestrained Growth/Too Many Humans/Population Override/Humans Vanish/ Cruel Reality of Nature/A Day Will Come/Earth Heals Herself/Clones/Super Human

The Cuckoo Clocks of Hell (2004)
Track-listing: Descent of the Damned/Spokes for the Wheel of Torment/Arc of the Pendulum/ Fountains of the Forgotten/The Treeman/ Pylegathon/Traveling Morgue/One Tooth of the Time Train/Bedlam's Bluff/Beaten with Sledges/ Woods of Suicides/Yellowed Hide/Moths to Flame/The Ravines of Falsehood/The Black Forest/Haven of Black Tar Pitch/The Escape Wheel

Enter the Chicken (2005)
Track-listing: Intro/We Are One/Botnus/Three Fingers/Running from the Light/Coma/Waiting Hare/Interlude/Funbus/The Hand/Nottingham Lace

Kaleidoscalp (2005)
Track-listing: Fankenseuss Laboratories/Stun Pike and the Jack in the Box Head/Music Box Innards/Breakfast Cyborg/The Bronze Bat/The Last Ride of the Bozomobile/Rack Maintenance/ The Sticker on Hallucinogens/Pylon Shift/Citadel/ The Slunk, the Gutter and the Candlestick Maker/The Android of Notre Dame/She Sells Sea Shells by the Slaughterhouse

Inbred Mountain (2009)

Track-listing: In Search of Inbred Mountain/ Johnny Be Slunk/Lotus Island/Flock Of Slunks/ Advance To The Summit/Plastination Station/ Escape From Inbred Mountain

The Elephant Man's Alarm Clock (2006)

Track-listing: Thai Fighter Swarm/Final Wars/ Baseball Furies/Elephant Man's Alarm Clock/ Lurker At The Threshold (Inspired By H.P. Lovecraft) Part 1/Lurker At The Threshold Part 2/Lurker At The Threshold Part 3/Lurker At The Threshold Part 4/Oakridge Cake (Tribute to Kool Keith)/Gigan/Droid Assembly/Bird With A Hole In Stomach/|Fizzy Lipton Drinks

Crime Slunk Scene (2006)

Track-listing (CD version): King James/Gory Head Stump 2006: The Pageant of the Slunks/The Fairy and the Devil/Buddy Berkman's Ballad/Mad Monster Party/Soothsayer/Col. Austin VS Col. Sanders AKA Red Track Suit/We Can Rebuild Him/Electronic Slight of Hand/Mecha Gigan/ Slunk Parade AKA Freaks in the Back
(Vinyl version): King James/Gory Head Stump 2006: The Pageant of the Slunks/The Fairy and

GUNS N' ROSES

the Devil/Buddy Berkman's Ballad/Mad Monster Party/Soothsayer/Col. Austin VS Col. Sanders AKA Red Track Suit/We Can Rebuild Him/ Electronic Slight of Hand

Pepper's Ghost (2007)
Track-listing: Pepper's Ghost/Carpal Tunnel Slug/ Magua's Scalp/Imprint (Dedicated to Takashi Miike)/Goblin Shark/Brewer In The Air/Exit 209/ Plankton/The Hills Have Headcheese/Bag Some Game/Towel In The Kitchen/Callbox/Embalming Plaza

Decoding the Tomb of Bansheebot (2007)
Track-listing: Materializing The Disembodied/ Asylum of Glass/Ghost Host/Killing Cone/ Bloodless/Checkerboard Incision/Circarama/ Disecto/Pickwick's Lost Chapter/I Can Only Carry 50 Chickens At a Time/Stretching Lighthouse/ . Hall Of Scalding Vats/Sail On Soothsayer (In Memory of Aunt Susie 1932-2007)

Cyborg Slunks (2007)
Track-listing: Sneak Attack/Reopening of the Scapula Factory/Infiltration/Aunt Suzie/A New War Is Underway

Albino Slug (2009)
Track-listing: The Redeem Team/Siege Engine/ Pink Eye/Dawn At The Deuce/Flee Flicker/ Symmetrical Slug/The Bight of Benin/Fear of Salt/Spooner Arks/Electric Bell Blanket/Tide Pools/Shell Substitutions/Forgotten Trail

Slaughterhouse on the Prairie (2009)
Track-listing: Lebron's Hammer/Blood Bayou/ Iceman [Tribute to George Gervin]/Don't Use Roosts If You Raise Broilers/Robot Checkerboard/Premonition/Crouching Stump Hidden Limb/Goat Host/The Streching Room/ Pumpkin Pike/Collecting Specimens/Rack Maintenance Part 2

A Real Diamond in the Rough (2009)
Track-listing: Broken Mirror/Big D's Touch/ Separate Sky/Dawn Appears/A Real Diamond In The Rough/Sundial/Squid Ink/Four Rivers/Allowed To Play/Formless Present/Squid Ink Part 2/The Miracle of Surrender/The Return of Captain E.O.

Forensic Follies (2009)
Track-listing: Forensic Follies/A-cycle Light-ray Cannons/Splinter In a Slunk's Eye/Under Sea Scalp/Whirlwind/Plunger/Trunk of the Tree/Slunk Shrine/Open Coffin Jamboree/(I'll Be) Taking Care of Grampa/Three Headed Troll/Splinter Disection/Mannequin Molds

Needle in a Slunk Stack (2009)
Track-Listing: Needle In a Slunk Stack/Interview With the Double Man/Carcass Cable/Next Stop, the Shell/Distilled Scalp/Furnace/Mego Frankenstein/Alpha Sea/Wormwood's Workshop Part 1/Pythagorus Sled/Slunk Smuggler/ Wormwood's Workshop Part 2/Astral Traveler

Shadows Between the Sky (2010)
Track-listing: Shadows Between The Sky/Inward Journey/Chaos of the Unconscious/Rim of the World/ Sea Wall/Sled Ride/Sunken Statue/Cookies for Santa/Andrew Henry's Meadow/Centrum/The Cliff's Stare/Greenskeeper/Wax Paper/Walk on the Moon

Spinal Clock (2010)
Track-listing: Lafayette's Landing/Whale On This/Four O'Clock For Dub Down/Spinal Clock/ Overnight The Animatronics/Gelatin Nerve/Spinal Cracker/Skeleton Dance/Bayou By You

Captain EO's Voyage (2010)
Track-listing: Captain EO's Voyage/Light/Infinity Appears/Stained Glass Hill/Trails of Moondust/ Star Chasing/Dancing the Dream/The Siphoning Sequence/Chase the Darkness Out/Backwards Footprint/Tarantula Crossing/Tears in the Mirror

GUNS N' ROSES

3 Foot Clearance (2010)
Track-listing: Griffin's Spike/Rammellzee: Hero of the Abyss/Floating Graveyard/Ballad of Jerry Mono/H.D. Autopsy/Droid Hunt/Battlefields/Handprint Ornament/Three Headed Guardian/Harpoon the Goon/Critical Leg Assignment/Siamese Butterfly/X-Ray
Limited edition version track-listing: Griffin's Spike/Rammellzee: Hero of the Abyss/Three Headed Guardian/Floating Graveyard/Ballad of Jerry Mono/H.D. Autopsy/Droid Hunt/Battlefields/Handprint Ornament/Harpoon the Goon/Critical Leg Assignment/Siamese Butterfly/X-Ray

Pike Series

It's Alive (2011)
Track-listing: Lebrontron/Tonka/Peeling Out/Barnyard Banties/Crack the Sky/The Hatch/Brooding Peeps/Picking the Feathers

Empty Space (2011)
Track-listing: Comb and Wattles/Wormers/Empty Space/Dummy Egg/Pullets/Perched/Hatched/Portable Pen/Leghorn/Scrape the Dirt Off

Underground Chamber (2011)
Track-listing: Underground Chamber

Look Up There (2011)
Track-listing: Golden Eyes/Look Up There

Electric Sea (2012)
Track-listing: Electric Sea/Beyond the Knowing/Swomee Swan/Point Doom/El Indio/La Wally/La Gavotte/Bachethead/Yokohama/Gateless Gate/The Homing Beacon

Balloon Cement (2012)
Track-listing: Balloon Cement/Red Water Colors/Transport Void/Thistle Museum/Alligator Eye Viewer/Veil of Tinfoil/Chestplate/Vast Mound/Replacement Nail/Shatter Shell/Bridge to Borg/Evaporate

The Shores of Molokai (2012)
Track-listing: Intro/The Shores of Molokai/The 5 Masters of Decapitation/Henry's New Home/Counter Clockwise/Stumps on Stilts/Mannequins Are My Friend/Smile Without a Face/Hatchet/Thermal Exhaust Port/Melting Man

Racks (2012)
Track-listing: The Snow Rabbit/Telekinite/Asbury Park Boardwalk/Castle of Dr. Cadaver/Sunbursts/Chamber of Slunks/Spiderwall/Coffin for a Penny/Fomahaut/The Patrolman

March of the Slunks (2012)
Track-listing: Magellan's Maze/Burying Toys/Malbert's Strut/Happy Landing/The Robot Who Lost Its Head/Thud/Satellite Invaders/The Other Side of the Island/Ghost Coop/The Raid/Vault

The Silent Picture Book (2012)
Track-listing: Dweller By the Dark Stream/Blind Cyclops/Flea Market/Three Steps/Beam of Omega/Whirlibird/Ropelight/Flashes/Melting Man Part 2

Forgotten Library (2012)
Track-listing: Disintergration/Corpse Be Animated/Faded from View/Yellowed Pages/Beginning Putrification/Decay/Forgotten Library

Propellar (2013)
Track-listing: Propellar/Room Of Shells/Meeting Of The Mummy/The Poultry Show/Launched/Dome

Pike 13 (2013)
Track-listing: 9 tracks, all untitled

The Mark of Davis (2013)
Track-listing: Ricochet/Nebula/The Canals/
Chickephant/Dry Ice Screeches/Death Star
Surface/Tree of Lanterns/Elephicken

View Master (2013)
Track-listing: Puzzle Box/Ran/Pullout Drawer/
Early Coin/View Master/First Day of Autumn/
Find/Dragon Shield/Big Little Book/Stock/Toys of
Jupiter/Learn Circle

The Boiling Pond (2013)
Track-listing: The Boiling Pond/Conductor/
Ancestors/Piledriver Impact/Subterranean/
Punmul/Flesh Tearing Cliffs/Life of a Fly/
Screaming Skull/Subterranean part 2

The Spirit Winds (2013)
Track-listing: The Spirit Winds/Petal/Frog
Charmer/The Pier/Cab Window

The Astrodome (2013)
Track-listing: The Astrodome/Airtight Garage/
Explorer Twin/Omega Wing/Hollow Eyes/
Beaming/Sun Heart/Light Mote

Teeter Slaughter (2013)
Track-listing: Teeter Slaughter part 1/Teeter
Slaughter part 2/Teeter Slaughter part 3/Teeter
Slaughter part 4/Teeter Slaughter part 5/Teeter
Slaughter part 6/Teeter Slaughter part 7/Teeter
Slaughter part 8/Teeter Slaughter part 9/Teeter
Slaughter part 10/Teeter Slaughter part 11

Thaw (2013)
Track-listing: Thaw/Melting Season/Room Of
Frozen Combs/Kept In Batteries/Dry/Fragmented/
Dust Filter/In The Bin/Fountains In A Wire

Spiral Trackway (2013)
Track-listing: Spiral Trackway/Center Platform/
Aluminum Hub/Fiber Optic Gateway/Solar

Satellite/Symphony of the Seed/Micro and
Macro World/Hyacinth

Sphere Façade (2013)
Track-listing: Monorail Stop/Sphere Façade/
Waterproof Membrane/Reflection Surface/
Viewing Deck/Spokes in Space/Bantam
Pavilions/Game Grid

Telescape (2013)
Track-listing: Pyramids Rising/Between Sea and
Sky/Land Drawings/Launch Pad/Telescape 1/
Telescape 2

Slug Cartilage (2013)
Track-listing: Four Ton Chandelier/Scowl Owl/
Previous Plate/Chip of Red/Pine Sap/Smudge
Mad/Zebra Stripe/Slug Cartilage/I. Wasnail

Pancake Heater (2013)
Track-listing: Pancake Heater/Spires of Space
Mountain/Crumbled or Pelleted/Topspin/Trough
Feeder/Omni Mover Assistance/Sprinkled/Beak
to Scoop/Storing Feed

Worms for the Garden (2013)
Track-listing: Worms for the Garden/Ridge Roll/
Owl on the Road/Learned the Land/Molt

Halls of Dimension (2013)
Track-listing: McDougal Street/Halls of Dimension
Part One - Hall 1/Hall 2/Hall 3/Hall 4/Hall 5/Part
Two - Falling Through the Vacuum/Suns Set

Feathers (2013)
Track-listing: Feathers/Claw Station/Mill/Faded/
Cactus Spines/Lake Whisperer/Rooster Row

Splatters (2013)
Track-listing: Splatters 1/Splatters 2/Splatters 3/
Splatters 4

GUNS N' ROSES

Mannequin Cemetery (2013)
Track-listing: Melted Glasses/Purse of Holes/
Cobwebs in the Calf/Faded Fingernail Polish/
Hat That Smells Like an Old Bookstore/Where
Rings Were/Piles of Parts/Shoes Without Socks/
Mannequin Cemetery

Pearson's Square (2013)
Track-listing: Pearson's Square/Eagle's Nest/
Eagle's Flight/Hearts

Delight

Rise of the Blue Lotus (2013)
Track-listing: Mountain Cabin/The Flooding of
Pain/Rise of the Blue Lotus

Pumpkin (2013)
Track-listing: Pumpkin Pikes 1/Pumpkin Pikes
2/Pumpkin Pikes 3/Pumpkin Pikes 4/Pumpkin
Pikes 5/Pumpkin Pikes 6/Pumpkin Pikes 7/
Pumpkin Pikes 8/Pumpkin Pikes 9/Pumpkin
Pikes 10/Pumpkin Pikes 11/Pumpkin Pikes 12/
Pumpkin Pikes 13/Pumpkin Pikes 14/Pumpkin
Pikes 15/Pumpkin Pikes 16/Pumpkin Pikes 17/
Pumpkin Pikes 18/Pumpkin Pikes

Thank You, Ohlinger's (2013)
Track-listing: Thank you Ohlinger's/Unopened Boxes/
Way in the Back/Manila Envelopes/Alphabetical
Order/Window Clip/Shoe Lock/Telling Number

The Pit (2013)
Track-listing: The Pit part 1/The Pit part 2/The Pit
part 3/The Pit part 4/The Pit part 5/The Pit part
6/The Pendulum

Hollowed Out (2013)
Track-listing: Low Rolling Hills/Lobster Hands/
One Foot In Front of the Other/Sideways Jaw
Trap/Mosquito on Stilts/Trading Post/Cyborg
Parking/Hollowed Out

It Smells Like Frogs (2013)
Track-listing: Gold Dragon part 1/Gold Dragon
part 2/Gold Dragon part 3/Gold Dragon part 4/
Gold Dragon part 5/Gold Dragon part 6/It Smells
Like Frogs

Twisterlend (2013)
Track-listing: The Closed Triptych/Ghouls of
the Sea/Canal System/Forbidden Fold/Gloomy
Emptiness/Bowling for Slaughters/Twisterlend

Pikes (2013)
Track-listing: Pumpkins Pikes 19/Pumpkins
Pikes 20/Pumpkins Pikes 21/Pumpkins Pikes
22/Pumpkins Pikes 23/Pumpkins Pikes 24/
Pumpkins Pikes 25/Pumpkins Pikes 26/
Pumpkins Pikes 27

Coat of Charms (2013)
Track-listing: Hall of Aluminum/Coat of Charms/
Jettison part 1/Jettison part 2/Jettison part 3/
Jettison part 4/Jettison part 5/Jettison part 6

Wishes (2013)
Track-listing: Ascending Soul/Sharing Space/The
Sky is Heavy/Wishes

Backwards Chimney (2014)
Track-listing: West of Arkham/Backwards
Chimney/Cloth Held/Sentinel Hill/Other Paths

Pike 43 (2014)
Track-listing: Six untitled instrumental tracks

**You Can't Triple Stamp a Double Stamp
(2014)**
Track-listing: You Can't Triple Stamp a Double
Stamp/Avalanche/Cripes/Silent City/Treedotted
Hillside/Wormfarm/Prominent Ghosts/Flickering
Lights/Extra Gloves/Portrait Gallery/Tea and
Strumpets/By The Moon/Snow Owl

The Coats of Claude (2014)
Track-listing: The Coats of Claude/Ghost in the Rocking Chair/Animatronic Party Goers/Dancing Backwards/Forked Beak/Dimly Backlit Eyeballs/Headless Reflection

Rainy Days (2014)
Track-listing: See-Through Cloud/Underwater Rain Drops/Light Through the Fog/Rainbow

Roller Coaster Track Repair (2014)
Track-listing: Room 7/Room 12

Hide in the Pickling Jar (2014)
Track-listing: Hide in the Pickling Jar/Countersunk/Squirrel on a Perch/Sabertooth Saw

Monument Valley (2013)
Track-listing: Monument Valley/Fembot/Attic Floor/Lirtson Nostril

Pitch Dark (2014)
Track-listing: Pitch Dark/Drifting Ice/Water Drops

Claymation Courtyard (2014)
Track-listing: Claymation Courtyard/Disintegration Mirrors/Chainsaw Slide/Eerie Canal

Factory (2014)
Track-listing: Factory Q/Factory R/Factory S/Factory T/Factory U/Factory V/Factory W/Factory X/Factory /Factory Z

City of Ferris Wheels (2014)
Track-listing: City of Ferris Wheels/Lost Toys/The Cape of Good Hope

The Frankensteins Monster Blinds (2014)
Track-listing: Boris/Kar/Loff

The Miskatonic Scale (2014)
Track-listing: M/I/S/K/A/T/O/N

Cycle (2014)
Track-listing: Repair Station/Cycle/Replacement Decal

Night Gallery (2014)
Track-listing: Painting 1/Painting 2/Painting 3/Painting 4

Outpost (2014)
Track-listing: Outpost/Minor Domo/Electric Umbrella/Pressed Pennies/Look Through

Ydrapoej (2014)
Track-listing: ID 1/ID 2/ID 3/ID 4/ID 5/ID 6/ID 7/ID 8/ID 9/ID 10

Footsteps (2014)
Track-listing: Footsteps

Citacis (2014)
Track-listing: Citacis 72/Citacis 73/Citacis 74/Citacis 75/Citacis 76/Citacis 77/Citacis 78/Citacis 79/Citacis 80

Outlined for Citacis (2014)
Track-listing: Citacis 63/Citacis 64/Citacis 65/Citacis 66/Citacis 67/Citacis 68/Citacis 69/Citacis 70/Citacis 71

Grand Gallery (2014)
Track-listing: Omplat/Monster Zero

Aquarium (2014)
Track-listing: Aquarium/Without Form/Attention Electric Cyclone/Beyond the Windmill/Hopper Feeding Mash

Hold Me Forever (In memory of my mom Nancy York Carroll) (2014)
Track-listing: N/Y/C/4/ev/er

Leave the Light On (2014)
Track-listing: Leave the Light On/Hospitality/The Bellman/This Room Sleeps One and a Half

Abandoned Slaughterhouse (2014)
Track-listing: A/C/C/1/3/6/5/6

Assignment 033-03 (2014)
Track-listing: 0/3/3/-/0/3

Category of Whereness (2014)
Track-listing: Second Lowest/Divide This Number/Numerous Experiments/Category of Whereness

Snow Slug (2014)
Track-listing: S 17/N 6/O 38/W 1/SL 52/U 12/G 81

Celery (2014)
Track-listing: Celery

Closed Attractions (2014)
Track-listing: Closed Attractions/Mecha Slunk Roller Coaster/Stump Cars/Lantern Alley/Antler Hill

Final Bend of the Labyrinth (2014)
Track-listing: FBOTL 1/FBOTL 2/FBOTL 3/FBOTL 4/FBOTL 5/FBOTL 6

Infinity Hill (2014)
Track-listing: Under Earth/Dark Moon/Ray Cast/ The Land Bleeds/The Mist/Forest Guardian/ Watchershand/Infinity Hill

Twilight Constrictor (2014)
Track-listing: For Your Safety/All Limbs/Inside/ Twilight Constrictor

Caterpillar (2104)
Track-listing: Reprint/Fountain/Hot Wheels/ Caterpillar/Mr. Toad's Wait Time/Ring/Dream Machine/Skizzy's Hot Rod

Bumbyride Dreamlands (2014)
Track-listing: Bumbyride Dreamlands/Torch/ Propshop/Hub and Spoke Plan/Sunken Claphouse/Asteroid Belt/Land/Bend/Sharp Drop

Pike 78 (2014)
Track-listing: four tracks numbered 1 – 4

Geppetos Trunk (2014)
Track-listing: Geppettos Trunk/Yellow Brick Mold/ South Chamber of Pit/Solar Sled/Landlakes/ Eyesblink/Emotion Detecter

Cutout Animatronic (2014)
Track-listing: Cut/out/An/ima/tronic

Carnival of Cartilage (2014)
Track-listing: Carnival of Cartilage

Calamity Cabin (2014)
Track-listing: Calamity Cabin/Walking In /The Forest Sings/Downpour/What a Weird Room/Found in the Tomb/Hollow Door/Beware of Quicksand

Dreamless Slumber (2014)
Track-listing: Dreamless Slumber part one/ Dreamless Slumber part two/Dreamless Slumber part three/Dreamless Slumber part four/Dreamless Slumber part five/Dreamless Slumber part six/Dreamless Slumber part seven/ Dreamless Slumber part eight/Dreamless Slumber part nine

GUNS N' ROSES

Whirlpool (2014)
Track-listing: AA/CC/EE/GG/II/KK/MM/OO/QQ/SS

Walk In Loset (2014)
Track-listing: Glass Eye/Long to Wave/Walk in Loset

Our Selves (2014)
Track-listing: Our Selves/Standing in the Field/Dew Drops/Looking From Afar

Interstellar Slunk (2014)
Track-listing: Barney Peeled Out/Coral Castle/Flat Fleet/0.5

Red Pepper Restaurant (2014)
Track-listing: Level 1/Level 2/Level 3/Level 4

The Time Travelers Dream (2014)
Track-listing: Channel 1/Channel 2/Channel 3/Channel 4/Channel 5/Channel 6/Channel 7/Channel 8/Channel 9

Listen for the Whisper (2014)
Track-listing: Listen for the Whisper/Crane

Sublunar (2014)
Track-listing: Peculiarity of Fire/Dryness of Earth/Moisture of Air/Frigidity of Water

The Splatterhorn (2014)
Track-listing: Horn 1/Horn 2/Horn 3/Horn 4/Horn 5/Horn 6/Horn 7/Horn 8/Horn 9

Coaster Coat (2014)
Track-listing: Coaster Coat/Flying Cat/Coastline

Magic Lantern (2014)
Track-listing: Magic Lantern/Chess Roof/First Corridor/Wind From Where/Land of the Lanterns

Northern Lights (2014)
Track-listing: Northern Lights/Flare

Yarn (2014)
Track-listing: H.V./Spindle 1/Spindle 2

Passageways (2014)
Track-listing: Passageway 1/Passageway 2/Passageway 3/Passageway 4/Passageway 5

Pilot (2014)
Track-listing: Pilot 1/Pilot 2/Pilot 3/Pilot 4/Pilot 5/Pilot 6/Pilot 7/Pilot 8/Pilot 9

Polar Trench (2014)
Track-listing: The Light in the Fog/Polar Trench/Heiro/Glyphics

The Mighty Microscope (2014)
Track-listing: The Mighty Microscope/Phase Yellow/Inner Space

In The Hollow Hills (2014)
Track-listing: In The Hollow Hills/Ghosts of Broken Eggs/Bumper Cars/Seas and Stars

Sideway Streets (2015)
Track-listing: Sideway Streets/Orbits/Pathless Road

Squid Ink Lodge (2015)
Track-listing: Old Lunch Pale/Squid Ink Lodge/Drawing in the Dirt

Project Little Man (2015)
Track-listing: Project Little Man/Thorne Room

The Moltrail (2015)
Track-listing: The Moltrail part 1/The Moltrail part 2/Woven Wire

Forest of Bamboo (2015)
Track-listing: Forest of Bamboo

Weird Glows Gleam (2015)
Track-listing: Weird/Glows/Gleam

Collect Itself (2015)
Track-listing: Collect Itself/Garden Mold

The Left Panel (2015)
Track-listing: The Left Panel/Strips of Paper

Wall to Wall Cobwebs (2015)
Track-listing: Runaway Carriage/The Miracle
Molecule/Wall To Wall Cobwebs

Night of the Snowmole (2015)
Track-listing: Phantom Steamboat/Night of the
Snowmole

Creaky Doors and Creaky Floors (2015)
Track-listing: Creaky Doors/Creaky Floors

Herbie Theatre (2015)
Track-listing: Herbie Theatre - First Act/
Intermission/Herbie Theatre - Second Act/Herbie
Theatre After Party

Glow in the Dark (2015)
Track-listing: Glow in the Dark/Vacant Space/
Underworld Maze

Marble Monsters (2015)
Track-listing: Marble Monsters/5 Sided
Chamber/Burning Eyes/Lost Cities

Infinity of the Spheres (2015)
Track-listing: Infinity of the Spheres/Liquid
Mantis

Vacuum (2015)
Track-listing: Basement Steps/Floating/Endless
Rain/Skyline/Sketched/Side Lake/Vacuum

Elevator (2015)
Track-listing: 10th Floor/11th Floor/12th
Floor/13th Floor/Flower and Headcheese Festival

Solar Sailcraft (2015)
Track-listing: Solar Sailcraft/Flying Saucer/
Toecutter's Cleaver part 1/Toecutter's Cleaver
part 2/Toecutter's Cleaver part 3/Toecutter's
Cleaver part 4/Toecutter's Cleaver part 5/
Toecutter's Cleaver part 6/Toecutter's Cleaver
part 7/Fragments

Louzenger (2015)
Track-listing: Louzenger/Backwords Circle/
Standing on a Sidewalk/Shade/Vehicleof/Hall
Mark/Airship

Shaded Ray (2015)
Track-listing: Shaded Ray/4 Lands/Junkyard
Ridge

The Other Side of the Dark (2015)
Track-listing: The Other Side of the Dark/Three
Wheeler

Scroll of Vegetable (2015)
Track-listing: Nest Boxes/Pirate Treasure/
Perchment/Scroll of Vegetable

Rotten Candy Cane (2015)
Track-listing: R/o/t/t/e/n/C/a/n/d/y/C/a/n/e

Along the River Bank (2015)
Track-listing: Along the River Bank/Mind Train/
View Masters/All Ashore/Starboard Bow/Shell

GUNS N' ROSES

Tourist (2015)
Track-listing: Glow Worm/Tourist/Ticket to Extinguish/Bookend Alley/Break for the Slide/Storage

Paint to the Tile (2015)
Track-listing: Paint to the Tile/Rattle/Shell/Faire Realm/Imprint 1

Tucked Into Dreams (2015)
Track-listing: Frontierland/Tucked Into Dreams/Gills/Fog/Pale Hill/Sand

Forever Lake (2015)
Track-listing: Forever Lake/Wooden Horses/Railroad Trail

Down in the Bayou Part Two (2015)
Track-listing: Critter/Marshmallow/Water Gardens/Down in the Bayou Part Two

Down the Bayou Part One (2015)
Track-listing: Down the Bayou Part One/Swamplands/Moss/Murky Waters

Chamber of Drawers (2015)
Track-listing: Chamber of Drawers/Where Winds Meet/To the Basement

Embroidery (2015)
Track-listing: Embroidery/8 Thousand Mirrors/Plunged

Digging Under the Basement (2015)
Track-listing: First Dig/Second Dig/Third /Fourth Dig/Fifth Dig/Sixth Dig/Oh no!

Haunted Roller Coaster Chair (2015)
Track-listing: Any/Volunteers/a/Ghost/Will/Fol/low/You/Home

Firebolt (2015)
Track-listing: bolt/e/r/i/f

Hideous Phantasm (2015)
Track-listing: Hideous Phantasm/Vessel/Glass Shade

Giant Claw (2015)
Track-listing: Giant/Claw/From/The/Cen/ter/Of/The/Earth/Giant Claw Returns to the Center of the Earth

Observation (2015)
Track-listing: ob/ser/vat/ion

Hats and Glasses (2105)
Track-listing: Hats/Glasses

Last Call for the E.P. Ripley (2015)
Track-listing: Stop 1/Stop 2/Stop 3/Stop 4/Stop 5/Stop 6/Stop 7/Stop 8/Stop 9

Nautical Nightmares (2015)
Track-listing: Shell 1/Shell 2/Shell 3/Shell 4/Shell 5/Shell 6/Shell 7/Shell 8/Shell 9

Blank Bot (2015)
Track-listing: QZ 1/QZ 2/QZ 3/QZ 4/QZ 5/QZ 6/QZ 7/QZ 8/QZ 9

Scream Sundae (2015)
Track-listing: Scream Sundae/Pop-Up Skull/Uncle Bubbles (inspired by Towel's dad)

Kareem's Footprint (2015)
Track-listing: Kareem's Footprint/Inosanto: Kali Master/Jabbar's Fly Swatter/Fake Beard Fight on Macau/Get Going Fella

Carrotcature (2015)
Track-listing: C-ret 1/C-ret 2/C-ret 3/C-ret 4/C-ret 5/C-ret 6/C-ret 7/C-ret 8

Popcorn Shells (2015)
Track-listing: Popcorn Shells/Stetzab/Yester

Invisible Forest (2015)
Track-listing: heaviness/speed/atmosphere/happiness

Chickencoopscope (2015)
Track-listing: Chickencoopscope/A Roosters Eye View/Chicken Fountains/Wire Reflections/The Wonders of Feathers

Heaven is your Home (For my Father, Thomas Manley Carroll) (2015)
Track-listing: Heaven is your Home/Always Watching

Fog Gardens (2015)
Track-listing: Ice Eclipse/Fog Gardens/The Bottle House/Track

Carnival Cutouts (2015)
Track-listing: Carnival Cutouts/Water Balloon Filling Station/Lasso the Slug

Whisper Track (2015)
Track-listing: Whisper Track/Hillsides/Such as Straw/Overgrown Shrubs

The Cellar Yawns (2015)
Track-listing: Side Less Well/Damp/Clothstraw/The Cellar Yawns

Ancient Lens (2015)
Track-listing: Ancient Lens/Fossilized Dunce Cap/2 x 6

Herbie Climbs a Tree (2015)
Track-listing: Herbie Climbs a Tree/Sealed Room/Lone Lagoon/Moving Walkway

Upside Down Skyway (2015)
Track-listing: Caterpillar Invasion/Skull Rock Cove/Suspension Bridge/Upside Down Skyway/Kendo Training Port/Braking Zones/Insects

Twisted Branches (2015)
Track-listing: Twisted Branches Part 1/Twisted Branches Part 2/Twisted Branches Part 3/Twisted Branches Part 4/Twisted Branches Part 5/Collapse Cliff/Mummy in the Wall/Swollen Trees

Half Circle Bridge (2015)
Track-listing: Half/Circle/Bridge/Tet

Land of Miniatures (2015)
Track-listing: Land of Miniatures/Loathsome Shape/Triceratoptron/Way Back When

Bats in the Lite Brite (2015)
Track-listing: Peg 1/Peg 2/Peg 3/Peg 4/Peg 5/Peg 6/Peg 7/Peg 8

Four Forms (2015)
Track-listing: Midnight Sun/Four Forms/Collapse Surface/Open Warp/Dripping Castle/Ricochet Laser/Thing From the Sea

Blue Tide (2015)
Track-listing: Blue/Tide

Ghoul (2015)
Track-listing: Ghoul 1/Ghoul 2

Orange Tree (2015)
Track-listing: Orange Tree/Town Hall Bell

GUNS N' ROSES

Region (2015)
Track-listing: Region/Castle Stairs/River of Liquid Fire/Clock Striking/Ancient Desert

Shapeless (2015)
Track-listing: Shapeless/Vague Lights/The Sleep Book

Ognarader (2015)
Track-listing: Og/na/ra/der

The Windowsill (2015)
Track-listing: The Moors/The Dunes/The Windowsill

Washed Away (2015)
Track-listing: Washed Away/Spike

A Ghost Took My Homework (2015)
Track-listing: A Ghost Took My Homework/A Man Visits Museum/Birds and Ladders

Crest of the Hill (2015)
Track-listing: Crest of the Hill/Clattering of Hooves/Antique Forest/Equestrian Statue

The Blob (2015)
Track-listing: Blob Enters the Room/Blob Digs a Hole/Blob Goes Upstairs/Blob Finds Ancient Scroll/Blob Gets Drink of Water/Blob Goes to Sleep

Last House on Slunk Street (2015)
Track-listing: Last House on Slunk Street/What's On The End of That Fork?/The Cupboards Are/There's a Stair Missing/The Mops Got Something On It/Popsicle Sticks and Ketchup/Clothesline with Stuff Hanging On It/Sandbox/Used Glasses/Doormat With Hole Underneath/Posters Covering Stuff/Stuff Hanging From The Ceiling/Wrapping Up Something/Unplugged Refrigerator/Sounds From Inside The Wall/Back Yard Chair

Quilted (2015)
Track-listing: Quilted

31 Days Til Halloween: Visitor From The Mirror (2015)
Track-listing: Visitor From The Mirror part 1/Visitor From The Mirror part 2/Visitor From The Mirror part 3/Visitor From The Mirror part 4/Visitor From The Mirror part 5/Visitor From The Mirror part 6/Visitor From The Mirror part 7

30 Days Til Halloween: Swollen Glasses (2015)
Track-listing: Swollen Glasses part 1/Swollen Glasses part 2/Swollen Glasses part 3/Swollen Glasses part 4/Swollen Glasses part 5/Swollen Glasses part 6/Swollen Glasses part 7/Swollen Glasses part 8/Swollen Glasses part 9/Swollen Glasses part 10

29 Days Til Halloween: Blurmwood (2015)
Track-listing: Blurmwood part 1/Blurmwood part 2/Blurmwood part 3/Blurmwood part 4

28 Days Til Halloween: The Insides of the Outsides (2015)
Track-listing: The Insides of the Outsides part 1/The Insides of the Outsides part 2/The Insides of the Outsides part 3/The Insides of the Outsides part 4/The Insides of the Outsides part 5/The Insides of the Outsides part 6

27 Days Til Halloween: Cavern Guide (2015)
Track-listing: Cavern Guide part 1/Cavern Guide part 2/Cavern Guide part 3/Cavern Guide part 4/Cavern Guide part 5/Cavern Guide part 6

26 Days Til Halloween: Bogwitch (2015)
Track-listing: Bogwitch part 1/Bogwitch part 2/
Bogwitch part 3/Bogwitch part 4/Bogwitch part
5/Bogwitch part 6/Bogwitch part 7/Bogwitch part
8/Bogwitch part 9

25 Days Til Halloween: Window Fragment
(2015)
Track-listing: Window Fragment part 1/Window
Fragment part 2/Window Fragment part 3/
Window Fragment part 4/Window Fragment part
5/Window Fragment part 6/Window Fragment
part 7/Window Fragment part 8/Window
Fragment part 9/Window Fragment part 10

24 Days Til Halloween: Screaming Scalp
(2015)
Track-listing: Screaming Scalp part 1/Screaming
Scalp part 2/Screaming Scalp part 3/Screaming
Scalp part 4/Screaming Scalp part 5/Screaming
Scalp part 6/Screaming Scalp part 7/Screaming
Scalp part 8/Screaming Scalp part 9

23 Days Til Halloween: Wax (2015)
Track-listing: Wax part 1/Wax part 2

22 Days Til Halloween: I Got This Costume
From The Sears Catalog (2015)
Track-listing: I Got This Costume From The Sears
Catalog part 1/I Got This Costume From The
Sears Catalog part 2/I Got This Costume From
The Sears Catalog part 3/I Got This Costume
From The Sears Catalog part 4/I Got This
Costume From The Sears Catalog part 5/I Got
This Costume From The Sears Catalog part 6/I
Got This Costume From The Sears Catalog part
7

21 Days Til Halloween: Cement Decay
(2015)
Track-listing: Cement Decay part 1/Cement
Decay part 2/Cement Decay part 3/Cement
Decay part 4/Cement Decay part 5/Cement

Decay part 6/Cement Decay part 7/Cement
Decay part 8

20 Days Til Halloween: Forgotten
Experiment (2015)
Track-listing: Forgotten Experiment part 1/
Forgotten Experiment part 2/Forgotten
Experiment part 3/Forgotten Experiment part
4/Forgotten Experiment part 5/Forgotten
Experiment part 6/Forgotten Experiment part 7/
Forgotten Experiment part 8

19 Days Til Halloween: Light in Window
(2015)
Track-listing: Light in Window part 1/Light in
Window part 2/Light in Window part 3/Light in
Window part 4/Light in Window part 5/Light in
Window part 6/Light in Window part 7/Light in
Window part 8/Light in Window part 9/Light in
Window part 10

18 Days Til Halloween: Blue Squared
(2015)
Track-listing: Blue Squared part 1/Blue Squared
part 2/Blue Squared part 3/Blue Squared part 4

17 Days Til Halloween: 1079 (2015)
Track-listing: 1079 part 1/1079 part 2/1079
part 3/1079 part 4/1079 part 5

16 Days Til Halloween: Cellar (2015)
Track-listing: Cellar part 1/Cellar part 2/Cellar
part 3/Cellar part 4/Cellar part 5/Cellar part 6/
Cellar part 7/Cellar part 8

15 Days Til Halloween: Grotesques (2015)
Track-listing: Grotesques part 1/Grotesques
part 2/Grotesques part 3/Grotesques part 4/
Grotesques part 5/Grotesques part 6/Grotesques
part 7

GUNS N' ROSES

14 Days Til Halloween: Voice From The Dead Forest (2015)
Track-listing: Voice From The Dead Forest part 1/ Voice From The Dead Forest part 2/Voice From The Dead Forest part 3/Voice From The Dead Forest part 4/Voice From The Dead Forest part 5/Voice From The Dead Forest part 6/Voice From The Dead Forest part 7/Voice From The Dead Forest part 8

13 Days Til Halloween: Maple Syrup (2015)
Track-listing: Maple Syrup part 1/Maple Syrup part 2/Maple Syrup part 3/Maple Syrup part 4/ Maple Syrup part 5/Maple Syrup part 6/Maple Syrup part 7/Maple Syrup part 8

12 Days Til Halloween: Face Sling Shot (2015)
Track-listing: Face Sling Shot part 1/Face Sling Shot part 2/Face Sling Shot part 3/Face Sling Shot part 4/Face Sling Shot part 5/Face Sling Shot part 6/Face Sling Shot part 7/Face Sling Shot part 8

11 Days Til Halloween: Reflection (2015)
Track-listing: Reflection part 1/Reflection part 2/Reflection part 3/Reflection part 4/Reflection part 5/Reflection part 6/Reflection part 7

10 Days Til Halloween: Residue (2015)
Track-listing: Residue part 1/Residue part 2/ Residue part 3/Residue part 4/Residue part 5/ Residue part 6/Residue part 7/Residue part 8

9 Days Til Halloween: Eye on Spiral (2015)
Track-listing: Eye on Spiral part 1/Eye on Spiral part 2/Eye on Spiral part 3/Eye on Spiral part 4/ Eye on Spiral part 5/Eye on Spiral part 6/Eye on Spiral part 7

8 Days Til Halloween: Flare Up (2015)
Track-listing: Flare Up part 1/Flare Up part 2/ Flare Up part 3

7 Days Til Halloween: Cavernous (2015)
Track-listing: Cavernous part 1/Cavernous part 2/Cavernous part 3/Cavernous part 4/Cavernous part 5/Cavernous part 6/Cavernous part 7/ Cavernous part 8

6 Days Til Halloween: Underlair (2015)
Track-listing: Underlair part 1/Underlair part 2/ Underlair part 3/Underlair part 4/Underlair part 5/Underlair part 6/Underlair part 7/Underlair part 8

5 Days Til Halloween: Scrapbook Front (2015)
Track-listing: Scrapbook Front part 1/Scrapbook Front part 2/Scrapbook Front part 3/Scrapbook Front part 4/Scrapbook Front part 5/Scrapbook Front part 6/Scrapbook Front part 7

4 Days Til Halloween: Silent Photo (2015)
Track-listing: Silent Photo part 1/Silent Photo part 2/Silent Photo part 3/Silent Photo part 4/ Silent Photo part 5/Silent Photo part 6

3 Days Til Halloween: Crow Hedge (2015)
Track-listing: Crow Hedge part 1/Crow Hedge part 2/Crow Hedge part 3/Crow Hedge part 4

2 Days Til Halloween: Cold Frost (2015)
Track-listing: Cold Frost part 1/Cold Frost part 2/ Cold Frost part 3/Cold Frost part 4/Cold Frost part 5/Cold Frost part 6/Cold Frost part 7

Happy Halloween: Silver Shamrock (2015)
Track-listing: Silver Shamrock part 1/Silver Shamrock part 2/Silver Shamrock part 3/Silver Shamrock part 4/Silver Shamrock part 5

365 Days Til Halloween: Smash (2015)
Track-listing: Smash

The Wishing Brook (2015)
Track-listing: Wish 1/Wish 2/Wish 3

Rooms of Illusions (2015)
Track-listing: Rooms of Illusions part 1/Rooms of Illusions part 2/Rooms of Illusions part 3/Rooms of Illusions part 4/Rooms of Illusions part 5

Sunken Parlor (2015)
Track-listing: Wall Slide/Sunken Parlor

Screen Door (2015)
Track-listing: Sc/Are/Ee/Nn/Do/Or

Hornet (2015)
Track-listing: Hornet part 1/Hornet part 2/Hornet part 3/Hornet part 4/Hornet part 5

Crumple (2015)
Track-listing: Crumple part one/Crumple part two

Trace Candle (2015)
Track-listing; Trace Candle

Teflecter (2015)
Track-listing: Teflecter/Q 12/Q 11/Q 10/Q 9/Q 8/Q 7/Q 6

Wheels of Ferris (2015)
Track-listing: Saw See/Forgotten Factory/Lamp/Wheels of Ferris/Stapler/B Train to Bronx/Wax Barrell

Pike Doors (2015)
Track-listing: Door One/Door Two/Door Three

Old Toys (2015)
Track-listing: Old Toys/Zone Ahead/Mount Shasta/Oak Island/Exit 46/Valley of the Fog

Rain Drops on Christmas (2015)
Track-listing: Rain Drops on Christmas (This song is dedicated to those that have lost loved ones)/Puddles/The Cookie Monster/I know you know what that present is . . ./ . . .But don't tell me

Mirror Realms (2016)
Track-listing: Blue Slide/Mirror Realms part one/Mirror Realms part two/Mirror Realms part three

Cove Cloud (2016)
Track-listing: Cove/Cloud

Out of the Attic (2016)
Track-listing: Chew Chew Train/Out of the Attic/Nowhere in Particular/Perilous Garden/Dank Dungeon/Giant Jellyfish/Gloom

Dragging the Fence (2016)
Track-listing: Dragging the Fence/Planted

Buildor (2016)
Track-listing: Buildor part 1/Buildor part 2

Florrmat (2016)
Track-listing: Florrmat part 1/Florrmat part 2/Florrmat part 3/Florrmat part 4/Florrmat part 5/Florrmat part 6/Florrmat part 7

Happy Birthday MJ 23 (2016)
Track-listing: Happy Birthday MJ 23/Groovie Goolies/Yellow Brick Snail/Rib Cage Wreath

Arcade of the Deserted (2016)
Track-listing: Arcade of the Deserted/Swung Vault/Cavernous/Sank

GUNS N' ROSES

The Creaking Stairs (2016)
Track-listing: The Creaking Stairs Part 1/The
Creaking Stairs Part 2/The Creaking Stairs Part 3

Cabs (2016)
Track-listing: Cabs/Sludging Through the
Slaughterhouse/Styrofoam Cut-Ups/Underneath
the Arctic

Rooftop (2016)
Track-listing: Hexagon/Rooftop

Drift (2016)
Track-listing: Fastpass/Drift/Tentaclon/Streamlet

Lightboard (2016)
Track-listing: Lightboard/Tales/Deep Within The
Sea

22222222 (2016)
Track-listing: 22222222/11111111

Coupon (2016)
Track-listing: Nail in the Clock/Coupon

Oneiric Pool (2016)
Track-listing: Oneiric Pool part 1/Oneiric Pool
part 2/Oneiric Pool part 3/Oneiric Pool part 4/
Oneiric Pool part 5/Oneiric Pool part 6/Oneiric
Pool part 7

Castle on Slunk Hill (2016)
Track-listing: Corridor 1/Corridor 2/Corridor 3/
Corridor 4/Corridor 5/Corridor 6

The Five Blocks (2016)
Track-listing: 0 Block/1 Block/2 Block/3 Block/4
Block/5 Block

Attic Garden (2016)
Track-listing: Drawer 1/Drawer 2/Drawer 3/
Drawer 4/Drawer 5/Drawer 6/Drawer 7/Drawer 8

The Mermaid Stairwell (2016)
Track-listing: The Mermaid Stairwell/Dancing
Sparkles/Fairy Boat/Silver Upon the Ocean

Chart (2016)
Track-listing: Chart/Granite Track/Glowing Gate

Sparks in the Dark (2016)
Track-listing: Sparks in the Dark/The Pond of
Peace/Garden at Twilight/A Long Days Walk

Hamdens Hollow (2016)
Track-listing: Section 1/Section 2/Section 3/
Section 4/Section 5/Section 6/Section 7/Section
8/Section 9/Section 10/Section 11

Santa's Toy Workshop (2016)
Track-listing: Roudy Elves in Workshop/Assembly
Line of Monsters and Robots/Winds Through
Antlers/Blitzen Goes Berserk/Santa's 20 Minutes
Away/Wrapped Mego Monsters Under the Tree/
Reindeer Rampage

Out Orbit (2017)
Track-listing: Invisible Railroad/To Infinity and
Beyond (dedicated to Craig Sager)/Out Orbit/
Assortments

Space Viking (2017)
Track-listing: Space Viking (To Bernie Worrell,
the greatest music maker of all)/Litten Well/Ever

Nettle (2017)
Track-listing: Nettle/Praying/Storms/Barren part
1/Barren part 2/Open Ancient/Leaving Shells

Rivers in the Seas (2017)
Track-listing: Rivers in the Seas/The Roles of
Uncertainty/Other Portals/Seven Planes

Adrift in Sleepwakefulness (2017)
Track-listing: Half See/Dreaming Frequencies/
Empty Scroll/Salvage the Fragments/Stare into
Trance/Adrift in Sleepwakefulness

The Moss Lands (2017)
Track-listing: The Moss Lands/Crescent Moon/
Antique Wall/City of Lutes/Groves/Sunless
Stream/Faint Clicking/Vague Visions/Ribbons

250 (2017)
Track-listing: Two/Hundred/And/Fifty

Waterfall Cove (2017)
Track-listing: Waterfall Cove/Whispers Way/The
Barren Plains/9001

Bozo in the Labyrinth (2017)
Track-listing: Mirrors of the Sleeping Mind/Cliff
Faces/Flooded Ballroom/Branch/The Chambers/
Bozo in the Labyrinth

Coop Erstown (2017)
Track-listing: Coop Erstown/Tinkertrack/
Quadruple Chicken Barn/Clay Hen/Rooms of
Brooms

Woven Twigs (2017)
Track-listing: Twig 1/Twig 2/Twig 3/Twig 4/Twig 5/
Twig 6/Twig 7/Twig 8/Twig 9

Abominable Snow Scalp (2017)
Track-listing: Abominable Snow Scalp/
Floorascents/Headless Reflection/Pluriverse/
Crator Ridge/Door Along the Wall/Pincushion

Meteor Firefly Net (2017)
Track-listing: Image From The Void/Mountainous
Mine/Meteor Firefly Net/Nail Bridge

Blank Slate (2017)
Track-listing: Blank Slate/Opened to the Air/Wind
of Hollow/Task in Trunk/Solar Staple/Lockun

Echo (2017)
Track-listing: Reaching/Echo/Table

Undersea Dead City (2017)
Track-listing: Undersea Dead City/Region of the
Unreal/Mangled/Odor of Book/Moonlit Decay/
Visitor From Tomb

Ferry to the Island of Lost Minds (2017)
Track-listing: Lost Minds Part 1/Lost Minds Part
2/Lost Minds Part 3/Lost Minds Part 4/Lost
Minds Part 5/Lost Minds Part 6/Lost Minds Part
7/Lost Minds Part 8

Portal to the Red Waterfall (2017)
Track-listing: Portal to the Red Waterfall/Spirits/
Roundtable/Crayon Factory

Nib Y Nool (2017)
Track-listing: Nib Y Nool 1/Nib Y Nool 2/Nib Y
Nool 3/Nib Y Nool 4/Nib Y Nool 5/Nib Y Nool 6/
Nib Y Nool 7/Nib Y Nool 8/Nib Y Nool 9/Nib Y
Nool 10

Glacier (2017)
Track-listing: Glacier/Relic/Flood/Evaporate/Plate

Poseidon (2017)
Track-listing: Poseidon part 1/Poseidon part 2/
Poseidon part 3/Poseidon part 4/Poseidon part
5/Poseidon part 6

Ride Operator Q Bozo (2017)

GUNS N' ROSES

Track-listing: R.O.Q Bozo 1/R.O.Q Bozo/R.O.Q Bozo 3/R.O.Q Bozo 4/R.O.Q Bozo 5/R.O.Q Bozo 6/R.O.Q Bozo 7/Ramp Ahead

Far (2017)
Track-listing: Far 1/Far 2/Far 3/Far 4/Far 5

Thoracic Spine Collapser (2017)
Track-listing: Thoracic Outlet Syndrome/Thoracic Sprain/Nerve Compression at T4/Nerve Compression at T5/Nerve Stability at T6/Complete Shutdown of Central Nervous System/Thoracic Park (home of the most spine shattering roller coasters)/Rejuvenation Chamber

Sonar Rainbow (2017)
Track-listing: Sonar Rainbow/The Maddening of Mercury/Debris/Venomous Fog

Decaying Parchment (2017)
Track-listing: Is/The Maps Inside/Wings of a Dead Moth/Pillar/Twister/Decaying Parchment

A3 (2017)
Track-listing: A3/Liquid Mirror

The Squaring of the Circle (2017)
Track-listing: The Squaring of the Circle/Osirion/Scalp Assail/Fork/Mosaic Silk/Decake

Coniunctio (2017)
Track-listing: Coniunctio

Guillotine Furnace (2017)
Track-listing: Guillotine Furnace Part 1/Guillotine Furnace Part 2/Guillotine Furnace Part 3/Guillotine Furnace Part 4/Guillotine Furnace Part 5/Guillotine Furnace Part 6/Guillotine Furnace Part 7/Guillotine Furnace Part 8

Fourneau Cosmique (2017)
Track-listing: Fourneau Cosmique/Endless Experiments

Dreamthread (2017)
Track-listing: Hypnagogia/Thread 1/Thread 2/Thread 3/Thread 4/Thread 5/Thread 6/Thread 7

Special Releases

In Search of The (2007)
13 albums spelling out the title – all tracks listed "Track 1", "Track 2" etc

Acoustic Shards (2007)
Track-listing: For Mom/Who Me?/Little Gracie/Ed's Rhapsody / Midnight Dance / Jars/Ganryu Island / Sasaki's Gone/Ghosts Upstairs/Spirals/Cubes, Chunks & Crumbles/Thugs/Dinging / Ah-Ji-Jee/Johnny/Stay Out of the Shed/Serape/Longing/Box Elders

Bucketheadland Blueprints (2007)
Track-listing: Blueprints Theme/Giant Robot VS Cleopat/Wonka in Slaughter Zone/Gorey Head Stump & Nosin'/Computer Master/Chicken for Lunch/Sterling Scapula/Seaside/Let's Go to Wally World/Robot Flight/Earthling Fools/Guts & Eyeballs/Haunted Farm/The Rack & Alice in Slaughterland/Skids Looking Where/Buddy on a Slab & Funeral Time/Decapitation/Virtual Reality [2nd Version]/Giant Robot Finale/Robotic Chickens/Intro to Bucketheadland Park [Theme]/Swamp Boy Square Dance/Pirate's Life for Me

From the Coop (2008)
Track-listing: Disembodied Part 1/Disembodied Part 2/Hog Bitch Stomp/Malagueña/Space Mountain/Excerpt #1/Excerpt #2/Excerpt #3/Excerpt #4/Eraserhead/La Grima/Funk Tune/Funkin' Freak/Hog Bitch Stomp/Return of Augustus Gloop/Malagueña/Lunartics/Scalpel Sled/Scraps

Extended Plays

KFC Skin Piles (2001)
Track-listing: A1/A2/A3/A4/B1/B2/B3/B4/B5

Death Cube K

Dreamatorium (1994)
Track-listing: Land of the Lost/Maps of
Impossible Worlds/Terror by Night/Maggot
Dream/Dark Hood

Disembodied (1997)
Track-listing: Disembodied/Embalmed/Terror
Tram/Hanging Gallows/Pre Hack

Tunnel (1999)
Track-listing: Thanatopsis/Tunnel/Leech/Post
Mortem/Hemloc/Scalding Tank/Loss Leper/
Karate/Draw & ¼/Gap/Death Of The Four
Horrors

DCK (2007)
Track-listing: 9 "Untitled" tracks

Monolith (2007)
Track-listing: 5 "Untitled" tracks

Torn From Black Space (2009)
Track-listing: Slow Descent/Hollow Ground/
Watchers/Path Of The Dead/Night Crawler/
Hidden Chamber

GUNS N' ROSES

With Bootsy Collins

Zillatron

Lord of the Harvest (1993)
Track-listing: C.B.I. Files (Central Bug Intelligence)/Bugg Lite/Fuzz Face/Exterminate/ Smell The Secrets/Count Zero/Bootsy And The Beast/No Fly Zone (The Devil's Playground)/The Passion Continues

With Brain

I Need Five Minutes Alone (As Pieces)
Track-listing: Peesez Monologue/Pieces/Danyel/ Ginger/8 Diagram Pole Fighter/Scoop Rack/I'll Wait/Carl Junghole/Twice With The Sledge/ Hazelnut Cream Pie/Slapatron/Bobafi Crucify/ Rap – Bobesett/General Butterfly

Kevin's Noodle House (2007)
Track-listing: Used Banana Box/Leg Warmer/ BK Lounge/Thin Crust/Who Flung Dung/Quad Compressor = Pete/Barnard/Dogens Quest/First Steps

Brain as Hamenoodle (2010)
Track-listing: Meet Hamen/Brad P/Door Handle/ Sunflower Seed/One To Five/Not Feelin' It

With Brain and Melissa Reese

Best Regards (2010)
Track-listing: 5 CDs – all tracks "Untitled"

Kind Regards (2010)
Track-listing: Authentic Uncle/After Hours/ Children At Play/Corn Thins/Dengeness Crab/ May You Help Me?/No Idea/Pop Chip/Team Garcia/Zit Ricken/Gonervill PT 1/Gonervill PT 2/

Gonervill PT 3/Gonervill PT 4/Gonervill PT 5/ Gonervill PT 6/PowPowPow/Bug Spray/Joan/Pac Man/Pea Body/Peak/The Jerk/Weird One/Year Of The Dragon/Your Boy/Zico

With Travis Dickerson

Chicken Noodles (2006)
Track-listing: Enter Tomorrow/Loss From A Distance/Sorrow Of Discord/False Directions

Chicken Noodles II (2007)
Track-listing: Chicken Or The Egg/Ovum Prophecy/Concentric Motion/Oyster Crackers/ Heat And Serve/Let It Cool/Chicken Nostrils

Iconography (2009)
Track-listing: Scansion/Amaranthine/Horology/ Legerdemain/Principia/Fourfold Continuum/ Commemoration/Wheedle/Hue And Cry/Pi/The Children Of Nyx

Left hanging (2010)
Track-listing: Continental Drift/Game Theory/ Archetype/Terra Firma/Cosmogony/What The Hell Was That/Box Beat Boom

With Jonas Hellborg & Michael Shrieve

Octave of the Holy Innocents (1993)
Track-listing: Rana And Fara/Death That Sleeps In Them/The Past Is A Different Country, I Don't Live There Anymore/Child King/Kidogo

With Alix Lambert and Travis Dickerson

Running After Deer (2008)
Track-listing: Becoming A Race Horse/The Liberian Boxing Team/What In The Fuck?/ Pregnant Men In America/Jockey/The African Toy/It Make No Goddam Sense/

Maybe It's Because You're An Asshole/Below The Belt/I'm Tired

With Viggo Mortensen

One Less Thing to Worry About (1997)
Track-listing: Writing/Cursive/Envidia/Cuttings/ Wading/Matinee/Independence/Edit/I'm Not A Singer/To Sleep/Opportunity/Recuerdo/Pioneers/ Necessity Of Lorca/Week Ends/Fat/Prepare/Blow/ Forgetful/Chaco/Eleonora/Parrillada/Ganas/Lagrimas Puras/The Show/Clear/Wet Dog/Parker/Meet/ Laureles/Tell Yourself/Reno/Cruelty/1959/The New Year/Otono Catalan/Single/Lunch (Him)/Stop/Henry, Age 2/Henry, Age 3/Lunch (Her)/The Night We Called It A Day/Bedtime Story For Henry/Reading

Recent Forgeries (1998)
Track-listing: Chaco/Show/Clear/Cuttings/ Wading/1/2/Red/Meet/Laureles/Reno/ Cruelty/1959/Week Ends/Matinee/Prepare/ Bedtime Story For Henry/Massage School/ (Untitled)

The Other Parade (1999)
Track-listing: Death Of A Dentist/Massage School/Trouble At The Launchpad/Strike At The Wig Factory/The Other Parade/Room For Nine/ Dream Of The See-Saw Repairman/Night In An Animal Hospital/...3,4...

One Man's Meat (1999)
Tracks: 10 Chicken Surgery

Pandemoniumfromamerica (2003)
Tracks: Den Gang Jeg Drog Afsted/ Pandemoniumfromamerica/Gone/ They Ate Your family/I Want Mami/Red River Valley/Leave it/ Holyhead/Fall of Troy/Shadow/Cuba On Paper/ Maybe/Half Fling

Please Tomorrow (2004)
Track-listing: Swallows To Bats/Nocturne/Dream One/ Dream Two/Dream Three/Frost/Moonset/Sunrise

This That and The Other (2004)
Track-listing: This/Edit/Massage School/Cuttings/ Necessity Of Lorca/Moonset/Laureles/Eleonora/ Leave It/Parker/The Show/Clear/Trouble At The Launchpad/Otono Catalan/Cursive/Chicken Surgery/That/To Sleep/Independence/Week Ends/ Jack's Box/Ganas/Wading/Matinee/Den Gang Jeg Drog Afsted/The New Year/Prepare/They Ate Your Family/Blow/The Other

Intelligence Failure (2005)
Track-listing: Demolition Of The Willing/Voice Of The People/Spain/Weapons Of Mass Distraction/ Why They Hate Us/It's The Economy/Recess Disappointment/What Kind Of Nation

At All (2008)
Track-listing: Blacksburg/Bomb This/Sorrow Acre/ Fear's Echo/Blind Rendition Fly-over/Shoreditch Nocturne/Thanks, China; Keep The Change/ Tokyo Doesn't Love Us Anymore/At All

Reunion (2011)
Track-listing: Hold My Ladder/Empty House/ It Wasn't Me/Why Not Now?/Lend Me Your Tightrope/Meet Me Outside/Nice Walking With You

Acá (2013)
Tracks 1 & 9

Seventeen Odd Songs (2016)
Track-listing: Don't Come Over/Confession/Den Gang Jeg Drog Afsted/Hold My Ladder/Arranca el Viernes/Berlin Poem/Fear's Echo/Summer's Here/Moonset/Ingeborg/Ashes/Nice Walking With You/Danube Poem/Seed/Ammends/ Thunderhead/Under The Weather

GUNS N' ROSES

Arcana

Arc of the Testimony (1997)
Tracks: Illuminator/Returning/Circles of Hell

Cobra Strike

The 13th Scroll (1999)
Track-listing: The 13th Scroll/Water Ceiling/7th Hall/6th Door/Blank Sky/Torn Face/Wound/Inferno/Braingate/CS-118/Torture Tunnel/Headstone/Hidden Tomb/32nd Degree/Helicopter Kick/Black Sea River/Silent Scream/Buried Alive/The 13th Scroll (Digging to the Devil)

Cobra Strike II: Y, Y+B, X+Y (2000)
Track-listing: Desert/False Radien Cross/Poison Wind/Hellchop to Blind Claw/The Funeral/Beware of the Holding Funnel/Traitors Gate/Moonflake/First Master/Splinter Pool/Notorious Swade/Blood Scroll/Yoshimitsu's Den/Cobra Cartlige/Slap to Branding Nunchuka/Spider Crawl

Colonel Claypool's Bucket of Bernie Brains

The Big Eyeball in the Sky (2004)
Track-listing: Buckethead/Thai Noodles/Tyranny of the Hunt/Elephant Ghost/Hip Shot from the Slab/Junior/Scott Taylor/The Big Eyeball in the Sky/Jackalope/48 Hours to Go/Ignorance is Bliss

Cornbugs

Spot the Psycho (1999)
Track-listing: Choptalk/Vegetable Man/Lord Lawnmower/Pigs Are People Too/Om Frog/Nature Trail/Clown Smile (Death Warmed Over)/Bone Apetit/Chicken & A Severed Hand/Chuckles/Chance/Zig Zag N Scream/Dust N Bones/Rip The Mask/Own That Jimmy/Box A Hair/Tower

Treasure/Head Wound/Power & The Gory/Old Bill/Can You Spot The Psycho?

Cemetery Pinch (2001)
Track-listing: Poker Face/Buried Child/Buckethead, The Scariest & Best Show Ever!/Gore Galore/Cadaver Cadaver/Pain Donkey/Brain Dead/Skeleton In The Closet/Bone Saw/Ed Gein/Hades' Greenish Crown Rag/The Woe Of The Sargasso Sea/Polka Hell/Belly Like A Snake/Happy Halloween/Cornbugs/Ain't No Devil (hidden track)

How Now Brown Cow (2001)
Track-listing: The End/Pipe Man/Bun Boy/Meat Rotten Meat/Sacramento/Brain Dead Too/Dog Town/I'm A Psycho/Tongue Tied/I Wanna/Spastic Song/Head Cheese/Hup You Little Puppet/Didja

Brain Circus (2004)
Track-listing: Riders Of The Whistling Skull/Wasteland/Mushroom Workers/Dirty Sperm Rag/Firin' Pin/Boots Upon The Ground/Crab Claw Maracas/Kingdom Come/Down, Down, Down/(I Want Me A) Clone/Arm Torn Off By A Train/Voodoo Muffin/Hippie Days Are Done/Truck Fire

Donkey Town (2004)
Track-listing: Daddy-O/Chicken Farm/Lawn Puppet/Billy Shakes/Druid Holiday/Pricker Hill/Stalker/Farm-to-Fork/Wiggle Dance/Bear/Sex Milk Mambo/Foundling

Compilations

Skeleton Farm (2002)
Track-listing: Sacramento/Hades' Greenish Crown Rag/Pipe Man/Om Frog/Nature Trail/Clown Smile (Death Warmed Over)/Skeleton In The Closet/Boxa Hair/The Woe Of The Sargasso Sea/Rip The Mask/Belly Like A Snake/Bun Boy/Whiskey Biscum/Cornbugs/Untitled Track

GUNS N' ROSES

Rest Home for Robots (2003)
Track-listing: Lord Lawnmower/Poker Face/
Brain Dead/Zigzag N Scream/Dust N Bones/Ed
Gein/Buried Child/Pigs Are People Too/Spot The
Psycho/Pain Donkey/Chance/I Wanna/Old Bill

Celebrity Psychos (2005)
Track-listing: Choptalk/Vegetable Man/I'm
A Psycho/Tongue Tied/Happy Halloween/
Buckethead Scariest & Best Show Ever!/Cadaver
Cadaver/Meat Rotten Meat/Bone Saw/Didja/
Brian Dead/Dog Town/Hup You Little Puppet/Own
That Jimmy

Deli Creeps

Deli Creeps (1991 Demo Tape) (1991)
Track-listing: Random Killing/Dream Girl/Tribal
Rites/Shadows/Can I Have A Ride

Dawn Of The Deli Creeps (2005)
Track-listing: Can I Have A Ride/Dream Girl/
Found Body/Flesh For The Beast/Hatchet/Time/
Grampa Bill/Chores/Beauty Of Life/Buns Of
Steel/Buried Deep Stays Buried Still/Boom Ch
Ka/Random Killing

El Stew

El Stew 'Extended Play 1.0' (1999)
Track-listing: B-Boy Showcase/Dark Side
Whiplash/Broken Skull/Vintage/Bonus Beats,
Scratches & Loops

No Hesitation (1999)
Track-listing: Reign Of Terror/C.O.K.E/Pelican
Boots/Brah/Dim Slim/T.H.T.S.L.E.E./Reef-Ill/Arab
Mafia/The Tower/Surf Mission (Invasion Of The
Duck Punk)/Darkside Whiplash/Igloo Condo/B-
Boy Showcase/Corn Leaf Smokin/Twoast/Warrior/
Vintage/Blu Kube King

The Rehearsal (2003)
Track-listing: 12 untitled tracks

Rehearsal #2 - The Dark Night Of A Million
Stains (2011)
Track-listing: B'ak'tun/Psilocybin Mushroom/
Tortuguero Moment/Shattered Frontal

Frankenstein Brothers

Bolt on Neck (2008)
Track-listing: Bolt on Neck/5 Second Minute/
Bought Big Ben/The Thief & the Prince/Wait/
Prototype #1

Giant Robot

Giant Robot (1996)
Track-listing: Doomride/Welcome To
Bucketheadland/I Come In Peace/Buckethead's
Toy Store/Want Some Slaw?/Warweb/Aquabot/
Binge And Grab (Instrumental Version)/Pure
Imagination/Buckethead's Chamber Of Horrors/
Onions Unleashed/Chicken/I Love My Parents/
Buckethead's TV Show/Robot Transmission/
Pirate's Life For Me/Post Office Buddy/Star Wars/
Last Train To Bucketheadland

Gorgone

Gorgone (2005)
Track-listing: Enter Gorgone/Siege/Aftermath

Praxis

A Taste of Mutation (1992)
Track-listing: Animal Behaviour/Dead Man
Walking/Crah Victim / Black Science Navigator/
Seven Laws Of Woo

Transmutation (Mutatis Mutandis) (1992)
Track-listing: Blast/War Machine Dub/Interface/
Stimulation Loop/Crash Victim/Black/Science
Navigator/Animal Behavior/Dead Man Walking/
Seven Laws of Woo/The Interworld and the New
Innocence/Giant Robot/Machines in the Modern
City/Godzilla/After Shock (Chaos Never Died)

Singles from Transmutation (Mutatis
Mutandis)

"Animal Behavior" (1992)

Sacrifist (1994)
Track-listing: Stronghold/Cold Rolled/Iron Dub/
Suspension/Rivet/Deathstar/The Hook/Nine
Secrets/Crossing

Metatron (1994)
Track-listing: Wake the Dead/Skull Crack (We
Are Not Sick Men)/Meta-Matic/Cathedral Space
(Soft Hail of Electrons)/Turbine/Vacuum-Mass/
Cannibal (Heart Shape of the Iron Blade)/
Inferno/Heatseeker/Exploded Heart/Warm
Time Machine/Low End Transmission/Over the
Foaming Deep/Double Vision/Armed (T.S.A.
Agent #5)/Warcraft (Bruce Lee's Black Hour of
Chaos)/Triad (The Saw is Family)/Space After
(The Consciousness That Dances and Kills)

Live in Poland (1997)
Track-listing: Live at Summer Jazz Days '96/
Metatron/Sacrifist/Tarab/Crash Victim/The Hook
/ Giant Robot

Transmutation Live (1997)
Track-listing: Movement 1/Movement 2/
Movement 3/Movement 4

Collection (1998)
Track-listing: Triad (The Saw Is Family)/Skull
Crack (We Are Not Sick Men)/Stronghold/Meta-
Matic/Rivet/Maggot Dream/Turbine/Suspension/
Warcraft (Bruce Lee's Hour Of Chaos)/Dark
Hood

Warszawa (1999)
Track-listing: Initiation/Flux And Reflux/Saturn/
Destroyer/Fifth Element

Zurich (2005)
Track-listing: Transmutation/Flame War/
Transmutation 2/Buckethead Audio Virus/
Theatre Of Eternal Turntables/Transmutation
3 - Fresh Impression/Telematic Circuit Break/
Low Bass Monster/Ekstasis/Flicker/Compressed
Signal Cuts/Transmutation 4/Cut-Chaos/Giant
Robot/Direct Hit/Transmutation 5 (Ascent)/
Undercurrent (Live At Knitting Factory)

Tennessee 2004 (2007)
Track-listing: Vertebrae/Spun/Night Of The Slunk/
Guitar Virus/Machine Gun/Haunted/Broken/
Fractal/Bent Light/Chopper/Optic/Magus

Profanation (Preparation for a Coming
Darkness) (2008)
Track-listing: Caution/Worship/Ancient World/
Furies/Galaxies/Sulfur and Cheese/Larynx/
Revelations Part 2/Ruined/Garbage God's/
Babylon Blackout/Endtime
(US release bonus tracks: Wedge/Subgrid)

Sound Virus (2015)
Track-listing: Suspension/Warcraft Triad/Skull
Crack / Cathedral/Inferno/Low Time Machine/
Stronghold/Turbine/Nine/Science Faxtion

Living on Another Frequency (2008)
Track-listing: Sci-Fax Theme/Lookin' for Eden/
At Any Cost/Chaos in Motion/Famous/L.O.A.F.

 183

GUNS N' ROSES

(Living On Another Frequency)/Gone Tomorrow/
Life-IS IN-Deliver/Take You Down/What
It Is/Fatally Flawed Flesh/I See Rockets/
ZIONPLANET10

Shin Terai

Unison (2001)
Track-listing: Clue/Dinner of Heaven/Emotional
Intelligence/Dusk/Tag of War/Dream Catcher/
From Texas

Heaven & Hell (2004)
Track-listing: Movement 1/Movement 2/
Movement 3/Movement 4/Movement 5/
Movement 6/Movement 7

Lightyears (2007)
Track listing: Grid/Transparent/Solitude/
Interwoven/Vector/Vertical/Accelerate/Impact/
Between/Erratum

Thanatopsis

Thanatopsis (2001)
Track-listing: Worm Hole/In Their Millions/Pyrrhic
Victory/Final Reparation/Mortheol/Myopia/Vertex/
Twinge/Last Rites/A Thanatopsis

Axiology (2003)
Track-listing: Nostrum/Pretzel Logic/Vicious
Circle/Cult Of One/Pyre/New War/Gnash/Axiology/
Non Sequitur/Top Of The World Ma

Anatomize (2006)
Track-listing: Counter Clockwise/Break Even
Point/Vitreous Humor/Pollyanna/Prolix Mood/
Common Ground/Unnerved/Simper/Broca's
Area/Cross Section

Requiem (2015)
Track-listing: Introit/La Calavera Catrina/
Resurrection/Veneration/Hypnosis And Thanatos/
Offering/Critical Mass

Guest appearances

Anton Fier
Dreamspeed (1993)
Tracks: Dreamspeed/Being and Time/Never
Come Morning/Dreamspeed (Realm of the
Senseless Mix) A Vague Sense of Order

Blindlight 1992–1994 (2003)
Track-listing: Dreamspeed/Being and Time/
Emotional Smear/Clouds Without Water/Time
Function/A Vague Sense of Order/Never Come
Morning/Dreamspeed/A Vague Sense of Order/
Smoke and Mirrors
(Disc 2): The Absence of Time/Djeema el
Fna/Blind Light/Our Completion/Midnight/The
Nostalgic Ache/Clairvoyance of Self (Seeing
Through)/Our Completion/Bait and Switch

Bernie Worrell

Pieces of Woo: The Other Side (1993)
Track-listing: Witness For The Defense/Set The
Tone / Victory/The Mask/Gladiator Skull/Moon
Over Brixton/Judie's Passion Purple/Fields of Play

Free Agent: A Spaced Odyssey (1997)
Track-listing: Hope Is Here/AfroFuturism (Phased
One)/In Pursuit/WOO Awakens, The Wizard
Cometh/Re-Enter Black Light (Entersection)/
Warriors Off to WOO

Bill Laswell
Axiom Collection II: Manifestation (1993)
Divination – Ambient Dub Volume 1 (1993)
Axiom Ambient – Lost in the Translation (1994)
Axiom Funk – Funkcronomicon (1995)

184

Axiom Funk – 'If 6 was 9' (Single) (1995)
Alien Ambient Galaxy (1996)
Valis II – Everything Must Go (1997)
Telesterion – Hall of Mysteries (1998)
Points of Order (2001)
Method Of Defiance – Inamorata (2007)

Bootsy Collins
Christmas Is 4 Ever (2006)
The Official Boot-Legged-Bootsy-CD (2008)
Tha Funk Capital of the World (2011)
World Wide Funk (2017)

Buckethead and Travis Dickerson
Dragons of Eden (2008)
Track-listing: The Cosmic Calendar/The Brain
And The Chariot/The Abstractions Of Beasts/
Tales Of Dim Eden/Lovers And Madmen/Future
Evolution/Draco/Knowledge Is Destiny

Company 91
1992 – Company 91 Volume 1
1992 – Company 91 Volume 2
1992 – Company 91 Volume 3

Phonopsychograph Disk
Ancient Termites (1998)
Live @ Slim's / Turbulence Chest (1999)
Unrealesed (Cassette Only) (1999)
Marsupial's Belly Flop Breaks (Remastered
version) (2009)
Unreleased (CD version) (2013)

Freekbass
The Air is Fresher Underground (2003)
A Sliver of Shiver (Live DVD) (2007)
Junkyard Waltz (2008)

Icehouse
'Big Wheel' (Single) (1993)
Spin One (EP) (1993)
Full Circle (1994)
'Great Southern Land' (German single) (1994)
Masterfile (Japanese release) (1997)

Lawson Rollins
Elevation (2011)

Mike Patton with Buckethead and DJ Flare,
forming Moonraker
Live @ The Knitting Factory (Bootleg only) (2000)

Refrigerator
'Somehow' (1997)

Single appearance with artist(s)
Henry Kaiser – Hope You Like Our New Direction
(1991)
Will Ackerman – The Opening of Doors (1992)
MCM and the Monster – Collective Emotional
Problems (1993)
Psyber Pop – What? So What? (1993)
Jon Hassell and Blue Screen – Dressing for
Pleasure (1994)
Hakim Bey – T.A.Z. (Temporary Autonomous
Zone) (1994)
Buckshot LeFonque – "No Pain No Gain"
(1995)
Julian Schnabel – Every Silver Lining Has a
Cloud (1995)
Bastard Noise – Split W/Spastic Colon (1998)
DJ Qbert – Wave Twisters (1998)
Banyan – Anytime at All (1999)
Ben Wa – Devil Dub (1999)
Double E – Audio Men (2000)
Tony Furtado Band – Tony Furtado Band (2000)
Meridiem – A Pleasant Fiction (2001)
Gonervill – Gonervill (2001)
Fishbone and the Familyhood – Nextperience
Present: The Friendliest Psychosis of All (2002)
Gemini – Product of Pain (2003)
Bassnectar – Mesmerizing The Ultra (2005)
Gigi – Gold & Wax (2006)
Melissa Reese – Lissa (2007)
Gaudi – Magnetic (2017)

Soundtracks
Last Action Hero (soundtrack) (1993)
Last Action Hero (score) (1993)
Johnny Mnemonic (1995)
Mighty Morphin Power Rangers (1995)

GUNS N' ROSES

Mortal Kombat (1995)
Myth – Dreams of the World (1996)
Stealing Beauty (1996)
Beverly Hills Ninja (1997)
Mortal Kombat: Annihilation (1997)
Ghosts of Mars (2001)
Dragon Ball Z: The History of Trunks (2001)
Scratch (2002)
Flesh for the Beast (score) (2004)
Masters of Horror (2005)
Saw 2 (2005)
Twisted Metal (2012)

Compilations
Guitar Zone (1997)
Guitars on Mars (1997)
Night and Day (1998)
Guitarisma 2 (1998)
Great Jewish Music: Marc Bolan (otherwise
unreleased cover of '20th Century Boy') (1998)
New Yorker Out Loud: Volume 2 (1998)
Crash Course in Music (1999)

Horizons (1999)
Music for the New Millennium (1999)
Innerhythmic Sound System (2001)
Bomb Anniversary Collection (2001)
Gonervill presents: The Freak Brothers (2001)
Guitars for Freedom (2002)
The Meta Collection (otherwise unreleased track
'Remember') (2002)
Urban Revolutions (2002)
Live from Bonnaroo 2002 – Volume 2
(otherwise unreleased C2B3 song 'Number
Two') (2002)
Blue Sueños (otherwise unreleased track
'Planeta') (2005)
Guitar Hero II ('Jordan') (2006)
The Longest Yard and Jack the Ripper (2006)
Fallen Soldiers Memorial (otherwise unreleased
track 'Buckets of Blood' with Bootsy Collins)
(2008)
Guitar Hero III ('Soothsayer') (2008)
Rock Band 2 ('Shackler's Revenge' with Guns N'
Roses) (2008)

BRYAN MANTIA

GN' R Albums
Chinese Democracy

Limbomaniacs

Stinky Grooves (1990)
Track-listing: Butt Funkin'/Maniac/Freestyle/
Porno/Shake It/That's The Way/The Toilet's
Flooded/Pavlov's Frothing Dogs

Praxis
See Buckethead discography

Bullmark
Interstate '76 (1996)

Giant Robot
See Buckethead discography

Godflesh
Songs of Love and Hate (1996)
Track-listing: Wake/Sterile Prophet/Circle of Shit/
Hunter/Gift from Heaven/Amoral/Angel Domain/
Kingdom Come/Time, Death and Wastefulness/
Frail/Almost Heaven

Pieces
See Buckethead discography

Tom Waits

Bone Machine (1992)
Track-listing: Earth Died Screaming/Dirt in the
Ground/Such a Scream/All Stripped Down/Who
Are You/The Ocean Doesn't Want Me/Jesus
Gonna Be Here/A Little Rain (for Clyde)/In the

Colosseum/Goin' Out West/Murder in the Red
Barn/Black Wings/Whistle Down the Wind (for
Tom Jans)/I Don't Wanna Grow Up/Let Me Get
Up on It/That Feel

Mule Variations (1999)
Track-listing: Big in Japan/Lowside of the Road/
Hold On/Get Behind the Mule/House Where
Nobody Lives/Cold Water/Pony/What's He
Building?/Black Market Baby/Eyeball Kid/Picture
in a Frame/Chocolate Jesus/Georgia Lee/Filipino
Box Spring Hog/Take It with Me/Come on Up to
the House

Real Gone (2004)
Track-listing: Top of the Hill/Hoist That Rag/Sins
of My Father/Shake It/Don't Go into That Barn/
How's It Gonna End/Metropolitan Glide/Dead
and Lovely/Circus/Trampled Rose/Green Grass/
Baby Gonna Leave Me/Clang Boom Steam/
Make It Rain/Day After Tomorrow/Chick a Boom
(Hidden track)

Orphans, Brawlers, Bawlers & Bastards
(2006)
Track-listing: Lie to Me/LowDown/Fish in the
Jailhouse/Bottom of the World/Lucinda/Ain't
Goin' Down to the Well/Lord I've Been Changed/
Puttin' on the Dog/Road to Peace/All the Time/
The Return of Jackie and Judy/Walk Away/Sea of
Love/Buzz Fledderjohn/Rains on Me
(Disc two) Bend Down the Branches/You Can
Never Hold Back Spring/Long Way Home/
Widow's Grove/Little Drop of Poison/Shiny
Things/World Keeps Turning/Tell It to Me/Never
Let Go/Fannin Street/Little Man/It's Over/If I
Have to Go/Goodnight Irene/The Fall of Troy/Take
Care of All My Children/Down There by the Train/
Danny Says/Jayne's Blue Wish/Young at Heart

(Disc three:) What Keeps Mankind Alive?/
Children's Story/Heigh Ho/Army Ants/Book of
Moses/Bone Chain/Two Sisters/First Kiss/Dog
Door/Redrum/Nirvana/Home I'll Never Be/Poor
Little Lamb/Altar Boy/The Pontiac/Spidey's Wild
Ride/King Kong/On the Road/Dog Treat (Hidden
track)/Missing My Son (Hidden track)

Additional tracks on LP version: Crazy 'Bout My
Baby/Diamond in Your Mind/Cannon Song/Pray/
No One Can Forgive Me/Outtake from Bone
Machine/Mathie Grove

Primus

Brown Album (1997)
Track-listing: The Return of Sathington
Willoughby/Fisticuffs/Golden Boy/Over the
Falls/Shake Hands with Beef/Camelback
Cinema/Hats Off/Puddin' Taine/Bob's Party
Time Lounge/Duchess and the Proverbial Mind
Spread/Restin' Bones/Coddingtown/Kalamazoo/
The Chastising of Renegade/Arnie

Singles from Brown Album:
'Shake Hands with Beef' (1997)
'Over the Falls' (1997)

Rhinoplasty (1998)
Track-listing: Scissor Man/The Family and the
Fishing Net/Silly Putty/Amos Moses/Behind My
Camel/Too Many Puppies/The Thing That Should
Not Be/Tommy the Cat/Bob's Party Time Lounge

Singles from Rhinoplasty:
'Behind My Camel' (1998)

Antipop (1999)
Track-listing: Intro/Electric Uncle Sam/Natural
Joe/Lacquer Head/The Antipop/Eclectic Electric/
Greet The Sacred Cow/Mama Didn't Raise No
Fool/Dirty Drowning Man/Ballad Of Bodacious/

Power Mad/The Final Voyage Of The Liquid Sky/
Coattails Of A Dead Man/The Heckler

Singles from Antipop:
'Lacquer Head' (1999)
'Electric Uncle Sam' (1999)

Buckethead
See Buckethead discography

El Stew
See Buckethead discography

No Forcefield

Lee's Oriental Massage 415-626-1837 (2000)
Track-listing: Lom/The John Rocker Redemption
Clause/Mr Jellyneck/The Blow Out/Claudius The
God/Vanessa From The Man Show/Marin Mating
Call/Babaak/Hitler Was My Co-Pilot/Squid In The
Shirt/Valeria Mazza/The Hard R/The Clam

God is an Excuse (2001)
Track-listing: Dimethyl Tryptamine/Ladies Night
In Buffalo/Money Savers/How To Purify Street
Heroin/Vanessa From The Man Show/Ray
Watson As Mr. Hand/You Are My Sunshine/Davey
Drum's Drum Solo

Colonel Claypool's Bucket of Bernie Brains
See Buckethead discography

Serj Tankian

Elect the Dead (2007)
Track-listing: Empty Walls/The Unthinking
Majority/Money/Feed Us/Saving Us/Sky Is Over/
Baby/Honking Antelope/Lie Lie Lie/Praise the
Lord and Pass the Ammunition/Beethoven's
Cunt/Elect the Dead

Singles from Elect the Dead:
'The Unthinking Majority' (2007)
'Empty Walls' (2007)
'Lie Lie Lie' (2007)
'Sky Is Over' (2008)

Imperfect Harmonies (2010)
Track 10: Left of Centre

Buckethead and Travis Dickerson
See Buckethead discography

Science Faxtion
See Buckethead discography

Travis Dickerson
See Buckethead discography

Brain & Melissa

Playstation Home – 'You and Me', 'My World', 'Forever' (2008)
Don King Presents: Prizefighter – 'Main theme' (2008)
ModNation Racers – 'Modnation Theme' (2010)
MLB 2K11 – 'MLB 2k Theme' (2011)
Detention soundtrack (2011)
Infamous 2 – 'Infamous 2 Theme', 'The Swamp', 'Eroico Con Moto' (2011)
Fear Not – 'Fear Not 1&2' (2011)
The Horror of Barnes Folly – 'Main Theme' (2011)
Twisted Metal – 'Race 2 Distruction', 'Ready to Die', 'Twisted Metal Theme' (2012)
Power/Rangers soundtrack (2015)
Bloodborne – 'Bloodborne', 'The Night Unfurls', 'Moonlit Melody' (2015)
Infamous: Second Son – 'BadAss Combat', 'Double Crossed', 'Higher Elevation' (2015)

GUNS N' ROSES

RICHARD FORTUS

GN' R Albums

Chinese Democracy
Appetite For Democracy 3D

The Eyes/Pale Divine

Freedom in a Cage (1990)
Track-listing: Flow My Tears/The Fog/Body Fall/
Way Strange/One Of A Kind/Freedom In A Cage/
Anything/Delicate Balance/I Know/So Far Away/
The Closet/Burn LIke The Sun/Prime/Lowest
High/Island/Nothing Turns Me On/Dream/My Only
You/Love Song/Tell Me God/Had A Girl/Poverty
Beach/Hunter/Together Alone

Straight to Goodbye (1991)
Track-listing: Straight To Goodbye/Something
About Me/My Addiction/Freedom In A Cage/
Cigarette/The Fog/Universe/Couldn't Happen To
You/Anything/Flow My Tears/Sorrow

Love Spit Love (1994)
Track-listing: Seventeen/Superman/Half a Life/
Jigsaw/Change in the Weather/Wake Up/Am I
Wrong/Green/Please/Codeine/St. Mary's Gate/
More

Trysome Eatone (1997)
Track-listing: Long Long Time/Believe/Well Well
Well/Friends/Fall on Tears/Little Fist/It Hurts
When I Laugh/7 Years/Sweet Thing/All God's
Children/More Than Money/November 5/How
Soon Is Now?

Tommy Stinson

See Tommy Stinson Discography

The Valance Project (2010)
Track-listing: Who Do You Love/No Way/Future
People/Afrobeat/In This Life/G'Nib G'Nub/Free
Form/If We Get It (We Know We're Getting'
Good)/Number One/The Hourglass of Time

The Dead Daisies (2013)
Track-listing: It's Gonna Take Time/Lock 'n' Load/
Washington/Yeah Yeah Yeah/Yesterday/
Writing On The Wall/Miles In Front Of Me/Bible
Row/Man Overboard/Tomorrow/Can't Fight This
Feeling/Talk To Me

Revolución (2015)
Track-listing: Mexico/Evil/Looking For The One/
Empty Heart/Make The Best Of It/Something I
Said/Get Up, Get Ready/With You And I/Sleep/My
Time/Midnight Moses/Devil Out Of Time/Critical

The Compulsions

Dirty Fun (2015)
Track-listing: Hellbound Babies/Silly Little
Woman/Evil Bastards/Lucky/House of Rock/Long
Tall Sally/The Feel/I Still Got the Hots for You,
Baby/Stay Eazy/Buzz Awhile

FRANK FERRER

GN' R Albums
Chinese Democracy
Appetite for Democracy 3D

The Beautiful (1990)
Track-listing: Sins in America/Highway/Sly Old
Fox/Fine Science of Chaos/Apart of Time

Story Book (1992)
Track-listing: Refrain Intro/Lighter Than/John
Doe/Ain't That Enough/Together/The We in Me/
Back Inside/Spyder Song/Storybook/Xenophobe/
Cocaine/Cold Turkey/I Am

Love Spit Love
See Richard Fortus discography

The Compulsions
See Richard Fortus discography

GUNS N' ROSES

RON THAL

GN' R Albums
Chinese Democracy
Appetite For Democracy

Solo (as Ron Thal)

The Adventures of Bumblefoot (1995)
Track-listing: Bumblefoot/Orf/Scrapie/Blue
Tongue/Limberneck/Q Fever/Strawberry Footrot/
Ick/Malignant Carbuncle/Rinderpest/Strangles/
Fistulous Withers/Poem (bonus track)/Shell On
The Sand (bonus track)

Hermit (1997)
Track-listing: Zero/Hermit/Fatback/Freak/
Sweetmeat/I Can't Play The Blues/Gray/
Unsound/Goodbye/Rowboat/Hangup/Every Time I
Shake My Head (It's Like Christmas)

Solo (as Bumblefoot)

Hands (1998)
Track-listing: Hands/Swatting Flies/What I Knew/
Shrunk/Dummy/Chair Ass/Noseplugs/Vomit/
Brooklyn Steakhouse/Drunk/Backfur/Tuesday in
Nancy/Dirty Pant'loons/Cactus - Hidden Track
(No.69)/Trainwreck - Hidden Track (No. 85)

9.11 (2001)
Track-listing: Fly in the Batter/Lost/Raygun/Hole
in the Sky/Children of Sierra Leone/Don Pardo
Pimpwagon/Legend of Van Cleef/Guitars SUCK/
Hall of Souls/Top of the World/R2/Time

Uncool (2002)
Track-listing: BBF Takes the Mic/Go/T Jonez/My
World Is You/Dominated/Kiss the Ring/What's

New Pussycat?/I Hate Me More Than I Love You/
Delilah/Ronald's Comin' Back Now/BBF Says
Goodnight/Can't Take My Eyes Off You/Hidden
Track

Forgotten Anthology (2003)
Track-listing: Old/Thought I Could Fly/Apathy/
Shell/Meat/Day To Remember/Bagged A Big
1/Mine/Heart Attack/Girl Like You/Crunch/
Maricona/She Knows/Myth/A Way Out/Wasted
Away/Mafalda/Bonus Track

Normal (2005)
Track-listing: Normal/Real/Turn Around/Rockstar
For A Day/Overloaded/Pretty Ugly/The Color of
Justice/Breaking/More/Awake/Life Inside Your
Ass/Shadow/Thank You

Abnormal (2008)
Track-listing: Abnormal/Glad To Be Here/Objectify/
Some Other Guy/Jenny B/Last Time/Simple Days/
Conspiracy/Piranha/Guitars Still Suck/Green/
Spaghetti/Misery/Redeye/The Day After/Dash

Barefoot – The Acoustic EP (2008)
Track-listing: Normal/Real/Turn Around/Rockstar
For A Day/Overloaded/Pretty Ugly/The Color of
Justice/Breaking/More/Awake/Life Inside Your
Ass/Shadow/Thank You

Little Brother is Watching (2015)
Track-listing: Clots/Little Brother Is Watching/
Argentina/Don't Know Who to Pray to Anymore/
Livin' the Dream/Cuterebra/Higher/Women Rule
the World/Sleepwalking/Eternity/Never Again

Solo singles
'Bernadette' (2011)
'Strawberry Fields Forever' (2011)
'Invisible' (2011)
'Goodbye Yellow Brick Road' (2011)
'Father' (2011)
'Cat Fight' (2011)
'There's A Kind of Hush' (2011)
'Let Your Voice Be Heard' (2011)
'The Pink Panther Theme' (2011)

Tony Harnell & the Wildflowers featuring

Bumblefoot (2013)
Track-listing: Paralyzed/Get Up Again/Runaround/
Devil Of A Healer/Burning Daylight/Somebody To
Love/What If/Wouldn't Be Human/Child's Play

Art of Anarchy (2015)
Track-listing: Black Rain/Small Batch Whiskey/
Time Everytime/Get on Down/Grand Applause/
Til the Dust Is Gone/Death of It/Superstar/
Aqualung/Long Ago/The Drift

The Madness (2017)
Track-listing: Black Rain/Small Batch Whiskey/
Time Everytime/Get on Down/Grand Applause/
Til the Dust Is Gone/Death of It/Superstar/
Aqualung/Long Ago/The Drift

Sons of Apollo

Psychotic Symphony (2017)
Track-listing: God of the Sun/Coming Home/
Signs of the Time/Labyrinth/Alive/Lost in
Oblivion/Figaro's Whore/Divine Addiction/Opus
Maximus

Guest appearances
Jessica Simpson 'Irresistible' (2001)
Q*Ball – Q*Ball in Space (2003)
Various Artists - Shawn Lane Remembered Vol
2 (2004)

Mistheria - Messenger of the Gods (2004)
Phi Yann-Zek - Solar Flare (2005)
Q*Ball - Fortune Favors The Bald (2005)
Freak Kitchen – Organic (2005)
Christophe Godin - Metal Kartoon (2005)
Julien Damotte & Fufux - Papa NoHell
(unreleased) (2005)
Mike Orlando - Sonic Stomp (2006)
24-7 Spyz - Face The Day (2006)
Guthrie Govan - Erotic Cakes (2006)
Various Artists - The Alchemists II (2007)
Q*Ball - This Is Serious Business (2007)
Jordan Rudess - The Road Home (2007)
Various Artists - We Wish You A Metal Christmas
(2008)
Orelsan - Perdu D'avance (2009)
Swashbuckle - Back To the Noose (2009)
Various Artists - OCC Rocks (2009)
Liberty N' Justice - Light It Up (2010)
Ty Tabor – Something's Coming (2010)
Indestructible Noise Command - Bleed the Line
(2010)
Scarlet Haze - Reach Down (2011)
Fredrik Pihl – Silhouettes (2011)
Rick Devin – 'Tush' (2011)
Various Artists - Embrace the Sun (2011)
Plug-In – Hijack (2011)
Don Jamieson - Live And Hilarious (2011)
Various Artists - Guitar Addiction, Vol. 1 (2011)
ElixirOnMute - The Last Halloween (2011)
Scarface – Work Ethic (2012)
Madonagun - Grovel At Her Feet (2012)
Liberty N Justice - The Cigar Chronicles (2012)
Rick Stitch 'LIV4EVR' (2012)
Cilver – 'In My Head' (2013)
The Feckers – It'd Be Rude Not To (2013)
Russ Dwarf – Wireless (2013)
Mattias Eklundh - Freak Guitar - The
Smorgasbord (2013)
Destrage - Are You Kidding Me? No. (2014)
DMC Generation Kill – 'Lot Lizard' (2015)
Carthagods – Carthagods (2015)
Bumblefoot & Milan Polak - Devil On My
Shoulder (2015)_
Fragile Mortals - Fired Up (2016)
Fragile Mortals – Suicide (2016)

GUNS N' ROSES

Thank You Scientist - *Stranger Heads Prevail* (2016)
Paul Personne - *Lost In Paris Blues Band* (2016)
Dobermann - *Pure Breed* (2017)

Compilations
Various Artists - *Ominous Guitarists From the Unknown* (1992)
Various Artists - *Guitar on the Edge No. 2* (1992)
Various Artists - *Guitar on the Edge No. 3* (1993)
Various Artists - *Guitar on the Edge No. 4* (1994)
Various Artists - *SEGA Power Cuts 1* (1996)
Various Artists - *Super Guitar Heroes Vol. 1, 2, & 3* (1996)
Various Artists - *Ondes De Choc* (1997)
Various Artists - *Hard Beats From Hell* (1997)
Various Artists - *Guitar & Bass No. 50* (1998)
Various Artists - Rock Sound, Volume 45 (2000)
Various Artists - *Fretless Guitar Masters* (2001)
Various Artists - *The Alchemists* (2002)

Soundtrack - *Outlaw Volleyball: Music From The Game* (2003)
Various Artists - *Village of the Unfretted* (2005)
Various Artists - *Artists for Charity – Guitarists 4 the Kids* (2006)
Various Artists - *CMJ – On Air, Vol. 12* (2006)
Various Artists - *FMQB – SubModern #021 Specialty Show Sampler* (2008)
Various Artists - *Guitars That Ate My Brain* (2009)
Various Artists - *This Is Shredding, Vol. 1* (2009)
Various Artists - *Rock 2 Live, Vol. 1* (2014)

Tribute CDs
Various Artists - *Crushing Days – A Tribute To Joe Satriani* (2000)
Various Artists - *Warmth in the Wilderness – A Tribute to Jason Becker* (2001)
Lounge Brigade - *Sabbath in the Suburbs: The Lounge Tribute to Ozzy Osbourne & Black Sabbath* (2002)
Lounge Brigade - *The Sweet Sounds of Slim Shady: The Lounge Tribute to Eminem* (2002)
Lounge Brigade - *The Lounge Below: The*

Lounge Tribute to Outkast (2003)
Various Artists - *The Spirit Lives On – The Music of Jimi Hendrix Revisited, Volume 1* (2004)
Various Artists - *A World With Heroes - A KISS Tribute* (2013)
Various Artists - *Thriller - A Metal Tribute To Michael Jackson* (2013)

Other Projects
AWOL - *AWOL – EP* (1987)
Soundtrack - *Wild Woody SEGA CD video game* (1995)
Carlin Music Publishing - *Library CD #331 Alternative: Punk vs. Nu-Metal* (2002)
Soundtrack - *Outlaw Volleyball Xbox video game* (2003)
Soundtrack - *Test Drive: Eve of Destruction PlayStation 2 video game* (2004)
Carlin Music Publishing - *Library CD #356 Rap & Hip Hop* (2005)
Soundtrack - *Rig 'N' Roll PC video game* (2010)
Soundtrack - *The Evangelist* (2016)

Producer
Boiler Room - *Low Society* (1996)
Various Artists - *God Shave the Queen* (1996)
Indecision – *Unorthodox* (1996)
Inhuman - *Evolver* (1997)
Indecision - *Most Precious Blood* (1998)
Evoken - *Embrace the Emptiness* (1998)
Various Artists - Lost Voices (1998)
Future Chicken Farmers - *Future Chicken Farmers* (1998)
Pat O'May - *Breizh / Amerika* (1999)
Inhuman - *Rebellion* (1999)

Various Artists - *Hell Rules 2 – A Tribute To Black Sabbath* (2000)
Anomos/Stealth - *From Here On . . .* (2000)
Various Artists - *Crushing Days – A Tribute To Joe Satriani* (2000)
Evoken - *Quietus* (2000)
Most Precious Blood - *Nothing in Vein* (2001)
One Second Thought - Self Inflicted (2001)

The Wage of Sin - Product of Deceit And Loneliness (2002)
Troy Kurtis – Demo (2002)
Engineered / Produced. Co-writing, performed all music
Q*Ball - *In Space* (2002)
Cathy-Ann - *Honey Wagon* (2003)
Q*Ball - *Fortune Favors the Bald* (2004)
Various Artists - *Bring You To Your Knees: A Tribute To Guns N' Roses* (2004)
The Nerve! - *The Nerve!* (2004)
Nikki Sorrentino - Demo (2014)
Evoken - *Antithesis of Light* (2005)
Zachary Fischer Band - *On Borrowed Time* (2005)
24-7 Spyz - *Face the Day* (2006)
Q*Ball - *This Is Serious Business* (2007)
Hurricane - *Abaybay* (Rock Re-mix) (2007)
Return To Earth - *Captains of Industry* (2007)
Talking Metal on Fuse – (FuseTV (November 2007 – March 2008) (2007)
Return To Earth - *Automata* (2010)
Alexa Vetere - *Breathe Again* (2012)
Poc - *Rise Above* (2012)
Art of Anarchy - *Art of Anarchy* (2015)
Art of Anarchy – 'The Madness' (2016)
Art of Anarchy - *The Madness* (2017)

GUNS N' ROSES

DJ ASHBA

GN' R Albums
Appetite For Destruction 3D

Solo

Addiction to the Friction (1996)
Track-listing: Over Drive/Day at the Beach/
Addiction to the Friction/Shredder's Shuffle/
If Only/G String Groove Thing/Bashin' With
Beethoven/Lax/Eyes of a Cherokee/Walk – Don't
Run/Cry for Freedom/Follow Your Heart

Eli Roth's Goretorium – Songs For The
Demented Mind (2012)
Track-listing: The Opening/Welcome to the
Delmont/Vacancy/The Lobby/Uneasy Greeting/
Hellevator/13th Floor/Bitter Suite/We're Gonna
Die/911/Bloodline/Basement/Ghost in the
Machine/Demise/Dancing With Demons/Suicide
Party/Nightmares Do Come True/Breaking News/
The Closing

Beautiful Creatures (2001)
Track-listing: 1 A.M./Wasted/Step Back/Ride/
Wish/Kick Out/Blacklist/Kickin' For Days/Time
and Time Again/Goin' Off/New Orleans/I Got It All

Sixx:A.M.

The Heroin Diaries Soundtrack (2007)
Track-listing: X-Mas in Hell/Van Nuys/Life Is
Beautiful/Pray for Me/Tomorrow/Accidents Can
Happen/Intermission/Dead Man's Ballet/Heart
Failure/Girl with Golden Eyes/Courtesy Call/
Permission/Life After Death

Singles from The Heroin Diaries
Soundtrack:
'Life Is Beautiful' (2007)
'Pray for Me' (2008)
'Tomorrow' (2008)
'Accidents Can Happen' (2008)

X-Mas in Hell EP (2008)
Track-listing: Life Is Beautiful/X-Mas in Hell Mix/
Life Is Beautiful/X-Mas in Hell Mix (w/ Spoken
Word)"/Life Is Beautiful (X-Mas Mix)

Live is Beautiful (2008)
Track-listing: X-Mas in Hell/Pray for Me/
Heart Failure/Intermission/Dead Man's Ballet/
Tomorrow/Accidents Can Happen/Life Is
Beautiful

This Is Gonna Hurt (2011)
Track-listing: This Is Gonna Hurt/Lies Of The
Beautiful People/Are You with Me Now/Live
Forever/Sure Feels Right/Deadlihood/Smile/Help
Is On The Way/Oh My God/Goodbye My Friends/
Skin/Codependence

Singles from This Is Gonna Hurt:
'Lies of the Beautiful People' (2011)
'This Is Gonna Hurt' (2011)
'Are You With Me' (2012)
'Help Is On The Way' (2012)
'Skin' (2012)

7 (2011)

Track-listing: Lies of the Beautiful People/This Is Gonna Hurt/Life Is Beautiful/Help is on the Way/Sure Feels Right/Pray for Me/Accidents Can Happen

Modern Vintage (2014)

Track-listing: Stars/Gotta Get It Right/Relief/Get Ya Some/Let's Go/Drive/Give Me a Love/Hyperventilate/High on the Music/Miracle/Before It's Over

Singles from Modern Vintage:

'Gotta Get It Right' (2014)
'Let's Go' (2014)
'Stars' (2014)
'Drive' (2014)

Prayers for the Damned Vol 1. (2016)

Track-listing: Rise/You Have Come to the Right Place/I'm Sick/Prayers for the Damned/Better Man/Can't Stop/When We Were Gods/Belly of the Beast/Everything Went to Hell/The Last Time (My Heart Will Hit the Ground)/Rise of the Melancholy Empire

Singles from Prayers for the Damned Vol. 1:

'Rise' (2016)
'Prayers for the Damned' (2016)

Prayers for the Blessed Vol. 2 (2016)

Track-listing: Barbarians (Prayers for the Blessed)/We Will Not Go Quietly/Wolf at Your Door/Maybe It's Time/The Devil's Coming/Catacombs/That's Gonna Leave a Scar/Without You/Suffocate/Riot in My Head/Helicopters

Production, songwriting and guest credits

Aimee Allen – *I'd Start a Revolution If I Could Get Up in the Morning* (2002)
Enuff Z'Nuff - *Welcome To Blue Island* (2003)
Outlaw Volleyball - Original Soundtrack (2003)
Marion Raven - *Heads Will Roll EP* (2005)
Marion Raven - *Set Me Free* (2007)
Drowning Pool - *Full Circle* (2007)
Mötley Crüe - *Saints of Los Angeles* (2007)
Neil Diamond - *A Cherry Cherry Christmas* (2007)
The Last Vegas - *Whatever Gets You Off* (2009)
James Durbin - *Memories of a Beautiful Disaster* (2011)

GUNS N' ROSES

MELISSA REECE

LISSA EP (2007)
Track-listing: Feel It/Girlfriend/Pretty Please/Ooh
La La/Old Skool/Remember The Times

The Valence Project
See Bryan Mantia discography

Brain & Melissa
See Bryan Mantia discography

Brain and Buckethead
See Buckethead discography

CHRIS PITMAN

GN' R Albums
Chinese Democracy

'Oh My God'

Musical collaborations
Tool – 'Third Eye' (1996)
Blinker the Star – 'Kween Kat' (1996)

PAUL TOBIAS

GN'R Albums
"Sympathy for the Devil"

"Oh My God" (End of Days OST)
Chinese Democracy
Chinese Democracy/Street of Dreams/There Was
a Time/Catcher in the Rye/Riad N' the Bedouins/
I.R.S./Prostitute

Hollywood Rose
'Shadow of your Love', 'Back off Bitch' (both
would be re-recorded by Guns N' Roses)

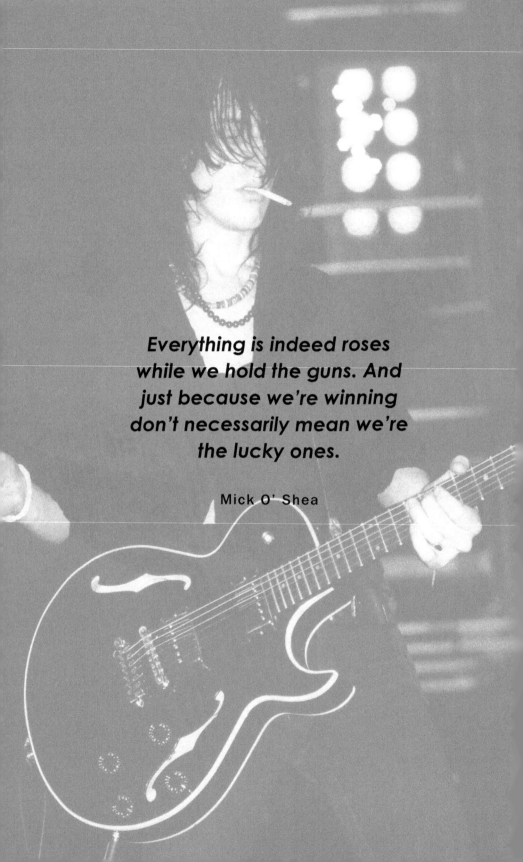

Everything is indeed roses while we hold the guns. And just because we're winning don't necessarily mean we're the lucky ones.

Mick O' Shea

GUNS N' ROSEOLOGY

80 Great Guns N' Roses Recordings

80. 'Hair of the Dog' The Spaghetti Incident?

Only three or four tracks from *The Spaghetti Incident?* make it beyond # 70 in my rankings, so it won't come as a surprise to learn I'm no fan of the album. Nor am I all that keen on Nazareth, either. Nazareth's lead guitarist, Manny Charlton, produced an early Guns N' Roses demo session at Sound City Studios in June 1986 and that, in my humble opinion, is where all association with the Scottish rockers should have ended.

79. 'Buick Mackane/Big Dumb Sex' The Spaghetti Incident?

T. Rex and Soundgarden were both great bands. All great bands, however, have off days. Guns were certainly off their game here. The repetitive riff at the centre of 'Buick Mackane' sounds like something Duff might have come up with the first time he picked up a bass guitar. To try polishing the turd by segueing into Soundgarden's 'Big Dumb Sex' was just, well . . . dumb.

78. 'Down on the Farm' The Spaghetti Incident?

My fundamental objection here is that I just don't get UK Subs – I never have, and never will. In fact, I'm astounded Axl and Co. had even heard of the Subs, let alone decide to cover one of their lesser-known songs. And don't even get me started on Axl's Dick van Dyke Mockney Poppins. Chim chim, cher fuckin' arghhhh!!!!

77. 'Human Being' The Spaghetti Incident?

When Guns first came crawling out of the West Hollywood gutter their look and sound positively shrieked "New York Dolls". Indeed, one has to wonder why they didn't incorporate a Dolls track into their early sets. By 1993, of course, Guns were as far removed from the Dolls as human beingly possible. This is a passable effort, but nobody does the Dolls quite like the New York Dolls.

76. 'My World' Use Your Illusion II

The words "and last but by no means least" certainly don't apply here. Whoever elected to tag 'My World' onto the end of *UYI II* should have at least had the grace to leave sufficient time for the listener to reach the stereo because this is execrable compared to other fare on the album. It's often been said that a killer single album lurks within *UYI* albums, and back in those sepia-toned days of cassette-recording I did exactly that. This one wasn't ever in the running.

GUNS N' ROSES

75. 'Sorry' Chinese Democracy

'Sorry' kinda encapsulates everything that needs to be said here, I'm afraid. *Chinese Democracy*'s taking up some 14 years of his life left Axl open to ridicule in certain quarters – and if this turgid plod-a-long was still considered worthy of making the album's final cut when there were enough songs left over from the *CD* sessions, then some of that ridicule is wholly justified.

74. 'Get in the Ring' Use Your Illusion II

This one would figure much higher had it not been for Axl's puerile "punks in the press" rant midway through what is otherwise a fist-pumping classic GN'R blues-fused groove. It's one thing to be pissed over a music journo's erroneous quotes, but quite another to verify every word of your gauntlet-throwing-down challenge to Vince Neil to "get in the ring" only to then deny said conversation ever took place. Memo to Axl: an apology to Mick Wall is long overdue . . .

73. 'Raw Power' The Spaghetti Incident?

There's nothing intrinsically wrong with this version of The Stooges' classic per se. It's just that Guns were masters of their craft by the time of *The Spaghetti Incident?* so Slash playing two-chord punk rock chug-a-longs is akin to having Orson Welles directing a high school end-of-year review on the back of *Citizen Kane*.

72. 'Black Leather' The Spaghetti Incident?

Let's get one thing straight here, 'Black

Leather' isn't a Sex Pistols song. John Lydon had long-since shed his punk persona – with Sid having left this mortal coil – by the time Guns' old mucker Steve Jones (and his sidekick Paul Cook) were conjuring up songs to pad out the woeful *The Great Rock 'N' Roll Swindle* soundtrack. That 'Black Leather' didn't make the soundtrack pretty much says all that needs saying here.

71. 'One In A Million' G N' R Lies

It's been written elsewhere that Guns N' Roses' career should have been dead in the water following the release of *GN'R Lies* because of 'One in a Million'. This one certainly sparked controversy at the time, but while there is no place in rock'n'roll – or indeed, anywhere else – for such blatant racist and xenophobic ravings, it's worth remembering Geffen Records could have refused to issue *GN'R Lies* unless 'One in a Million' was replaced with another song – any song. That they didn't do so suggests they were happy to put dollars before common decency.

70. 'I Don't Care About You' The Spaghetti Incident?

I suspect choosing a Fear track was a means of Guns tipping their hat to the LA punk scene but, again, they don't quite pull it off. It's not that they play the song badly – how could they play any song badly? It's just that Fear were of their time and 'I Don't Care About You' encapsulated that early Eighties feel. It would have fit nicely on *Live ?!*@ Like a Suicide,* or maybe even *GN'R Lies*. Going off on a slight tangent, Fear were once signed to Slash Records.

69. 'Scraped' Chinese Democracy

I don't mind admitting I had to re-familiarise myself with this one – and it took several plays before I decided it was just about worthy of scraping into a higher tier. Like every other GN'R fan I was checking the net regularly once Axl (or whoever it was) started leaking the songs intended for *Chinese Democracy* online. 'Scraped' was one of the few to remain under wraps until the album finally hit the shelves. I can't say listening to it again enriched my day.

68. 'New Rose' The Spaghetti Incident?

Again, the only criticism I have with Guns choosing to cover 'New Rose' is that The Damned's '76 original is the better recording – which kinda defeats the whole purpose of covering a song. Then again, I defy any band to come anywhere close to the original.

67. 'Garden of Eden' Use Your Illusion I

Guns N' Roses meet The Dickies only without the humour. I mean, I'm all for experimentation, but this one should never have got beyond a soundcheck mess-about. Listening to 'Garden of Eden' one can't help but question the quality of the songs that didn't make the *UYI* final cut. Didn't anyone ponder the sanity of placing 'Garden of Eden' directly after 'The Garden' in the track-listing on *UYI I*? And with 'Bad Apples' also appearing on the same album one cannot help but wonder whether Axl has some latent Adam and Eve fixation?

66. 'Nice Boys' G N'R Lies

I didn't think much of 'Nice Boys' on first listening to *GN'R Lies* and my opinion ain't changed much since. Indeed, its only merit is that it shows Guns' early potential. Wannabe bad boy Angry Anderson would go on to pen syrupy power ballads for naff Aussie soaps. 'Suddenly', I'm feeling a tad nauseous . . .

65. 'Mama Kin' G N' R Lies

The comparisons betwixt early Aerosmith and early Guns N' Roses are endless and very apt. We also owe Steve Tyler and Co a huge debt of gratitude as *Rocks* was the album that turned Slash onto lead guitar. While Guns crank their way through this classic blues grind ably enough, imagine what they could have done with 'Back in the Saddle' or 'Get the Lead Out'?

64. 'You Can't Put Your Arms Around a Memory' The Spaghetti Incident?

The French novelist Gustave Flaubert advised us against touching our idols for fear of the gilt coming away on our hands. Johnny "Too-Kool-for-Skool" Thunders was Duff's ultimate boyhood rock idol growing up in Seattle. Duff would even get to jam with Thunders in his pre-GN'R days. By the time Guns came to share the same bill as Johnny (at Fender's Ballroom in March 1986) much of the latter's gilt had eroded away. Hopefully, the inclusion of 'You Can't Put Your Arms Around a Memory' on *The Spaghetti Incident?* introduced Johnny to a new audience.

63. 'This I Love' Chinese Democracy

This I don't love . . . yet don't exactly dislike either – which, again, pretty much sums up my feeling for *Chinese Democracy* as a whole. There's undoubtedly the seeds of a decent song here, but after endless toying in the studio it ends up getting lost in its own pomposity. Axl was very much in a 'November Rain'/'Estranged' vibe when he sat himself down at the piano. Bumblefoot Thal's solo is passable enough, but Slash would have elevated it to far greater heights.

GUNS N' ROSES

62. 'If The World' Chinese Democracy

Is it just me or is this Axl's attempt at a James Bond theme song? "Anything Chris Cornell can do, I can do better, right?" Chris Pitman has to take much of the credit here as he pretty much does everything other than sing and play drums on this one.

61. 'Look At Your Game, Girl' The Spaghetti Incident?

For those of you who don't know, 'Look At Your Game, Girl' was penned by Charlie Manson back when chasing the popstar dream seemed more appealing than enticing his extended "Family" of runaway, starry-eyed elfin waifs into embarking on a crazed killing spree that burst the late Sixties love and peace bubble. Guns weren't the first to record a Manson ditty, of course, as 'Never Learn Not To Love' (the B-side to the Beach Boys' 1968 single 'Bluebirds over the Mountain'), was a reworking of Manson's 'Cease to Exist'. As with 'One in a Million', 'Look At Your Game, Girl' brought condemnation from certain quarters, but as Norman Mailer so rightly opined: "Art demands to be free regardless of who's creating it."

60. 'Attitude' The Spaghetti Incident?

'Attitude' is 87 seconds of pumped-up punk rock and is perhaps the only track from *The Spaghetti Incident?* that you can imagine the Hell House-era Guns having penned. If one can look beyond the blatant misogynistic lyric, the tune is a four-to-the-floor foot-stomper. And it's still proving a crowd-pleaser on the Not in This Lifetime . . . Tour.

59. 'You Ain't the First' Use Your Illusion I

'You Ain't the First' is so reminiscent of 'Used to Love Her' that it would have sat perfectly on Side 2 of *GN'R Lies*. It's pure Izzy and one can picture him sitting crossed-legged on the studio floor with his acoustic nestled in his lap and a joint dangling from his lips while strumming the tune, oblivious to his surroundings.

58. 'Shackler's Revenge' Chinese Democracy

Axl wouldn't be human if at some point he didn't lose sight of what he was trying to achieve with *Chinese Democracy*. It's easy to see that 'Shackler's Revenge' showed some promise but endless hours of tweaking and twiddling spoils things somewhat.

57. 'I.R.S.' Chinese Democracy

Contrary to what you might hear elsewhere, 'I.R.S' doesn't stand for "Irritable Rose Syndrome", though I'm sure the powers-that-be at Interscope became ever more irritated with Axl as the studio costs rose ever higher.

56. 'Sympathy for the Devil' Interview with the Vampire Soundtrack

Given they had a $60 million budget to make *Interview with the Vampire* one cannot help but wonder why the production company didn't simply commission the original Stones version of 'Sympathy for the Devil' – that is until one learns the production company in question was, yes, you've guessed it, Geffen Pictures. By the time Guns came to record the song Axl and Slash – like the film's main protagonists Lestat

 204

and Louis – were at each other's throats. So much so, they recorded their respective parts separately. The lyric was perfectly suited to Axl's mindset circa December 1994, however, as everyone around him was left bemused by the nature of his game.

55. 'Oh My God' End of Days Soundtrack

The twentieth century was coming to a close when it was announced a brand-new Guns N' Roses composition was set to feature in Arnie's latest cinematic offering, *End of Days*. Axl would subsequently claim 'Oh My God' was an unfinished demo that was rushed so as to be ready for inclusion on the film's soundtrack. All Slash had to say about the song was that it merely confirmed he'd made the right decision in walking away from Guns as he and Axl were no longer on the same wavelength. But who was by then?

54. 'So Fine' Use Your Illusion II

The last thing anyone might have expected from Guns N' Roses was Axl and Duff sharing vocal duties on such a saccharine-soaked ditty such as 'So Fine'. But that's what made them so goddamn interesting, I suppose.

53. 'It's Alright' Live Era '87-'93

'It's Alright' is the only song within the GN'R canon that features on an official album yet wasn't actually recorded by the band. Whenever Axl started tinkling away the intro to the Black Sabbath piano-led ditty you just knew the next song on the set-list was gonna be 'November Rain'. Cue lighters . . .

52. 'Back Off Bitch' Use Your Illusion I

When Axl co-wrote this misogynistic rant with his buddy Paul Tobias he was still living in Lafayette and, according to Izzy at least, wasn't "getting any pussy". Given its frenetic pace, 'Back Off Bitch' would have perhaps been more suited to *Appetite for Destruction*, but the song had long-since been dropped from the set by the time Guns headed into the studio to record their much anticipated debut. Which again begs the question . . .

51. 'Shotgun Blues' Use Your Illusion II

I might be going out on a limb here but 'Shotgun Blues' sounds like another soundcheck free-for-all that was guaranteed to get the blood pumping ready for showtime – a catchy blues-rocking riff that Axl would extemporise whatever words came into his head at the time. Had someone at Geffen possessed the *cojones* to stand up to Axl and convince him that sometimes less is indeed more, then *Use Your Illusion* might still have been a killer single album and the 'Shotgun' riff could have been saved for another day.

50. 'Move to the City' G N' R Lies

Right, I'm not gonna say I've sorted the wheat from the chaff as we are talking Guns N' Roses here . . . so let's just say we're moving through the gears. The lyric to 'Move to the City' is self-explanatory. It's Izzy and Axl's rite of passage journey from the Indiana backwaters to LA set to a lilting boogie-woogie swing.

GUNS N' ROSES

49. 'Reckless Life' G N' R Lies

The opening track on the *Live ?!*@ Like a Suicide EP*, 'Reckless Life' gives the world its first chance to "Suck on Guns N' fuckin' Roses!". And what a taste! While it's nothing special compared with what was to come on both the *Appetite* and *UYI* albums, it nonetheless deserves to crack the Top 50.

48. 'Anything Goes' Appetite for Destruction

Axl penned this one while with Hollywood Rose, so I imagine it being one of the songs he and the rest of the nascent Guns would have played during those early gettin'-to-know-each-other rehearsals. A decent enough chug-a-long rocker but Guns would soon drop it from the set.

47. 'Dead Horse' Use Your Illusion I

'Dead Horse' is classic GN'R in that it starts off with a slow 'Patience' vibe, with Axl griping about some woman that done him wrong. It could well be an autobiographical musing, given that his short-lived marriage to Erin Everly was already on the skids by the time the band were writing up new material for the *UYI* albums.

46. 'Riad N' the Bedouins' Chinese Democracy

Certainly the most exotic song title in the GN'R oeuvre yet, other than its mention in the lyric, makes no more sense now than when *Chinese Democracy* was released. Maybe Axl had a tent set up in one of the myriad of recording studios? I don't profess to have the foggiest as to what 'Riad N' the Bedouins' is about, but it's a song that grows on you the more times you hear it.

45. 'Think About You' Appetite for Destruction

'Think About You' is another of those "Izzy songs" Slash always found endearing. It kinda gets lost on *Appetite* but would have slotted in nicely alongside 'Move to the City' and 'Reckless Life' on *GN'R Lies*. Hindsight is a wonderful thing . . .

44. 'Double-Talkin' Jive' Use Your Illusion I

Another *UYI* song where the driving riff – aided and abetted by Axl's low-menace delivery – is enough to elevate it from filler to thriller. And I, for one, would have loved to see Guns make more use of Slash's lilting flamenco guitar skills.

43. 'Prostitute' Chinese Democracy

This is another *Chinese Democracy* number that sounds as if Axl was toying with a Daniel Craig-era James Bond theme song – though this was unlikely to happen given its peculiar title. But Axl's intentions are often misunderstood.

42. 'The Garden' Use Your Illusion I

Slash: "Hey dude, you sound a little like Alice on this one."
Axl: "You really think so?"
Duff: "Yeah, man."
Axl: "Maybe we should get Alice in to sing on it . . . You still got his number?"

41. 'Bad Apples' Use Your Illusion I

Despite starting off like a cheesy car

commercial, 'Bad Apples' really gets into the swing once Slash's kickass riff kicks in. This is Guns at maximum swagger, with the Nicky Hopkins-esque boogie-woogie roadhouse piano taking things to a whole other level.

40. 'Catcher in the Rye' Chinese Democracy

As every conspiracy theorist knows, J.D. Salinger's *Catcher in the Rye* is the novel Mark Chapman stood patiently reading while awaiting the arrival of the police after gunning down John Lennon outside the Dakota Building in New York. Whether Axl was viewing himself as a latter-day Holden Caulfield surrounded by Geffen "phonies", he's always at his gun-slinging best when writing in a haunting 'November Rain'/'Estranged' vain.

39. 'Coma' Use Your Illusion I

The mere fact that Guns N' Roses would dare pen a track that comes in at ten minutes-plus that has a solitary verse and lacks a chorus says much about their creativity at the time of writing the *UYI* albums – a creativity that clearly wasn't in need of defibrillation. 'Coma' was aired live just a handful of times back in the day but is proving a surprising crowd-pleaser second time around.

38. 'Don't Damn Me' Use Your Illusion I

Don't go damning me for speaking my mind here, but this is another *UYI* filler that might have made more of an impression had the lyric matched the powerhouse riff.

37. 'Chinese Democracy' Chinese Democracy

More power to Slash for saying he enjoys

playing the songs from *Chinese Democracy* live. He could just be blowing smoke up Axl's ass to keep the feelgood factor going but imagine how great the title track would have sounded had he not woken up one morning and realised he was the guitar player in a band whose leader made Josef Stalin appear open-minded.

36. 'You're Crazy' (Acoustic) GN'R Lies

While the acoustic version of 'You're Crazy' pales against the original *Appetite* barn-burner, it's easily more sinister and threatening than most of what their late-Eighties poodle-haired peers could come up with.

35. 'Better' Chinese Democracy

If memory serves, this might well have been the first *Chinese Democracy* track leaked onto the net. I knew in that moment that *Chinese Democracy* couldn't hope to hold a candle to any of the Slash/Duff-era albums. However, amid the squawking, squeaking grind, Axl suddenly emits a trademark screech that redeems the song yet evokes a yearning for what the parent album could and *should* have been.

34. 'Out Ta Get Me' Appetite For Destruction

Through no fault of its own 'Out Ta Get Me' is one of the songs that tends to get overlooked when people start talking about *Appetite for Destruction*. This is perhaps to be expected given the competition. Yet it's one of the few songs where Axl is telling it exactly how he saw it. "Every time you turn around, someone is trying to screw you over financially, or the cops are banging on your door and you didn't do anything. It's just being railroaded into something and trying to get out from underneath it. You know – parents, teachers, preachers . . . everybody." Take that wonder heart . . .

33. 'Madagascar' Chinese Democracy

Having listened to *Chinese Democracy* in its entirety for the first time in years, I'm even more convinced the track-listing is the soundtrack to an imaginary film that only Axl could see. The Sally Army brass band intro is a little left-field, as indeed is the seemingly endless parade of film snippets: *Mississippi Burning*, *Casualties of War*, *Cool Hand Luke*, *Braveheart*, *Seven* et al. The excerpts from Martin Luther King, Jr.'s 'I Have a Dream' and 'Why Jesus Called a Man a Fool' could also be construed as self-indulgence on a certain someone's part. Whatever else you think about W. Axl Rose, you have to admire his ambition and scope.

32. 'Perfect Crime' Use Your Illusion I

This one has a special place in my heart as it's the first song I saw Guns play live. It's a jackhammer stomp that would have sat easily on either *Appetite* or *GN'R Lies*. It would have also served as the perfect opener on *UYI I*, In and out in 2 mins 23 seconds and on with the show.

31. 'You're Crazy' Appetite For Destruction

'You're Crazy' follows straight after 'Sweet Child O' Mine'. So one minute Axl's crooning about Erin having eyes of the bluest skies and the next he's looking for a lover in a world that's much too dark. 'You're Crazy' was penned long before Erin came into Axl's life, of course, but the dark world he was inhabiting was one entirely of his own making.

30. 'Ain't It Fun' The Spaghetti Incident?

This is one of the two tracks that almost makes *The Spaghetti Incident?* bearable . . . almost. It's so good in fact that it gives 'Knockin' on Heaven's Door' and 'Live and Let Die' a very close run in the GN'R best cover stakes. It's also the only Guns recording that contains the "C-word", which makes it all the more amusing that it scored them a transatlantic Top 10.

29. 'Bad Obsession' Use Your Illusion I

Forget the bloated production, pretentious lyrics and audacious video concepts – it was being a gritty rock'n'roll band teetering on the edge of near-collapse that gave Guns their fire. 'Bad Obsession' is another Izzy ditty brimming with understatement that helps keep *UYI I* chugging along on an even keel.

28. 'Used To Love Her' GN'R Lies

One of the more enduring urban myths surrounding Guns N' Roses is that the lyric to 'Used to Love Her' is about another of Axl's doomed romances. Another version of GN'R history has it Izzy came up with the lyric in response to a conversation he'd heard on the radio where some guy was "whining about a broad". So, it could well be about Axl . . .

27. 'There Was a Time' Chinese Democracy

This was another early "leaked file" from the long-running *Chinese Democracy* saga, and yet another reason why the finished album proved so utterly maddening! With its orchestral sweeps and sublime chorus, 'There Was a Time' verges on GN'R greatness. Yet by the time the album was deemed ready for the big bad world it had been buried under layer upon layer of dross. Still very listenable though . . .

26. 'Dust N' Bones' Use Your Illusion I

Gilby Clarke had the chops but he would be the first to admit he was no Izzy Stradlin. Then again, there is only one Izzy. 'Dust N' Bones' shows – and achingly so – just what Guns lost when Izzy finally decided enough was enough.

25. 'Right Next Door to Hell' Use Your Illusion I

Choosing the opening track for your album can't be easy – especially when your debut has sold more than ten million copies and counting. Thankfully, Axl's highly strung, high-rise neighbour (a lady by the name of Gabriella Kantor) provided the inspiration behind this upfront-in-yer-face rocker by having him arrested for reportedly whomping her with a wine bottle – an empty bottle one would assume . . . It's also the mix that got Bill Price the gig producing the *UYI* albums. Go Bill!

24. 'Nightrain' Appetite For Destruction

'Nightrain' just goes to show you never know when inspiration will strike. Slash, Duff, and Izzy had worked up the music, but the song frustratingly remained incomplete . . . at least until it was Axl's turn to take a slurp of a certain cheap Californian fortified wine that provided the band with one of their five a day. Bottoms up, fill that man's cup . . .

23. 'Pretty Tied Up' Use Your Illusion II

As the song goes, 'Pretty Tied Up (The Perils of Rock N' Roll Decadence)' is centred around an eye-popping experience Izzy had while calling in on a dominatrix friend that lived "down on Melrose". I wonder if poor Iz visualised the obese dude in drag and duct tape with an onion stuffed in his pie-hole every time Guns played the song live . . .?

22. 'Locomotive' Use Your Illusion II

A hard and brutal Jack N' Coke-fused rocker in the 'Welcome to the Jungle'/'You Could Be Mine' vein. It's another paean to unrequited love, but Slash's hypnotic, piledriving riff burrows into your brain like a derailed locomotive. Should have been a single.

21. 'Street of Dreams' Chinese Democracy

By far and away the best track on *Chinese Democracy*. Axl's vocal flitting betwixt rage, longing, fury, and raw emotion. Another stark reminder of how great an album *Chinese Democracy* might have been.

20. '14 Years' Use Your Illusion II

It's said that Izzy penned '14 Years' to denote the time he and Axl had known each other. It's infinitely more amusing, however, picturing Axl humming the tune while sat at the *Chinese Democracy* console.

GUNS N' ROSES

19. 'Rocket Queen' Appetite For Destruction

A closer worthy of bringing any album to its finale – and that's without the coital clatter of Axl banging away at Steven Adler's supposed ex, Adriana Smith, on the studio floor. The accommodating Miss Smith reportedly received a bottle of Jack Daniels for rendering her services. Make mine a double . . .

18. 'It's So Easy' Appetite For Destruction

According to a 1988 interview Axl gave to *Hit Parader*, the inspiration for 'It's So Easy' came from an ad for Easy Dates that he happened upon in some adult magazine or other. "It's this girl bent over so her ass is up in the air and it says, 'It's so easy.' According to Wendy Lou Gosse, who was dating West Arkeen at the time he and Duff co-wrote the song, 'It's So Easy' was a "hippy, la-la song" before Axl made it "more rock'n'roll".

If Axl had had his way, the song's promo video would have shown Erin Everly with her ass on display as she hung suspended from a doorframe sporting a mouth-gag and very little else. Unsurprisingly, the video was never given an official release. Oh, and Axl also laid into Bowie on the video shoot for daring to flirt with Erin. Hopefully, she'd been untied and had the mouth-gag removed by that point.

17. 'Mr. Brownstone' Appetite For Destruction.

At the time of writing 'Mr. Brownstone', Guns N' Roses were an exciting rock'n'roll band dabbling in nefarious substances. By the time of *Appetite*'s release, however, three of the band were drug addicts dabbling in rock'n'roll. "I used to do a little, but the little wasn't doing, so the

little got more and more . . ." The pitfalls of heroin addiction effortlessly encapsulated in a single couplet.

16. 'My Michelle' Appetite For Destruction

I imagine the conversation going something like this as Elton's 'Your Song' drifts out of the car stereo:
Michelle: "I just love this song, Axl; I wish someone would write a song about me one day." Axl: "Hmm, okay; give me somethin' to work with"
Michelle: "Let's see . . . Well, as you know, mom died of a heroin overdose . . . oh, and daddy works in the porn industry."
Axl: "Don't forget you get to do your coke for free, Bitch . . ."

15. 'Since I Don't Have You' The Spaghetti Incident?

This was the third single from *The Spaghetti Incident?* but as I didn't buy the album – either out of some misguided principle or more likely because I had more pressing ways of spending £15 or whatever the hell the retail price was – this syrupy spoonful of croon took me completely by surprise when I first heard it on the radio. I haven't heard the Skyliners' original, but I'm willing to bet I won't hear a muttered "Yep, we're fucked" at the start of the guitar solo.

14. 'Live and Let Die' Use Your Illusion I

Roger Moore only just outpoints Timothy Dalton in the worst James Bond stakes, so *Live and Let Die* doesn't rate too highly on my all-time Bond movie list – although Jane Seymour saves it from being a total bore. I remember an MTV interview where Axl recounts how the idea for Guns to cover the song came about. He'd rented the movie and upon hearing Macca's dulcet tones, he'd grabbed the phone and called Slash. Thankfully, Guns ramp everything up to 11 to make the song their own.

13. 'Don't Cry' (Original) Use Your Illusion I

This is undoubtedly a great song and ticks all the power ballad boxes. What I didn't get at the time – and still don't understand – is why include alternate versions of 'Don't Cry' on each of the *UYI* albums? What they should have done is record an acoustic version as they did with 'You're Crazy'.

12. 'Don't Cry' (Alternate) Use Your Illusion II

And just where else were you expecting this one to land?

11. 'November Rain' Use Your Illusion I

It's only by listening to the original piano-only version of 'November Rain' that you get a sense of what Axl had in mind. By the time it made it to the *UYI* masters, however, it had undergone the Jim Steinman rock operatic treatment. Axl had been dreaming of performing 'November Rain' to a sea of cigarette lighters since he first parked his butt on the piano stool. And more power to him 'cos it craps on anything from *Bat Out of Hell*.

10. 'Civil War' Use Your Illusion II

What we got here is . . . a great fuckin' song. With the exception of 'Sweet Child O' Mine', the lyrical content on *Appetite* was pure West

Hollywood gutter rock designed to appeal to the lowest common denominator. 'Civil War' was a revelatory insight into Guns' true songcraft potential . . . and they didn't disappoint.

9. 'Welcome to the Jungle' Appetite for Destruction

It's hard to imagine W. Axl Rose ever being an impressionable hick from the sticks, but then again, who would have guessed Slash spent time living in Stoke-on-Trent? I've never been bitten by the wanderlust bug myself, but a solitary listen to 'Welcome to the Jungle' might well have had me boarding a Greyhound bus bound for the City of Angels.

8. 'Knockin' on Heaven's Door' Use Your Illusion II

Dylan's '73 classic appears on the soundtrack to Sam Peckinpah's gritty Western drama, *Pat Garrett and Billy the Kid*. Guns had first fucked about with 'Knockin'on Heaven's Door' during a soundcheck at the Marquee Club during the summer of 1987. The UK music press would soon proclaim Guns as the latest gunslingers aiming to shoot the Stones from off of their lofty cloud. They'd do it as well . . .

7. 'Patience' GN'R Lies

Izzy apparently penned 'Patience' as a way of exorcising the ghosts of a failed romance – well, they do say the best art is born out of misery. I've always been a sucker for a blues ballad and this one ranks up there with the best.

6. 'You Could Be Mine' Use Your Illusion II

Any song that contains the line "With your bitch slap rapping and your cocaine tongue" is

GUNS N' ROSES

enough to grab my interest. 'You Could Be Mine' was earmarked for inclusion on *Appetite*, and one has to wonder how it lost out to lower order tracks such as 'Out Ta Get Me' or 'Anything Goes'? Or just maybe a synthetic android arrived from the future, sought out the band, and suggested they set the track aside because the long-anticipated sequel to *The Terminator* was about to go into pre-production?

5. 'Yesterdays' Use Your Illusion II

Seeing this one featuring so prominently might come as a surprise to some of you but there's just something about the lyric that grabbed me by the short n' curlies and has never quite let go. Time might well be fading the pages in my own book of memories but ones that centre around Guns N' Roses thankfully remain as sharp as ever.

4. 'Breakdown' Use Your Illusion II

And another personal favourite that still sends a shiver down my spine. To my mind this is the most underrated track on the *UYI* albums – maybe in the whole GN'R canon. I don't know where Axl's head was at while penning the lyric but boy, he was bang on the button. Everything is indeed roses while we hold the guns. And just because we're winning don't necessarily mean we're the lucky ones. Think on that a spell . . .

3. 'Paradise City' Appetite For Destruction

The G/C/F/C/G intro to 'Paradise City' is without doubt one of the most instantly recognisable in the annals of rock. Guns came up with the song while making their way back to LA from playing a show in San Francisco, conjuring up lines while

snorting others – allegedly! It's often said that the most memorable songs are the easiest to write. Guns didn't know it at the time, but they'd just come up with the ultimate set closer. Take. Me. Home . . .

2 . 'Estranged' Use Your Illusion II

It could just be that the relationship I happened to be in at the time the *UYI* albums were released had hit the skids (Hi, Heather . . .), but it really did feel as if Axl had crawled inside my mind. I know I wasn't talking so loud or walking quite so proud as before anyways. But that's what's so magical about Axl's songwriting – his unerring ability to pinwheel betwixt maniacal rage and vulnerable desperation. While 'Don't Cry' and 'November Rain' tug at the heartstrings, 'Estranged' rips them out of your throat and spits in your eye.

1. 'Sweet Child O' Mine' Appetite For Destruction

Could there really be any other choice? Every band of renown has a signature song and to think this one might have remained a string-skipping exercise had Slash had his way . . .? All that really needs to be said here is that life sure is grand if you're lucky enough to be with a lady whose face takes you away to that special place . . .

UNRELEASED

Appetite For Destruction Sessions

'Sentimental Movie'
'Cornshucker'

Use Your Illusion Sessions

'Bring It Back Home'
'Crash Diet' (Co-written with West Arkeen)
'It Tastes Good, Don't It'
'Just Another Sunday'
'Too Much Too Soon'
'Untitled' (Features in the Making of Estranged video, subsequently reworked as 'Back and Forth Again' on It's Five O'Clock Somewhere)

The Spaghetti Incident? Sessions

'A Beer And A Cigarette' (Hanoi Rocks cover recorded during the Use Your Illusion sessions for possible inclusion on The Spaghetti Incident?)
'Down on the Street'

Chinese Democracy Sessions

'Atlas Shrugged'
'Better Gone' (A Bryan Mantia remix of 'Better' that was leaked to the internet in 2013)
'Blood in the Water' (A Bryan Mantia remix of 'Prostitute' that was leaked to the internet in 2013)
'Down By the Ocean' (Co-written with Izzy Stradlin)
'Elvis Presley and the Monster of Soul' (featuring American film and television composer and conductor Marco Beltrami)
'Going Down' (Sung by Tommy Stinson and leaked to the internet in 2013)
'Ides of March'
'Oklahoma'
'Quick Song'
'Silkworms' (Written by Dizzy Reed and Chris Pitman and leaked to the internet in 2018)
'The General' (featuring Marco Beltrami)
'Thyme' (featuring Marco Beltrami)
'We Were Lying'
'Zodiac'

GUNS N' ROSES

GN'R CONSPIRATORS
WEST ARKEEN

Aaron West Arkeen was born in the Parisian suburb of Neuilly-sur-Seine but grew up in San Diego, California. He was born with craniosynostosis, a birth defect in which the skull grows irregularly, often constricting brain growth. The condition required surgery that left him with an ear-to-ear scar over the crown of his head. Arkeen's parents divorced when he was four. His father Morris, a former sergeant in the US Army, got custody of West and his older brother Abe, while their two sisters remained with the mother. On relocating to San Diego with his boys, Arkeen senior opened a pool hall called The Silver Cue, Speaking with the *LA Weekly* in July 2017, Abe Arkeen said their mother's being a "non-factor" in their lives had proved the underlying root of West's substance abuse issues in later life. "We were abandoned at a very critical time," he explained. "When you're a child of abandonment you do one of two things: You either explode at the world or you implode. My brother was an imploder."

It was around the age of 14 that Arkeen developed a yearning to learn to play the guitar. His father dutifully presented him with a cheap acoustic, and after one solitary lesson Arkeen settled down to teaching himself the rest playing along to Morris' record collection – notably Jimi Hendrix and Earth, Wind & Fire. Subsequent guitar heroes would include B.B. King, John Lennon, and Deep Purple's Tommy Bolin. "West was on that guitar constantly," Abe continued. "He just had a gift."

Having worked for a time in the oil industry in Texas, Arkeen spent several months working as a slot-machine repairman in Las Vegas before heading for the bright lights of LA (circa 1982) in the hope of making it in the music industry. During the day he eked out a living as a house painter. At night he played in bars and anywhere else on the Strip that would have him. He was still looking to make his mark when Duff McKagan fortuitously moved into the apartment next to his own at El Cerrito Place in Hollywood (funk pioneer Sly Stone was a resident eleswhere in the block). The two quickly became friends and Duff would soon introduce Arkeen to the other ragtag musicians in his band.

Arkeen was responsible for teaching Duff the open E tuning style he would use on 'It's So Easy' (for which Duff ensured Arkeen received a song-writing credit on *Appetite For Destruction*. When sales of *Appetite* really started soaring on the back of 'Sweet Child O' Mine' topping the *Billboard* 100, Duff and the rest of GN'R helped Arkeen get a publishing deal with Virgin Records. Arkeen would also receive co-writing credits on the *Use Your Illusion* albums for 'Yesterdays', 'Bad Obsession' and 'The Garden'. Other songs he co-wrote with Axl – 'Crash Diet', 'Just Another Sunday', and 'Sentimental Movie' – remain unreleased.

When Guns went out touring with The Cult they invited Arkeen along for the ride. When Geffen insisted that Arkeen earn his keep on the tour, the band arranged it so that he ended up being paid $300 per week for supplying them with water bottles during the shows. Alan Niven remembers Arkeen travelling back to LA from New Orleans after the final Cult show on the tour bus sporting nothing other than a pink nightgown and cowboy boots.

Although Arkeen was happy playing in the GN'R barroom band, The Drunk Fux, alongside Duff and Izzy (and Del James), as well as helping out playing guitar in the recording studio, Duff says their friend never made any noises about wanting to join Guns N' Roses. Contrary to Duff's assertions, Arkeen would have liked nothing better than to be invited to join the band – at least according to one-time Outpatience keyboardist, Gregg Buchwalter. "Unfortunately in LA at that time MTV was happening, and everyone wanted band members that had a look," he told the *LA Weekly* in July 2017. "And poor West was really thrilled that his friends in Guns N' Roses were playing some of his tunes and writing with him. They wouldn't let him in the band because he was too short and fat. He didn't look right. His girlfriend told me. She said, 'He's asked them a bunch of times to join the band, but they told him, 'No, you're too short and fat man, you don't look right.' Isn't that sick?"

Arkeen would eventually find an outlet for his songwriting creativity with The Outpatience, a hard rockin' LA-based quintet that recorded one album – *Anxious Disease* (a Japan-only release in 1996) – and would surely have gone on to record more records had it not been for his untimely demise in May 1997, aged just 36.

Arkeen was found dead at his Fruitland Drive apartment in Studio City. According to the Los Angeles County coroner's report the cause of death was acute heroin, morphine and cocaine intoxication. The cause of death was ruled an "accidental opiate overdose", but many of Arkeen's friends – including Duff – suspect foul play as the people that were with him on the day of his death reportedly made off with his guitars, home recordings, and lyric notebooks instead of dialling 911.

At the time of his death Arkeen was recovering from severe burns from his indoor barbecue having exploded. He'd last spoken to his brother from the burns unit where he was receiving treatment. "I heard a lot of rumours but all I know is that he got torched pretty bad," said Abe. "The sad thing is that they gave him a prescription opiate to deal with the pain and he had kicked drugs.

"Duff was gracious, kind, sympathetic and respectful as were all of GN'R at my family's loss," Abe continued. "They lost a close friend and I a brother. West was wild and crazy, but he had a talent from God. And like a lot of artists, they just burn out."

Guns N' Roses would dedicate *Live Era: '87-'93* to Arkeen's memory.

GUNS N' ROSES

DEL JAMES

Del James was born Adelberto James Mirando in New Rochelle, New York on February 5, 1964 – coincidentally sharing the same birthday as Duff – but grew up in neighbouring Mamaroneck. He relocated to West Hollywood sometime during 1985 to begin working for *RIP* magazine which was dedicated to championing the West Hollywood metal scene. (He would rise to the position of senior editor at the now long-defunct magazine.)

James had only been in town a few days when he met West Arkeen, who in turn introduced him to the then unsigned Guns N' Roses. Speaking about his "close" relationship with the band in *RIP* in April 1989, James said how he'd served as "roadie, roommate, confidant, reporter and a friend" to each band member. "My relationship with Axl is still very close," he continued. "It's a friendship, and out of that friendship comes a shared trust. The following represents Axl's trust in me to report the unwritten truth about W. Axl Rose and the rock'n' roll phenomenon known as Guns N' Roses. My job was rather easy: I just let Axl do most of the talking."

James also had a passion for penning psychological horror novellas. One of his short stories, *Without You*, was to prove the inspiration for the promo video to 'November Rain', of course. James' stories were published in 1995 as *The Language of Fear* by Dell Books and features an intro by Axl.

James receives co-writing credits on 'The Garden' and 'Yesterdays' – which appear on *Use Your Illusion I* and *II* respectively. His songwriting talents have also been utilised by the likes of TNT, Testament, Dizzy Reed, The Almighty and Ricky Warwick.

James still counts himself as one of Axl's closest associates. His continuing association with Guns N' Roses saw him serving as road manager on the Not in This Lifetime . . . Tour.

DIZZY REED

Dizzy Reed (born Darren Arthur Reed in June 1963) was brought into Guns N' Roses at Axl's behest in early 1990 to help augment the songs that would make up the *Use Your Illusion* albums. (Aside from Axl, he's the longest serving member of Guns N' Roses.) On being asked why he'd always been treated as an integral cog of the GN'R wheel during live performances, in a March 2018 interview with www.metalwani.com, Reed explained that it was primarily down to Axl. "He wanted me in the band, and I think he saw that I really wanted to be a part of the band. I'm not saying that the other guys didn't wanna put me behind a curtain on stage; I don't know that for sure, [and] I can't say that for sure. There was a little bit of talk of possibly me being a little bit . . . my head poking out from behind the curtain. But Axl, I think, saw how badly I wanted it and wanted to be a part of the band and wanted to add to it, and I give him all the credit for that, man."

Though he was born in Hinsdale, Illinois, Reed's family relocated to Colorado while he was still a toddler. Like most kids with dreams of achieving musical stardom, Reed pestered his parents for a guitar. With his doting grandmother having also taught him the rudiments of the organ, Reed found he could pick and choose from the plethora of low-rent, local garage bands. On deciding his future lay elsewhere, he loaded up his car and headed for LA. His first gig upon arriving in West Hollywood was playing guitar in Johnny Crash alongside Matt Sorum. Indeed, the two soon-to-be GN'R buddies stayed around long enough to record an album (the aptly titled *Unfinished Business* would remain unreleased till 2008).

It was while playing with The Wild that Reed was first introduced to Guns N' Roses as both bands were rehearsing out of the same decrepit, breeze-block garage-like 10 x 14 self-storage spaces at the back of Gardner Street. "I had been with [The Wild] for about five years," Reed told www.gnrlies.com in July 2004. "We were just trying to get a deal. I had a few deals, they fell through, but we were doing really good playing the clubs. We were basically just drinking a lot and chasing girls.

While Slash, Duff, Izzy, and Steven offered little more than a polite nod whenever the two bands bumped into each other, a shared passion for keyboards led to Reed and Axl striking up a friendship; the two keeping in touch all the way through GN'R's meteoric rise on the back of *Appetite* and *GNR Lies*. "Axl would always tell me when they [Guns N' Roses] added a keyboard player that I was going to be the guy," said Reed. "And when it was time, he found me, tracked me down, and said, 'It's time to do it.'"

Reed, of course, was perfectly positioned to witness the behind-the-scenes powerplays and spats that would bring about the demise of GN'R's *Use Your Illusion* line-up. Knowing how prickly Axl could get whenever anyone mentioned the "old Guns N' Roses", Reed chose his words carefully. "I don't think there was an actual downfall as much as everybody sort of outgrew what was going on," he said in the aforementioned www.gnrlies.com interview. "People lost track of how they got there. Sometimes when you're that young and you have that much success that fast you grow out of it. I think that had a lot to do with it. There was a definite lack of communication also, which when you have a group of people that work together that closely all the time, communication is extremely important.

GUNS N' ROSES

When there is a lot of money to be made, sometimes the powers that be will keep that communication from happening for fear that it might break up what's going on. Thus, the money machine will shut down."

Aside from keeping it in the GN'R family, so to speak, by guesting on Slash's Snakepit's *It's Five O'Clock Somewhere*, Duff's *Believe in Me*, Gilby Clarke's *Pawnshop Guitars* and *Gilby Clarke*, and Tommy Stinson's *Village Gorilla Head* and *One Man Mutiny*, Reed has also appeared on albums by the likes of one-time Rolling Stone Mick Taylor, Motörhead, Bang Tango, and Christian rock pioneer, Larry

Norman. He also played in The Dead Daisies alongside Richard Fortus, of course.

Speaking with the Nothing Shocking podcast in August 2018, Reed said that while he loved being in a recording studio he preferred being out on the road. So much so, in fact, that when he's not touring with Guns N' Roses he goes out with his hard rock covers act Hookers N' Blow, in which he plays keyboard, guitar and occasionally gets behind the mic.

Reed's debut solo album, *Rock N' Roll Aint Easy*, was released in February 2018 via Golden Robot Records.

PAUL TOBIAS

Guns N' Roses were making their first live appearance in eight years at the House of Blues in Las Vegas on January 1, 2001 when Axl introduced Tobias to the audience as being the guy who'd helped him "keep the band together" following Slash and Duff's respective departures. A press release issued August 15, 2002, at the start of the Chinese Democracy Tour, quoted Axl as saying how the public got a different story about Tobias from "the other guys" (Slash, Duff and Matt) who supposedly had their own agendas for doing so. "The original intentions between Paul and myself were that Paul was going to help me for as long as it took to get this thing together in whatever capacity that he could help me in. So when he first was brought into this, he was brought in as a writer to work with Slash."

Axl's working relationship with Tobias stretched back to co-writing 'Back Off Bitch' and 'Shadow of Your Love' during the former's days in Hollywood Rose. In October 1994, without bothering to consult Slash, Duff, or Matt, Axl invited Tobias to join Guns N' Roses in the studio to play guitar on their cover of the Stones' 'Sympathy for the Devil', which was set for inclusion on Neil Jordan's *Interview with the Vampire*. Axl viewed Tobias as a potential replacement for Gilby Clarke; the latter having been served notice sometime the previous year.

Slash, however, didn't particularly like Tobias as a person. Nor did he think much of Tobias's playing and said as much to Axl. Duff and Matt had also taken a dislike to Tobias but they tried their utmost to get along with him, if only to keep Axl from throwing another hissy fit. Slash wouldn't prove as amenable, however. And it was discovering Tobias had overdubbed one of his guitar parts on 'Sympathy for the Devil' that triggered his exit from Guns N' Roses. Matt's derisive comments about Tobias being capable of filling Slash's shoes was to herald his own departure from the band soon thereafter.

Together with Dizzy Reed, Tobias co-wrote 'Oh My God', which appeared on the *End of Days* soundtrack in November 1999. Many of the guitar parts (and at least one piano part) that Tobias laid down during the *Chinese Democracy* sessions would survive to the final mix – despite his departure from Guns N' Roses during the summer of 2002 (when he was replaced by Richard Fortus). The reason for Tobias's departure was said to be due to his aversion to touring – his final GN'R show coming at the Hard Rock Café in Las Vegas on December 31, 2001. Tobias's links with Guns N' Roses would extend to subsequently working with Bryan Mantia on a 2013 various artists album called *Eclectic Cinema*. The album also features future GN'R keyboardist Melissa Reese.

Tobias's being in Guns N' Roses had elevated his stature somewhat. So much so, that shortly after his departure from GN'R his one-time bandmates in Mank Rage set about trying to secure record company interest in an album's worth of material. Nothing would come of their endeavours, but many of these songs can be heard via Mank Rage's Facebook page.

GUNS N' ROSES

FRANK FERRER

Frank "Thunderchucker" Ferrer was originally invited to fill in for Bryan Mantia on the Chinese Democracy Tour in July 2006; the latter having returned to the US to be at his wife's side when she gave birth. He subsequently replaced Mantia full time later that same year. His getting the nod over both Steven Adler and Matt Sorum for the GN'R "regrouping" makes him Guns N' Roses' longest-serving drummer.

Ferrer was born in New York City in March 1966, his earliest musical memories coming with pulsating Latino rhythms blaring out from neighbouring apartments, storefronts, and car stereos. Indeed, his father played percussion in a Latino band. Ferrer's musical epiphany would come seeing Kiss performing on TV when he was 11 years old. He duly set about badgering his father to take him to see Simmons and Co. at Madison Square Garden. "That's when I knew I wanted to play," he told *Online Drummer* in 2011. "[But] I thought I wanted to play guitar because they were up front and running around. The drummer just sat there."

Armed with a set of bongos borrowed from his father, Ferrer joined a youth choir in middle school. He soon progressed to a full drum kit and, encouraged by his music teacher to follow his dreams, began playing in clubs and bars. A chance meeting during the mid-Eighties saw Ferrer join forces with singer/guitarist Jonathan Lacey and bassist Perry Bottke to form The Beautiful, a dynamic alternative rock outfit that ended up being signed to Warner Music on the strength of a cassette demo. They subsequently released a self-titled EP in 1990, their debut album, *Storybook*, coming two years later.

Following on from The Beautiful, Ferrer teamed up with ex-Psychedelic Furs brothers, Richard and Tim Butler, and future GN'R collaborator Richard Fortus to form Love Spit Love. The band would release their eponymously titled album in 1994 but are perhaps best known for their cover version of The Smiths' 'How Soon is Now' which was selected as the theme tune for the long-running US TV series *Charmed*.

When he's not touring with Guns N' Roses, Ferrer plays with The Compulsions, which features fellow GN'R member Richard Fortus and ex-Hanoi Rocker Sami Yaffa. He can also be found kicking out the punk-rock jams in his personal project, Pisser. "I'm playing for myself in Pisser," he told *The Classic Metal Show* in 2014. "I don't care if there are 20 or two people in the room. In NYC, it's a live thing. It's a city of live drumming. You've got to play live to get put on and to get noticed. That's how I got my first band . . . and that's how I ended up with Guns."

ROBIN FINCK

At the time he joined Guns N' Roses in 1997, the then 25-year-old, Georgia-born Robin Finck was playing guitar for the Cirque du Soleil (where he met his future wife, Bianca). What most likely brought him to Axl's attention as a replacement for Slash, however, was his having toured with Nine Inch Nails on their Self-Destruct and Further Down the Spiral tours following the departure of Richard Patrick.

Having signed a two-year contract at the beginning of 1997, Finck threw himself into the recording of Chinese Democracy. The album was still light years away from completion when his two-year conscription came to an end, of course. But as with Paul Tobias, many of Finck's guitar parts survived through to the final mixing. (He also receives a songwriting credit on 'Better'.) There is some dispute as to whether Finck appeared on 'Oh My God'. Axl is of the opinion that he does appear on the track, while the guitarist himself still begs to differ.

Finck would end up rejoining Nine Inch Nails in time for the Fragility v1.0 and Fragility v2.0 tours in support of their latest album, The Fragile. He also played on Still, the accompanying studio album to Live on the All That Could Have double album. Shortly after the NIN tours came to an end in 2000, Finck returned to duty with Guns N' Roses for tours across Europe and Asia. He also performed with the band at that year's MTV Video Music Awards. (During his second tenure with GN'R, Finck and Buckethead contributed to the soundtrack to John Carpenter's 2001 film Ghosts of Mars.)

Finck declined an offer to rejoin Nine Inch Nails to tour in support of their 2005 album With Teeth but would, however, accept an offer to rejoin as a member of their live band in April 2008. He would subsequently opt to remain with Nine Inch Nails rather than rejoin Guns N' Roses to tour in support of Chinese Democracy. In March 2009, Finck was officially replaced in Guns N' Roses by DJ Ashba.

Following the departures of his fellow live band members Alessandro Cortini and Josh Freese, at the end of 2008 Finck and bassist Justin Meldal-Johnsen re-grouped [10] with band leader Trent Reznor and new drummer Ilan Rubin and the four-piece band completed an eight-date tour of Australia and New Zealand between February and March 2009. Finck continued to perform with the band throughout the 2009 Nine Inch Nails/Jane's Addiction (NIN|JA) tour, with shows throughout North America, and the subsequent Wave Goodbye tour through Europe and Asia. The band then returned to the US to play a series of shows culminating in the final live appearance of Nine Inch Nails.

Though no longer part of Guns N' Roses, in 2009 Finck's name would appear alongside those of Axl, Tommy Stinson, and Buckethead in a $1 million lawsuit launched against Guns N' Roses and Interscope-Geffen by the British label, Independiente, and the US arm of the Domino Recording Company. Both labels alleged GN'R had committed copyright infringement in using segments of the German electronic musician Ulrich Schnauss's compositions – 'Wherever You Are' and 'A Strangely Isolated Place' – in 'Riad 'N the Bedouins'.

GN'R's then manager, Irving Azoff, denied any wrongdoing. "The band believed when the record (Chinese Democracy) came out and still believes that there are no unauthorised

GUNS N' ROSES

samples on the track," said Azoff. "The snippets of 'ambient noise' in question were provided by a member of the album's production team who has assured us that these few seconds of sound were obtained legitimately." The matter would be settled amicably.

RICHARD FORTUS

Guns N' Roses' incumbent rhythm guitarist joined the band in July 2002, replacing the outgoing Paul Tobias. Fortus was touring Europe with Enrique Iglesias when he got a call from his friend Tommy Stinson asking him to fly back to LA to audition for the band. Fortus was originally sounded out to audition as a potential replacement for Robin Finck three years earlier (the role eventually going to Buckethead.) Fortus' ability to play both lead and rhythm would lead an ebullient Axl to sing his praises. "He's an amazing lead player and very technically skilled," he enthused in a press release shortly after Fortus' inclusion. "He really likes the pocket that Brain sets and the two of them click with Tommy so we finally have the real deal rhythm section, as Richard is a proven professional. Basically, Richard's the guy that we always were looking for." However, had Izzy deigned not to take himself out of the running at the time of GN'R's late 2015 "regrouping", then in all likelihood Fortus' tenure with Guns N' Roses would have ended after the final Appetite for Democracy Tour date in Las Vegas in June 2014.

Fortus hails from St Louis, Missouri, where his musical path started with violin lessons at the tender age of four. Within a year or so he was also showing an aptitude for the drums – even if his beating out rhythms on anything that came to hand drove his family to distraction. By the time he enrolled at the Conservatory of the Arts in St. Louis – during which time he played in several local youth symphonies – he'd added guitar to his repertoire. Upon leaving the Conservatory he set about forming his own band, The Eyes, from among friends and like-minded acquaintants.

The Eyes steadily built up a local following

playing local clubs such as Kennedy's, Mississippi Nights, and Off Broadway before venturing over the state line. They self-released an album called *Freedom in a Cage*, before securing a record deal with Atlantic Records in early 1990. Upon discovering they shared their name with at least another two bands, the four-piece underwent a change of name to Pale Divine. They released their debut album, *Straight to Goodbye*, for Atlantic in October 1990. They may as well have called their album *"Straight to Siberia"* as Atlantic reportedly did little to promote either the album or the band.

Having switched to Atlantic's sister label, Atco, Pale Divine were invited to open for the Psychedelic Furs who were touring the US in support of their latest album, *World Outside*. Despite gaining some much-needed exposure, friction within the band – primarily betwixt Fortus and frontman Michael Schaerer – proved problematic when it came to recording a follow-up album and they left Atco by mutual consent. When the Furs went into "extended hiatus" in 1992, Fortus joined forces with Richard and Tim Butler – as well as future GN'R collaborator, Frank Ferrer – in the short-lived Love Spit Love.

Love Spit Love would score a minor hit with 'Am I Wrong?' (the lead single from their eponymous debut album). The band's follow-up album, *Trysome Eatone* (released via Madonna's Maverick Records) failed to capitalise on this exposure, however, and when the Butler brothers opted to reform the Psychedelic Furs, Fortus – and Ferrer – were happy to tag along. The duo appear on the Furs 2001 album, *Beautiful Chaos: Greatest Hits Live*.

When Guns N' Roses' summer 2013 North American leg of their Appetite for Democracy Tour came to an end, Fortus, together with

GUNS N' ROSES

Ferrer and Dizzy Reed, joined the Dead Daisies as a side project. Betwixt further legs of the Appetite for Democracy Tour, the GN'R trio recorded two albums – *Dead Daises* (2013) and *Revolucion* (2015).

MELISSA REESE

The latest – and by far the prettiest – edition to the GN'R clan was born in Seattle, Washington. Reese is the youngest of three girls born into a mixed-race household of Chinese, English, Spanish, Japanese, Filipino, Irish, Scottish and Danish descent. One of her sisters was already singing in a local choir and Reese says she initially took up singing simply to mimic her sibling but quickly fell in love with performing in front of others. As she explains on her website: "I ended up going on a similar path as she; joined girls' choir and began piano lessons (being able to play Bach by ear aged just three), but as I got older, I went down a different road. My sister continued on a classical course and now sings opera whereas I took up songwriting and directionally went more pop, R & B, and hip hop."

While enrolled at Roosevelt High, Reese deviated from the classical music training of her formative years and joined the school's vocal jazz ensemble. The ensemble competed at both the Reno and Lionel Hampton Jazz Festivals and ended up taking first place in both competitions, while Reese won an outstanding soloist award at the latter festival. Upon leaving high school she set about furthering her musical prowess by experimenting with recording her own material. Having mastered a vintage Boss BR-8 and a Roland Groovebox she invested in the same Pro Tools, Logic and Reason, that had captivated Axl's attention when first starting out on his *Chinese Democracy* odyssey. Within two years, she'd penned, performed and produced hundreds of songs in her own home studio. Three of the six tracks from her 2007 EP, *LISSA* (in collaboration with Bryan Mantia and featuring Buckethead on one of the tracks) – 'Ooh La La', 'Pretty Please' and 'Old Skool' – featured in

various network cable series such as *Cashmere Mafia*, *Gossip Girl*, and *Keeping Up with The Kardashians*. Another of her songs, 'Girlfriend', was selected as the theme song for the Just Fab Shoe commercial campaign.

Reese would subsequently work with Mantia as Brain and Melissa, primarily composing original game themes for Sony Playstation. The duo's first full length major Playstation series release, *Infamous 2*, would be nominated for "Outstanding Achievement in Original Composition" by the AIAS (Academy of Interactive Arts and Sciences). They would also score a TV commercial for Johnnie Walker Blue (featuring a computer-generated Bruce Lee).

Brian and Melissa were thrilled to be invited to work on the score/remix for Taylor Swift's 'Bad Blood' music video which premiered at the opening of the 2015 *Billboard* Music Awards. 'Bad Blood' would also take home the Grammy for Best Music Video in 2016, the same year she was invited to join Guns N' Roses as the band's second keyboardist, replacing Chris Pitman.

Reese would have just two weeks to learn and master 50 songs in preparation for the Not in This Lifetime . . . Tour. She spent upwards of 15 hours a day poring over and dissecting each song in turn – especially Axl's phrasing which she "studied like a hawk". While admitting she had no idea what she was getting herself into, Reese says she's "eternally grateful to Axl and the rest of the band for taking a chance on me." Though eternally grateful for such a once-in-a-lifetime opportunity, she waited until after the GN'R tour was under way before telling her parents as she didn't want to "stress them out".

Reese's role in GN'R has been described as the "enhancer" as she uses Akai samplers

GUNS N' ROSES

(among other state-of-the-art tools) to produce sounds from certain of the songs on *Chinese Democracy*, as well as playing Moog synthesiser on 'Paradise City'. She also plays synthesiser, sub-bass, and provides onstage programming during the tour.

Speaking to *LA Weekly* in May 2017, Reese said how she didn't want to get in the way of such iconic songs. "On the keys, I add sonic layers to thicken our sound without sticking out like a sore thumb. Anything from synths [to] organic patches and samples." She then goes on to reveal how she washes down a full box of See's Candy with Diet Coke – a trait carried over from her Brain and Melissa days – to get herself "jacked" for GN'R's customary three-hour sets. Things didn't go according to script at the MetLife Stadium in New Jersey, however, and she was forced to swallow her puke rather than risk getting her rig console covered in sticky Coke-soaked candy. The rest of the band duly presented her with a blue bucket – to match her dyed tresses ("Blue" being her GN'R nickname) – should such an unsavoury occasion happen again.

Betwixt legs on the GN'R tour she's penned the end credits theme to Walter Hill's 2016 crime thriller, *The Assignment*, while she and Mantia would work together on the musical score to Joseph Khan's 2018 film, *Bodied*. "I love that I've had the chance to do so many different things outside recording my own music as an artist," Reese says on her website. "I always want to do what feels right to me and what I'm good at. Embrace my diversity, and not limit myself. I view my work as an extension of my ethnic heritage – there are so many parts that make up me. And delving into all these areas is the only way that I can be completely true to who I am."

BUCKETHEAD

The enigmatic multi-instrumentalist joined Guns N' Roses in 2000. He remained with the band for four years, during which time he recorded various guitar parts on *Chinese Democracy* (all tracks except for 'Catcher in the Rye' and 'This I Love'). He would only make a handful of live appearances with the band, however.

The inverted KFC bucket and plastic facemask-wearing "guitar mutant virtuoso" (his own words) was born Brian Carroll in Pomona, California in May 1969. He was said to be an introverted child who spent most of his time holed up in his bedroom either watching Kung Fu flicks or poring over comic books. His only forays outdoors were visits to nearby Disneyland in neighbouring Anaheim. Indeed, such was his love of roller-coasters that he would insist on Axl accompanying him to the theme park to sign his GN'R contract.

Buckethead first came to prominence in Praxis, the experimental rock/funk project fronted by Bill Laswell and featuring Bryan "Brain" Mantia. Praxis combined elements of various musical genres such as funk, jazz, hip-hop and heavy metal into highly improvised music, and their 1992 debut album, *Transmutation (Mutatis Mutandis)*, was well received by the critics. That same year, Buckethead released his own debut solo album, *Bucketheadland*, via his fellow multi-instrumentalist John Zorn's Japanese Avant label. Though only available on import, the album received positive reviews, earning Buckethead his first notices.

In May 1994, while still actively part of Praxis – recording both *Sacrifist*, and *Metatron* –Buckethead released *Dreamatorium* under the name of Death Cube K (an anagram

of Buckethead) owing to certain legal complications with Sony Music. He was already proving himself a prolific writer as his follow-up solo album, *Giant Robot*, came out just six months later in November 1994.

By the time Axl came calling, Buckethead had released three other solo albums – *The Day of the Robot* (April 1996), *Colma* (March 1998), and *Monsters and Robots* (April 1999). He'd also released two further Death Cube K albums – *Disembodied* and *Tunnel*. To date, he's recorded some 306 studio albums (including 275 in the Pike Series), clocking up an amazing 163 hours – give or take five minutes. He started work on what is said to be his "most precious personal project", *Buckethead Plays Disney*, in 1997 but the album has yet to be completed.

Unlike most lead guitarists, Buckethead has proved something of an introvert. Indeed, it was his dislike of being in the spotlight that led to his formulating his trademark alter ego: the plastic facemask being an homage of sorts to fictional psychopathic slasher, Michael Myers, from the *Halloween* franchise, while the inverted-bucket-on-the-head idea came to him out of the blue one evening after eating some fried chicken. (It's said that his original bucket came from a lesser-known deli chicken chain, and that he only made the switch to KFC some time later.) The chicken fetish didn't end there, however, as he would subsequently claim in interviews that he'd been raised in a coop by chickens. He also had those same gullible reporters believe that his long-term goal was to bring attention to the ongoing chicken holocaust in fast-food outlets across the globe. His stage antics have proved equally bizarre, as he often breaks into robotic break dance routines or treats the audience to

GUNS N' ROSES

random nunchaka displays.

In hindsight, it's easy to see that Axl and Buckethead were never likely to make lasting bedfellows. When it was announced that Guns N' Roses were having to postpone their much anticipated opening European leg of the Chinese Democracy World Tour owing to Buckethead having suffered internal haemorrhaging of the stomach, many pundits believed the postponement was simply an excuse for the *Chinese Democracy* release date being put back till later in the year. However, rumours soon began to fly that the real reason behind the tour's eleventh-hour postponement was due to Buckethead's intention to release his latest solo offering, *Somewhere Over the Slaughterhouse*, within days of the tour getting under way – and that Axl feared the album's release would deflect attention away from *Chinese Democracy*.

Buckethead quit Guns N' Roses without warning in May 2004 on the eve of the band's scheduled appearance at Rock in Rio Lisboa I.

DJ ASHBA

DJ (Daren Jay) Ashba replaced the outgoing Robin Finck in Guns N' Roses in March 2009. He remained with the band until July 2015, making his last live appearance at The Joint on the final night of the Appetite for Democracy Las Vegas residency on June 7, 2014. In a handwritten letter (that would subsequently be translated to Japanese, Portuguese, Spanish and French) issued at the time of his departure, the then 32-year-old Ashba said he'd "reached a point in my life where I feel it's time to dedicate myself to my band Sixx:A.M., my adoring wife and family, and to the many new adventures that the future holds for me."

One has to wonder whether Axl was standing over his shoulder while he was penning his gushing ode, as he waxes on about his arriving at the audition with no real expectations of his getting the gig. And of his "shock and surprise" at receiving the call that was to take him on "the most incredible journey I could have possibly imagined."

Ashba was born in Monticello, Indiana, but grew up in Fairbury, Illinois. As with Josh Freese, his mother was a classically trained pianist who set about helping him on his own artistic bent as soon as he could walk. Indeed, he performed in his first piano recital – Beethoven's 'Ode to Joy' – aged just five. Again, as with Freese, he developed an early fascination for the drums, assembling his first kit from an assortment of pots and pans until finally acquiring a bona fide kit replete with skins and bass pedal. The guitar was also to prove an early obsession, his fixation stretching so far as to take a job detassling corn to save up to procure an instrument from his mother's Sears catalogue, despite only being eight years old at the time.

His first live music experience came when he was 16 catching Mötley Crüe on their 1987 Girls, Girls, Girls Tour, little realising he'd one day end up working with Nikki Sixx. Recalling that night years later, Ashba said: "The crowd, the music, the lights! It was the night I realised that no matter what it takes, I was gonna be on that stage one day." Within two years he'd packed up his worldly goods and moved to where the action was in West Hollywood.

Having played for two years or so with a long-forgotten outfit called Barracuda, Ashba released his debut album in 1996, an instrumental-only offering titled *Addiction to the Friction*. Preferring to be part of something rather than continue ploughing a lone furrow, he auditioned and was accepted into BulletBoys, a heavy metal act that featured a certain Steven Adler in the line-up. Within a year, however, Ashba quit BulletBoys to form Beautiful Creatures with Joe Lesté of Bang Tango.

Beautiful Creatures subsequently secured a recording deal with Warner Bros. and released their self-titled debut in August 2001. (The album was produced by Sean Beavan, who also for a time worked on *Chinese Democracy*.) The album would reach # 29 on the *Billboard* Top Heatseekers chart. When Warners subsequently dropped Beautiful Creatures from their roster, Ashba decided he might have better luck fronting his own hand-picked outfit. He was fronting ASHBA when Nikki Sixx invited him to join his short-lived side-project Brides of Destruction (which featured Tracii Guns in the line-up). Ashba surprisingly declined. His name would come up in connection with Mötley Crüe when rumours began circulating that he and Josh Freese had stood in for Mick Mars and Tommy Lee respectively on the Crüe's February

GUNS N' ROSES

2005 compilation album, *Red, White & Crüe*. Ashba was also rumoured to be taking Mar's place on Crüe's forthcoming reunion tour – a rumour he wasted little time in quashing.

Ashba's long-standing collaboration with Sixx got under way in 2006 when the duo set up Funny Farms Studios – a state-of-the-art facility which included three full-service studios and a photography studio – and began writing, producing, and performing together. It was this collaboration, of course, that gave rise to Sixx:A.M.

Sixx:AM's first release was *The Heroin Diaries Soundtrack*, which served as an accompaniment to Sixx's critically acclaimed 2007 autobiography, *The Heroin Diaries: A Year in the Life of a Shattered Rock Star*. Initially, Sixx had no intention of taking Sixx:A.M. out on the road but continuing pressure from Crüe fans saw him finally relent. While touring with Guns N' Roses, Ashba recorded two further Sixx:A.M. albums, *This Is Gonna Hurt*, (the title of Sixx's second literary offering, published 2011), and *Modern Vintage* (October 2014).

Following Ashba's return in 2015, Sixx:A.M. released *Prayers for the Damned, Vol. 1* (April 2016) and *Prayers for the Blessed, Vol. 2* (November 2016) before going into hiatus.

Ashba is currently collaborating with Sixx:A.M. frontman, James Michael in Pyromantic.

JOSH FREESE

Having been born on December 25, the then 24-year-old Josh Freese couldn't have been blamed for thinking all his Christmases had come at once on being invited to replace Matt Sorum in Guns N' Roses in the spring of 1997 (signing a two-year contract similar to that of Robin Finck's). Yet while Freese recorded 30 songs for possible inclusion on *Chinese Democracy* – co-writing the title track with Axl – his only drumming credit is on 'Oh My God'.

"The Bruce Lee of Drums", as Freese would come to be known, was surrounded by music from an early age, his mother being a classically trained pianist while his father was the conductor of the Disneyland Band. He first began playing the drums aged eight and, following in dad's footsteps, started his professional music career aged 12 playing in a Disneyland Top 40 band. Within three years, however, Freese had waved a fond farewell to Mickey, Donald, and Goofy et al to tour with The Vandals. He's continued playing with the Orange County punk perennials to the present day.

Aside from his ongoing Vandals' commitments, Freese supplied the beat on

Suicidal Tendencies' *The Art of Rebellion* (June 1992) and the Infectious Grooves' *Sarsippius' Ark* (February 1993). In January 1996, he joined a reformed Devo, making his debut at the Sundance Film Festival. He's continued as their primary onstage drummer ever since – and also played on the kitsch Akron synth-popsters' 2010 album, *Something for Everybody*. He has since gone on to work with Perry Farrell, Paul Westerberg, Chris Cornell, Juliana Hatfield, Nine Inch Nails, The Offspring, and Sting to name but a few. To date, he's appeared on upwards of 200 records. His standing is such that, in 2015, LA's mayor, Eric Garcetti, declared July 24 "Josh Freese Day".

While Bryan Mantia was holed up in the makeshift Masonic hall above Village Recorders re-writing Freese's drum parts on *Chinese Democracy*, the latter formed A Perfect Circle with Tool frontman, Maynard James Keenan (and guitarist Billy Howerdel). He appears on all the band's studio albums – with the exception of 2018's *Eat the Elephant* – and is still considered an integral member of the band.

GUNS N' ROSES

BRYAN MANTIA

Born and raised in the South Bay city of Cupertino, California, Mantia became fixated with the groove-laden sounds at an early age – especially the beats laid down by Led Zeppelin's John Bonham, Mitch Mitchell (Jimi Hendrix Experience), and Clyde Stubblefield (James Brown). He wouldn't start playing drums himself till he was 16, however. His enduring nickname came courtesy of the guys in his high school band owing to his obsession with percussionist and composer Anthony J. Cirone's book, *Portraits in Rhythm* (50 studies for snare drum). Having continued perfecting his drumming technique studying at the Percussion Institute of Technology in Hollywood, Mantia joined San Francisco party band, The Limbomaniacs, a funk-rock outfit that would break up soon after Mantia's inclusion. (They would reform again without Mantia in the late-Eighties and released the album *Stinky Grooves* in 1990.)

Following on from The Limbomaniacs, Mantia played with a variety of Bay Area bands before hooking up with Bill Laswell, Bootsy Collins, and Buckethead to form the funk/experimental supergroup Praxis. It was at Buckethead's behest that Mantia replaced Josh Freese in Guns N' Roses. "Buckethead told me that Josh had quit and said, 'Axl's an awesome dude; you should come check it out," Mantia told www.moderndrummer.com in March 2009. "So I went in there, and I didn't hear back from them for a while. And then one day I remember Axl calling me and saying, 'You know, if you want the gig you can have it and you can still be on other stuff. You can still do Primus or whatever you want to do.'"

Mantia accepted, little realising what he was getting himself into as his drum kit would spend the next six years or so set up at Village Recorders in Santa Monica. He recalls driving around Los Angeles with Roy Thomas Baker in the latter's Rolls-Royce searching for the exact drums they wanted for re-recording Freese's parts on *Chinese Democracy*. "We went to every company and it wound up being a mash-up of all the best drums we could find around LA," he explained. "We pretty much gathered the most ridiculous kit you could ever have to re-record Josh's parts. Josh had come up with some pretty good parts for the album. Axl was like, 'Hey, I like what Josh did so could we start out by you doing his parts, but with your feel? Because your feel's different.'"

Mantia's endless striving for perfection saw him head over to Sony Music to seek out the guy responsible for orchestrations on their films to see if he could transcribe Freese's drum parts. The process took around five months as the guy could only transcribe six songs a month owing to his other commitments.

When Mantia first assembled the kit he and Baker and amassed at Village he wasn't happy with the vibe in the main studio. Having first cleared it with the studio's owner, he moved into the upstairs theatre which the local Freemasons were using as their temple.

Mantia toured several legs of the Chinese Democracy Tour before quitting to spend time with his wife and newborn daughter.

CHRIS PITMAN

The then 22-year-old Los Angeles-based multi-instrumentalist was drafted into Guns N' Roses in early 2008 as a second keyboardist. (He also stood in for Tommy Stinson at the Rodeo Drive Walk of Style Induction Ceremony in honour of Versace on February 8, 2007.) He receives a number of credits on *Chinese Democracy*, ranging from keyboards and synthesisers, 12-string guitar and mellotron, through to bass and drum programming and digital editing. He also receives a co-writing credit on 'If the World' and 'Madagascar', and appears on 'Oh My God'.

Pitman was born in Independence, Missouri in February 1976 and studied at both the Art Institute of Kansas City and the University of Missouri. Upon finishing his schooling, Pitman worked for a time with post-conceptual artist Les Levine and Dr. Dre before forming alternative metallists Replicants with ex-Tool bassist Paul D'Amour. Replicants would release a self-titled album consisting entirely of covers of songs by famous bands active in the Seventies and Eighties, before going into permanent hiatus. His next venture, the short-lived electronica outfit ZAUM, would also prove Tool-related as he worked alongside the band's drummer Danny Carey. ZAUM would only get as far as recording a four-track, self-titled demo, but Pitman's collaboration with Carey led to his being invited to go out on tour with Tool, as well as provide additional synthesiser on the track 'Third Eye' from the band's 1996 album, *Ænima*.

While recording *Chinese Democracy* and touring with Guns N' Roses, Pitman played synthesiser on the Electric Company's 2004 album, *Creative Playthings*. The following year saw him again join forces with Danny Carey in Source of Uncertainty, an experimental project involving recording material solely using pre-Sixties musical recording devices.

Another of Pitman's ongoing side-projects was SexTapes, whose eponymously titled debut album was released a couple of weeks prior to *Chinese Democracy*. "I'm glad to finally get this album out there as it was just finished this summer," he enthused. "Between my involvement with Guns N' Roses and the band's high expectations for a solid and unique hard rock sound, we're stoked to finally have a great record that we're proud to release to our fans."

Pitman would be rather less stoked upon discovering he wouldn't be involved in the 2016 Guns N' Roses "regrouping", however. So much so, he issued an angry tweet labelling the GN'R reunion a "cash grab" and a "nostalgia trip". Though he would subsequently issue an apology for his Twitter rant, he subsequently insisted that he'd quit the "oldies band" because "they just want to repeat that 30-year-old music over and over."

In August 2016, Pitman launched a lawsuit against Axl for $167,000 -$125,000 in unpaid wages dating back to 2011 plus interest – which Axl supposedly couldn't afford to pay him at the time. According to Pitman, Axl wrote him a promissory note in October 2011 for the $125,000 to be paid by the following October. That Pitman waited five years before asking for his money suggests he was earning very nicely from GN'R in the interim. The suit was settled in November 2016, with Pitman reportedly having to settle for less than the $167,000 he was seeking.

GUNS N' ROSES

TOMMY STINSON

Aside from his 18-year tenure with Guns N' Roses (1998-2016), Tommy Stinson is perhaps best known for his time in The Replacements, the legendary Minneapolis-based garage punksters that have since come to be regarded as one of alternative rock's foremost pioneers. Stinson had barely hit puberty when his guitar-playing older brother, Bob, and his high school dropout buddy Chris Mars coerced him into joining their fledgling band Dogbreath – despite his never having before played bass. The trio set about covering songs by the likes of Aerosmith, Ted Nugent and Yes in the basement of the Stinson household, but the music reportedly came in a poor second behind booze and drugs. The line-up was soon augmented by Paul Westerberg on guitar. They also found a singer, but Westerberg's ego was such that he orchestrated a move which allowed him to take over the mic.

Having ditched Dogbreath in favour of The Impediments, the fledgling band – sans the younger Stinson – made their drunken debut at a local church hall and ended up being banned from the venue owing to their unruly behaviour. This would be their only outing as The Impediments as the quartet soon underwent another name change to their more enduring name. The newly christened Replacements recorded a four-song demo which they handed to Peter Jesperson, the manager of a local record store that specialised in punk rock that had recently co-founded Twin/Tone Records.

The band had only handed Jesperson a copy of the demo in the hope of securing a gig at Jay's Longhorn Bar, a local venue where Jesperson worked as a DJ. Jesperson only had to hear the opening song, 'Raised in the City', to know The Replacements had the potential

to be huge, however. He called Westerberg the following day asking if they wanted to record a single or album for Twin/Tone. The Replacements duly signed with Twin/Tone and headed into the studio to record their debut album, *Sorry Ma, Forgot to Take Out the Trash*. Owing to the label's finances, however, the album wouldn't be released until the following August. The band's follow-up album, *Hootenanny*, would receive mainstream positive reviews with *Village Voice*'s Robert Christgau going so far as to deem it the "most critically independent album of 1983".

It would be The Replacements' third album, *Let It Be*, that brought the major record labels sniffing round. They eventually signed with Sire Records, home of The Ramones. Tommy Ramone would produce The Replacements first Sire album, *Tim*. *Tim* was to prove Bob Stinson's swansong with The Replacements as he would be dismissed in 1986 because of his debilitating drink and drug addictions – he died in 1995.

Another mooted reason for Stinson senior's sacking was his dislike of The Replacements' shift away from punk. This was certainly evident in the band's 1989 album, *Don't Tell a Soul*. While costing them many of their early hardcore fans, the album exposed them to wider mainstream success – with the lead single, 'I'll Be You', topping the *Billboard* Modern Rock chart (and reaching # 51 on the *Billboard* 100). By this juncture, however, The Replacements were riven with internal friction. The situation was hardly helped by Westerberg's decision to record a new album's worth of material largely with session musicians – and it took some serious arm-twisting by Sire for him to agree to it being released as a Replacements album.

All Shook Down brought The Replacements

further mainstream attention (receiving a Grammy nomination for "Best Alternative Music Album"). Westerberg's use of session players – coupled with Chris Mars' sudden departure soon after the album's release – led many fans to ponder the band's future. New drummer Steve Foley was brought in, but the writing was on the wall for all to see and The Replacements duly embarked on a drawn-out farewell tour until the summer of 1991; the final show coming at Chicago's Taste of Chicago food festival on July 4. (The Replacements would reform in 2012 and continue until 2015).

Stinson's first post-Replacements outfit was the short-lived Bash & Pop (with Steve Foley on drums) who were signed to Sire and released one album, *Friday Night Is Killing Me*, in January 1993. Following the breakup of Bash & Pop in 1994, Stinson formed Perfect, and signed the band to Peter Jesperson's Medium Cool Records. The band's debut EP, *When Squirrels Play Chicken*, was released in 1996 to mainly positive reviews. The band's debut album, tentatively titled *Seven Days a Week*, would end up being shelved indefinitely, however, which ultimately heralded their demise in 1998. (The album would receive a belated release via Rykodisc in 2004 under the title *Once, Twice, Three Times a Maybe*.)

Stinson's invitation to replace Duff in Guns N' Roses came via Josh Freese. Duff didn't make any comment at the time – at least not publicly – but it's hard to imagine him not smiling upon hearing the news of Stinson's appointment as he was a huge Replacements fan. Stinson features prominently on *Chinese Democracy*, playing bass on all but one track, 'If the World', as well as providing backing vocals on several songs. He also played on 'Oh My God', of course.

During the Chinese Democracy World Tour, Stinson was given a solo slot during which he played either 'My Generation', or The Dead Boys' 'Sonic Reducer'. He was even known to belt out one of his own compositions on occasion – 'Motivation' from his 2004 debut solo album, *Village Gorilla Head*. (His second solo album, *One Man Mutiny*, was released in 2011.)

Axl had also come to rely on Stinson's judgement in the recording studio but sitting at Axl's right hand wasn't without its occasional prickly moments. During GN'R's performance at Cleveland's Quicken Loans Arena on the North American leg of the Chinese Democracy Tour on November 24, 2006, Axl reportedly called support act, Eagles of Death Metal, the "Pigeons of Shit Metal". Speaking with the *NME*, EoDM's frontman, Jesse Hughes, said how Stinson had thrown his bass to the floor in disgust at Axl's putdown and had threatened to quit GN'R. (While Stinson didn't carry out his threat, EoDM would be dismissed from the tour.)

Stinson would subsequently feel compelled to issue a statement in which he made no mention of his onstage outburst. Instead, he said that while it had been his suggestion to offer a support slot to Eagles of Death Metal, he'd since come to realise they were the wrong band for a GN'R audience. He then went on to add that although he'd been known to thrown off his bass in the past, he'd never yet thrown it at Axl or anyone else in Guns N' Roses. He finished off by saying how Axl has been a dear friend for nine years, that the two had no problem communicating with each other, and that he wished people "would stay the fuck out of shit they don't know anything about."

Stinson officially remained a member of Guns N' Roses until the January 2016 "regrouping", but he most likely started planning an exit strategy from the moment Duff agreed to stand in for him during the Latin American leg of the Appetite For Democracy Tour in April 2014.

GUNS N' ROSES

RON THAL

There aren't many guitarists that would think to adopt the name of a bacterial infection and inflammatory reaction on the feet of birds, rodents, and rabbits. (His wife, Jennifer, was studying for her veterinary exams at the time.) Then again, nor are there many guitarists that can boast being endorsed by Joe Satriani, but Ron "Bumblefoot" Thal can count himself among that elusive clique. "I had gotten an email from Joe and it said, 'I have recommended you to Guns, so in case you want to check it out just so you know if they get in touch it's not a joke or anything,' he revealed to www.uberrock.co.uk in August 2010. "Then a few hours later I got an email from one of the guys in the band (GN'R's then resident keyboardist Chris Pitman) and then I got a call from the producer of *Chinese Democracy* and then management got in touch and we ended up chatting on and off for maybe two months or so."

Born and raised in Brooklyn, Thal first developed a gameplan on hearing the *Kiss Alive* album – even though he was just six years old at the time of the album's release. "It was like a little spark came on and I was like, 'that is what I gotta do with my life!'" he would enthuse. "So, immediately, I need to get a band together, writing songs, doing promotion, making demos, and make it happen!"

Borrowing an old acoustic guitar from one of the older neighbourhood kids he set about writing rudimentary ditties revolving around the planets and solar system (the first being a rip off of The Sweet's 1975 UK Top 3 hit 'Fox On The Run' called 'Jupiter is Nice'). His fascination with Kiss – especially Gene Simmons – was all-consuming, however. (As with Frank Ferrer, Thal's first live concert came with seeing Kiss

at Madison Square Garden.) "I really wanted to play bass because, out of everyone in Kiss, it was Gene Simmons that wowed me the most. I wanted to spit blood, fly up to the rafters, breathe fire and play a bass!"

A visit to a local music store didn't pan out quite as he'd hoped. Though he came away with his own acoustic guitar, he felt the owner had conned him into the purchase by saying he'd need to play acoustic for a couple of years before he could even think about taking on the bass guitar. He threw himself into reading all the "learn-how-to-play-guitar" books he could get his hands on, while a sympathetic teacher at his elementary school showed him the odd chord structure. The first song he learned by rote was 'Rock and Roll Hoochie Koo'. (Coincidentally, Rick Derringer's 1973 hit would prove the first song Richard Fortus learned to play on the guitar.)

By the time he was 16, Thal had progressed from penning his own compositions on his home eight-track studio, to engineering and producing his music. Two years later, he won a Sam Ash Guitar Solo Contest with what he describes as a "spontaneous solo". He was also playing GN'R songs in a New York-based covers band called Legend, never imagining he'd one day be playing those songs for real alongside Axl in stadiums around the world.

Despite Thal's opening lines of dialogue with Chris Pitman and GN'R's management, there was some initial confusion as to whether he would in fact be joining Guns N' Roses. Though he was careful to stress that it was early days on his website, and that both parties were still in the "just feelin' it out" stage, GN'R's management nonetheless took exception to his upfront musings and issued a press release stating that no one had as yet been approached to fill the spot recently vacated by Buckethead. "I was feeling it out," Thal reiterated in the www.uberrock.co.uk, but I was also teaching at SUNY Purchase College [and] producing a ton of bands at my studio. I was putting out my own music and touring, licensing music to TV shows and my world was pretty complete and I was happy with it. I knew that if I joined Guns I would have to give a lot of that up, and this was around the time when everything happened with Dimebag (Darrell) and I started thinking, 'Do I really wanna be the guy that gets shot for stopping the old band from getting back together?'

"You know there was a lot to consider and at first I kind of turned them down," he continued. "Then we didn't speak for about a year and a half and then they had a tour coming up and we all got back in touch and we decided to get together and rehearse in NY and I brought my guitar and jammed to three songs, said that's cool, let's do it again tomorrow. We just did that for three weeks, and then we hit the road and played 27 countries! The whole thing I realised is not to over think it – just jump in and learn how to swim and see where it goes and see what happens. Don't worry about the 'what ifs' and that's what I did."

Thal's GN'R debut came at the first of the four Hammerstein Ballroom Chinese Democracy Tour "warm-up" dates on May 12, 2006. As with Tommy Stinson, he would be invited to take centre stage for renditions of songs from his forthcoming 2008 solo album, *Abnormal* – 'Objectify', 'Glad to Be Here', and 'Abnormal', as well as covering Henry Mancini's 'Pink Panther Theme' on occasion. (Strange that Axl

would throw his toys out of the pram over the possibility of Buckethead promoting *Somewhere Over the Slaughterhouse* while on tour with GN'R, yet allow Thal to spotlight songs for his as-yet-unreleased album?)

If Thal is to be believed, he wasn't exactly welcomed into the GN'R fold with open arms. In a 2013 interview with *HereTodayGoneToHell. com*, he said that certain "other members" were unhappy about having a third guitarist in the line-up, and that he'd had to "get a little violent" to gain their respect. Though Thal clearly earned the respect of his petulant peers, he was surplus to requirements once Axl and Slash settled their long-standing differences. When asked about his status in Guns N' Roses during an interview promoting the release of his latest solo album, *Little Brother Is Watching*, in February 2015 Thal refused to take the bait, saying that he was "honouring a request to not make any public statements".

Thal wouldn't go public about the parting of the ways until July 2016, by which time, of course, the "regrouped" Guns N' Roses were midway through the North American leg of the Not in This Lifetime . . . Tour.

Following on from Guns N' Roses, Thal formed Art of Anarchy, whose eponymous 2015 album featured Scott Weiland on vocals – though the latter would subsequently distance himself from the project. While with Art of Anarchy, Thal underwent surgery to have a cancerous tumour removed. Art of Anarchy's follow-up album, *The Madness*, was released in March 2017. That same year, Thal joined progressive metal act Sons of Apollo, whose sole album to date, *Psychotic Symphony*, was released in October 2017.

GUNS N' ROSES

A BRIEF
GN'R CHRONOLGY

THE RISE, THE FALL, THE REGROUPING

1985

Mar 26. The flyer for the first Guns N' Roses show at The Troubadour announces "L.A Guns and Hollywood Rose presents the band Guns N' Roses". The line-up is: Axl Rose (vocals), Tracii Guns (lead guitar), Izzy Stradlin (rhythm guitar), Ole Beich (bass guitar), Rob Gardner (drums).

June 6. The *Appetite for Destruction*-era Guns N' Roses play together for the first time at the Troubadour: Axl (vocals), Slash (lead guitar), Izzy (rhythm guitar), Duff McKagan (bass guitar), Steven Adler (drums)

June 8. Guns N' Roses support The Fastbacks at the Omni Room (Gorilla Gardens) in Seattle – their one and only performance on the fabled "Hell Tour".

June 20. Guns N' Roses perform 'Welcome to the Jungle' for the first time at the Troubadour.

Oct 10. Guns N' Roses perform 'Paradise City' for the first time at the Troubadour.

1986

Feb 28. Geffen Records' A&R man Tom Zutaut sees Guns N' Roses for the first time at the Troubadour.

Mar 25. Guns N' Roses sign with Geffen Records for $750,000.

Aug 23. Guns N' Roses perform 'Sweet Child O' Mine' for the first time at the Whisky A Go Go.

August. (exact date unknown) Guns N' Roses hire New Zealand-born Alan Niven as their manager. The band enters Rumbo Studios with producer Mike Clink to begin work on *Appetite For Destruction*.

Dec 16. Guns N' Roses release the four-track EP, *Live ?!*@ Like a Suicide*, on their own UZI Suicide label.

 238

1987

June 15. Geffen release 'It's So Easy' / 'Mr. Brownstone' as a double A-side single in the UK.

June 19. Guns N' Roses make their UK debut with the first of three shows at London's legendary Marquee Club on Wardour Street. (The other shows were June 22 and June 28.)

July 21. Geffen release *Appetite For Destruction* in the US. The album is released in the UK the following month.

Aug 1-2. The promo video for 'Welcome to the Jungle' is shot at Park Plaza and 450 S. La Brea in Hollywood.

Aug 14. Guns N' Roses open for The Cult at the Halifax Metro Centre in Halifax, Nova Scotia on the latter act's North American tour.

Sept 28. Geffen releases 'Welcome to the Jungle'.

Sept 29. Guns N' Roses kick off their "European Tour" with a show at Hamburg's Markethalle with fellow West Hollywood rabble-rousers Faster Pussycat in support. (Aerosmith were set to headline but pulled out at the last minute.)

Oct 4. Guns N' Roses play the first of five UK shows, at Newcastle's City Hall. The other dates are Nottingham Rock City (Oct 5), Manchester Apollo (Oct 6), Colston Hall, Bristol (Oct 7), Hammersmith Odeon, London (Oct 8).

Oct 28. Guns N' Roses make their debut on MTV's *Headbanger's Ball*.

Oct 30. Guns N' Roses give their one and only performance of the controversial 'One in a Million' at the CBGBs Record Canteen.

Nov 3. Guns N' Roses open for Mötley Crüe at the Cajundome in Louisiana (LA) on the Crüe's North American tour.

GUNS N' ROSES

1988

Jan 31. Guns N' Roses' headlining Appetite For Destruction Tour commences with a show at The Limelight in New York City. (Axl walked out of the band only to return three days later.)

January (exact date unknown). Guns N' Roses enter Rumbo Studios with Mike Clink to record 'Patience', 'Used To Love Her', 'One In A Million', along with an acoustic reworking of 'You're Crazy', which all subsequently appear on GN'R Lies. (Another acoustic song, 'Cornshucker', is recorded but remains unreleased.)

Feb 2. Guns N' Roses' performance at The Ritz in New York is filmed by MTV. (An edited version is subsequently broadcast.)

Apr 11. Guns N' Roses shoot the promo video for 'Sweet Child O' Mine' at the Huntington Park Ballroom in Huntington Park (CA).

Apr 23. Appetite For Destruction enters the Billboard 200 Top 10 for the first time.

May 13. Guns N' Roses open for Iron Maiden at the Moncton Coliseum in Moncton, New Brunswick (Canada) on the British heavy metal act's North American tour.

June 3. Geffen releases 'Sweet Child O' Mine'.

July 9. Guns N' Roses open for Aerosmith on the Permanent Vacation Tour at the Celebrity Theatre in Phoenix, Arizona.

Aug 6. Appetite For Destruction tops the Billboard 200 for the first time.

Aug 20. Guns N' Roses appear at the Monsters Of Rock Festival at Castle Donington, England. Two fans die as a result of injuries sustained in the crush at the front of the stage.

Sept 7. Guns N' Roses perform 'Welcome to the Jungle' at the MTV Video Music Awards. The song wins the "Best New Artist" category.

Sept 10. 'Sweet Child O' Mine' reaches # 1 on the Billboard Hot 100.

Nov 17. Guns N' Roses appear on the front cover of Rolling Stone for the first time (Issue # 539).

Nov 30. Geffen releases GN'R Lies. (The album's original title was Lies! The Sex, The Drugs, The Violence, The Shocking Truth.)

1989

Feb 11. Appetite For Destruction reclaims the # 1 spot on the Billboard 200.

Feb 18/19. The promo video for 'Patience' is shot at the Record Plant and The Ambassador Hotel in LA. (The Ambassador was the scene of Robert Kennedy's assassination in June 1968.)

Mar 25. Guns N' Roses score their first UK Top 10 hit with 'Paradise City'. (Peak position # 6.)

April (exact date unknown) Geffen releases 'Patience' in the US. (Peak position on the Billboard Hot 100 # 4.)

June 26. Geffen releases 'Patience' in the UK. (Peak position # 10.)

Aug 27. Izzy is arrested at Phoenix Sky Harbor International Airport en route to LA for "making a public disturbance". (He is reported to have urinated on the floor, verbally abused a stewardess, and lit a cigarette in the non-smoking section.)

Sept 11. Guns N' Roses scoop the award for "Best Heavy Metal/Hard Rock Video" for 'Sweet Child O' Mine' at the MTV Video Music Awards. (Izzy and Axl get involved in a backstage altercation with Mötley Crüe frontman Vince Neil.)

Oct 10-11. The promo video for 'It's So Easy' is shot at The Cathouse. (The video wasn't released until 2018, as part of the *Appetite for Destruction: Locked N' Loaded* box set.)

Oct 18. Guns N' Roses open for the Rolling Stones at the LA Memorial Coliseum. Midway through their set Axl threatened to quit the band unless certain members didn't stop "dancing with Mr. Brownstone". The other dates were October 19, 21, 22.

Dec 17. Axl and Izzy join the Stones onstage for a version of 'Salt Of The Earth' at the Stones show at the Convention Hall in Atlantic City, New Jersey. It's the first time the Stones have performed the song live.

1990

February. (exact date unknown) Keyboardist Darren "Dizzy" Reed joins Guns N' Roses.

Mar 28. Steven Adler signs an agreement forfeiting his rights as a partner in Guns N' Roses. The agreement essentially puts him on notice for a 30-day probation period, during which time he is urged to seek treatment for his heroin addiction.)

Apr 7. Guns N' Roses appear at Farm Aid IV at the Hoosier Dome in Indianapolis. The set includes a first airing of 'Civil War'. (This will prove Steven's last show with Guns until making a guest appearance during the Not in This Lifetime . . . Tour at the Paul Brown Stadium in Cincinnati, Ohio on July 6, 2016. Steven joined the band onstage for 'Out Ta Get Me' and 'My Michelle'. (Steven makes other guest appearances in Nashville, LA, and Buenos Aires.)

Apr 28. Axl and Erin Everly get married in Las Vegas. Axl reportedly threatened to kill himself unless Erin accepted his proposal.

June 26. Guns N' Roses' cover of Bob Dylan's 'Knockin' On Heaven's Door' is released on the *Days Of Thunder* film soundtrack.

July 11. Steven is officially sacked from Guns N' Roses. He is replaced by The Cult's Matt Sorum.

July 24. 'Civil War' appears on the benefit album *Nobody's Child: Romanian Angel Appeal*.

Oct 30. Axl is arrested for allegedly assaulting his next-door neighbour, Gabriella Kantor, with a wine bottle at his West Hollywood condominium complex on Shoreham Drive West. The incident will provide the basis for the song 'Right Next Door to Hell', the opening track on *Use Your Illusion I*.

GUNS N' ROSES

1991

Jan 20. Guns N' Roses headline Rock in Rio II at the Maracanã stadium in Rio de Janeiro, Brazil. The show marks Matt and Dizzy's live debut.

May 24. Guns N' Roses kick off the Use Your Illusion Tour with the first of two shows at the Alpine Valley Music Theatre in East Troy, Wisconsin.

May. (exact date unknown) Alan Niven is fired as manager. He is replaced by Doug Goldstein.

June 21. Geffen releases 'You Could Be Mine' in the US as the first single from the forthcoming *Use Your Illusion* albums. The song features in *Terminator 2: Judgement Day*.

July 2. Axl jumps into the audience at the Riverport Performance Arts Centre in St. Louis, Missouri, sparking a riot. The local authorities issue a warrant for Axl's arrest.

Aug 17. Axl keeps the crowd – as well as the rest of the band – waiting for over an hour-and-a-half at the Globen in Stockholm while he watches a firework display at the Swedish capital's Vattenfestivalen.

Aug 31. Guns N' Roses play Wembley Stadium in London, England. It is Izzy's last show as a full-time member of Guns N' Roses. (The 72,000 tickets sell out in record time, prompting the band to run a poster campaign prior to the show which read: "Guns N' Fuckin' Roses, Wembley Fuckin' Stadium, Sold Fuckin' Out".

Sept 10. Geffen release 'Don't Cry' as the second single from the *Use Your Illusion* albums.

Sept 16. Geffen release *Use Your Illusion I* and *II* simultaneously in Europe.

Sept 17. Geffen release *Use Your Illusion I* and *II* in the US. The albums debut at # 1 and # 2 on the *Billboard* 200.

Oct 5. *Use Your Illusion II* tops the Billboard 200.

October. (exact date unknown) Steven Adler launches a lawsuit against Guns N' Roses.

Nov 7. Izzy Stradlin officially leaves Guns N' Roses. He is replaced by one-time Kills for Thrills guitarist Gilby Clarke.

Dec 5. Gilby makes his GN'R debut at the Centrum in Worcester, Massachusetts – the opening show of the second US leg of the Use Your Illusion Tour. The band's onstage entourage is swelled to include session keyboardist Ted Andreadis, a three-piece horn section, and a trio of female backing singers.

Dec 9. Guns N' Roses play the first of three sell-out shows at Madison Square Garden in New York City. The other MSG dates are December 10 and 13.

1992

Feb 19. Guns N' Roses play the first of three sell-out shows at the 55,000-capacity Tokyo Dome. The other Tokyo Dome dates are February 20 and 22.

Mar 7. Geffen releases 'November Rain' in the UK. The single gives Guns N' Roses another UK Top 5 hit, peaking at # 4.

Apr 20. Guns N' Roses perform at The Freddie Mercury Tribute Concert for AIDS Awareness at Wembley Stadium in London. They were originally set to play three songs, but due to technical problems earlier in the show they only play 'Paradise City' and 'Knockin' On Heaven's Door'. Axl also duets with Elton John on 'Bohemian Rhapsody', and 'We Will Rock You' with Queen, while Slash joins Queen onstage for 'Tie Your Mother Down'. (Mercury had succumbed to AIDS the previous November.)

May 12. Slash and Metallica's Lars Ulrich stage a press conference at The Gaslight in Hollywood to unveil plans for a joint headline Guns N' Roses/Metallica stadium US tour.

June 2. Geffen releases 'November Rain' in the US. The single gives Guns N' Roses another *Billboard* Hot 100 Top 5 hit, peaking at # 3.

June 6. Guns N' Roses play a pay-per-view show at the Hippodrome Vincennes in Paris. They are joined onstage by Lenny Kravitz for a version of 'Always On The Run', while Steven Tyler and Joe Perry from Aerosmith join them to perform The Yardbirds' 'Train Kept A-Rollin'' and Aerosmith's 'Mama Kin'.

June 19. Axl is hassled by an overzealous security guard at Heathrow Airport. It's the second time the airport's security have singled him out for harassment (the other coming while the band were arriving in London for the Freddie Mercury Tribute concert).

July 12. Axl is arrested at New York's JFK Airport after St. Louis County authorities issue

fugitive warrants seeking his arrest over the outstanding warrant for the riot at the Riverport Amphitheatre the previous July.

July 14. In court Axl pleads innocent to four counts of misdemeanor assault and one count of property damage stemming from the Riverport Amphitheatre riot. A trial is set for October 13. The judge tells Axl that the impending Guns N' Roses/Metallica tour can proceed as scheduled.

July 17. The 26-date Guns N' Roses/Metallica joint headline tour gets under way with a show at the RFK Stadium in Washington D.C.

Aug 8. Metallica's James Hetfield is injured by onstage pyrotechnics during the band's performance at Montreal's Olympic Stadium. During Guns N' Roses' set, Axl stops the show and leaves the stage, bringing about another riot. Seven dates have to be rescheduled owing to Hetfield's injuries.

Sept 9. Guns N' Roses perform at the MTV Video Music Awards. Elton John joins the band to perform 'November Rain'. Backstage, Axl gets into a war of words with Nirvana's Kurt Cobain and his wife Courtney Love.

Oct 12. Geffen releases Izzy Stradlin And The Ju Ju Hounds' debut album.

Nov 28. A torrential downpour brings Guns N' Roses' six-tonne stage roof – complete with lighting rig – crashing to the ground at the Estadio El Campín, Bogotá, Colombia. Mercifully, no one is injured. With no time to build a new roof before the following evening's show, the road crew redesign the stage set, repositioning those lights that survived the crash to the stage's side walls.

GUNS N' ROSES

Dec 3. Officers from the Chilean Department Of Investigation visit Guns N' Roses' hotel searching for drugs in response to rumours fuelled by the Chilean media. The officers leave empty-handed.

1993

Feb 23. Guns N' Roses kick off the "Skin and Bones" leg of the Use Your Illusion Tour at the Frank Erwin Centre in Austin, Texas. (This leg is so-called because Guns have dispensed with Teddy Andreadis, the horn-section and backing singers.)

Apr 3. The show at the ARCO Arena in Sacramento is cut short after 90 minutes owing to Duff being struck on the head with a plastic water bottle, according to MTV. Slash is rather more succinct, describing the projectile as a "bottle of piss".

Apr 29. Gilby breaks his left wrist in a motorcycling accident while practising for a celebrity charity race in honour of the TJ Martell Foundation for leukemia, cancer and AIDS research. His injury forces Guns N' Roses to cancel the last four remaining dates on the Skin and Bones leg. Rather than reschedule any of the forthcoming European dates, Axl calls upon Izzy to help out until Gilby's injury has sufficiently healed.

May 22. Izzy makes his first of five stand-in appearances at Hayarkon Park in Tel Aviv, Israel.

May 30. Izzy takes his bow at the National Bowl in Milton Keynes, England.

July 5. Prior to the show at the Estadi Olímpic Lluís Companys in Barcelona, Slash and Duff are coerced into signing documents that give Axl the right to keep the name Guns N' Roses should either of them decide to leave the band.

July 17. The mammoth Use Your Illusion Tour comes to a climactic finale at the River Plate Stadium in Buenos Aires, Argentina. The show is broadcast live on TV in Argentina and neighbouring Uruguay.

Sept 28. Geffen releases Duff's solo debut album *Believe In Me*.

Oct 21. Axl reaches an out-of-court settlement with William "Stump" Stephenson, the audience member he'd attacked when jumping offstage at the Riverport Amphitheatre riot in July 1991.

Nov 23. Geffen releases *The Spaghetti Incident?*

1994

Jan 20. Axl performs 'Come Together' with Bruce Springsteen at Elton John's induction into the Rock and Roll Hall of Fame. It will prove to be his last public appearance for four years.

May 10. After years of living a reckless rock'n'roll lifestyle, Duff almost dies when his pancreas explodes.

June. (exact date unknown) Gilby is officially notified he is no longer a member of Guns N' Roses.

July 26. Virgin Records releases Gilby's debut solo album *Pawnshop Guitars*. Axl, Slash, and Duff all make guest appearances on the album.

Dec 13. Geffen releases Guns N' Roses' version of the Stones' classic 'Sympathy for the Devil'. The track features on the *Interview With a Vampire* film soundtrack.

1995

Feb 14. Geffen releases Slash's Snakepit's *It's Five O' Clock Somewhere*. The album stalls at # 70 on the *Billboard* 200 but sells more than one million copies worldwide.

Mar 10. Duff and Matt perform with Teddy Andreadis as part of an ad hoc house band (Wayne Neutron) at the opening of the Hardrock Hotel in Las Vegas. Izzy will also join them onstage, as do ex-Sex Pistol Steve Jones, Duran Duran's John Taylor, Billy Idol, and Iggy Pop. From this eclectic gathering, the Neurotic Outsiders are born.

Oct 31. Axl's cousin, Blind Melon frontman Shannon Hoon, dies of a heart attack brought on by suspected cocaine use in New Orleans. Hoon sang backing vocals on several tracks on the *Use Your Illusion* albums, 'Live and Let Die', 'November Rain', and 'Don't Cry'. He also appears in the promo video for 'Don't Cry'.

1996

August. (exact date unknown) Madonna's Maverick Records releases the Neurotic Outsiders' eponymous debut album.

Oct 16. Speaking on an online chat, Slash reveals he and Axl were "deliberating over the future of our relationship."

GUNS N' ROSES

Oct 30. Slash sends a fax to MTV News stating that he'd no longer be in Guns N' Roses. "Axl and I have not been capable of seeing eye to eye on Guns N' Roses for some time," the guitarist explained. "We recently tried to collaborate, but at this point, I'm no longer in the band. I'd like to think we could work together in the future if we were able to work out our differences."

Oct 30. Axl retaliates by sending a fax to MTV stating Slash hasn't been a part of Guns N' Roses since 1995.

Nov 22. Slash's new band, Slash's Blues Ball, makes its debut at The House Of Blues in Hollywood.

1997

January. (exact date unknown) Axl obtains the rights to the Guns N' Roses name.

January. (exact date unknown) One-time Nine Inch Nails guitarist, Robin Finck, is brought in to replace Slash in Guns N' Roses. He won't officially become a member of the band until August.

Feb 24. Steven's new band, Freaks in the Room, makes its debut as the Monday night house band at Billboard Live (formerly Gazzarri's) in West Hollywood.

May 30. Guns N' Roses' close associate and co-songwriter, West Arkeen, is found dead at his LA home. His death is subsequently ruled "accidental opiate overdose".

July. (exact date unknown) Matt leaves Guns N' Roses following an argument with Axl.

July. (exact date unknown) Multi-instrumentalist Josh Freese replaces Matt in Guns N' Roses.

August. (exact date unknown) Duff informs Axl that he's quitting Guns N' Roses. Duff's replacement is one-time Replacements' bassist Tommy Stinson.

1998

Feb 11. Axl is arrested at Phoenix Sky Harbor Airport after allegedly threatening a security worker. It's the first time he's been spotted in public since attending Elton John's induction into the Rock and Roll Hall of Fame in January 2004.

Mar 10. Geffen releases Izzy's first bona fide solo album, *117°*, in the US.

1999

Feb 18. Axl pleads guilty to the misdemeanor charge of disturbing the peace relating to his arrest at Phoenix Sky Harbor Airport. He receives a $500 fine and is sentenced to one day in jail, which he has already served on the day of his arrest.

Mar 16. Guns are presented with the new "Diamond Award" from the RIAA commemorating *Appetite For Destruction*'s sales of 15 million. The award is accepted on behalf of the band by Steven Adler.

May 27. Duff's new ouit, Loaded, self-release their debut album *Episode 1999: Live*. The album can only be ordered through the band's website.

Aug 1. Robin Finck leaves Guns N' Roses to rejoin Nine Inch Nails.

Sept 9. A clip of a new Guns N' Roses song called 'Oh My God' appears in a trailer at the MTV Video Music Awards for Arnold Schwarzenegger's latest film, *End Of Days*.

Nov 30. Geffen releases *Live Era '87-'93* in the US.

November. (exact date unknown) Geffen releases Izzy's second solo album, *Ride On*.

Dec 14. Guns' management company, Big F D Entertainment, launch a lawsuit against Slash and Duff for "monies owed".

2000

Jan 10. *Rolling Stone* publishes an interview with Axl in which he unveils four new songs – 'Catcher in the Rye', 'I.R.S.', 'The Blues', and 'There Was a Time' – set for inclusion on Guns N' Roses' forthcoming new album *Chinese Democracy*.

March. (exact date unknown) Josh Freese leaves Guns N' Roses.

June 22. Axl stuns revellers at the Cat Club on Sunset Boulevard by getting up onstage with the club's house band, The Starfuckers, for renditions of the Stones' 'Wild Horses' and 'Dead Flowers'. The Starfuckers' guitarist is Gilby Clarke.

Oct 9. Slash's Snakepit's second album, *Ain't Life Grand*, is released via Koch International.

Oct 25. Roberto Medina, head of the Rock in Rio festival, informs Brazilian TV network Globo that Axl has agreed to play at Rock in Rio 3 in January 2001 with his new Guns N' Roses line-up, which now includes guitar virtuoso Brian Patrick Carroll a.k.a. "Buckethead". The same month, Big F. D. confirms that Bryan "Brain" Mantia has replaced Josh Freese, and that Robin Finck has rejoined the band.

Dec 6. Guns N' Roses announce they will play the House Of Blues in Las Vegas on New Year's Day. Tickets go on sale the same day and sell out almost immediately.

2001

Jan 1. The new-look Guns N' Roses play the House Of Blues in Las Vegas. The line-up, aside from Axl, is: Buckethead (lead guitar), Robin Finck (guitar), Tommy Stinson (bass), Brain Mantia (drums). It's the first GN'R show since the final Use Your Illusion tour date in Buenos Aires in July 1993.

Jan 14. Guns N' Roses play Rock in Rio III in the City of Rock in Rio de Janeiro, Brazil.

May 10. Big F. D. confirms that a proposed Guns N' Roses European tour – set to

GUNS N' ROSES

commence on June 1, has been postponed until December.

May 21. Sanctuary Records releases Izzy's third solo album, *River*, in Europe. The album isn't released in the US until late August.

July. (exact date unknown) Loaded self-release their debut studio album, *Dark Days*.

Oct 15. Slash marries girlfriend Perla in Maui.

Nov 8. The rescheduled European tour is cancelled indefinitely.

Dec 29. Guns N' Roses play The Joint in Las Vegas.

Dec 31. Guns N' Roses play a second show at The Joint in Las Vegas. Slash happens to be in Vegas with Perla but is refused admission as per Axl's instructions.

2002

Apr 29. Slash, Duff, and Matt play together (with Buckcherry's Josh Todd and Keith Nelson) at the Randy Castillo Tribute at the Key Club in LA. It's the first time the trio have played in public together since the Use Your Illusion Tour. This proves the seed from which Velvet Revolver will grow.

June 27. Slash, Duff, and Matt join Shooter Jennings (son of Waylon Jennings) onstage at the opening of Club Vodka in West Hollywood for renditions of 'It's So Easy', 'Paradise City', and AC/DC's 'Whole Lotta Rosie'.

Aug 14. Guns N' Roses play the Hong Kong International Trade And Exhibition Centre Star Hall, the first date on the Chinese Democracy World Tour.

Aug 17. Guns N' Roses play the first of two consecutive shows at the Summersonic festival in Urayasu, Japan. The following night's show is in Osaka.

Aug 21. JVC – Victor release Izzy's fourth solo album, *On Down the Road*. Duff plays bass on the record.

Aug 23. Guns N' Roses headline the Leeds Festival.

Aug 26. Guns N' Roses play the London Arena. During the show Axl announces that *Chinese Democracy* is completed and ready for release.

Aug 29. Guns N' Roses bring MTV's Video Music Awards to a close with a three-song medley: 'Welcome To The Jungle', 'Madagascar', and 'Paradise City'.

Nov 7. The opening date of the North American leg of the Chinese Democracy World Tour at the GM Place in Vancouver is cancelled at the eleventh hour, causing some fans to vent their anger by smashing windows. Riot police are called in to quell the disturbance.

Dec 6. Following a sell-out date at Madison Square Garden in New York the previous evening, Guns N' Roses were set to bring the US leg of the Chinese Democracy World Tour to a close at the First Union Center in Philadelphia. When venue officials announce the show is postponed, some fans storm the stage and start trashing the band's equipment. Police units are again called in restore order.

2003

Jan 7. Slash is nominated for a Grammy Award in the "Best Rock Instrumental" category for his version of 'Speak Softly, Love' (the theme from *The Godfather*) he'd played during the Use Your Illusion Tour. He loses out to The Flaming Lips' 'Approaching Pavonis Mons By Balloon (Utopia Planitia)'.

Jan 21. Slash, Duff and Matt play the Sundance Film Festival in Park City, Utah. With actress Gina Gershon on vocals, they perform songs such as Nancy Sinatra's 'These Boots Are Made for Walkin'' and The Stooges' 'I Wanna Be Your Dog'. The trio are then joined onstage by Shooter Jennings for renditions of Bad Company's 'Feel Like Makin' Love', The Damned's 'New Rose', the Stones' 'Sympathy for the Devil', as well as the GN'R classics 'It's So Easy' and 'Paradise City'.

Mar 1. Steven Adler joins Suki Jones, an outfit formed by one-time Slash's Snakepit guitarist Keri Kelli. Their sets are primarily made up of tracks from *Appetite For Destruction* and *GN' R Lies*, as well as songs from AC/DC, Thin Lizzy, Aerosmith, Led Zeppelin, and Queen. They subsequently change their name to Adler's Appetite.

Apr 28. Robert John sues Axl for allegedly refusing to honour a long-standing contract in which the singer agreed to pay $80,000 for hundreds of photos of Guns N' Roses that John had taken since 1985.

May 13. Stone Temple Pilots' frontman, Scott Weiland, confirms to *Rolling Stone* that he is joining forces with Slash, Duff, and Matt. He also informs the magazine that the band is to be called Reloaded. This will soon be amended to Velvet Revolver.

June 17. *The Hulk* film soundtrack – featuring Velvet Revolver's soon-to-be-released debut single 'Set Me Free' – is released via Decca Records.

June 19. Velvet Revolver make their live debut at the El Rey Theatre in LA. Their setlist includes new compositions 'Slither' and 'Set Me Free', as well as 'It's So Easy' and STP's 'Sex Type Thing', and cover versions of the Sex Pistols' 'Bodies' and Nirvana's 'Negative Creep'. The exclusive invitation-only show was preceded by a media question-and-answer session.

July 16. Axl reportedly previews several new songs intended for *Chinese Democracy* at the Crazy Horse Too strip club in Las Vegas.

GUNS N' ROSES

Aug 22. Velvet Revolver sign with RCA Records.

Aug 30. New York Mets catcher, Mike Piazza, appears on *Friday Night Rocks* . . . with Eddie Trunk. He has a CDR marked "Guns N' Roses, "I.R.S." which he says he'd received in the mail three weeks prior. Trunk played the song on his show and subsequently received a "cease and desist" order via GN'R's management.

Sept 21. Slash and Izzy join Adler's Appetite onstage at the Key Club in Hollywood for renditions of 'Mr. Brownstone', 'Knockin' On Heaven's Door', and 'Paradise City'.

Oct 27. Scott Weiland is arrested in Hollywood on charges of driving under the influence of alcohol and drugs and misdemeanor hit-and-run following a traffic collision. He is later ordered to report to a live-in detox programme followed by six months in a residential drug rehab centre.

Oct 31. Matt's debut solo album, *Hollywood Zen*, is released. Slash makes a guest appearance on the track 'The Blame Game'.

Nov 8. The Guns N' Roses *Welcome To The Videos* DVD enters the *Billboard* Top Music Video chart at # 5.

2004

Jan 16. Gibson introduces a "Slash Signature" Les Paul guitar.

Mar 23. Geffen releases *Greatest Hits* in the US. The GN'R compilation album peaks at # 3 on the *Billboard* 200. The album reaches # 1 in the UK and elsewhere across the globe.

Mar 30. Guns N' Roses pull out of the forthcoming Rock In Rio - Lisbon. According to a press release the band were forced to withdraw owing to Buckethead's departure. Buckethead is replaced by Ron "Bumblefoot" Thal.

June 8. RCA releases Velvet Revolver's debut album, *Contraband*, in the US. The album sells in excess of 250,000 copies in its first week of release, entering the *Billboard* 200 at # 1.

July 5. VH1 premieres *Guns N' Roses: Behind The Music*. Slash, Steven, Gilby and Matt all make appearances in the show.

2005

Jan 26. Axl signs a publishing deal with the Sanctuary Music Group. The deal covers future material as well as GN'R's back catalogue.

July. (exact date unknown) *Contraband* is certified double-platinum by the Recording Industry Association of America (RIAA) for shipments in excess of two million copies in the US.

Aug 22. MTV reports that Slash and Duff have launched a lawsuit against Axl over unpaid publishing royalties. They accuse Axl of changing the publisher of GN'R's copyrighted songs – to Sanctuary Music Group from Warner Chappell – without their consent.

Oct 15. Izzy's fifth solo album, *Like a Dog*, is made available by mail order via the Scootersteez website.

2006

Jan 13. Axl makes a surprise appearance at the launch party for Korn's See You on the Other Side Tour at the Hollywood Forever Cemetery.

May 12. Ron "Bumblefoot" Thal makes his Guns N' Roses debut at the first of four sold-out shows at the Hammerstein Ballroom in New York. The other dates are May 14, 15, and 17. The shows are billed as "warm-ups" for the impending European tour. Izzy joins the band onstage for 'Think About You', 'Patience', and 'Nightrain'.

May 25. Guns N' Roses' European tour gets under way with a show in Madrid at the Auditorio Parque Juan Carlos I.

May 27. Guns N' Roses are one of the headline acts at Rock In Rio 2006, staged at the Parque da Bela Vista in Lisbon.

June 11. Guns N' Roses headline the Sunday bill at the Download Festival at Donington Park (formerly the Monsters of Rock Festival). Izzy joins the band on stage for several numbers.

June 24. Frank Ferrer stands in for Brain Mantia at the Graspop Metal Meeting in Dessel, Belgium.

June 27. Axl is arrested in the lobby of his hotel in Stockholm following an altercation with a security guard.

July 29. Guns N' Roses surprise the crowd at the first of two sold-out shows at London's Wembley Arena by attempting "proper English songs" – The Stones' 'Sway', Rod Stewart's 'Sailing', and The Beatles' 'Back in the USSR'.

Sept 23. Guns N' Roses headline KROQ's Inland Invasion 2006 at the Hyundai Pavilion in Devore, California.

Dec 14. Axl issues an open letter to fans saying *Chinese Democracy* has a tentative release date of March 6, 2007.

2007

Feb 8. Guns N' Roses play a two-song set at the Rodeo Drive's Walk of Style ceremony in Beverly

GUNS N' ROSES

Hills in honour of Gianni and Donatella Versace.

Feb 22. GN'R's official website announces *Chinese Democracy* is currently being mixed.

May 30. Izzy self-releases his sixth solo album, *Miami*, via the internet.

June 2. Guns N' Roses play the opening date of their revised world tour at the Monterrey Arena in Monterrey, Mexico. The tour was supposed to have commenced in Japan in April.

July 3. RCA release Velvet Revolver's second album, Libertad. The album debuted – and peaked – at # 5 on the Billboard 200, selling 92,000 copies in its first week.

July 14. Guns N' Roses perform 'Don't Cry' for the first time in 14 years at the Makuhari Messe in Chiba, Japan. The first of the five revised Japanese dates.

Nov 19. Izzy self-releases his seventh solo album, *Fire, the Acoustic Album*, via iTunes.

2008

Mar 27. Axl announces that he and Guns N' Roses are now being represented by Irving Azoff and Andy Gould.

July 13. Izzy self-releases his eighth solo album, *Concrete*, via iTunes. Duff plays bass on three tracks.

Sept 14. Rock Band 2 is released for Microsoft Xbox 360. The game features 'Shackler's Revenge', the first officially released track from *Chinese Democracy*.

Sept 22. Loaded release the *Wasted Heart* EP.

Oct 10. Ridley Scott's *Body Of Lies* is premiered in the US. 'If The World', from *Chinese Democracy* runs over the end-of-film credits.

Oct 22. Geffen releases 'Chinese Democracy' as the lead track from *Chinese Democracy*. The track is debuted on KROQ-FM's *Opie and Anthony* show.

Nov 23. *Chinese Democracy* is released in the US as a Best Buy exclusive. The album will reach # 3 on the *Billboard* 200.

Nov 24. *Chinese Democracy* scores a record 8.4 million streams when the album is debuted on MySpace from 12am Friday, November 20 through to 12am Monday, November 23. The premiere of *Chinese Democracy* is the biggest promotion in MySpace's five-year history to date, with every MySpace territory signing on to participate.

2009

Mar 21. Sixx A.M. guitarist, DJ Ashba, replaces Robin Finck in Guns N' Roses (Finck having rejoined Nine Inch Nails).

Mar 30. Loaded release their second studio album, *Sick*. The album peaks at # 43 on the *Billboard* 200.

Dec 9. Izzy self-releases his ninth solo album, *Smoke*, via iTunes.

Dec 11. Guns N' Roses play the first show of their Asian tour at the Taipei City Stadium in Taipei, Taiwan. DJ Ashba makes his GN'R live debut.

2010

Jan 13. The ongoing Chinese Democracy Tour gets under way again with a clutch of Canadian dates, starting with a show at the MTS Centre in Winnipeg, Manitoba. Axl's old friend, Sebastian Bach, serves as one of the support acts.

Feb 11. Guns N' Roses play a surprise acoustic set at the John Varvatos store on the Bowery in New York – the former site of CBGBs. The band plays a second surprise NYC acoustic show at the Rose Bar on Lexington Avenue.

Mar 7. The South American leg of the Chinese Democracy Tour commences with the first of five Brazilian shows at the Ginásio Nilson Nelson in Brasília.

Mar 31. Slash's eponymous debut solo album is released. The record will go Top 3 on the *Billboard* 200 and reach # 17 on the UK chart.

June 6. Guns N' Roses play the Ledovy Dvorets Arena in Saint Petersburg. It's the band's first Russian show.

July 15. Izzy self-releases his tenth solo album, *Wave of Heat*, via iTunes. Duff plays on seven tracks.

Aug 27. Guns N' Roses headline the Reading Festival, the opening date of the tour's second European leg. Owing to the band arriving late at the venue (Little John's Farm), they are informed by the organisers that they won't be allowed to play their normal set – much to the crowd's displeasure.

Oct 14. Guns N' Roses are joined onstage by Duff at the second of two shows at London's O2 Arena. This comes to pass owing to Duff and Axl staying in the same hotel.

GUNS N' ROSES

Oct 29. Guns N' Roses play a "surprise" private show at Mosfilm studios in Moscow.

2011

Feb 5. Axl scotches all rumours of a GN'R classic line-up reunion via his Twitter account: "Contrary to anyone's claims there are no concrete plans nor were there ever for a tour, a relaunch or sponsors (n' certainly not to replace anyone in the band) beyond a collection of random ideas thrown out by various individuals w/out any real foundation or negotiations in place other than our prior involvements (which wouldn't take a rocket scientist to put together). N' b4 it's twisted "prior involvements" has nothing to do with old GN'R.

Oct 2. Guns N'Roses headline the final night of the Rock In Rio festival at the City of Rock in Rio de Janeiro, Brazil. The band perform 'Estranged' for the first time since the Use Your Illusion Tour.

Oct 18. Guns N' Roses kick off the 36-date third North American leg of the ongoing Chinese Democracy Tour, also the first of two consecutive shows at the Palacio de los Deportes in Mexico City.

Dec 7. The news breaks that Guns N' Roses are to be inducted into the Rock and Roll Hall of Fame.

Dec 31. Guns N' Roses bring the Chinese Democracy Tour to a close with a New Year's Eve show at the Hard Rock Hotel in Las Vegas.

2012

Feb 10. Guns N' Roses get the North American leg of the Up Close and Personal Tour under way with a show at the Roseland Ballroom in New York.

Mar 12. Guns N' Roses bring the North American leg to a close at the House of Blues in West Hollywood.

Apr 11. Axl pens a "To whom it may concern" letter to the Rock and Roll Hall of Fame stating his feelings about GN'Rs impending induction.

Apr 14. Axl proves a no-show at Guns N' Roses' induction into the Rock and Roll hall of Fame in Cleveland. Slash, Duff, Steven, and Matt do attend, however, and get up onstage for several GN'R classics.

May 11. Guns N' Roses start the European leg of the Up Close and Personal Tour at the Stadium Live Club in Moscow.

May 22. Slash's second solo album, *Apocalyptic Love* (billed as Slash feat. Myles Kennedy & The Conspirators) is released. The album peaks at # 4 on the *Billboard* 200 and # 12 on the UK chart.

July 22. Izzy makes a guest appearance on the final night of the European leg at the Son Fusteret in Palma, Spain.

Oct 31. Guns N' Roses play the first show of the 12-night Appetite For Democracy residency at Hard Rock Hotel in Las Vegas.

2013

Feb 13. Guns N' Roses play a surprise acoustic show at the Tommy Hilfiger after party at Soho House in West Hollywood.

Mar 9. The Appetite For Democracy Tour heads Down Under for the first of six Australian dates at the Perth Arena.

May 24. The Appetite For Democracy Tour returns to North America with a headline appearance at the Rocklahoma 2013 Festival in Pryor, Oklahoma.

June 8. Guns N' Roses headline the Governors Ball Music Festival on Randall's Island in New York.

2014

Apr 2. GN'R's management announce Duff will step in for Tommy Stinson on the last six shows on the Latin American leg of the Appetite For Democracy Tour. Stinson is committed to playing shows in the US with the reformed Replacements.

Apr 6. Duff plays his first GN'R show since the Use Your Illusion Tour at the Estadio Ferro in Buenos Aires, Argentina.

Apr 23. Guns N' Roses play a nine-song set at the 2014 Revolver Golden Gods at Club Nokia in LA. Before the show, Axl receives the Ronnie James Dio Lifetime Achievement Award from actor Nicolas Cage.

May 21. Guns N' Roses return to the Hard Rock Hotel & Casino in Las Vegas for the first show of a nine-date No Trickery! An Evening of Destruction residency.

July 1. Appetite For Democracy 3D: Live at the Hard Rock Casino is released on Blu-ray and DVD in the US.

Sept 16. World on Fire, the second Slash feat. Myles Kennedy and The Conspirators is released. The album peaks at # 10 on the Billboard 200 and # 7 on the UK chart.

2015

Feb 6. Rumours that Axl and Slash have buried their differences after 19 years were confirmed by the guitarist's tweeted birthday message: "Happy Birthday @AxlRose iiii];)"

July 27. DJ Ashba announces that he is leaving Guns N' Roses to focus on his family and Sixx A.M.

Sept 17. Richard Fortus suffers multiple injuries in a motorcycle accident. Aside from breaking a shoulder blade, collar bone, six ribs and a toe, he also suffers a bruised lung and a lacerated liver.

September. (exact date unknown) Having heard rumours about a possible Guns N' Roses "regrouping", Matt meets with Duff to have said rumours confirmed and see about his possible involvement.

Dec 26. A teasing trailer is shown at US cinemas screening Star Wars: The Force Awakens. The trailer features 'Welcome to the Jungle' over black and white footage of crowds at early GN'R shows. The trailer is later added to the official GN'R website.

2016

Jan 4. Guns N' Roses are announced as one of the headliners at the Coachella Festival in April. Rumours abound that the line-up is set to include Duff and Slash.

Jan 5. GN'R's management issues a press release to the media confirming the "regrouping" of Axl, Duff and Slash.
Jan 19. Guns N' Roses announce two opening

GUNS N' ROSES

weekend shows at the new T-Mobile Arena in Las Vegas on April 8 and 9.

Mar 25. A teaser video clip listing 21 cities across the US and Canada that will be included on an upcoming summer US tour appears on GN'R's official website.

Apr 1. Guns N' Roses return to their roots with a special show at the Troubadour in West Hollywood; the first occasion Axl, Slash, and Duff have appeared on the same stage since July 1993. Tickets for the show are fixed at $10. The line up is: Axl, Slash, Duff, Richard Fortus, Frank Ferrer, and keyboardist Melissa Reese (making her GN'R debut). During the show Axl tumbles from a monitor breaking an ankle.

Apr 1. Tour dates are announced for the North American leg of the Not in This Lifetime . . . Tour. The tour will open at the Ford Field in Detroit on June 23.

Apr 8. Guns N' Roses plays the first of two sold-out shows at the T-Mobile Arena in Las Vegas. Owing to the injury he sustained at the Troubadour, Axl is forced to sing while perched on a specially designed throne borrowed from Dave Grohl.

Apr 16. Guns N' Roses play the first of their two headline appearances at the Coachella Festival in Indio, CA. Angus Young joins the band on stage for renditions of AC/DC's 'Whole Lotta Rosie' and 'Riff Raff'. Earlier in the day, it's announced (much to everyone's surprise) that Axl will be standing in for Brian Johnson on the last two legs of AC/DC's Rock or Bust World Tour. The second headline date is April 23.

Apr 19. Guns N' Roses play the first of two consecutive sold-out shows at the Sol Forum in Mexico City. The Cult open both shows.

May 7. Axl makes his first appearance with AC/DC at the Passeio Maritimo De Alges in Lisbon.

June 23. The first date of the Not in This Lifetime . . . Tour at Ford Field, Detroit.

July 6. Steven Adler makes the first of several guest appearances at the Paul Brown Stadium in Cincinnati. The songs performed are 'Out Ta Get Me' and 'My Michelle'.

Aug 22. The North American leg of the Not in This Lifetime . . . Tour comes to a close with a show at the Qualcomm Stadium in San Diego.

Aug 27. The North American leg of AC/DC's Rock Or Bust World Tour gets under way at the Greensboro Coliseum in Greensboro, North Carolina.

Oct 27. The Latin American leg of the Not in This Lifetime . . . Tour commences at the Estadio Monumental in Lima, Peru.

Nov 4. Guns N' Roses play the first of two consecutive shows at the River Plate Stadium in Buenos Aires, Argentina. It's the first occasion the band has visited the River Plate since the final show on the Use Your Illusion Tour in July 1993. Steven Adler makes a guest appearance on 'Out Ta Get Me'.

Nov 30. The Latin American leg is brought to a finale with the second of two consecutive shows at the Palacio de los Deportes in Mexico City.

2017

Jan 21. The Asia/Oceana leg of the Not in This Lifetime . . . Tour gets under way with a show at the Kyocera Dome in Osaka, Japan.

Feb 11. Guns N' Roses are joined onstage by Angus Young ('Whole Lotta Rosie' and 'Riff Raff') and Rose Tattoo's Angry Anderson ('Nice Boys') at the ANZ Stadium in Sydney.

Mar 3. The Asia/Oceana leg comes to a close at the Autism Rocks Arena in Dubai, UAE.

Mar 8. Guns N' Roses are announced as one of the headline acts at the Rock in Rio Festival in Rio de Janeiro on September 23.

May 27. The European leg of the Not in This Lifetime . . . Tour commences at Slane Castle in Ireland.

July 12. The final show on the European leg is at Goffertpark in Nijmegen, Netherlands.

July 20. Guns N' Roses play a "special invite-only" show at the Apollo Theater in Harlem New York.

July 27. The second North American leg of the Not in This Lifetime . . . Tour gets under way with a show at The Dome at America's Center in St. Louis, Missouri.

Sept 8. The North American leg comes to a close at the Alamodome in San Antonio, Texas.

Sept 23. Guns N' Roses headline Rock in Rio in Rio de Janeiro.

Oct 11. Guns N' Roses play the first of three shows at Madison Square Garden in New York. The other two MSG dates are October 15 and 16.

GUNS N' ROSES

Nov 29. Guns N' Roses bring their 2017 tour commitments to a close at The Forum in Inglewood CA. The set runs to almost four hours.

2018

June 3. The opening date of the second European leg of the Not in This Lifetime . . . Tour is at Berlin's Olympiastadion. Guns N' Roses perform Velvet Revolver's 'Slither' for the first time on the tour.

June 14. Axl, Slash, and Duff join The Foo Fighters onstage at the Firenze Rocks Festival (at the Visarno Hippodrome) in Florence for a rendition of 'It's So Easy'. Guns N' Roses headline the festival the following evening.

June 29. Universal Music Group releases *Appetite for Destruction: Locked N' Loaded.*

July 24. The final show of the European leg is at the Laugardalsvöllur in Reykjavik. Guns N' Roses' first visit to Iceland.

Sept 21. *Living the Dream*, the third Slash feat. Myles Kennedy and The Conspirators album is released. The album peaks at a rather disappointing # 27 on the *Billboard* 200 and # 4 on the UK chart.

Nov 3. The final leg of the Not in This Lifetime . . . Tour kicks off with a show at the Parque Fundidora in Monterrey, Mexico.

Nov 20. Guns N' Roses play the first of two consecutive shows at the AsiaWorld-Expo in Hong Kong.

Dec 8. Guns N' Roses bring the Not in This Lifetime . . . Tour to a close with a show at the Aloha Stadium in Honolulu, Hawaii.

GUNS N' ROSES

GN'R
GIG GUIDE

1985

Mar 26	The Troubadour	West Hollywood, CA. USA
Apr 11	Radio City	Anaheim, CA. USA
Apr 24	The Troubadour	West Hollywood, CA. USA
Apr 25	Dancing Waters Club	San Pedro, CA. USA
Apr 27	Radio City	Anaheim, CA. USA
May 11	Timbers Ballroom	Glendora, CA. USA
May 12	Joshua's Parlour	Los Angeles, CA. USA
June 6	The Troubadour	West Hollywood, CA. USA
June 8	Gorilla Gardens	Seattle, WA. USA
June 12	The Stone	San Francisco, CA. USA
June 28	Stardust Ballroom	Los Angeles, CA. USA
July 4	Madame Wong's East	Los Angeles, CA. USA
July 20	The Troubadour	West Hollywood, CA. USA
July 21	UCLA Frat Party	Los Angeles, CA. USA
Aug 30	Stardust Ballroom	Los Angeles, CA. USA
Aug 31	Roxy Theatre	West Hollywood, CA. USA
Sept 20	The Troubadour	West Hollywood, CA. USA
Sept 28	8th Annual Street Scene Festival	Los Angeles, CA. USA
Oct 10	The Troubadour	West Hollywood, CA. USA
Oct 18	Reseda Country Club	Reseda, CA. USA
Oct 31	Radio City	Anaheim, CA. USA
Nov 22	The Troubadour	West Hollywood, CA. USA
Dec 20	Music Machine	Los Angeles, CA. USA

1986

Jan 4	The Troubadour	West Hollywood, CA. USA
Jan 18	Roxy Theatre	West Hollywood, CA. USA
Feb 1	The Troubadour	West Hollywood, CA. USA
Mar 11	Music Machine	Los Angeles, CA. USA
Mar 21	Fender's Ballroom	Long Beach, CA. USA
Mar 28	Roxy Theatre	West Hollywood, CA. USA
Mar 29	Fender's Ballroom	Long Beach, CA. USA
Apr 5	Whisky a Go Go	West Hollywood, CA. USA
May 1	The Central	Los Angeles, CA. USA
May 3	Roxy Theatre	West Hollywood, CA. USA
May 13	Raji's	Hollywood, CA. USA
May 31	Gazzarri's	West Hollywood, CA. USA
July 11	The Troubadour	West Hollywood, CA. USA
July 21	Bogart's	Long Beach, CA. USA
July 24	Club Lingerie	Los Angeles, CA. USA
July 31	Timbers Ballroom	Glendora, CA. USA
Aug 15	Scream	Los Angeles, CA. USA
Aug 23	Whisky a Go Go	West Hollywood, CA. USA
Aug 28	The Stone	San Francisco, CA. USA
Aug 30	Santa Monica Civic Auditorium	Santa Monica, CA. USA
Sept 13	Music Machine	Los Angeles, CA. USA
Sept 20	9th Annual Street Scene Festival	Los Angeles, CA. USA
Oct 23	Arlington Theatre	Santa Barbara, CA. USA
Oct 31	Ackerman Hall	Los Angeles, CA. USA
Nov 15	Fender's Ballroom	Long Beach, CA. USA
Dec 23	The Cathouse	Hollywood, CA. USA
Dec 31	Glamour	Los Angeles, CA. USA

1987

Mar 16	Whisky a Go Go	West Hollywood, CA. USA
Mar 29	Roxy Theatre	West Hollywood, CA. USA
May 10	Stardust Ballroom	Hollywood, CA. USA
June 19	Marquee Club	London, UK
June 22	Marquee Club	London, UK
June 28	Marquee Club	London, UK
Aug 14	Halifax Metro Centre	Halifax, Nova Scotia
Aug 15	Moncton Coliseum	Moncton, Canada

GUNS N' ROSES

Aug 17	Verdun Auditorium	Montreal, Canada
Aug 18	Super Skate 7	Kitchener, Canada
Aug 19	CNE Stadium	Toronto, Canada
Aug 21	Detroit State Theatre	Detroit, MI, USA
Aug 22	Aragon Ballroom	Chicago, IL, USA
Aug 25	Winnipeg Arena	Winnipeg, Canada
Aug 26	Edmonton Convention Centre	Edmonton, Canada
Aug 27	Max Bell Arena	Calgary, Canada
Aug 29	Pacific Coliseum	Vancouver, Canada
Aug 30	Paramount Theatre	Seattle, WA. USA
Sept 2	Warfield Theatre	San Francisco, CA. USA
Sept 3	Santa Cruz Civic Auditorium	Santa Cruz, CA. USA
Sept 4	SDSU Open Air Theatre	San Diego, CA. USA
Sept 5	Long Beach Arena	Long Beach, CA. USA
Sept 7	The Mason Jar	Phoenix, AZ. USA
Sept 8	El Paso County Coliseum	El Paso, TX. USA
Sept 11	The Sunken Gardens	San Antonio, TX. USA
Sept 12	Palmer Auditorium	Austin, TX. USA
Sept 13	Bronco Bowl Auditorium	Dallas, TX. USA
Sept 16	Houston Music Hall	Houston, TX. USA
Sept 17	Saenger Theatre	New Orleans, LA. USA
Sept 29	Markthalle	Hamburg, Germany
Sept 30	Gate 3	Düsseldorf, Germany
Oct 2	Paradiso	Amsterdam, Holland
Oct 4	Newcastle City Hall	Newcastle, UK
Oct 5	Nottingham Rock City	Nottingham, UK
Oct 6	Apollo Theatre	Manchester, UK
Oct 7	Colston Hall	Bristol, UK
Oct 8	Hammersmith Odeon	London, UK
Oct 16	The Sundance	Bay Shore, NY. USA
Oct 17	Airport Road Music Hall	Allentown, PA. USA
Oct 18	Hammerjack's	Baltimore, MD. USA
Oct 20	Trocadero Theatre	Philadelphia, PA. USA
Oct 21	Palace Theatre	Albany, NY. USA
Oct 22	Obsessions	Randolph, NJ. USA
Oct 23	The Ritz	New York, NY. USA
Oct 25	The Chance	Poughkeepsie, NY. USA
Oct 26	The Living Room	Providence, RI. USA
Oct 27	Paradise Rock Club	Boston, MA. USA
Oct 29	L'Amour	New York, NY. USA
Oct 30	CBGBs Record Canteen	New York, NY. USA
Oct 31	The Lost Horizon	Syracuse, NY. USA

Nov 1	The Bayou	Washington DC. USA
Nov 3	Mobile Municipal Auditorium	Mobile, AL. USA
Nov 4	Albany Civic Center	Albany, NY. USA
Nov 6	Cajundome	Lafayette, LA. USA
Nov 7	Lakefront Arena	New Orleans, LA. USA
Nov 8	Mississippi Coliseum	Mississippi, MS. USA
Nov 10	Von Braun Civic Center	Huntsville, AL. USA
Nov 11	Charlotte Coliseum	Charlotte, NC. USA
Nov 13	Savannah Civic Center	Savannah, GA. USA
Nov 14	Carolina Coliseum	Columbia, SC. USA
Nov 15	Greensboro Coliseum	Greensboro, NC. USA
Nov 17	Knoxville Civic Coliseum	Knoxville, TN. USA
Nov 18	Jefferson Civic Center	Birmingham, AL. USA
Nov 20	Omni Coliseum	Atlanta, GA. USA
Nov 21	UTC Arena	Chattanooga, TN. USA
Nov 22	Omni Coliseum	Atlanta, GA. USA
Nov 24	Lakeland Civic Center	Lakeland, FL. USA
Nov 25	Lakeland Civic Center	Lakeland, FL. USA
Nov 27	Jacksonville Coliseum	Jacksonville, FL. USA
Nov 28	Lee County Civic Arena	Fort Myers, FL. USA
Nov 29	Hollywood Sportatorium	Pembroke Pines, FL.
Dec 3	La Villa Real Convention Center	McAllen, TX. USA
Dec 4	Fair Park Coliseum	Dallas, TX. USA
Dec 5	Sam Houston Coliseum	Houston, TX. USA
Dec 7	HemisFair Arena	San Antonio, TX. USA
Dec 9	Chaparral Center	Midland, TX. USA
Dec 11	Show Me Center	Cape Girardeau, MO. USA
Dec 12	Louisville Gardens	Louisville, KY. USA
Dec 17	Roy Wilkins Auditorium	St. Paul, MN. USA
Dec 18	UIC Pavilion	Chicago, IL. USA
Dec 19	Dane County VM Coliseum	Madison, WI. USA
Dec 26	Perkins Palace	Pasadena, CA. USA
Dec 27	Perkins Palace	Pasadena, CA. USA
Dec 28	Perkins Palace	Pasadena, CA. USA
Dec 30	Perkins Palace	Pasadena, CA. USA
Dec 31	The Glamour	Los Angeles, CA. USA

GUNS N' ROSES

1988

Jan 5	Santa Monica Civic Auditorium	Santa Monica, CA. USA
Jan 14	Coconut Teaszer	Los Angeles, CA. USA
Jan 21	The Cathouse	Los Angeles, CA. USA
Jan 31	The Limelight	New York City, NY. USA
Feb 2	The Ritz	New York City, NY. USA
Feb 4	Crest Theatre	Sacramento, CA. USA
Feb 5	Warfield Theatre	San Francisco, CA. USA
Feb 6	Warnors Theater	Fresno, CA. USA
Feb 8	Montezuma Hall	San Diego, CA. USA
Feb 9	The Celebrity Theatre	Anaheim, CA. USA
Feb 10	The Celebrity Theatre	Anaheim, CA. USA
Feb 12	Celebrity Theatre	Phoenix, AZ. USA
Apr 26	Burlington Memorial Auditorium	Burlington, IA. USA
Apr 28	Oshkosh Conference Hall	Oshkosh, WI. USA
Apr 29	Coronado Theatre	Rockford, IL. USA
Apr 30	Danville Civic Center	Danville, IL. USA
May 1	Toledo Sports Arena	Toledo, OH. USA
May 3	DeVos Performance Hall	Grand Rapids, MI. USA
May 5	Cleveland Music Hall	Cleveland, OH. USA
May 6	Wendler Arena	Saginaw, MI. USA
May 7	Detroit State Theatre	Detroit, MI. USA
May 9	Felt Forum	New York City, NY. USA
May 10	Tower Theatre	Upper Darby, PA. USA
May 11	Orpheum Theater	Boston, MA. USA
May 13	Moncton Coliseum	Moncton, New Brunswick, Canada
May 14	Halifax Metro Centre	Halifax, Nova Scotia, Canada
May 16	Quebec Coliseum	Quebec, Canada
May 17	Montreal Forum	Montreal, Canada
May 18	Ottawa Civic Arena	Ottawa, Canada
May 20	CNE Stadium	Toronto, Canada
May 23	Winnipeg Arena	Winnipeg, Canada
May 25	Northlands Coliseum	Edmonton, Canada
May 27	The Saddledome	Calgary, Canada
May 30	Pacific Coliseum (2 Shows)	Vancouver, Canada
May 31	Spokane Coliseum	Spokane, WA. USA
June 1	Seattle Coliseum	Seattle, WA. USA
June 3	Salt Palace	Salt Lake City, UT. USA
June 5	Shoreline Amphitheatre	Mountain View, CA. USA
June 6	Cal Expo Amphitheatre	Sacramento, CA. USA

July 9	Celebrity Theatre	Phoenix, AZ. USA
July 10	Celebrity Theatre	Phoenix, AZ. USA
July 17	Poplar Creek Music Theater	Hoffman Estates, IL. USA
July 19	Richfield Coliseum	Richfield, OH. USA
July 20	Wheeling Civic Center	Wheeling, OH. USA
July 22	Show Me Center	Cape Girardeau, MI. USA
July 24	Starplex Amphitheatre	Dallas, TX. USA
July 26	Sandstone Amphitheatre	Bonner Springs, KS. USA
July 27	Hilton Coliseum	Ames, IA. USA
July 29	Alpine Valley Music Theatre	East Troy, WI. USA
July 30	Val Du Lakes Amphitheatre	Mears, MI. USA
Aug 1	Riverbend Music Center	Cincinnati, OH. USA
Aug 2	Market Square Arena	Indianapolis, IN. USA
Aug 4	The Spectrum	Philadelphia, PA. USA
Aug 5	The Spectrum	Philadelphia, PA. USA
Aug 6	Saratoga Performing Arts Center	Saratoga Springs, NY. USA
Aug 7	Orange County Fairgrounds Stadium	Middletown, NY. USA
Aug 9	Weedsport Speedway	Weedsport, NY. USA
Aug 11	Pine Knob Music Theatre	Clarkston, MI. USA
Aug 12	Pine Knob Music Theatre	Clarkston, MI. USA
Aug 13	Pine Knob Music Theatre	Clarkston, MI. USA
Aug 16	Giants Stadium	East Rutherford, NJ. USA
Aug 17	Merriweather Post Pavilion	Columbia, MD. USA
Aug 20	Monsters of Rock Festival	Castle Donington, UK
Aug 24	Great Woods Amphitheatre	Mansfield, MA. USA
Aug 25	Great Woods Amphitheatre	Mansfield, MA. USA
Aug 26	Great Woods Amphitheatre	Mansfield, MA. USA
Aug 28	Buckeye Lake Music Center	Thornville, OH. USA
Aug 30	Pocono Downs	Wilkes Barre, PA. USA
Aug 31	Pittsburgh Civic Arena	Pittsburgh, PA. USA
Sept 2	Starwood Amphitheatre	Antioch, TN. USA
Sept 3	St. Louis Arena	St. Louis, MI. USA
Sept 8	Concord Pavilion	Concord, CA. USA
Sept 9	Cal Expo Amphitheatre	Sacramento, CA. USA
Sept 10	Shoreline Amphitheatre	Mountain View, CA. USA
Sept 12	Compton Terrace	Chandler, AZ. USA
Sept 14	Pacific Amphitheatre	Costa Mesa, CA. USA
Sept 15	Pacific Amphitheatre	Costa Mesa, CA. USA
Sept 17	Texas Stadium (Survival of the Fittest 1988)	Irving, TX. USA
Dec 4	NHK Hall	Tokyo, Japan
Dec 5	Osaka Festival Hall	Osaka, Japan
Dec 7	Nakano Sun Plaza Hall	Tokyo, Japan

GUNS N' ROSES

Dec 9	NHK Hall	Tokyo, Japan
Dec 10	Budokan	Tokyo, Japan
Dec 14	Melbourne Sports & Entertainment Centre	Melbourne, AUS
Dec 15	Melbourne Sports & Entertainment Centre	Melbourne, AUS
Dec 17	Sydney Entertainment Centre	Sydney, AUS
Dec 19	Mount Smart Stadium	Auckland, NZ

1989

Oct 13	Park Plaza Hotel	Los Angeles, CA. USA
Oct 18	Los Angeles Memorial Coliseum	Los Angeles, CA. USA
Oct 19	Los Angeles Memorial Coliseum	Los Angeles, CA. USA
Oct 21	Los Angeles Memorial Coliseum	Los Angeles, CA. USA
Oct 22	Los Angeles Memorial Coliseum	Los Angeles, CA. USA

1990

| Apr 7 | Hoosier Dome (Farm Aid IV) | Indianapolis, IN. USA |

1991

Jan 20	Maracanã Stadium (Rock in Rio II)	Rio de Janeiro, Brazil
Jan 23	Maracanã Stadium (Rock in Rio II)	Rio de Janeiro, Brazil
May 9	Warfield Theatre	San Francisco, CA. USA
May 11	Pantages Theatre	Los Angeles, CA. USA
May 16	The Ritz	N ew York City, NY. USA
May 24	Alpine Valley Music Theatre	East Troy, WI. USA
May 25	Alpine Valley Music Theatre	East Troy, WI. USA
May 28	Deer Creek Music Center	Noblesville, IN. USA
May 29	Deer Creek Music Center	Noblesville, IN. USA
June 1	Capital Music Center	Grove City, OH. USA
June 2	Toledo Speedway	Toledo, OH. USA
June 4	Richfield Coliseum	Richfield, OH. USA
June 5	Richfield Coliseum	Richfield, OH. USA
June 7	CNE Grandstand	Toronto, Canada
June 8	CNE Grandstand	Toronto, Canada
June 10	Saratoga Performing Arts Center	Saratoga Springs, NY
June 11	Hersheypark Stadium	Hershey, PA. USA
June 13	The Spectrum	Philadelphia, PA. USA

June 17	Nassau Veterans Memorial Coliseum	Uniondale, NY. USA
June 19	Capital Centre	Landover, MD. USA
June 20	Capital Centre	Landover, MD. USA
June 22	Hampton Coliseum	Hampton, VA. USA
June 23	Charlotte Coliseum	Charlotte, NC. USA
June 25	Greensboro Coliseum	Greensboro, NC. USA
June 26	Thompson–Boling Arena	Knoxville, TN. USA
June 29	Rupp Arena	Lexington, KY. USA
June 30	Birmingham Race Course	Birmingham, AL. USA
July 2	Riverport Amphitheatre	Maryland Heights, MI. USA
July 3	Riverport Amphitheatre	Maryland Heights, MI. USA
July 4	World Music Theatre	Tinley Park, IL. USA
July 6	Sandstone Amphitheatre	Bonner Springs, KS. USA
July 8	Coca-Cola Starplex Amphitheatre	Dallas, TX. USA
July 9	Coca-Cola Starplex Amphitheatre	Dallas, TX. USA
July 11	McNichols Sports Arena	Denver, CO. USA
July 12	Fiddler's Green Amphitheatre	Englewood, CO. USA
July 13	Salt Palace Arena	Salt Lake City, UT. USA
July 16	Tacoma Dome	Tacoma, WA. USA
July 17	Tacoma Dome	Tacoma, WA. USA
July 19	Shoreline Amphitheatre	Mountain View, CA. USA
July 20	Shoreline Amphitheatre	Mountain View, CA. USA
July 23	ARCO Arena	Sacramento, CA. USA
July 25	Pacific Amphitheatre	Cosa Mesa, CA. USA
July 29	Great Western Forum	Inglewood, CA. USA
July 30	Great Western Forum	Inglewood, CA. USA
Aug 2	Great Western Forum	Inglewood, CA. USA
Aug 3	Great Western Forum	Inglewood, CA. USA
Aug 13	Helsinki Ice Hall	Helsinki, Finland
Aug 14	Helsinki Ice Hall	Helsinki, Finland
Aug 16	Globen	Stockholm, Sweden
Aug 17	Globen	Stockholm, Sweden
Aug 19	Forum Copenhagen	Copenhagen, Denmark
Aug 24	May Market Area	Mannheim, Germany
Aug 31	Wembley Stadium	London, UK
Dec 5	Worcester Centrum	Worcester, MA. USA
Dec 6	Worcester Centrum	Worcester, MA. USA
Dec 9	Madison Square Garden	New York City, NY. USA
Dec 10	Madison Square Garden	New York City, NY. USA
Dec 13	Madison Square Garden	New York City, NY. USA
Dec 16	The Spectrum	Philadelphia, PA. USA
Dec 17	The Spectrum	Philadelphia, PA. USA

GUNS N' ROSES

Dec 28	Suncoast Dome	St. Petersburg, FL. USA
Dec 31	Joe Robbie Stadium	Miami Gardens, FL. USA

1992

Jan 3	LSU Assembly Center	Baton Rouge, LA. USA
Jan 4	Mississippi Coast Coliseum	Biloxi, MS. USA
Jan 7	Pyramid Arena	Memphis, TN. USA
Jan 9	The Summit	Houston, TX. USA
Jan 10	The Summit	Houston, TX. USA
Jan 13	Nutter Center	Fairborn, OH. USA
Jan 14	Nutter Center	Fairborn, OH. USA
Jan 21	Target Center	Minneapolis, MN. USA
Jan 22	Target Center	Minneapolis, MN. USA
Jan 25	Thomas & Mack Center	Paradise, NV. USA
Jan 27	San Diego Sports Arena	San Diego, CA. USA
Jan 28	San Diego Sports Arena	San Diego, CA. USA
Jan 31	Compton Terrace	Chandler, AZ. USA
Feb 1	Compton Terrace	Chandler, AZ. USA
Feb 19	Tokyo Dome	Tokyo, Japan
Feb 20	Tokyo Dome	Tokyo, Japan
Feb 22	Tokyo Dome	Tokyo, Japan
Apr 1	Palacio de los Deportes	Mexico City, Mexico
Apr 2	Palacio de los Deportes	Mexico City, Mexico
Apr 6	Myriad Arena	Oklahoma City, OK. USA
Apr 9	Rosemont Horizon	Rosemont, IL. USA
Apr 20	Wembley Stadium	London, UK
May 16	Slane Concert	Slane, Ireland
May 20	Strahov Stadium	Prague, Czechoslovakia
May 22	Népstadion	Budapest, Hungary
May 23	Donauinsel Stadium	Vienna, Austria
May 26	Olympiastadion	Berlin, Germany
May 28	Cannstatter Wasen	Stuttgart, Germany
May 30	Müngersdorfer Stadion	Cologne, Germany
June 3	Niedersachsenstadion	Hanover, Germany
June 6	Paris Hippodrome	Paris, France
June 13	Wembley Stadium	London, UK
June 14	Maine Road	Manchester, UK
June 16	Gateshead International Stadium	Gateshead, UK
June 20	Talavera-Mainwiese	Würzburg, Germany
June 21	St. Jakob Stadium	Basel, Switzerland

June 23	Feijenoord Stadion	Rotterdam, Holland
June 27	Stadio delle Alpi	Turin, Italy
June 30	Estadio Benito Villamarín	Seville, Spain
July 2	Estádio José Alvalade	Lisbon, Portugal
July 17	RFK Stadium	Washington, D.C. USA
July 18	Giants Stadium	East Rutherford, NJ. USA
July 21	Pontiac Silverdome	Pontiac, MI. USA
July 22	Hoosier Dome	Indianapolis, IN. USA
July 25	Rich Stadium	Orchard Park, NY. USA
July 26	Three Rivers Stadium	Pittsburgh, PA. USA
July 29	Giants Stadium	East Rutherford, NJ. USA
Aug 8	Olympic Stadium	Montreal, Canada
Aug 25	Phoenix International Raceway	Avondale, AZ. USA
Aug 27	Aggie Memorial Stadium	Las Cruces, NM. USA
Aug 29	The Superdome	New Orleans, LA. USA
Sept 2	Florida Citrus Bowl	Orlando, FL. USA
Sept 4	Astrodome	Houston, TX. USA
Sept 5	Texas Stadium	Irving, TX. USA
Sept 7	Williams-Brice Stadium	Columbia, SC. USA
Sept 11	Foxboro Stadium	Foxborough, MA. USA
Sept 13	CNE Grandstand	Toronto, Canada
Sept 15	Hubert Humphrey Metrodome	Minneapolis, MN. USA
Sept 17	Arrowhead Stadium	Kansas City, KS. USA
Sept 19	Mile High Stadium	Denver, CO. USA
Sept 24	Oakland Coliseum	Oakland, CA. USA
Sept 27	LA Memorial Coliseum	Los Angeles, CA. USA
Sept 30	Jack Murphy Stadium	San Diego, CA. USA
Oct 3	Rose Bowl	Pasadena, CA. USA
Oct 6	Kingdome	Seattle, WA. USA
Nov 25	Caracas Polyhedron	Caracas, Venezuela
Nov 29	Estadio El Campín	Bogotá, Colombia
Dec 2	Estadio Nacional de Chile	Santiago, Chile
Dec 5	River Plate Stadium	Buenos, Argentina
Dec 6	River Plate Stadium	Buenos, Argentina
Dec 10	Arena Anhembi	São Paulo, Brazil
Dec 12	Arena Anhembi	São Paulo, Brazil
Dec 13	Autódromo Internacional Nelson Piquet	Rio de Janeiro, Brazil

GUNS N' ROSES

1993

Jan 12	Tokyo Dome	Tokyo, Japan
Jan 14	Tokyo Dome	Tokyo, Japan
Jan 15	Tokyo Dome	Tokyo, Japan
Jan 30	Eastern Creek Raceway	Sydney, Australia
Feb 1	Calder Park Raceway	Melbourne, Australia
Feb 6	Mount Smart Stadium	Auckland, New Zealand
Feb 23	Frank Erwin Center	Austin, TX. USA
Feb 25	Jefferson Civic Arena	Birmingham, AL. USA
Mar 6	New Haven Coliseum	New Haven, CT. USA
Mar 8	Cumberland County Civic Center	Portland, ME. USA
Mar 9	Hartford Civic Center	Hartford, CT. USA
Mar 12	Copps Coliseum	Hamilton, Canada
Mar 16	Augusta Civic Center	Augusta, ME. USA
Mar 17	Boston Garden	Boston, MA. USA
Mar 20	Carver–Hawkeye Arena	Iowa City, IA. USA
Mar 21	Fargodome	Fargo, ND. USA
Mar 24	Winnipeg Arena	Winnipeg, Canada
Mar 26	Saskatchewan Place	Saskatoon, Canada
Mar 28	Northlands Coliseum	Edmonton, Canada
Mar 30	BC Place	Vancouver, Canada
Apr 1	Memorial Coliseum	Portland, ME. USA
Apr 3	ARCO Arena	Sacramento, CA. USA
Apr 4	Lawlor Events Center	Reno, NV. USA
Apr 7	Delta Center	Salt Lake City, UT. USA
Apr 9	Don Barnett Arena	Rapid City, SD. USA
Apr 10	Omaha Civic Auditorium	Omaha, NE. USA
Apr 13	The Palace of Auburn Hills	Auburn Hills, MI. USA
Apr 15	Roanoke Civic Center	Roanoke, VA. USA
Apr 16	Dean Smith Center	Chapel Hill, NC. USA
Apr 18	Virginia Beach Amphitheatre	Virginia Beach, VA. USA
Apr 21	Estadio Jalisco	Guadalajara, Mexico
Apr 23	Palacio de los Deportes	Mexico City, Mexico
Apr 24	Palacio de los Deportes	Mexico City, Mexico
Apr 27	Estadio Universitario	Monterrey, Mexico
May 22	Hayarkon Park	Tel Aviv, Israel
May 24	Olympic Stadium	Athens, Greece
May 26	Inonu Stadium	Istanbul, Turkey
May 29	National Bowl	Milton Keynes, UK
May 30	National Bowl	Milton Keynes, UK
June 2	Praterstadion	Vienna, Austria

June 5	Goffertpark	Nijmegen, Holland
June 6	Goffertpark	Nijmegen, Holland
June 8	Gentofte Stadion	Copenhagen, Denmark
June 10	Valle Hovin	Oslo, Norway
June 12	Stockholm Olympic Stadium	Stockholm, Sweden
June 16	St. Jakob Stadium	Basel, Switzerland
June 18	Weserstadion	Bremen, Germany
June 19	Müngersdorfer Stadion	Cologne, Germany
June 22	Wildparkstadion	Karlsruhe, Germany
June 25	Waldstadion	Frankfurt, Germany
June 26	Olympiastadion	Munich, Germany
June 29	Stadio Comunale	Modena, Italy
June 30	Stadio Comunale	Modena, Italy
July 5	Estadi Olímpic Lluís Companys	Barcelona, Spain
July 6	Vicente Calderón Stadium	Madrid, Spain
July 8	Zénith de Nancy	Nancy, France
July 9	Halle Tony Garnier	Lyon, France
July 11	Rock Werchter	Werchter, Belgium
July 13	Palais Omnisports de Paris-Bercy	Paris, France
July 16	River Plate Stadium	Buenos Aires, Argentina
July 17	River Plate Stadium	Buenos Aires, Argentina

2001

Jan 1	House of Blues	Paradise, NV. USA
Jan 14	Maracanã Stadium	Rio de Janeiro, Brazil
Dec 29	The Joint	Paradise, NV. USA
Dec 31	The Joint	Paradise, NV. USA

2002

Aug 14	Exhibition Centre	Hong Kong, China
Aug 17	Chiba Marine Stadium	Chiba, Japan
Aug 18	WTC Open Air Stadium	Osaka, Japan
Aug 23	Temple Newsam Park	Leeds, UK
Aug 24	Pukkelpop Field	Hasselt, Belgium
Aug 26	London Docklands Arena	London, UK

GUNS N' ROSES

Nov 8	Tacoma Dome	Tacoma, WA. USA
Nov 10	Idaho Center	Nampa, ID. USA
Nov 14	Target Center	Minneapolis, MN. USA
Nov 15	Fargodome	Fargo, ND. USA
Nov 17	The MARK of the Quad Cities	Moline, IL. USA
Nov 18	Allstate Arena	Rosemont, IL. USA
Nov 21	The Palace of Auburn Hills	Auburn Hills, MI. USA
Nov 22	Mellon Arena	Pittsburgh, PA. USA
Nov 24	Gund Arena	Cleveland, OH. USA
Nov 25	Nationwide Arena	Columbus, OH. USA
Nov 27	Pepsi Arena	Albany, NY. USA
Nov 29	Air Canada Centre	Toronto, Canada
Nov 30	John Labatt Centre	London, Canada
Dec 2	Fleet Center	Boston, MA. USA
Dec 3	Hartford Civic Center	Hartford, CT. USA
Dec 5	Madison Square Garden	New York City, NY. USA

2006

May 12	Hammerstein Ballroom	New York City, NY. USA
May 14	Hammerstein Ballroom	New York City, NY. USA
May 15	Hammerstein Ballroom	New York City, NY. USA
May 17	Hammerstein Ballroom	New York City, NY. USA
May 18	The Plumm	New York City, NY. USA
May 25	Parque Juan Carlos	Madrid, Spain
May 27	Parque da Béla Vista	Lisbon, Portugal
May 31	Budapest Arena	Budapest, Hungary
June 2	Nürburgring	Nürburg, Germany
June 4	Idroscalo	Milan, Italy
June 7	Hammersmith Apollo	London, UK
June 9	RDS Arena	Dublin, Ireland
June 11	Donington Park	Castle Donington, UK
June 13	Sazka Arena	Prague, Czech Republic
June 15	Stadion Legii	Warsaw, Poland
June 17	Pannonia Fields II	Burgenland, Austria
June 20	POPB	Paris, France
June 24	Graspop Metal Meeting	Dessel, Belgium
June 26	Globen	Stockholm, Sweden
June 28	Oslo Spektrum	Oslo, Norway
June 29	Animal Showgrounds	Roskilde, Denmark
July 1	Hallenstadion	Zürich, Switzerland

July 2	Goffertpark	Nijmegen, Holland
July 5	Hartwall Areena	Helsinki, Finland
July 6	Hartwall Areena	Helsinki, Finland
July 8	Oslo Spektrum	Oslo, Norway
July 10	Terra Vibe Park	Athens, Greece
July 12	Kurucesme Arena	Istanbul, Turkey
July 14	Kobetamendi	Bilbao, Spain
July 15	Playa De Guardias Viejas	El Ejido, Spain
July 18	Hallam FM Arena	Sheffield, UK
July 19	Metro Radio Arena	Newcastle, UK
July 21	SECC	Glasgow, UK
July 23	MEN Arena	Manchester, UK
July 25	NEC Arena	Birmingham, UK
July 27	Nottingham Arena	Nottingham, UK
July 29	Wembley Arena	London, UK
July 30	Wembley Arena	London, UK

2007

Feb 8	Rodeo Drive	Beverly Hills, CA. USA
June 2	Monterrey Arena	Monterrey, Mexico
June 3	Arena VFG	Guadalajara, Mexico
June 5	Palacio de los Deportes	Mexico City, Mexico
June 10	Burswood Dome	Perth, Australia
June 13	Entertainment Centre	Adelaide, Australia
June 15	Rod Laver Arena	Melbourne, Australia
June 16	Rod Laver Arena	Melbourne, Australia
June 20	Entertainment Centre	Brisbane, Australia
June 21	Entertainment Centre	Brisbane, Australia
June 23	Acer Arena	Sydney, Australia
June 24	Acer Arena	Sydney, Australia
June 29	Vector Arena	Auckland, New Zealand
June 30	Vector Arena	Auckland, New Zealand
July 3	Westpac Arena	Christchurch, New Zealand
July 14	Makuhari Messe	Chiba, Japan
July 15	Makuhari Messe	Chiba, Japan
July 17	Nippon Gaishi Hall	Nagoya, Japan
July 18	Nippon Budokan	Tokyo, Japan
July 21	Intex Osaka	Osaka, Japan

GUNS N' ROSES

2009

Dec 11	Banqiao Stadium	Taipei, Taiwan
Dec 13	Olympic Arena	Seoul, South Korea
Dec 16	Osaka Dome	Osaka, Japan
Dec 19	Tokyo Dome	Tokyo, Japan

2010

Jan 13	MTS Centre	Winnipeg, Canada
Jan 16	Pengrowth Saddledome	Calgary, Canada
Jan 17	Rexall Place	Edmonton, Canada
Jan 19	Credit Union Centre	Saskatoon, Canada
Jan 20	Brandt Centre	Regina, Canada
Jan 24	Copps Coliseum	Hamilton, Canada
Jan 25	John Labatt Centre	London, Canada
Jan 27	Bell Centre	Montreal, Canada
Jan 28	Air Canada Centre	Toronto, Canada
Jan 31	Scotiabank Place	Ottawa, Canada
Feb 1	Colisée Pepsi	Quebec City, Canada
Feb 3	Moncton Coliseum	Moncton, Canada
Feb 4	Metro Centre	Halifax, Nova Scotia
Mar 7	Ginásio Nilson Nelson	Brasília, Brazil
Mar 10	Mineirinho	Belo Horizonte, Brazil
Mar 13	Estádio Palestra Itália	São Paulo, Brazil
Mar 16	Estacionamento da Fiergs	Porto Alegre, Brazil
Mar 18	Estadio Centenario	Montevideo, Uruguay
Mar 20	Movistar Arena	Santiago, Chile
Mar 22	Estadio José Amalfitani	Buenos Aires, Argentina
Mar 25	Estadio Monumental	Lima, Peru
Mar 27	Poliedro de Caracas	Caracas, Venezuela
Mar 30	Parque Jaime Duque	Bogotá, Colombia
Apr 1	Estadio Olímpico	Quito, Ecuador
Apr 4	Praça da Apoteose	Rio de Janeiro, Brazil
Apr 7	Figali Convention Centre	Panama City, Panama
Apr 11	Estadio Cuscatlán	San Salvador, El Salvador
Apr 15	Coliseo Roberto Clemente	San Juan, Puerto Rico
May 31	Vestlandshallen	Bergen, Norway
June 2	Oslo Spektrum	Oslo, Norway

June 5	Käpylä Sportspark	Helsinki, Finland
June 6	Ice Palace	St. Petersburg, Russia
June 8	Olympiysky Stadium	Moscow, Russia
June 12	Norje Havsbad	Sölvesborg, Sweden
June 14	Gigantium	Aalborg, Denmark
Aug 13	Monkey Rock USA	Sturgis, SD. USA
Aug 27	Little John's Farm (Reading Festival)	Reading, UK
Aug 29	Bramham Park	Leeds, UK
Aug 31	Odyssey Arena	Belfast, UK
Sept 1	The O2	Dublin, Ireland
Sept 4	Palalottomatica	Rome, Italy
Sept 5	Mediolanum Forum	Milan, Italy
Sept 8	Hallenstadion	Zürich, Switzerland
Sept 10	Galaxie	Amnéville, France
Sept 13	Bercy	Paris, France
Sept 16	Geneva Arena	Geneva, Switzerland
Sept 18	Wiener Stadthalle	Vienna, Austria
Sept 21	Romexpo	Bucharest, Romania
Sept 23	Belgrade Arena	Belgrade, Serbia
Sept 24	Arena Zagreb	Zagreb, Croatia
Sept 27	O2 Arena	Prague, Czech Republic
Sept 30	Sportpaleis	Antwerp, Belgium
Oct 2	Zénith de Lille	Lille, France
Oct 3	GelreDome XS	Arnhem, Holland
Oct 6	Pavilhão Atlântico	Lisbon, Portugal
Oct 9	Palacio de Vistalegre	Madrid, Spain
Oct 10	Velódromo de Anoeta	San Sebastián, Spain
Oct 13	The O2 Arena	London, UK
Oct 14	The O2 Arena	London, UK
Oct 17	LG Arena	Birmingham, UK
Oct 18	M.E.N. Arena	Manchester, UK
Oct 22	Pabellón Príncipe Felipe	Zaragoza, Spain
Oct 23	Palau Municipal	Barcelona, Spain
Dec 1	Reid Park	Townsville, Australia
Dec 4	ANZ Stadium	Sydney, Australia
Dec 7	Entertainment Centre	Adelaide, Australia
Dec 11	Perth Motorplex	Perth, Australia
Dec 16	Yas Arena	Abu Dhabi, UAE

GUNS N' ROSES

2011

Oct 2	Cidade do Rock	Rio de Janeiro, Brazil
Oct 5	Movistar Arena	Santiago, Chile
Oct 8	Estadio de La Plata	La Plata, Argentina
Oct 10	Salón Metropolitano	Rosario, Argentina
Oct 12	Orfeo Superdomo	Córdoba, Argentina
Oct 15	Hipódromo de Asunción	Asunción, Paraguay
Oct 18	Palacio de los Deportes	Mexico City, Mexico
Oct 19	Palacio de los Deportes	Mexico City, Mexico
Oct 22	Arena VFG	Guadalajara, Mexico
Oct 23	Monterrey Arena	Monterrey, Mexico
Oct 28	Amway Center	Orlando, FL. USA
Oct 29	American Airlines Arena	Miami, FL. USA
Oct 31	BI-LO Center	Greenville, SC. USA
Nov 2	Philips Arena	Atlanta, GA. USA
Nov 4	Toyota Center	Houston, TX. USA
Nov 5	Gexa Energy Pavilion	Dallas, TX. USA
Nov 8	Qwest Centre Omaha	Omaha, NE. USA
Nov 9	Lloyd Noble Center	Norman, OK. USA
Nov 12	Sprint Center	Kansas City, KS. USA
Nov 13	Target Center	Minneapolis, MN. USA
Nov 15	Allstate Arena	Rosemont, IL. USA
Nov 17	Izod Centre	East Rutherford, NJ. USA
Nov 19	The Comcast Theatre	Hartford, CT. USA
Nov 20	Mohegan Sun Arena	Wilkes-Barre, PA. USA
Nov 25	DCU Center	Worcester, MA. USA
Nov 26	Susquehanna Bank Center	Camden, NJ. USA
Nov 28	Copps Coliseum	Hamilton, Canada
Dec 1	The Palace of Auburn Hills	Auburn Hills, MI. USA
Dec 2	U.S. Bank Arena	Cincinnati, OH. USA
Dec 4	Bridgestone Arena	Nashville, TX. USA
Dec 7	Covelli Centre	Youngstown, OH. USA
Dec 8	Conseco Fieldhouse	Indianapolis, IN. USA
Dec 11	1stBank Center	Broomfield, CO. USA
Dec 13	Maverik Center	West Valley City, UT. USA
Dec 16	KeyArena	Seattle, WA. USA
Dec 17	Pacific Coliseum	Vancouver, Canada
Dec 21	The Forum	Inglewood, CA. USA
Dec 27	Comerica Theatre	Phoenix, AZ. USA
Dec 30	The Joint	Paradise, NV. USA
Dec 31	The Joint	Paradise, NV. USA

2012

Feb 10	Roseland Ballroom	New York City, NY. USA
Feb 12	Terminal 5	New York City, NY. USA
Feb 15	The Ritz Webster Hall	New York City, NY. USA
Feb 16	Hiro Ballroom	New York City, NY. USA
Feb 19	House of Blues Chicago	Chicago, IL. USA
Feb 21	The Fillmore Detroit	Detroit, MI. USA
Feb 23	The Fillmore Silver Spring	Silver Spring, MD. USA
Feb 24	House of Blues	Atlantic City, NJ. USA
Feb 27	Electric Factory	Philadelphia, PA. USA
Mar 1	The Tabernacle	Atlanta, GA. USA
Mar 3	House of Blues	Lake Buena Vista, FL. USA
Mar 5	Jackie Gleason Theater	Miami, FL. USA
Mar 9	Hollywood Palladium	Los Angeles, CA. USA
Mar 11	The Wiltern	Los Angeles, CA. USA
Mar 12	House of Blues	Los Angeles, CA. USA
May 11	Stadium Live Club	Moscow, Russia
May 12	Stadium Live Club	Moscow, Russia
May 17	The O2	Dublin, Ireland
May 19	Capital FM Arena	Nottingham, UK
May 20	Echo Arena Liverpool	Liverpool, UK
May 23	Metro Radio Arena	Newcastle, UK
May 25	SEC	Glasgow, UK
May 26	LG Arena	Birmingham, UK
May 29	Manchester Arena	Manchester, UK
May 31	The O2 Arena	London, UK
June 1	The O2 Arena	London, UK
June 4	Ahoy Rotterdam	Rotterdam, Holland
June 5	Palais Omnisports de Paris-Bercy	Paris, France
June 8	Warsteiner Park	Mönchengladbach, Germany
June 10	Halle Tony Garnier	Lyon, France
June 11	Zénith de Strasbourg	Strasbourg, France
June 14	Zénith de Toulouse	Toulouse, France
June 16	Val de Moine	Clisson, France
June 18	Park & Suites Arena	Montpellier, France
June 19	Zénith Oméga de Toulon	Toulon, France
June 22	Fieramilano	Milan, Italy
June 24	Festivalpark Stenehei	Dessel, Belgium
June 27	St. Jakobshalle	Basel, Switzerland
June 29	Schwarzl Freizeitzentrum	Graz, Austria
July 1	Romexpo Arena	Bucharest, Romania

GUNS N' ROSES

July 3	Yarkon Park	Tel Aviv, Israel
July 6	Parkorman	Istanbul, Turkey
July 8	Vasil Levski National Stadium	Sophia, Bulgaria
July 11	Rybnik Municipal Stadium	Rybnik, Poland
July 13	Pieš any Airport	Pieš any, Slovakia
July 15	Petrovaradin Fortress	Novi Sad, Serbia
July 17	Spaladium Arena	Split, Croatia
July 20	Benicàssim Festival Grounds	Benicàssim, Spain
July 22	Son Fusteret	Palma, Spain
Oct 31	The Joint	Las Vegas, NV. USA
Nov 2	The Joint	Las Vegas, NV. USA
Nov 3	The Joint	Las Vegas, NV. USA
Nov 7	The Joint	Las Vegas, NV. USA
Nov 9	The Joint	Las Vegas, NV. USA
Nov 10	The Joint	Las Vegas, NV. USA
Nov 14	The Joint	Las Vegas, NV. USA
Nov 17	The Joint	Las Vegas, NV. USA
Nov 18	The Joint	Las Vegas, NV. USA
Nov 21	The Joint	Las Vegas, NV. USA
Nov 23	The Joint	Las Vegas, NV. USA
Nov 24	The Joint	Las Vegas, NV. USA
Dec 7	Bhartiya City	Bangalore, India
Dec 9	MMRDA Grounds	Mumbai, India
Dec 12	Leisure Valley Gurgaon	Delhi, India
Dec 16	Mata Elang Stadium	Jakarta, Indonesia
Dec 18	Zepp Tokyo	Tokyo, Japan

2013

Feb 13	Soho House	Los Angeles, CA. USA
Mar 9	Perth Arena	Perth, Australia
Mar 12	Allphones Arena	Sydney, Australia
Mar 13	Newcastle Entertainment Centre	Newcastle, Australia
Mar 16	Sidney Myer Music Bowl	Melbourne, Australia
Mar 17	Sidney Myer Music Bowl	Melbourne, Australia
Mar 20	Brisbane Entertainment Centre	Brisbane, Australia
Mar 24	Sepang International Circuit	Sepang, Malaysia
Mar 28	du Arena	Abu Dhabi, UAE
Mar 30	Forum de Beirut	Beirut, Lebanon
May 24	Pryor Creek Festival Grounds	Pryor Creek, OK. USA

May 26	AT&T Center	San Antonio, TX. USA
May 28	House of Blues	Houston, TX. USA
May 29	House of Blues	Dallas, TX. USA
June 1	Lonestar Pavilion	Lubbock, TX. USA
June 2	Midland Theatre	Kansas City, KS. USA
June 5	Outer Buffalo Harbor	Buffalo, NY. USA
June 6	Brooklyn Bowl	New York City, NY. USA
June 8	Randalls Island	New York City, NY. USA
July 12	Festival d'été de Québec	Quebec, Canada
July 14	Métropolis	Montreal, Canada
July 17	Sound Academy	Toronto, Canada

2014

Mar 20	HSBC Arena	Rio de Janeiro, Brazil
Mar 22	Mineirão Stadium	Belo Horizonte, Brazil
Mar 25	Ginásio Nilson Nelson	Brasília, Brazil
Mar 28	Anhembi Convention Centre	São Paulo, Brazil
Mar 30	Vila Capanema Stadium	Curitiba, Brazil
Apr 1	Stage Music Park	Florianópolis, Brazil
Apr 3	Fiergs Pavilion	Porto Alegre, Brazil
Apr 6	Ferro Stadium	Buenos Aires, Argentina
Apr 9	Jockey Club	Asunción, Paraguay
Apr 12	Estadio Hernando Siles	La Paz, Bolivia
Apr 15	Chevrolet Hall	Recife, Brazil
Apr 17	Centro de Eventos do Ceará	Fortaleza, Brazil
April 23	Club Nokia	Los Angeles, CA. USA
May 13	Sands Bethlehem Event Center	Bethlehem, PA. USA
May 16	Columbus Crew Stadium	Columbus, OH. USA
May 21	The Joint	Las Vegas, NV. USA
May 24	The Joint	Las Vegas, NV. USA
May 25	The Joint	Las Vegas, NV. USA
May 28	The Joint	Las Vegas, NV. USA
May 30	The Joint	Las Vegas, NV. USA
May 31	The Joint	Las Vegas, NV. USA
June 4	The Joint	Las Vegas, NV. USA
June 6	The Joint	Las Vegas, NV. USA
June 7	The Joint	Las Vegas, NV. USA

GUNS N' ROSES

2016

Apr 1	The Troubadour	West Hollywood, CA. USA
Apr 8	T-Mobile Arena	Las Vegas, NV. USA
Apr 9	T-Mobile Arena	Las Vegas, NV. USA
Apr 16	Empire Polo Club	Indio, CA. USA
Apr 19	Foro Sol	Mexico City, Mexico
Apr 20	Foro Sol	Mexico City, Mexico
Apr 23	Empire Polo Club	Indio, CA. USA
June 23	Ford Field	Detroit, MI. USA
June 26	FedExField	Landover, MD. USA
June 29	Arrowhead Stadium	Kansas City, KS. USA
July 1	Soldier Field	Chicago, IL. USA
July 3	Soldier Field	Chicago, IL. USA
July 6	Paul Brown Stadium	Cincinnati, OH. USA
July 9	Nissan Stadium	Nashville, TN. USA
July 12	Heinz Field	Pittsburgh, PA. USA
July 14	Lincoln Financial Field	Philadelphia, PA. USA
July 16	Rogers Centre	Toronto, Canada
July 19	Gillette Stadium	Foxborough, MA. USA
July 20	Gillette Stadium	Foxborough, MA. USA
July 23	MetLife Stadium	East Rutherford, NJ. USA
July 24	MetLife Stadium	East Rutherford, NJ. USA
July 27	Georgia Dome	Atlanta, GA. USA
July 29	Camping World Stadium	Orlando, FL. USA
July 31	Mercedes-Benz Superdome	New Orleans, LA.
Aug 3	AT&T Stadium	Arlington, TX. USA
Aug 5	NRG Stadium	Houston, TX. USA
Aug 9	AT&T Park	San Francisco, CA. USA
Aug 12	CenturyLink Field	Seattle, WA. USA
Aug 15	University of Phoenix Stadium	Glendale, AZ.
Aug 18	Dodger Stadium	Los Angeles, CA. USA
Aug 19	Dodger Stadium	Los Angeles, CA. USA
Aug 22	Qualcomm Stadium	San Diego, CA. USA
Oct 27	Estadio Monumental	Lima, Peru
Oct 29	Estadio Nacional	Santiago, Chile
Nov 1	Estadio Gigante de Arroyito	Rosario, Argentina
Nov 4	River Plate Stadium	Buenos Aires, Argentina
Nov 5	River Plate Stadium	Buenos Aires, Argentina
Nov 8	Estádio Beira-Rio	Porto Alegre, Brazil
Nov 11	Allianz Parque	São Paulo, Brazil
Nov 12	Allianz Parque	São Paulo, Brazil

Nov 15	Estádio Olímpico	Rio de Janeiro, Brazil
Nov 17	Pedreira Paulo Leminski	Curitiba, Brazil
Nov 20	Estádio Mané Garrincha	Brasília, Brazil
Nov 23	Estadio Atanasio Girardot	Medellín, Columbia
Nov 26	Estadio Nacional	San José, Costa Rica
Nov 29	Palacio de los Deportes	Mexico City, Mexico
Nov 30	Palacio de los Deportes	Mexico City, Mexico

2017

Jan 21	Kyocera Dome	Osaka, Japan
Jan 22	World Memorial Hall	Kobe, Japan
Jan 25	Yokohama Arena	Yokohama, Japan
Jan 28	Saitama Super Arena	Saitama, Japan
Jan 29	Saitama Super Arena	Saitama, Japan
Feb 2	Westpac Stadium	Wellington, New Zealand
Feb 4	Western Springs Stadium	Auckland, New Zealand
Feb 7	Queensland Athletics Centre	Brisbane, Australia
Feb 10	ANZ Stadium	Sydney, Australia
Feb 11	ANZ Stadium	Sydney, Australia
Feb 14	Melbourne Cricket Ground	Melbourne, Australia
Feb 18	Adelaide Oval	Adelaide, Australia
Feb 21	Domain Stadium	Perth, Australia
Feb 25	Changi Exhibition Centre	Singapore
Feb 28	SCG Stadium	Bangkok, Thailand
Mar 3	Autism Rocks Arena	Dubai, UAE
May 27	Slane Castle	Slane, Ireland
May 30	San Mamés Stadium	Bilbao, Spain
June 2	Passeio Marítimo de Algés	Lisbon, Portugal
June 4	Vicente Calderón Stadium	Madrid, Spain
June 7	Letzigrund	Zürich, Switzerland
June 10	Autodromo Enzo e Dino Ferrari	Imola, Italy
June 13	Olympiastadion	Munich, Germany
June 16	London Stadium	London, UK
June 17	London Stadium	London, UK
June 20	Stadion Energa Gda sk	Gda sk, Poland
June 22	Hanover Fairground	Hanover, Germany
June 24	Werchter Festival Park	Werchter, Belgium
June 27	Telia Parken	Copenhagen, Denmark
June 29	Friends Arena	Stockholm, Sweden
July 1	Kantola Event Park	Hämeenlinna, Finland

GUNS N' ROSES

July 4	Let any	Prague, Czech Republic
July 7	Stade de France	Paris, France
July 10	Ernst-Happel-Stadion	Vienna, Austria
July 12	Goffertpark	Nijmegen, Holland
July 15	Yarkon Park	Tel Aviv, Israel
July 20	Apollo Theatre	New York City, NY. USA
July 27	The Dome at America's Center	St. Louis, MO. USA
July 30	U.S. Bank Stadium	Minneapolis, MN. USA
Aug 2	Sports Authority Field	Denver, CO. USA
Aug 5	War Memorial Stadium	Little Rock, AR. USA
Aug 8	Marlins Park	Miami, FL. USA
Aug 11	BB&T Field	Winston-Salem, NC. USA
Aug 13	Hersheypark Stadium	Hershey, PA. USA
Aug 16	New Era Field	Orchard Park, NY. USA
Aug 19	Parc Jean Drapeau	Montreal, Canada
Aug 21	TD Place Stadium	Ottawa, Canada
Aug 24	Investors Group Field	Winnipeg, Canada
Aug 27	Mosaic Stadium	Regina, Canada
Aug 30	Commonwealth Stadium	Edmonton, Canada
Sept 1	BC Place	Vancouver, Canada
Sept 3	The Gorge Amphitheatre	George, WA. USA
Sept 6	Sun Bowl	El Paso, TX. USA
Sept 8	Alamodome	San Antonio, TX. USA
Sept 23	Barra Olympic Park	Rio de Janeiro, Brazil
Sept 26	Allianz Parque	São Paulo, Brazil
Sept 29	Estadio Monumental	Santiago, Chile
Oct 1	Estadio Ciudad de La Plata	La Plata, Argentina
Oct 8	Wells Fargo Center	Philadelphia, PA. USA
Oct 11	Madison Square Garden	New York City, NY. USA
Oct 12	Prudential Center	Newark, NJ. USA
Oct 15	Madison Square Garden	New York City, NY. USA
Oct 16	Madison Square Garden	New York City, NY. USA
Oct 19	Capital One Arena	Washington, D.C. USA
Oct 22	TD Garden	Boston, MA. USA
Oct 23	XL Centre	Hartford, CT. USA
Oct 26	Quicken Loans Arena	Cleveland, OH. USA
Oct 29	Air Canada Centre	Toronto, Canada
Oct 30	Air Canada Centre	Toronto, Canada
Nov 2	Little Caesars Arena	Detroit, MI. USA
Nov 3	KFC Yum! Center	Louisville, KY. USA
Nov 6	United Center	Chicago, IL. USA
Nov 7	BMO Harris Bradley Center	Milwaukee, WI. USA

Nov 10	Toyota Center	Houston, TX. USA
Nov 13	Bridgestone Arena	Nashville, TN. USA
Nov 14	BOK Center	Tulsa, OK. USA
Nov 17	T-Mobile Arena	Las Vegas, NV. USA
Nov 18	Golden 1 Center	Sacramento, CA. USA
Nov 21	Oracle Arena	Oakland, CA. USA
Nov 24	Staples Centre	Los Angeles, CA. USA
Nov 25	The Forum	Inglewood, CA. USA
Nov 28	Valley View Casino Center	San Diego, CA. USA
Nov 29	The Forum	Inglewood, CA. USA

2018

June 3	Olympiastadion	Berlin, Germany
June 6	Dyrskuepladsen	Odense, Denmark
June 9	Donington Park	Castle Donington, UK
June 12	Veltins-Arena	Gelsenkirchen, Germany
June 15	Ippodromo del Visarno	Florence, Italy
June 18	Brétigny-sur-Orge Air Base	Paris, France
June 21	Festivalpark Stenehei	Dessel, Belgium
June 24	Maimarktgelände	Mannheim, Germany
June 26	Matmut Atlantique	Bordeaux, France
June 29	Caja Mágica	Madrid, Spain
July 1	Estadi Olímpic Lluís Companys	Barcelona, Spain
July 4	Goffertpark	Nijmegen, Holland
July 7	Leipziger Festwiese	Leipzig, Germany
July 9	Stadion Slaski	Chorzow, Poland
July 13	Otkritie Arena	Moscow, Russia
July 16	Tallinn Song Festival Grounds	Tallinn, Estonia
July 19	Valle Hovin	Oslo, Norway
July 21	Ullevi Stadium	Gothenburg, Sweden
July 24	Laugardalsvöllur	Reykjavik, Iceland
Nov 3	Parque Fundidora	Monterrey, Mexico
Nov 8	Gelora Bung Karno Stadium	Jakarta, Indonesia
Nov 11	Philippine Arena	Santa Maria, Philippines
Nov 14	Sunway Lagoon	Kuala Lumpur, Malaysia
Nov 17	Taoyuan Baseball Stadium	Taoyuan, Taiwan
Nov 20	AsiaWorld–Expo	Hong Kong, China
Nov 21	AsiaWorld–Expo	Hong Kong, China
Nov 25	du Arena	Abu Dhabi, UAE
Nov 29	FNB Stadium	Johannesburg, South Africa
Dec 8	Aloha Stadium	Honolulu, HI. USA

GUNS N' ROSES

Professional thanks to:

Mark Neeter and everyone at Red Planet Publishing.

Special mention to:

Tasha "Bush" Cowen, Shannon "Mini B" Stanley, Matt Whapshott, Lisa "T-bag" Bird, Ziggy P & Mel King, Paul Young (not the singer), Tony Makin & Pads, Drezzie & Catherine, Kev Gray, Joel & Aggie and everyone at The Old House at Dorking and The Star, Luke Dillon (and Delia and Willow), Gemma and Donna (a.k.a. "The Girls"), "Blowback Annie" Chamberlain, Dan, Jeannie & "Pinks", Roop & Debs, "Scouse Mark" Rudge, Andy Cole, and Stuart "GN'R" Furlonger.

SOURCES

Books:

McKagan, Duff: It's So Easy (and other lies): The Autobiography (Orion, 2012); Slash: Slash: The Autobiography (Harper, 2008); Adler, Steven: My Appetite for Destruction: Sex & Drugs & Guns 'N' Roses (Harper Collins, 2011); Wall, Mick: Last of the Giants: The True Story of Guns N' Roses (Trapeze, 2017); Wall, Mick: W. Axl Rose: The Unauthorized Biography (Pan, 2008); Canter, Marc: Reckless Road: Guns N' Roses and The Making of Appetite for Destruction (Shoot Hip Press, 2008); Sugarman, Danny: Appetite for Destruction: Days of Guns N' Roses (Arrow Books Ltd, 1992); Sixx, Nikki: The Heroin Diaries: A Year in the Life of a Shattered Rock Star (Pocket Books, 2008).

Magazines, periodicals and TV documentaries:

LA Weekly, Daily Mail, New York Times, Sounds, NME, Kerrang!, Rolling Stone, Billboard, Birmingham Mail, Rockline, Musician, Metal Hammer, Q Magazine, Fortune, Classic Rock, MTV News, Guitar Player, Washington Post, Mail on Sunday, The Guardian, Afronbladet, Globo TV, The Independent, LA Times, LA Weekly, Sweden Rock, Slash: Raised on the Sunset Strip.

Websites and podcasts:

www.gunsnfnroses.com, On Down The Road, Appetite for Distortion, www.maxim.com, www. legendaryrockinterviews.com, www.loudersound.com, www.heretodaygonetohell.com, www.musicradar. com, www.rocknworld.com, www.mygnrforum.com, www.gunsnroses.com, www.velvetrevolver.com, www.indiatoday.in, www.bbc.co.uk, www.gnrfrance.net, VerdamMnis, Stormbringer, The Current, www.newrocktimes.com, www.metalwani.com, www.nationalrockreview.com, www.bumblefoot. com, www.bucketheadpikes.com, www.slashonline.com, www.duffonline.com, /izzystradlin999, www. moderndrummer.com

AVAILABLE NOW

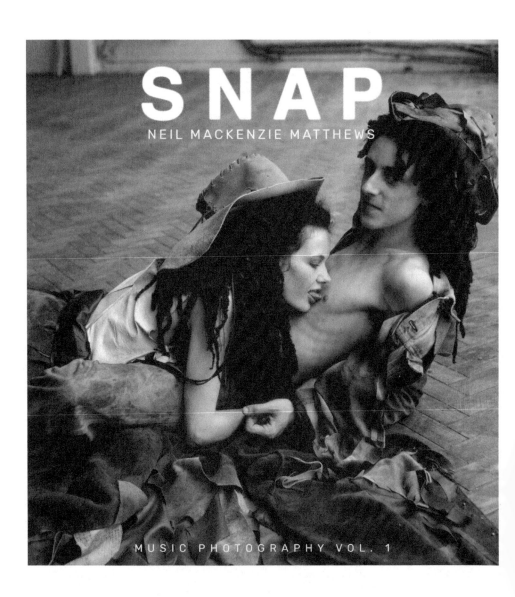

www.redplanetmusicbooks.com

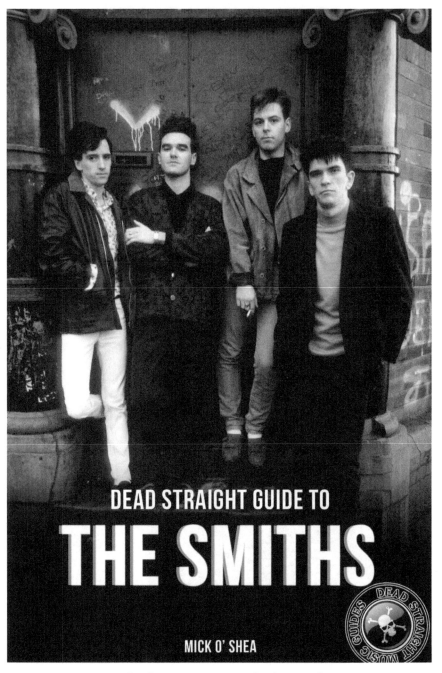